ASPECTS OF EDUCATIONAL
TECHNOLOGY

Aspects
of Educational Technology
Volume XIII

Educational Technology
Twenty Years On

*Edited for the Association for Educational
and Training Technology by*
G Terry Page and Quentin A Whitlock

General Editor:
R E B Budgett *Department of Teaching Media,
University of Southampton*

**Kogan Page, London/Nichols Publishing
Company, New York**

First published 1979
by Kogan Page Limited
120 Pentonville Road, London N1 9JN

Copyright © The Association for Educational
and Training Technology, 1979
All rights reserved

Printed in Great Britain by
Anchor Press, Tiptree, England

ISBN 085038 247 5 (UK)
ISBN 0-89397-073-5 (USA)
ISSN 0141-5956

Published in the USA by Nichols Publishing Company
PO Box 96 New York, NY 10024

Contents

Editorial   9

Keynote Address   11

Section 1: Learning Strategies and Tactics   19

1.1 Simulation-Games and Case Studies — Some Relationships
    between Objectives and Structure
    H I Ellington, F Percival and E Addinall   20

    'Power for Elaskay' (Workshop)
    H I Ellington, F Percival and E Addinall   29

1.2 Psychological Troubleshooting Diagnostics as a Basis for Deeper
    Adaptive Instruction
    L Landa   31

1.3 A Micro-Analytical Procedure to Improve Instructional Materials
    P D Mitchell   36

1.4 Creativity and Control — Neglected Factors within Self-Instruction
    Programme Design
    A J Romiszowski and B Atherton   45

1.5 A Competency-Based Approach to Course Development in
    Teacher Education
    E A Soremekun   53

1.6 How do Students Use Lecture Handouts?
    M Trueman and J Hartley   62

1.7 The Evaluation of Educational Projects and Programmes
    (Workshop)
    C A Hawkins   67

Section 2: Resource-Based Learning (Including Distance Education)   71

2.1 Distance Study in Educational Theory and Practice
    B Holmberg   72

2.2 Home Environment and Learning — Educational Technology at a
    Distance (Paper and Workshop)
    J Megarry   77

2.3 Providing Environments for Resource-Based Learning in Colleges
of Further Education
P Noble   87

2.4 Flexistudy — Further Education College-Based Distance Learning
with Face-to-Face Tutorials (Workshop)
B Green   94

Section 3: Media Design   97

3.1 The Television Phoenix at San Francisco State University
F X Moakley   98

3.2 Some Observations on Producing and Measuring Readable Writing
(Paper and Workshop)
J Hartley and M Trueman   102

3.3 Songs and Slides in the Teaching of English as a Foreign Language
(Workshop)
V R Belsey and J Wellington   108

3.4 Establishing a CCTV System (Workshop)
L Pettman   109

3.5 Better Tape-Slide Programmes for the Amateur (Workshop)
*F J Webb, with E Hudson, N Cooper, J T Mills, G Corfield and
J Clarke*   111

Section 4: The Development of Learning Packages   115

4.1 The Design, Development and Assessment of a Learning
Programme for Part-Time Adult Education
E W Anderson   116

4.2 Training Design for Manager Skills
R J Le Hunte   123

4.3 Developing a Self-Instructional Course on How to Develop
Self-Instructional Courses!
D Rowntree   131

4.4 Packaging a Workshop
L F Evans   136

4.5 Peer Instruction in Learning Packages
G M Wilkinson   143

4.6 Self-Instruction for Hotel and Catering Skills (Workshop)
L M Bray   148

Section 5: Applications in Primary and Secondary Education   150

5.1 The Development of the Kent Mathematics Project (Paper and
Workshop)
B Banks, A J Larcombe and A Tourret   151

5.2 Can Keller Plan Work in Schools?
D W Daly   158

5.3 Instructional Design by the COMET Method *T Sakamoto* 164

5.4 Evaluation of the Schools Council Avon/Bath University Modular Courses in Technology Project (Paper and Workshop)
N D C Harris and P J Watts 172

Section 6: Applications in Tertiary Education 179

6.1 Educational Technology for the Teacher Education Curriculum
E Nunan 180

6.2 Mediated Self-Instruction: Its History and Continuing Development at the University of Connecticut 185

6.3 A Modular System of Self-Instruction in Educational Technology within a Course of Teacher Training *A Wood* 189

6.4 An Objective Approach to Teaching Physical Chemistry *W P Race* 195

6.5 Making Large Group Instruction Effective: a Case Study *E E Green* 203

6.6 The Learning Environment in Chemistry: the Contribution of the Educational Techniques Subject Group of the Chemical Society
P J Hills and R B Moyes 208

6.7 Teaching Adults in Higher Education (Workshop) *R J McDonald* 213

Section 7: Some Applications of Training Technology 215

7.1 Programmed Instruction - Promise, Propagation and Progress
S N Marson 216

7.2 The American Military Educational Technology Complex: Focus, Research and Development *F X Moakley* 222

7.3 From Panacea Programme to Peripatetic Package *P R Symes* 226

7.4 An Evaluation of the Royal Navy Training System and Implications for Future Development
Lt Cdr J D S Moore and Lt Cdr M J Kitchin 230

7.5 Come into My Parlour, Said the Spider . . . *I Townsend* 237

7.6 A Systematic Approach to the Future of Educational Technology (Workshop) *R M Adamson* 240

7.7 Twenty Years On — The Development of Instructional Technology in The British Army *Maj J R J Goose and Maj P T Nolan* 242

Section 8: Computer-Based Instruction 244

8.1 The Application of Random-Access Back Projection in Computer Assisted Instruction *C F A Bryce and A M Stewart* 245

8.2 The Need, Provision and Use of a Computer-Assisted Interactive Tutorial System *A Cooper and F Lockwood* 252

8.3 Some Educational Uses of Computers in UK Schools
K Shaw 258

8.4 Computer-Based Training for Office Tasks (Workshop)
A Roebuck 269

8.5 Computer-Assisted Instruction (CAI) and Programmed Learning in British Airways *H S Butcher* 271

8.6 Computer-Managed Learning in a Postgraduate Service Course
T R Black 274

Section 9: The Management of Education and Training 277

9.1 Time Off for Innovation
K J Adderley, J Pearce, J Tait and D Williams 278

9.2 A Model for Evaluating Educational Programmes *D C Moors* 287

9.3 Course Planning Teams: the Roles of Participants (Paper and Workshop) *J Scobbie and R McAleese* 297

9.4 Getting it All Together: or a Systems Approach to Technical Education Curricula *T Wyant* 304

9.5 The Dynamics of an Information System for Educational Technology *D P Ely* 310

Using the ERIC System (Workshop) *D P Ely* 316

9.6 Use of an Optical Mark Reader in Army Selection
D R F Hammond and P L Wilson 318

9.7 A Technology for Job Mobility Through Training and Education (Workshop)
P J Edney 326

9.8 The Management of Large-Scale Instructional Technology Projects (Workshop)
A J Romiszowski 328

Section 10: The Role of Educational Technology 332

10.1 Information Processing: a Model for Educational Technology
C J Lawless 333

10.2 Staffing and Consultancy: UNESCO Enquiry into Modern Educational Techniques
J Leedham 343

10.3 Educational Technology and Significant Learning? (Workshop)
T Boydell and M Pedler 349

10.4 Mapping the Field of Educational Technology (Workshop)
J Green and A Morris 354

10.5 Educational Technology to Educational Development — A Bid for Survival? (Workshop)
D Rowntree 358

10.6 Evaluation: Dialogue between Education and Technology (Workshop)
D Walsh 358

Closing Address 360

Keyword Index 363

Author Index 365

Editorial

The Proceedings of the International Conference on Educational Technology

Twenty years ago saw the beginnings of research and development in the field of programmed self-instruction in the UK. In particular, among several ventures initiated in various parts of the country, the Science Research Council funded a project at the Department of Psychology, Sheffield University, which was to establish the city as a centre of innovation in educational technology. It was, therefore, especially appropriate that the man most closely associated with that research, Harry Kay, should return to Sheffield to open a conference on the theme 'Educational Technology 20 Years On'.

As Dr Kay observed in his opening address, one cannot look back at the attitudes and activities of educational technologists of the late 1950s without experiencing something of a shock. While many familiar landmarks survive, the landscape has changed dramatically. The 1979 ETIC programme teemed with topics and techniques nameless even 10 years ago. On the other hand, catch-words like 'frame writing', 'card trial', even 'objectives', once the everyday currency of ETIC delegates, seemed now as outdated as the farthing in this age of decimalization. While ETIC '79 reflected this change, the vigilant delegate could still detect faint echoes of remote teaching machines and other robots of the classroom.

As Dr Kay pointed out, whereas in those early years of experimentation with models of self-instruction, the theoretical base of the technology (basically the programmed instruction model) was, or seemed to be, a stronger and more lasting influence than the technological devices for presenting learning, that same model eventually was revealed as insufficient to bear the structure which was being imposed upon it. The programmed instruction model worked and still works in a micro, one-task, training situation. In the macro-situation of curriculum planning and course development the methodology has been found wanting. On the other hand, the technology of hardware design has continued to develop and by now has far outstripped the evolution of learning theory. The recently developing interests in the large-scale organization and planning of instruction was well reflected in a number of contributions to ETIC '79 on such themes as staff development and educational development. An interesting paper on the organization and promotion of educational technology within a large scale institution was given by the team from Brighton Polytechnic. Other significant contributions concerned the professional role of the educational technologists (Leedham) and the problems of learning life skills (Boydell and Pedler) as well as the roles of participants in course planning teams (Scobbie and Macaleese).

The overwhelming trend in conference contributions was towards the practical. Significantly, there were over 20 workshop contributions — far more than in previous conferences. Few if any contributions paused to consider the rationale and philosophy of educational technology, a striking confirmation of Dr Kay's observation on the current paucity of thinking on the methodology of this subject.

A few contributions did describe applications of a self-instructional approach based on the programmed instruction model. The papers by Le Hunte, Butcher and Rowntree and the workshop by Bray were good examples.

The 1979 conference might be said to be something of a watershed in the development of the Association. The gradual absorption over the years of techniques and methods from different disciplines and the widespread misgivings about the applicability of the programmed instruction model for education have led finally and inevitably to a change of title for the association, ratified at the Sheffield Annual General Meeting. At the same time it is interesting to note that the association has acknowledged its debt to its origins by inviting Dr Kay to become its new president. In Dr Kay's own words, 'whether we like it or not, yesterday's history will influence, if not govern, tomorrow's learning'.

Indeed, in his closing address to ETIC '79 Norman Willis saw yesterday's history as the foundation for tomorrow's learning. He concluded, 'I welcome the idea that this conference this year should be retrospective, bringing back to your minds the opportunities the past has given . . . I look forward to ETIC '80 when you will . . . discuss . . . the ways in which you will push forward into the twenty-first century, building upon the experience which you have gained as educational technologists over the last 20 years.'

G Terry Page
Quentin A Whitlock
Sheffield City Polytechnic, June 1979

Keynote Address
Educational Technology 20 Years on
— Sheffield Revisited

Dr Harry Kay
Vice-Chancellor, University of Exeter; President, Association for Educational and Training Technology (APLET)

Introduction

Recently there has been an exhibition on Paddington Railway Station to celebrate the 125 years since the great Brunel built the station in 1854. The whole edifice is, of course, a wonderful technological achievement. The photographic exhibition is of beautiful quality and portrays the past glories of the Great Western Railway. One exhibit in particular fascinated me. There were two photographs; the one on the right showed platforms numbers 4, 5 and 6 as they are in 1978-79 and the one on the left had been taken from exactly the same point and showed platforms 4, 5 and 6 as they were — 70 years previously — in 1908. The shock as we look back and see the original, not blurred by the kindly eye of memory but the stark reality of 70 years ago, with all its differences of fashion and scale, makes the comparison overwhelming. You look at yesterday and today, side by side.

In one sense, I am asking you to do something similar. I suppose one reason why it was suggested that I should give this lecture is because 20 years ago I was setting up a University Department in Sheffield and our first major piece of research was on the Psychology of Adaptation, Programmed Instruction and Teaching Machines. From this same city, I am now asking you to look back with me over this period and see what has emerged. I am not intending to make a detailed review. There is no need for that. There have been several excellent papers by Annett (1973), Hartley (1974) and Hawkridge (1976) and others. What I hope we may achieve at the beginning of this conference is to take a wide perspective on some of the major issues facing educational technology, and to examine how the position has shifted during the course of time and hazard a few guesses about the future.

Let us consider the last 20 years and look at the period in the same overall manner that we might look at our Paddington Station picture. I wish to focus on two features: first, the technical changes that have taken place over these 20 years; second, the change in our educational ideas.

Firstly then, the changes in our technical equipment. Today, we have so many pieces of hardware that had not even been thought of at that time. Now this may seem to be surprising, for one of the phrases of the period that is treated with derision is Harold Wilson's white-hot technological revolution — it seemed to burn its speaker more than its listeners. But from the vantage point of 1979, the 20 years have indeed witnessed remarkable technical innovation, so much so that many everyday gadgets of our world were unknown when we first were discussing what would now be called educational technology. I am thinking of video-tape recorders, copying machines, pocket calculators, overhead projectors, desk computers, the linking of television with the telephone and with the computer to give us versions of Prestel, Viewdata and the like, not forgetting cable television. Of course, throughout this period there were forecasts of technological revolution and, in particular, we used to hear much about the impact of automation, just as we hear about microprocessors today. Indeed, we heard so much that many came to believe it would never happen, but this is to misunderstand the nature of socio-technical revolutions. Political revolutions have their D-days when a government collapses, when a ruler steps down. Events happen dramatically at the centre of power. Technological change has to permeate through society and, though we can chronicle the day when something is invented, it is rare for it to make an overnight impact. Not everyone goes out and buys a pocket calculator on the day after it is invented; what we find is that gradually it is being used more and more. A few years ago, forward-looking Senates were discussing whether calculators should be allowed in examinations and wondering whether they would be too noisy. A year or two later, the question has become redundant; everyone has a calculator, they are all silent and small enough for the pocket. And so it has been with a number of machines. Not every office bought a copying machine immediately, but no large office today can do without one. And indeed, the general question has to be asked — how far do we control the machine, or does it control us? Social technical changes of this kind, like the tide, come in gradually, sometimes imperceptibly, but inexorably. Over the last 20 years we have witnessed this process again and again. And all the evidence indicates that the speed of introduction of such changes is accelerating.

The total result is that if we compare our 1979 picture with our 1959 picture, we find the technical changes are bigger than some of us, in our pessimism, might think. Figure 1 gives an impressionistic illustration of this increased usage. The technical resources that are now available to us in education are immense and would have seemed a pipe-dream when we started out on this road where, in the main, we were designing and constructing our own machines. If I may make a link with last year's conference by quoting the opening speaker, Geoffrey Hubbard, 'technology is in advance of our capacity to use it'. And of how many areas besides education is that so! As Marshall McLuhan said, 'Our technologies are generations ahead of our thinking'.

So much for the technical changes. Let us now turn to the second feature — the changes in educational ideas. I wish to try to correct a widespread impression that the early days were completely taken up by enthusiasts constructing teaching machines and the like. I recall listening to Skinner speaking in Washington on education not long after he had published his Harvard Review article. The impact was enormous. Here was a cogently reasoned case against educational methods that required an answer; here also was an alternative procedure, powerfully argued and supported apparently by experimental data. It hammered a new empirical philosophy into teaching. I found myself stimulated by the importance of his subject and challenged by my doubts over his extrapolation to the human learning situation. On returning to Britain the only person I knew who was working in the subject was Gordon Pask whose cybernetic approach with SAKI was entirely different from Skinner's. So when John Annett, Max Sime and I moved from Oxford to Sheffield we found ourselves in unmapped territory — speaking metaphorically, not geographically! (May I add in passing that it is never wise to get too far ahead of the field in a new development? The number of times we explained our ideas to publishers, industrialists, educationalists, to be met by evident incredulity, only to have the same people return later for a repeat session, was endless.)

USAGE IN EDUCATION

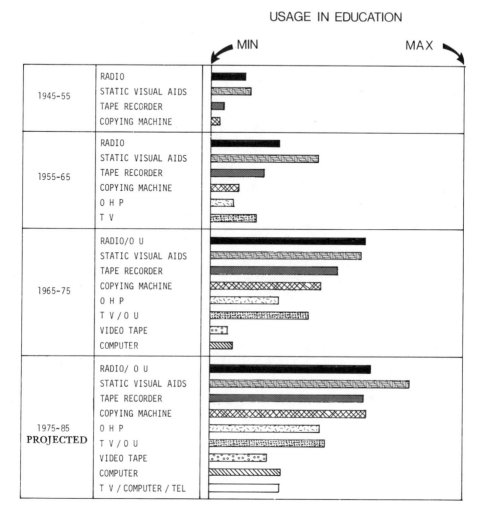

Figure 1. *Technology in education*

But I do wish to convey to you that those early days were exciting and I want to say why, because from my analysis I hope to move the wheel full circle and pose the question — what of today? I would explain the excitement of those beginnings in terms of our tackling an old problem with new ideas. This is not always the approach; in many fields such as education or medicine, significant forward steps may be taken from two very different origins. On the one hand, a new idea, a concept or theory points in a new direction. The worker looks around for the tools to do the job and they may be readily available or he may have to create them. He may, and this is so often the case, have to compromise and the idea gets blunted in the execution because the tools do not quite match up to the specification. He makes do. The second approach is from the other side. A new instrument or tool has been created. New possibilities are opened up and advances take place in one subject. Then someone from a totally different discipline with a totally different problem appreciates how the new tool might be used in his subject and so he introduces it into the new discipline. And often the new introduction is more important than the purpose for which the tool was originally conceived. The problem is the link between tool and new subject. You can think of your own examples — for instance, the widespread use of lasers from techniques in surgery to communication with satellites.

Now the significance of the early days in programmed learning was that it exemplified the former example; the direction we were taking was dictated by new ideas. We were not in the game because we had discovered a new gadget but because we believed we could make the appropriate hardware. I have often seen it stated that the tools took over; that is not the whole truth, though it may be fair criticism. Certainly, in the early days of programmed instruction, the tools had a mesmeric effect. The press were fascinated by 'a teaching machine'. They loved to call it 'a robot' or some similar idiotic name. And those workers who had been a long time in the field of visual aids felt that there was nothing new in educational technology. But indeed there was, even if the realization that the machine itself was unimportant and that the ideas for teaching behind the machine were what mattered.

In passing I should observe that it may have been because of its empirical origins, or it may be because traditional education felt itself threatened by the newcomer, but one of the most persistent features was the frequency with which we early workers were asked to evaluate or assess our teaching contribution. It was certainly a fair question but after a time we came to wonder why it had never been asked, and even to this day it is still not always asked of more traditional methods. Teaching is very much a personal exercise and defence mechanisms are quickly roused. I heard a professor say recently, 'Information retrieval sounds like something I ask the dog to do; I prefer to read a book'. How sacrosanct is the technology of a former time, how suspect the technology of our own!

To return to my theme: if the significance of our early movement lay in its empirical theory rather than in its hardware technology, then success or failure would depend on the quality or otherwise of those theoretical ideas. I believe the history of the subject confirms this. It soon became apparent that the theoretical models were insufficient to bear the structure which was being imposed upon them. The theories failed because they did not predict different results in the macro-situations with which they had to contend. As descriptions of what might be taking place on micro-areas of behaviour they were adequate enough but it became more and more obvious, as we moved into the macro-situations of continuous, adaptive behaviour that reinforcement, knowledge of results, confirmation, and the like were all predicting consequences. They gave no guidance as to how to develop teaching beyond the very limited initial learning situations from which they had been developed.

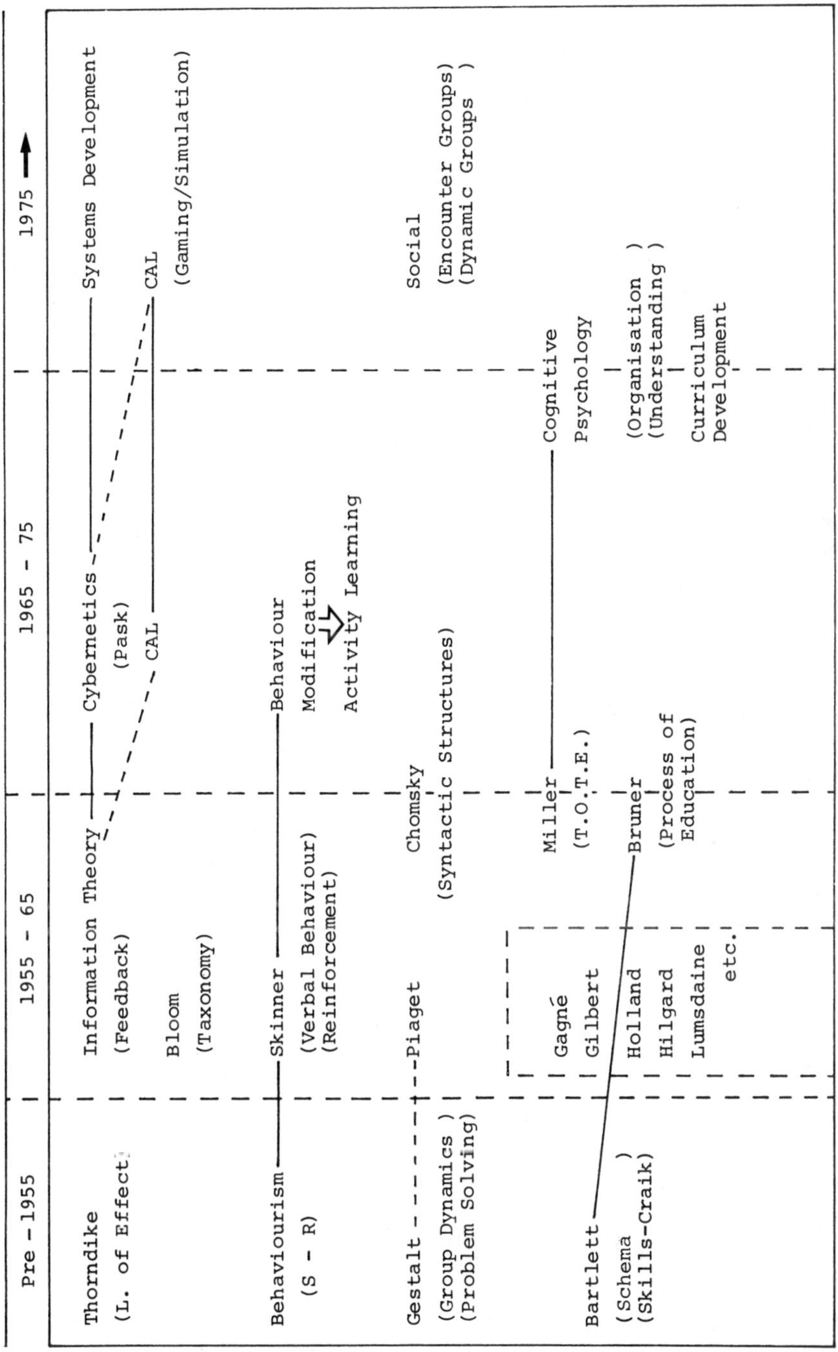

Figure 2. *Educational theories*

Fortunately in other branches of education there were developments from different standpoints. In Figure 2, I have indicated a few of them and I would stress their interaction on the one hand and their limited application on the other. The adoption of Piagetian philosophy was slow to begin but widespread once it got started. Bloom's taxonomies, very different in their concepts, were influential throughout the 1960s, whilst Bruner's 'process of education' typified the more liberal approach to transmit knowledge and create intellectual skills. It was a short step from them to put the stress on systems development, curriculum development and group dynamics.

Let us now focus on the 1979 picture and continue our two-subject story of educational theory and technical development by beginning this time with theory. If educational theory is to make progress, then it must hold on to the empirical tradition of its origins and cut out the woolly theorizing that is too general to be of use. Today, I read with scepticism that in educational technology, sociology and cybernetics are taking over from psychology. This seems to indicate a misconception. All disciplines have large overlapping areas and certainly in our field of study are not sharply divided from one another. Even in their history they are joined; social psychology through Kurt Lewin was stressing group dynamics in the mid-1930s, whilst on the other front, the young and very influential Cambridge psychologist, Kenneth Craik, had examined negative feedback, the central concept of cybernetics, in the very early 1940s before cybernetics had been 'christened'.

We are right to examine the various conditions under which learning will take place and to try and identify those that are most favourable — the group situation, the active participation of the student, the satisfactory closing or solution of the problem. But I think we should pause for a moment to set out the magnitude to the task of understanding man's learning abilities. Educational technology, no less than any other branch of education, has to accept that man's learning takes place in a neurophysiological system and that such a biological mechanism is fundamentally different from any hardware system as yet devised by man. In contrast to the computer analogy, the software is carried around with the hardware; yesterday's programme cannot be taken out and, whether we like it or not, yesterday's history will influence, if not govern, tomorrow's learning.

Now this is saying that any learning theory will have to be based on a bio-social model. We cannot account for learning in terms of biology alone, nor can we accept an explanation that relies entirely on a social standpoint. Many theories have foundered because they have only considered the one, in much the same way as the nature-nurture, hereditary-environment argument has concentrated upon one side to the exclusion of the other. Man as an adaptive organism can only be understood when both his biological and social attributes are considered.

I have stressed the point because there is nothing to be gained by hoping that a general theory of learning as to how man's adaptive behaviour is formed is just around the corner. If tomorrow the combination of neuro-anatomy and biochemistry unlocks the secret of how the nervous system stores information at the molecular level, in a way analogous to that of Crick and Watson solving the genetic code, it would not make our task any the easier in the immediate future. In spite of all the efforts that our Figure 2 illustrates, there is no simple theory, no easy solution as to how man learns or how he can best be taught.

On the other hand, we have travelled and are travelling very fast indeed down the road of technological invention. Distance learning has been achieved; time storage has been mastered (video-cassette); retrieval of information is nearly instantaneous. If we think of our two travellers setting out together in 1959, the theorist was giving a helping hand to his technology partner. In 1979 the positions are very different. The technologist is looking back down the road and saying to the theorist. 'Everything is possible, if only you know what you want'. Seductive language, indeed!

You will have noticed that I have reached this position without any direct reference to Computer Assisted Learning. All I need to say here is that the computer with its ever decreasing costs in hardware, and as the most adaptive tool man ever devised, is destined to play an ever-increasing role in education at all levels, and the microprocessor will only make it more widespread. Teaching is often the art of adapting to the needs of a student. A computer with perfect memory and instantaneous 'attention' stands ready for the job — it needs only the human programmer.

If the relative positions are something akin to what I have described, where does this leave us? If technical development is way out in front and educational theory will take a long, long time before it catches up, how we proceed? We can certainly expect many different approaches to be tried — as they should. Amongst my general priorities would be the following four.

1 Attitudes, Predilections and Prejudices

We must be more aware that not everybody in education loves educational technology. We need more support, particularly on the research side. Perhaps I stress this, coming from the universities. I wish, as a Vice-Chancellor, I could tell you that every time the subject of educational technology is mentioned, a warm glow of sympathy and support circulates through out Senate Chambers. Alas, it does not. We still hear, as one academic put it, 'I have never felt the need for advice on how to teach'. The defence mechanisms are as impregnable as the walls of Troy — you will only get inside by a combination of skill, sympathy and subtlety. Be prepared for a long seige, for you are assaulting a private world and there must be no casualties on either side. As was said long ago, 'teachers rarely watch teachers teaching'.

2 Problem-Oriented Research

In the absence of clear theoretical guidance we shall sharpen our thinking most by making it problem-oriented. This is a well-tried method. It works. And it works in the area of complex human behaviour, as in the case of the Cambridge Laboratory's successful studies of high level skills in 1940.

3 Motivation

The more one ponders the problem of motivation, the more important and the more ubiquitous it seems. What is the relationship between our phylogenetic development as a species with its accent upon survival-and-adaptation and, on the other side, ontogenetic development as we learn to adapt? 'Ontogeny repeats phylogeny'. We can appreciate that in a biological system the twin contiguities of time and space are likely to play a major part in individual development. In many ways close proximity of events in the two dimensions provides the simplest means of indicating a relationship. But we do not know why a reward assists the learning of the two contiguous events or why in human examples when we have moved to symbolic material the same consequences apply. Some see the reward as terminating the behaviour. Then why should the termination aid learning? Again, what is it that makes for intrinsic motivation? We see it most evidently when students can learn some material that is patently difficult but which they like; as against their failure to learn much simpler material, which they dislike. As Miller puts it, 'every educator knows, the central problem of education is to make the students want it'. Learner-controlled studies offer us a lot of scope in this field.

4   Growth of Knowledge

I have not time to make the case, so let me quote Bruner (1977), 'the advances in knowledge in the last half century have been such as to lead any thoughtful man, especially one interested in education, to seek fresh ways of transmitting to a new generation the fund of learning that has been growing at such a rapid rate'. We all know the truth of that. The growth has been enormous over the last few decades. And the great danger to society will be the division between those who have some understanding of the world in which they live and those who have not.

Never before has the knowledge grown so fast; never before has there been so much to know; never before have we lived so close to the changing world created by our own technology. Indeed, to make the obvious parody, 'never have so many known so little about so much'! We face the responsibility of transmitting that knowledge to younger generations and of continuing to do so throughout their lives as new knowledge is added to the old. I believe passionately with Bruner that, 'any subject can be taught to any child at any age in some form that is honest'. We must try, and educational technology must share that responsibility. We need every tool and every idea we can muster to that end. Without that knowledge many of our society will never have the enjoyment that understanding could give them and many will become more alienated from the world we have created. We *all* need to learn so much more than we did a few years ago.

We began with a railway station. The Army used to have a sign, and may still have, at an HQ entrance to speed the departing soldier. It read: 'Where are you going? When will you be back?' I think we can say we have come a long way over the last 20 years. It has turned out differently from what we expected. It always does. There is no doubt that we are in a much stronger position on one front. 'Give us the tools . . .' Yes, we have certainly got them. But we cannot expect to 'finish the job' just yet. To that extent, we cannot risk saying when we will be back. For this is very much the kind of job where knowing how best to use the tools is far more difficult than making the tools. We have seen in 20 years the technology of tool-making change out of all recognition so that it offers us today what was not even dreamt of when we began. We have seen in 20 years the philosophy of education tack and shift and become more human, less assertive, and ever more aware of the difficulties confronting it. Some of us then, in the early days, were lucky; we apparently worked on the easier stretch; you face the tougher section. I hope this conference will be one source of inspiration to speed you on your task.

References

Annett, J (1973) The psychological bases of educational techology. In Budgett, R and Leedham, J (eds) *Aspects of Educational Technology*, **VI**. Pitman.

Bruner, J (1977) *The Process of Education.* Harvard University Press, Cambridge, Massachusetts.

Hartley, J (1974) Programmed Instruction 1954-74. *Programmed Learning & Educational Technology,* 11, 6, pp 278-97.

Hawkridge, D G (1976) Next year, Jerusalem! The rise of educational technology. *British Journal of Educational Technology,* 7, pp 7-30.

Section 1:
Learning Strategies
and Tactics

1.0 Introduction

ETIC '79 Tracks

Most of the papers in this Section were presented in Track 2, 'Learning Design', at ETIC '79. The only exception is Trueman and Hartley (1.6) which was presented to the Conference in Track 3, 'Learning Environment, Practice and Technique'.

Categories and Special Interests

Ellington *et al* (1.1), Landa (1.2), Mitchell (1.3), Romiszowski and Atherton (1.4), Soremekun (1.5) and Trueman and Hartley, all appeared in the 'Strategies and Presentation of Learning (Strats)' category at Sheffield (indeed, this was the sole category for Landa and for Romiszowski and Atherton). The only contribution in this Section not from the 'Strats' category is Hawkins' workshop (1.7) which was categorized as 'Evaluation (Eval)'.

There is a strong tertiary education interest, coded 'Tert' at Sheffield, in this Section, particularly in Mitchell, Soremekun, and Trueman and Hartley. Ellington *et al* also provide a strong secondary education interest, particularly perhaps in the workshop based on their simulation game, 'Power for Elaskay'.

Links with Other Sections

Readers with a particular interest in Section 1 are also likely to be interested in the following contributions from other sections:

Section 4: Anderson (4.1), Le Hunte (4.2), Rowntree (4.3), Evans (4.4), Wilkinson (4.5), Bray (4.6).
Section 5: Daly (5.2), Harris and Watts (5.4).
Section 6: Wood (6.3), Green, E E (6.5), McDonald (6.7).
Section 10: Green and Morris (10.4).

1.1 Simulation–Games and Case Studies — Some Relationships between Objectives and Structure

Dr H I Ellington, Dr F Percival and Dr E Addinall
Robert Gordon's Institute of Technology, Aberdeen

Abstract: The range of possible educational objectives that can be achieved by simulation-games and case studies is discussed, and it is shown how these can be related to basic structural features. In particular, the characteristics of exercises that can be described as having 'linear', 'radial' and 'composite' features are examined, both in general terms and with reference to specific examples of science-based simulation-games and case studies with whose development the authors have been associated.

1 Introduction

At the APLET Conference held in the Polytechnic of Wales, Pontypridd in April 1978, the authors presented a paper entitled 'Building science-based educational games into the curriculum' (Ellington, Percival and Addinall, 1979). During the presentation of the paper, the structures of several of the exercises developed by the authors were briefly described. Subsequently, a number of delegates expressed great interest in this aspect of the presentation and suggested that a paper dealing specifically with the structures of the games would be of considerable value to the educational community. The present paper has been written in response to this request.

2 Classification of the Game Structures Developed by the Authors

Virtually all of the simulation-games and case studies developed by the authors to date have structures which can be classified under one of the following three broad headings: (a) *simple linear structures,* (b) *simple radial structures* and (c) *composite structures.* These basic structures have been found to be suitable for the achievement of distinct (although not mutually exclusive) sets of broad educational aims and objectives, as will be explained in the subsequent sections. It should be emphasized that, although all the individual exercises described have a content that is more or less science-based, the sets of educational aims and objectives specific to each type of structure would be equally valid for content which is non-scientific in nature. It is therefore hoped that the analysis presented in this paper will be of interest to all who are involved in the design or use of games, simulations and case studies, and not merely to fellow scientists and technologists.

3 Simple Linear Structures

The essential structural characteristics of exercises that have a simple linear format are seen by the authors to be as follows:

☐ the participants progress systematically through a predetermined series of activities;

☐ all participants have the same basic resource materials and carry out the same basic set of activities.

In common with all other types of game, simulation and case study, simple linear exercises can be used to achieve a wide range of cognitive objectives related to their subject content. In addition, they have the following specific educational characteristics:

☐ the progressive nature of their structure enables a complicated case study to be broken down into easily manageable stages and clearly illustrates the relationship of each part to the whole;

☐ they can be used to foster the development of problem-solving analytical and decision-making skills.

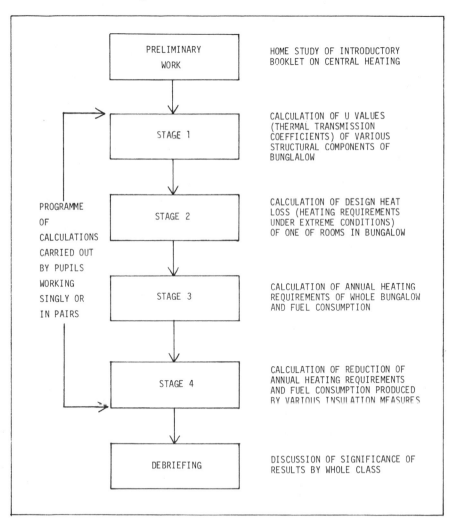

Figure 1. *Central heating game, project 1*

These characteristics will now be illustrated by examining two specific exercises, namely, the first project in the 'Central Heating Game' Multi-Project Pack and 'What Happens When The Gas Runs Out?'

Project 1 in the 'Central Heating Game' Multi-Project Pack

The 'Central Heating Game' (Cowking, Ellington and Langton, 1978) is an example of a new type of educational package recently developed in Robert Gordon's Institute of Technology — the multi-disciplinary multi-project pack. In such packages, the same basic scenario and set of resource materials are exploited in a variety of projects designed for use in the teaching of a wide range of academic disciplines (Ellington and Addinall, 1977). All the projects in the 'Central Heating Game' are concerned with domestic central heating, and are based on the study of a typical bungalow.

Project 1 in the package is designed for use in the teaching of physics, engineering and architecture, and involves carrying out a detailed technical appraisal of the heating requirements of the bungalow. The exercise (which is shown schematically in Figure 1) takes the form of a highly structured linear case study in which the class (working either singly or in pairs) progress systematically through four successive stages, each of which builds upon its predecessor. At the start of each stage, the members of the class are issued with a detailed instruction sheet which (a) gives the answers to the calculations carried out in the previous stage (if appropriate), (b) gives the background theory and technical data needed for the work of the stage and (c) gives detailed instructions on how to carry out this work. In this way, the members of the class are led easily through what would otherwise be an extremely difficult set of calculations, and are also given a clear understanding of what the calculations are all about.

What Happens When the Gas Runs Out?

This is a structured case study developed at Glasgow University primarily for use with junior science undergraduates, its main purpose being to demonstrate the social relevance of science and technology (Johnstone, Percival and Reid, 1978). The exercise involves appraising Britain's likely reserves of natural gas and formulating a policy for providing a suitable replacement when these reserves become exhausted (see Figure 2). The participants work in co-operative groups of 4 to 8, each student being provided with an individual copy of the resource/work sheet for each stage of the exercise; these are handed out prior to the start of each stage.

As can be seen from Figure 2, the exercise is essentially a linear programme in which the participants are led through a series of activities that start in the lower levels of Bloom's cognitive domain and finish up in the higher levels. Such a progression is a feature of many exercises of this type, and is something that the authors believe can be well achieved by employing a strictly linear structure of the type shown; the structure enables each stage to build upon the work of its predecessors, thus enabling a progression from simple to complex ideas and activities to take place easily and naturally.

4 Simple Radial Structures

The essential structural characteristics of exercises that have a simple radial format are seen by the authors to be as follows:

☐ each participant (or group of participants) carries out a set of activities specific to a different role in a scenario or different point of view in a problem situation and then presents information or argues a case at a plenary session or simulated meeting;

☐ the various participants (or groups of participants) have different resource material and carry out different (albeit often related) activities.

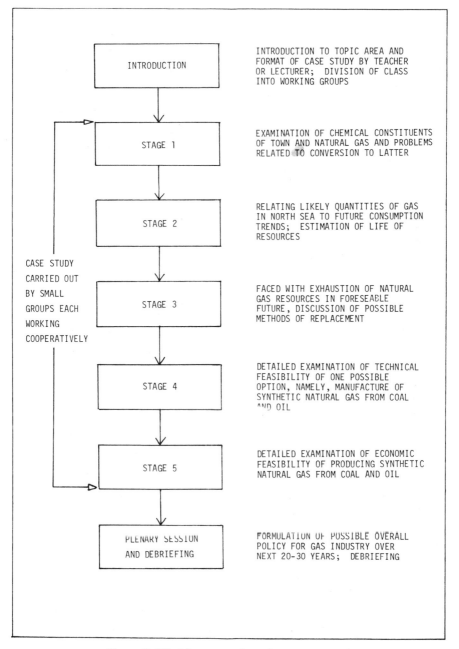

Figure 2. *What happens when the gas runs out?*

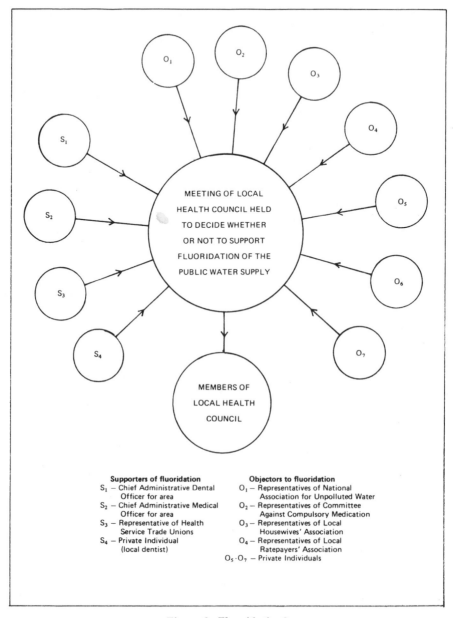

Figure 3. *Fluoridation?*

The educational characteristics specific to exercises with this type of structure are given below:

☐ they enable the different arguments or points of view in a complicated problem situation to be identified, examined in detail and subjected to informed criticism and discussion;

☐ they foster the development of useful communication skills, particularly those related to presentation and defence of arguments, and can be used to develop a wide range of desirable attitudinal traits, such as willingness to listen to the points of view of others.

These characteristics will now be illustrated by examining two specific exercises, namely, 'Fluoridation?' and 'The Amsyn Problem'.

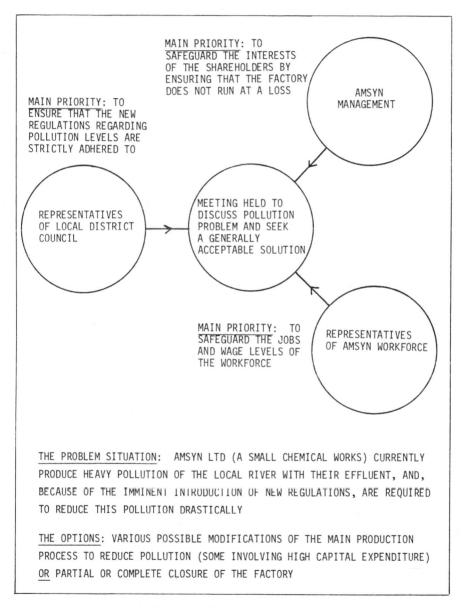

Figure 4. *The Amsyn Problem*

Fluoridation?

This is a role-playing simulation game developed at Robert Gordon's Institute of Technology, Aberdeen for use in the teaching of science, health education and general studies at upper secondary and tertiary level (Percival and Ellington, 1978). It is based on the hypothesis that an Area Health Board are considering adding fluoride to their public water supply, and takes the form of a simulated public meeting called by one of the Local Health Councils to discuss the matter. Arguments for and against fluoridation are first prepared by various interested parties (see Figure 3) and are then presented at the meeting, where the members of the Local Health Council decide whether or not to support fluoridation when the issue is discussed by the Area Health Board. The exercise is designed for an optimum of 18 people (minimum 13, maximum 24). All participants are issued with a common introductory sheet together with resource material specific to their role.

'Fluoridation?' is a typical radial exercise in that it (a) provides the participants with the basic facts regarding the issue being examined, and (b) shows that these basic facts can be looked at from more than one point of view. In particular, it highlights the type of conflict that almost invariably arises between the protagonists of a controversial measure, who generally produce detailed arguments to show that it would be technically or economically beneficial to the community as a whole, and its opponents, who generally claim that its introduction would violate the rights of the individual or produce unacceptable (albeit often unquantifiable) environmental or social side effects. Such issues, whose resolution has nearly always to be based on the formulation of value judgements rather than on the rational appraisal of facts, are ideally suitable for treatment using a radial rather than a linear approach.

The Amsyn Problem

This is a role-playing simulation-game developed at Glasgow University for use in teaching the social relevance of science to senior secondary pupils and junior undergraduates (Ellington and Percival, 1977). The exercise is based on a typical industrial problem situation, in which a small chemical firm situated in a depressed area is confronted with a range of options to combat environmental pollution. Three interested parties (Management, Local District Council and Trade Unions) first discuss the various possibilities from their own respective points of view (see Figure 4) and then meet in an attempt to find a solution compatible with their conflicting priorities. The exercise, which is designed for an optimum number of 16, is introduced by means of a short tape-slide programme after which the members of the three groups are issued with resource material specific to their role.

As in the case of 'Fluoridation', 'The Amsyn Problem' provides a vehicle whereby a complex issue, involving a number of apparently incompatible technical, economic and social issues, can be examined from the points of view of the various interested parties. In this case, however, the object of the exercise is to produce a generally acceptable compromise solution to a problem situation rather than to reach a decision on a straightforward 'either-or' issue. Such situations also lend themselves to treatment using a radial approach of the type outlined in this paper.

5 Composite Structures

An exercise can be said to have a composite structure if its overall design embodies both linear and radial features, thus enabling it to combine the educational advantages of the two basic structures described above. Such exercises are typically more complicated than those described so far, and their characteristics are best illustrated by looking at specific examples.

Power for Elaskay

This is a structured lesson on alternative energy resources that was developed at

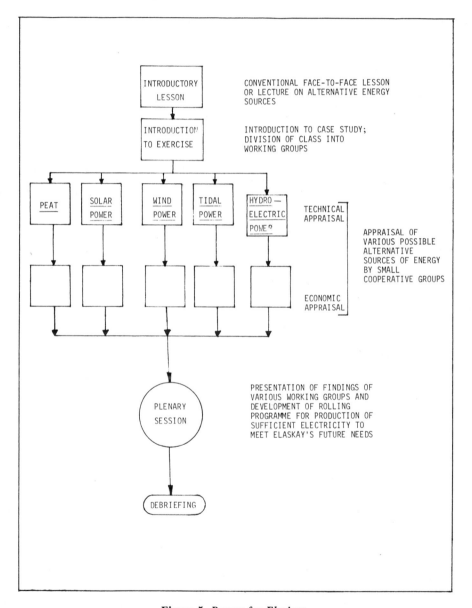

Figure 5. *Power for Elaskay*

Robert Gordon's Institute of Technology for use with science, engineering and general studies classes at upper secondary and lower tertiary level (Ellington and Addinall, 1978). The problem faced by the designers of the exercise was that of:

(a) giving all members of a class a general appreciation of the basic technical principles underlying the various alternative energy sources available to man;

(b) enabling the class to carry out a fairly detailed appraisal of the technical and economic feasibility of exploiting each of these various sources of energy;

(c) completing the work in a period of roughly three hours.

Since (c) clearly precluded detailed study of all the various sources of energy by all members of the class, it was decided to adopt the approach outlined in Figure 5, and to combine an introductory lesson on the basic principles of alternative energy with a case study carried out by the class. This case study involves developing a rolling programme for meeting the electricity requirements of the hypothetical offshore island of Elaskay over the next 50 years by exploiting the island's natural energy resources (peat, solar energy, wind energy, tidal energy and hydroelectric power). It combines detailed systematic study of each of the five possible resources by small working groups (the linear elements of the exercise) with a plenary session in which the various groups report their findings and the class then uses these to develop a viable rolling programme (the radial element). Each member of the class is issued with an introductory sheet describing the scenario and structure of the case study together with resource material specific to the particular form of alternative energy that he is to examine (a work book and a work sheet). The exercise can be used with a class of up to 25.

The Power Station Game

A second example of an educational game with a composite structure is 'The Power Station Game', developed in Robert Gordon's Institute of Technology on behalf of the Scottish Education Department. The structure of this exercise, which deals with the decisions that have to be made when a new power station is being planned, is described in detail elsewhere (Ellington and Langton, 1975), while the relationship between the educational aims and objectives and the various elements of the structure are discussed in a later paper (Ellington and Langton, 1978).

Postscript

All the exercises described or referred to above are now generally available, and can be obtained from the sources listed below.

The 'Central Heating Game', 'Fluoridation?', 'Power for Elaskay' and 'The Power Station Game': Mrs D Winfield, Qualifications Department, IEE, Savoy Place, London WC2R 0BL.

'What Happens When The Gas Runs Out?': Education Division, The Chemical Society, Burlington House, Piccadilly, London W1V 0BL.

'The Amsyn Problem': The Scottish Council for Educational Technology, 16 Woodside Terrace, Glasgow G3 7XM.

References

Cowking, A, Ellington, H I and Langton, N H (1978) The central heating multi-project pack. *Physics Education,* 13, pp 214-216

Ellington, H I and Addinall, E (1977) The multi-disciplinary multi-project pack — a new concept in simulation gaming. *Programmed Learning & Educational Technology,* **14**, 3, pp 213-222.

Ellington, H I and Addinall, E (1978) Power for Elaskay — a learning package on alternative energy resources for use by science teachers. *School Science Review,* June, pp 747-750.

Ellington, H I and Langton, N H (1975) The power station game. *SAGSET Journal,* **5**, 1, pp 31-35.

Ellington, H I and Langton, N H (1978) The applications of multi-disciplinary educational games in schools. In Megarry, J (ed) *Perspectives on Academic Gaming and Simulation 1 & 2* pp 76-79. Kogan Page, London.

Ellington, H I and Percival, F (1977) Educating 'through' science using multi-disciplinary simulation games. *Programmed Learning and Educational Technology,* **14**, 2, pp 117-126.

Ellington, H I, Percival, F and Addinall, E (1979) Building science-based educational games into the curriculum. In Race, W P (ed) *Aspects of Educational Technology,* **XII,** Kogan Page, London.

Johnstone, A H, Percival, F and Reid, N (1978) Simulations and games in the teaching of chemistry. In Megarry, J (ed) *Perspectives on Academic Gaming and Simulation 1 & 2,* pp 92-97. Kogan Page, London.

Percival, F and Ellington, H I (1978) Fluoridation? — a new role-playing game for use in schools and colleges. *SAGSET Journal,* **8**, 3, pp 93-99.

Workshop Report
'Power for Elaskay'
A Simulated Case Study Based on the Exploitation of Alternative Energy Sources

Presenters: **Dr H I Ellington and Dr E Addinall.** *Rapporteur:* **Dr F Percival**
Robert Gordon's Institute of Technology, Aberdeen

Introduction

The 'Power for Elaskay' simulated case study is part of a structured lesson on alternative energy sources developed by H I Ellington and E Addinall for use in the Association for Science Education's 'Science in Society' course. This course is an AO level course for use with sixth-form pupils and is designed to highlight the social, economic and environmental implications of science upon society.

The case study involves students in carrying out technical and economic appraisals of the various alternative energy resources (peat, solar power, wind power, tidal power and hydro-electric power) available on the hypothetical offshore island of Elaskay. The students then co-operate in devising a rolling programme whereby a selection of these alternative energy resources can be used to meet the electricity needs of Elaskay over the next 50 years.

The Workshop Session

The workshop was intended to support the more formal paper given earlier at the conference, entitled 'Simulation-games and case studies — some relationships between objectives and structure' by H I Ellington, F Percival and E Addinall, all at Robert Gordon's Institute of Technology. Originally Drs Ellington and Addinall had planned a joint presentation in the workshop; however, a late illness meant that Eric Addinall could not be present at the session.

Twelve people attended the session, a number which turned out to be ideal for the full participation of group members. Henry Ellington began the session by explaining the background and educational objectives of the case study, before describing in detail the scenario of the exercise. He then went on to explain, in layman's terms, how each of the five possible alternative energy strategies included in the exercise could be used to meet, at least in part, the island's anticipated future energy requirements. (In schools, a double period, ie approximately 80 minutes, is given to this part of the exercise before the students even look at the case study.)

Workshop participants were then split into five sub-groups each of which studied in some detail *one* of the five possible alternative energy sources for the island. As time was relatively short, the sub-groups were not required to do the technical and economic calculations for each alternative, but were handed out sheets containing the answers for various possible energy schemes. The participants' main task therefore was to interpret the tables and costs and to co-operate in formulating a rolling programme for the next 50 years' energy requirements. (The exercise is structured such that one alternative cannot *on its own* meet Elaskay's needs.)

Having digested and discussed their information, each sub-group appointed a spokesperson who reported the optimum set of variables for their particular scheme. These included the site of the main scheme (each participant was given a detailed map of the island), the peak generating capacity of the scheme (in MW), the annual electrical output of the scheme (in million kWh), the time needed to build, the capital cost, and the cost per unit generated over the first 25 years. Dr Ellington noted down the optimum variables for the five possible schemes on an overlay for the group to assimilate.

Several of the findings caused considerable discussion among the group. For example, it was discovered that electricity from solar power was very much more expensive than all the other schemes (over £2 per unit at current costs, compared to under 4p per unit from a peat-fired power station). This highlighted the sort of common misconception about energy supplies which an exercise like this can clearly illustrate.

Having obtained this 'central pool' of information the group set about formulating an energy policy for the island. Before this could be done they had to agree which criteria they were going to consider important during their deliberations. For example, how strongly would environmental considerations affect their decision? Was economics going to be the key issue? Was it morally justifiable to use up the island's only non-renewable energy resource (peat) to provide a cheap but short term energy answer or would it be more sensible to keep it in reserve in case of future emergency?

After some discussion it was decided to keep peat in reserve and concentrate on obtaining a reasonable balance between economic and environmental constraints. The final rolling programme decided upon by the group involved initially building a 15 MW hydro-electric scheme followed by a combined tidal/pumped storage scheme a few years later. Finally, a second hydro-electric scheme would be required at a later date to meet increasing demand.

The Discussion

Following completion of the case study a wide ranging discussion ensued which carried on well over the allotted time for the workshop. Topics covered included the extent to which the overall objectives of the exercise were content-related, the relation of objectives to structure in such exercises, and the possible strategies in the process of decision-making. Dr Ellington pointed out that youngsters are far more ready to co-operate in the decision-making process than older (more sophisticated?) participants who may have been raised in an autocratic environment. Interest was expressed in the other case study material used in the 'Science in Society' course, and how these exercises complemented each other in helping to accomplish the overall aims of the course.

1.2 Psychological Troubleshooting Diagnostics as a Basis for Deeper Adaptive Instruction

L Landa
The University of Iowa

Abstract: This paper discusses how programmed learning and other instructional methods, including CAI, have been developed into deeper adaptive teaching devices through psychological troubleshooting diagnostics.

New trends and systems in instruction began to develop during the post-war era because conventional classroom instruction was unable to adapt to the individual needs and characteristics of students. One of the major tasks of programmed instruction and educational technology was to overcome this cardinal shortcoming of conventional instruction.

Without discussing in detail the relationships between adaptation and individualization, it may be maintained that adaptation is a means of individualization, and that characteristics and level of individualization depend on the characteristics and level of adaptation.

The characteristics of adaptation may, however, be different. Adaptation, as with many other phenomena, has its own parameters and may be described and evaluated on the basis of these parameters.

One of the parameters of adaptation is, for example, *the nature of its object.* Instruction may be adaptive to the students' knowledge, their abilities, motivation, character traits and the others. Another parameter is the *width* of adaptation, ie the number of students' characteristics which are taken into account in an instructional process. Still another parameter is the *depth* of adaptation, ie the level of students' characteristics which is taken into consideration in an instructional process and adapted to. There exist other parameters as well.

In this presentation we will choose only one characteristic of students for examination and analysis; namely cognitive processes and, more specifically, thought processes. This concerns the parameter of adaptation we referred to above as the object of adaptation.

Another parameter we will use here is the depth of adaptation. In other words, we will consider in this presentation differences in instructional processes from the point of view of how adaptive they are to the learner's thought processes in terms of the level on which they are examined and analyzed by an instructional agent (man or machine) for further tailoring to them and their adaptive development.

Thought processes, as it is widely recognized, are the result of interaction of knowledge and operations. Knowledge may appear in the form of images, concepts and propositions; operations in the form of practical or cognitive actions. Practical actions are transformations of material, tangible objects; cognitive operations are transformations of material objects' images, concepts or propositions about objects' attributes or their relationships. Differently stated, they are transformations of internal, psychological objects rather than external material ones.

Knowledge is a necessary but not a sufficient condition of thinking, as to think means not simply 'to know' something or to reproduce this something but to be able to transform the knowledge (images, concepts or propositions) in order to solve certain problems and to achieve goals that are set. The thinking may consist in setting goals as well, but in this case goal-setting appears as a specific goal which should be achieved and as a specific problem which should be solved.

Adaptation in general, and instruction in particular, is inherently associated with diagnostics and represents one of its results. Adaptation to some object is possible only on the basis of a certain information about its characteristics. Gathering this information with the purpose of attributing the object to some class or category which then determines how this object should be specifically, ie adaptively, handled is a diagnostic process.

The characteristics of adaptation itself and the direction of diagnostics are closely connected with the objective(s) of instruction and the instructor's conception of what is the object of instruction and what should be developed in a student as a result of instruction.

The dominant object of instruction in the framework of behaviorism was students' behavioral acts. With regard to thinking it was students' responses or answers to specific stimuli or questions or problem conditions. The major instructional objective in the behavioristic approach to instruction was the eliciting of correct responses, their maximizing and strengthening. The basic techniques of instruction in this approach were determined by 'fill in blank' techniques, prompting, assessment of students' responses as correct or wrong on the basis of operative feedback, repetition of correct responses and some others.

We may refer to instruction based on this approach as 'instruction oriented at eliciting and learning correct responses' or 'response oriented instruction'.

What was the object of diagnostics in this approach to instruction? It was mainly responses (answers) and their characteristics (correct or wrong, stable or unstable, the retention rate and some others).

What was the object of adaptation in the response-oriented instruction? It was characteristics of responses.

Linear programmed instruction primarily took into account such characteristics of responses as their correctness or incorrectness. The adaptation expressed itself, if it is appropriate to speak in this case of adaptation at all, in providing students with feedback about the correctness or incorrectness of their answers. In some varieties of linear programme the rate of stability of correct responses and some other characteristics were also taken into account. In this case a minimal adaptation to students' learning took place. The material presented to the student at the next step depended on the degree of acquisition in the preceding step.

Branched programs took into account one more, very important, characteristic of responses: the nature of error if the response was erroneous. The diagnostics here were wider which permitted to make instruction adaptive not to just correctness or incorrectness of response but to the nature of a mistake should it occur.

The well known logic of branched programmed instruction was this:

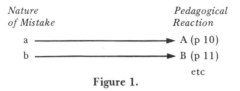

Figure 1.

Branched programmes were a considerable step forward in both psychological diagnostics and adaptivity of instruction where psychological diagnostics of the nature of mistakes was a basis for more adaptive instruction.

Why, however, was the level of diagnostics and adaptivity even in branched programmes insufficient and why could it not be a base for a deeper, more effective and individualized instruction?

It is well known that one and the same mistake may be caused by different and sometimes most diverse deficiencies in psychological processes, ie be a result of different psychological causes. For example, one and the same mistake may be made because one person does not have a necessary knowledge, another because his knowledge is wrong, the third because it is incomplete, the fourth because it is not sufficiently generalized, the fifth because he does not know how to apply the knowledge he has (ie which operations to perform), the sixth because his operations are incomplete in their composition, non-systematized, insufficiently generalized etc, although he may know which operations are to be applied in some particular case. There may be other causes, or varieties of causes, or their combinations.

Behavioristically response-oriented instruction was aimed at teaching *responses* rather than internal psychological *processes* leading to these responses. It is now widely recognized by many psychologists and educationists that one of the major objectives of instruction should be teaching students how to think, ie processes of the independent *generation* of responses, procedures of *arriving* at them, even if they were never learned before.

In contrast to response-oriented instruction we will call instruction oriented at formation of processes that underly the ability to come to responses 'process-oriented instruction'.

Process-oriented instruction, as we understand it, does not underestimate the significance of correct, well-systematized and generalized knowledge and the role of correct responses in answering questions and solving problems. (Instead of 'correct responses', it would be more precise to talk about better answers, solutions or decisions because, in many cases, several answers, solutions or decisions are possible and correct, although not all of them may be equally optimal.) Process-oriented instruction sets as its objective the development of the processes, general methods of algorithmic and heuristic thinking, leading to an ability to produce correct or better responses rather than just teaching the responses themselves.

But in order to be able to teach processes effectively in an adaptive manner, it is necessary to be able to diagnose not only the nature of responses given by a student but his psychological mechanisms. In case of a mistake it means that it is necessary to diagnose not only the nature of the mistakes but the deficiencies in the processes leading to these mistakes.

Deeper adaptive instruction should adapt pedagogical reactions and influences to the psychological causes of mistakes rather than to the mistakes themselves. And what is more important here is that pedagogical reactions to one and the same mistake should be different depending on the psychological reason for this mistake. This however, presupposes development, availability and application of diagnostic methods which would enable an identification in each particular case of the psychological reason for a mistake and not only just its nature.

In 1966 we called this type of psychological diagnostics 'psychological troubleshooting diagnostics' (Landa, 1976) by anology with technical diagnostics, where one and the same malfunction in some technical device may result from different deficiencies in its mechanism. In order to repair the device it is necessary to troubleshoot a specific cause which brought about this malfunction in each particular case.

Thus, in contrast to the logic of adaptation characteristic of conventional branched programming where pedagogical reaction to a mistake depends only on the nature of the mistake (and where one and the same mistake always leads to one and the same pedagogical reaction), the logic of adaptation on the basis of psychological troubleshooting is quite different. It presupposes different pedagogical reactions to one and the same mistake if its psychological causes are different and it is directed to the cause of the mistake rather than to the mistake itself.

Diagrammatically, this logic may be described as follows:

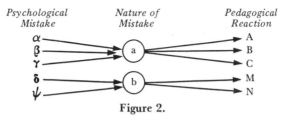

Figure 2.

This level of adaptation and the resulting level of individualization is much deeper than that of conventional branched programmes, since, as has been mentioned, the instruction in this case is adaptive not only to the incorrect responses (outcomes) of some processes but even more to the processes themselves.

The significance of this level of adaptive instruction and its implications may be easily seen by analogy with medical treatment.

The logic of conventional branched programmes described in medical terms looks like this:

Headache ⟶ Treatment A
Toothache ⟶ Treatment B
etc

Figure 3.

It is evident, however, that a headache or toothache may have different patho-physiological and even anatomical causes and in order to get someone cured of, say, a headache a physician should diagnose its cause and treat the cause rather than just its external manifestation, the symptom. If he limits himself to the diagnosis of a symptom of symptoms, does not try to make a diagnosis of a cause and treats therefore only the symptom(s) or, at best, a probable disease which may be the cause of the symptom(s), he may never be able to get the patient cured and thus remove the unhealthy symptoms. He may be lucky if the patient has the probable (most frequent) disease. In this case his treatment may lead to a positive result. But if the patient suffers from a different, less probable disease, then he would be treated for a disease he does not have and would not be treated for the disease he actually suffers from.

This analogy describes a situation in terms of the effectiveness of conventional branched programmes based on the diagnosis of only psychological symptoms rather than the processes leading to those symptoms. From this follows that individualization of instruction may be, in itself, as ineffective as individual medical treatment based on the diagnostics of just symptoms. The critical point here is whether the individualization is based on psychological troubleshooting diagnostics and treats, figuratively speaking, identified psycho-pedagogical 'diseases', or whether it is based on the diagnosis of just the nature of responses and proceeds only from the knowledge of psycho-pedagogical symptoms.

There is no space here to describe the methods and techniques of psychological troubleshooting diagnostics which was developed by the present author about 15 years ago while he was still working in the USSR. A part of the methods and techniques has been described in chapters 9 and 11 of his book (Landa, 1976)[1], another part in the doctoral dissertation of his former doctoral student and associate O Yudina (Yudina, 1973a), partially published in Yudina, 1972 and Yudina, 1973b. It can only be mentioned here that one of the prerequisites for psychological troubleshooting diagnostics is building an algorithmic or heuristic model of an ideally functioning process in order then to identify deviations from this model by means of special diagnostic probes. (The type of model to be built — algorithmic or heuristic — depends on the algorithmic or heuristic nature of the processes involved in producing responses or answers, ie processes which would be the object of psychological troubleshooting diagnostic procedures.) That is why it can be maintained that psychological troubleshooting diagnostics and the resulting methods of constructing deeper adaptive instructional programmes are a part of algorithmico-heuristic theory and methods of learning and instruction initiated in the USSR about 25 years ago (see Landa, 1974, 1976, 1978) and are now being successfully developed further by a number of authors both in the USSR and the West.

In the USSR, on the basis of the psychological trubleshooting diagnostic methods, our associate O Yudina wrote (in collaboration with G Granik) a programmed textbook where pedagogical reactions to students' mistakes were determined not by their nature only but by their psychological causes as well, identified on the basis of psychological troubleshooting diagnostics (Granik and Yudina, 1970). So it was proved that psychological troubleshooting diagnostic procedures may be not only algorithmized but carried out by specially designed programmed textbooks. The latter, and not only man, can provide the level of adaptation where pedagogical reactions and strategies of instruction are determined not only by the nature of students' answers but by characteristics of processes leading to these answers and producing certain behavioral outcomes. Thus, this textbook is able to identify and treat 'diseases' underlying and generating certain symptoms rather than being limited to diagnosing and reacting to symptoms themselves.

Algorithmization of psychological troubleshooting diagnostic procedures can be conducted not only by means of programmed textbooks but computers as well. It is a matter of technical implementation of algorithms for psychological troubleshooting diagnostic procedures. CAI based on psychological troubleshooting diagnostic methods will make computers both better diagnostic, and deeper adaptive, teaching devices where the 'diagnostic part' of a computer will provide information on a 'treatment part' concerning a student's 'diseases', and the 'treatment part' would be able to 'cure' causes of 'unhealthy symptoms' of students and not only the symptoms themselves.

---

[1] In both chapters, especially in chapter 11, there are a lot of translation and printing mistakes, including mistakes in formulas which distort the meaning and make some of the formulas wrong and even incomprehensible. The publisher has a list of errata which he sends on request.

References

Annet, J (1964) The relationship between theories of learning and theories of instruction. *Programming '63*. Sheffield University, Department of Education.

Austwick, K (ed) (1963) *Teaching Machines and Programming*. Pergamon Press.

Clauss, G (1965) Zur Handlungas analyse durch Algoritmen und ihre Anwendung im Unterricht. *Padagogik*, 4.

Granik, G and Yudina, O (1970) Russian language. Programmed textbook and workbook. *Pedagogica*. Moscow. (In Russian)

Landa, L N (1976) *Instructional Regulation and Control: Cybernetics, Algorithmization and Heuristics in Education*. Educational Technology Publications, Englewood Cliffs.

Yudina, O (1972) Research into the efficiency of diagnostic teaching in the classroom environment. In Ways of increasing the efficiency of Russian language teaching in secondary school. *Pedagogica*, 3. Moscow.

Yudina, O (1973a) Diagnostics of psychological causes of students' errors by means of a programmed textbook. Doctoral dissertation. Moscow. (In Russian)

Yudina, O (1973b) Diagnostics of psychological causes of students' errors in algorithmic and non-algorithmic instruction. In Landa, L (ed) Problems of algorithmization and programming of instruction. *Pedagogica*, 2. (In Russian)

1.3   A Micro-Analytical Procedure to Improve Instructional Materials

P David Mitchell
Director, Graduate Programme in Educational Technology, Concordia University, Departmnent of Education, Montreal, Quebec, Canada

Abstract: It is common to hear complaints that one instructional programme was boring, another interesting. If instructional materials are to teach, they must first induce or reinforce looking and listening. A programme that induces more attention than another is a more effective instructional system (other factors, eg content, being equal). How can we design instructional programmes which promote both viewing/listening and communicate knowledge?

Interest in, or attention to, instructional materials involves a sustained relation between the person and the material (or information). Both programme content and production techniques might control attention. But how can the effects of individual programme elements be isolated in practice?

A laboratory procedure is described which enables us to investigate moment-by-moment fluctuations in attention (using TV viewing behaviour as the exemplar) and to relate attention to both the content and the production techniques used in the programme segments. The viewer sits before a TV receiver which has been modified so that the brightness of the screen is controlled by his viewing behaviour. Each press of a microswitch held in his hand produces a momentary increase in brightness; this defines a viewing response. Lack of responding produces a blank screen within a second or so (depending on original brightness). A steady rate of responding maintains regular brightness. A graphic cumulative record is made of viewing behaviour.

Analysis of viewing records can reveal programme segments which do not maintain students' interests. Causal relationships can be identified between individual components of the programme and their effects on post-tests.

Introduction

As Landa (1962) showed, instruction is a process with poor feedback. To improve teaching and learning Landa argued for the development of cybernetic teaching devices. Such devices are not yet common. Here we begin with the same concern but rely on exploiting existing structures within which we can establish tighter feedback loops. Whether this will facilitate a major increase in educational effectiveness remains problematical. Our initial results are most encouraging. For instance, using the method to be described, our investigation of Educational Television (ETV) aims not only to provide basic reasearch into educational communications but also to provide feedback to the ETV producer. We now operate with time delay but anticipate a real-time cybernetic system which provides the producer with a visual display indicating the extent to which a sample of viewers is interested in the programme *being recorded*. Thus he can attempt to regulate output (attention-elicitation) and not simply inputs during the production.

How Effective are Instructional Materials in Attracting and Maintaining Students' Interest?

An important question is seldom asked, much less answered by researchers on instructional design, that is, to what extent will this instructional material (eg TV programme, booklet) interest the student in a non-institutional situation, where he is free to look at any page or book or TV channel — or, equally, to ignore the instructional material?

It is common to hear students complain that one book, CAL lesson or television programme was 'boring' and another was 'interesting'. Can 'boredom' or 'interest' be operationally defined? Is instructional effectiveness related to interest? If educational materials are to teach, they must first induce looking and/or listening. If one version of a lesson induces more attention than another, then it should be more effective.

Intuitively, we use the concept of *'interest'* to reflect the extent to which a person is engaged in some form of sustained interplay with the subject matter presented by print or other media. Thus the theoretical notion of high interest in the subject or, more appropriately, information stream, implies a relatively high probability of choosing or continuing to view or listen to the stored knowledge once the interaction is established. Conversely, low interest implies a low probability of selecting or continuing to attend to the subject matter.

Without high interest in (ie selecting and paying relatively continuous attention to) the messages printed, the efficacy of instructional communications is questionable regardless of test results under *controlled study*. Interest in, or attention to, instructional materials involves a sustained relationship between the person and the material (or information contained therein). Both content and presentation techniques or format might control attention. However these change throughout the lesson. How can the effects of individual programme elements be isolated for research? Is there a causal relationship between attention to individual components of an instructional programme and learning?

Laboratory for Conjugate Analysis of Attention to Communications

How Can We Investigate an Instructional Programme's Ability to Promote Attention?

Is there any method available to the educational technologist for pre-testing instructional material under non-compulsory conditions, one which might yield data on the student's interest in the subject matter *as presented* — preferably on a dynamic (ie moment-by-moment) basis rather than only retrospectively by interview or post-test?

In the Educational Technology Laboratory at Concordia University in Canada we have established just such a procedure. It provides a continuous and precise recording of a person's attention to (ie interest in) a sequence of mediated instructional communications. This technique can supplement or replace other attempts to measure interest or attention (eg subjective reports, unobserved monitoring of time spent attending to stimulus, monitoring of time spent looking at a distracting stimulus, physiological measures of arousal).

A key research problem concerns the isolation of individual elements in a lesson and their effects on students' capability. Using television as an exemplary case we have established a laboratory for monitoring moment-by-moment variations in viewing behaviour (as an operational definition of attention to, or interest in, the instructional messages). We are beginning to extend this research to slide/tape presentations and plan to analyze Computer-Aided Learning and textual materials.

Conjugate Programmed Analysis of Behaviour

Conjugate reinforcement procedures differ from standard operant reinforcement which usually provides a discrete event (eg candy, new stimulus) contingent upon some action. Instead, the contingent 'stimulus' is *continuously available* (eg a TV programme). In conjugate reinforcement the person's behaviour controls directly and immediately the *intensity* of the stimulus. To illustrate, at a noisy cocktail party one can attend to another person's speech and ignore extraneous information or noise. Yet one can shift attention easily. By definition, the other person's speech (or content thereof) serves to reinforce attending behaviour. Similarly, attending to a TV screen may be reinforced by its content (cf Lindsley, 1962).

This *dynamic* (as contrasted with the usual static) reinforcement procedure is highly sensitive to moment-by-moment fluctuations in the person's behaviour because the stimulus intensity is controlled by the person's *rate* of responding. Thus, it is especially valuable for examining the reinforcing value of *continuous* or *narrative stimuli* such as a symphony, TV programme or other information which cannot be broken into discrete segments for episodic presentation because this would violate the nature of the narrative stimulus itself. (Imagine attempting to use a five-second burst of Beethoven's violin concerto or a few seconds of TV news as a reinforcer!)

The technique of conjugately programmed reinforcement satisfies many criteria; it provides efficient, automatic and precise recording of behaviour and an operational definition of interest. By making the contingent stimulus *continuously* available, where the *intensity* of this stimulus varies directly and immediately with the rate of response, conjugate analysis provides a direct, immediate and fine-grained analysis of moment-by-moment changes in the reinforcing value of the contingent stimulus.

A response is defined functionally. Pressing a sequence of keys on a typewriter may be considered as typing a word, not simply as so many keys pressed. Similarly, if pressing a microswitch illuminates a TV screen momentarily, it is a television-viewing response. A record of this provides a measure of attention and an operational definition of interest.

In our lab the viewer sits before a TV receiver which has been modified so that the brightness of the screen is controlled by his viewing behaviour (which is defined functionally). Each press of a microswitch held in his hand produces a momentary increase in brightness; this defines a viewing response. Lack of responding produces a blank screen within a second or two, depending on original brightness. A steady rate of responding (which becomes as automatic as eye movements after a few minutes) maintains regular brightness. A cumulative record is made of this viewing behaviour automatically. The degree of resolution of the graph is less than five seconds. We also use counters and printing counters. Thus we can relate isolated events in a TV programme to viewing behaviour. (This technique was developed by Lindsley in 1962 who used it to study the effectiveness of commercial messages.)

Using current response stations, the feedback loop to the educational materials producer must be provided by the researcher. This delay can be eliminated if several stations are yoked together and fed directly from the TV studios during a production. The average viewing behaviour would be displayed to the producer who could try different presentation formats, etc if attention is decreasing. Such cybernetic TV production remains untested.

Microanalytic Investigation of Instruction

Attention

Applied at the micro-analytic level, where engaging the attention of students is a *sine qua non,* instructional design should benefit from continuous feedback-controlled decisions about what instructional events to present next. Instructional theory fails to provide an adequate explanation of how a person's capability is modified by interplay with his environment but it is clear that attention to the message stream is essential. Attention may be controlled not only by instructional messages but also by the manner of presentation. (Perhaps learning how to teach or to design effective instructional materials involves the manner of presentation as much as the content.)

If a common meaning is to be shared by the instructional designer and student it is necessary to use attention-eliciting techniques especially if the information stream is externally paced, because the student is unable to review the material. It is also useful if not essential even if we accept the view of cognitive researchers that the student is responsible for his own attention. Attending behaviour should be reinforced.

Entertainment

Though producers of educational television materials often talk about the entertainment aspect of their work (for example, 'Sesame Street is intended to entertain as well as to educate'), it is difficult to discern exactly what is meant. If entertainment implies not simply to amuse but to engage the attention of people then any communication (which *must* engage attention of the intended recipient) might be called entertainment. What can we learn about instructional communications by analyzing the manner of presentation of professional entertainers? Is it possible to examine TV programmes that capture attention in order to discover critical factors that might be used to design instructional communications?

TV Production Techniques

It is common knowledge that people watch entertaining TV programmes even when there is something better to do. This involvement is believed to be less common with 'educational' TV. Content differences notwithstanding, production techniques may contribute to this.

Unlike commercial television, where new production techniques and formats are introduced to attract viewers' attention, educational TV changes little and relies on slower pacing. Yet short, fast programme segments; strobe lights; amplified guitars; and long sequences of fast stills commonly are viewed by young people who then find ETV boring. Whether such techniques can, or ought to, be used in ETV is a moot point.

ETV, compared with its entertainment counterpart, is more concerned with attitude change, motivating viewers to read textual material and promoting the growth of knowledge. Whether and when techniques used in entertainment TV are compatible with these aims is an important area for research.

Evaluation of ETV Programme Effectiveness

Most studies of Educational Television (ETV) examine post-viewing scores on tests of recognition or recall. Also, they rely on aggregate data from many viewers. Typically there is considerable variance in the level of individual student achievement. To what extent can these individual differences be explained by differences in attention to, or interest in, the instructional communications? Expressed otherwise, if the viewer does *not observe* information pertinent to post-viewing test items then that could explain why his score is lower than it otherwise might have been. It could also help to explain confusing reports about the instructional effectiveness of 'television'.

Another complicating factor in ETV evaluation studies is that identical composite scores on a post-test do *not* imply shared knowledge about identical segments of the programme. Different viewers may selectively recall different portions of a programme. Such aggregate scores may be useful for predicting class performance but they shed little light on the underlying dynamics of learning from watching television.

Do Students Pay More Attention to Complex than to Simple ETV Images?

Research

We have produced and analyzed three versions of an instructional TV programme. They have a common audio track but different video tracks. One consists solely of a presenter (intended as a baseline for comparison). The others contain mixed video segments: presenter; motion picture film footage; slides; or graphics (including simple movement of a pointer or cut-outs). Ten instructional concepts were presented either by presenter alone (simple video) in one mixed version or by complex video (film or slides or graphics) in the other. Because the audio channel of educational (and other) television often carries most of the significant information all concepts were presented aurally (audio was not regulated by the viewer). Thus we investigated relative attractiveness of the different video production techniques.

In each of the 10 programme blocks attention was higher for the complex version of the video presentation. Comparing mean attention scores for all simple video blocks with complex video, the latter produced 19 per cent more viewing behaviour ($p < .01$), graphics segments being most attention-provoking. (See Figure 1.) Mean scores averaged over several lengthy video segments obscure many interesting details. Individual differences were common (*cf* Shears, 1978). Note that attention rises and falls as production techniques change.

Figure 2 shows a cumulative record typical of many 'viewers' of a mixed video programme; a horizontal line indicates non-viewing and slope is a function of viewing rate. The vertical line is a trace left by the pen as it re-cycled from the top to the bottom of the page. Notice that the second half of the programme began with a graphics shot and viewing rate was high throughout most of this shot, fading near the end and then recovering. With the next shot, of the presenter, visual attention

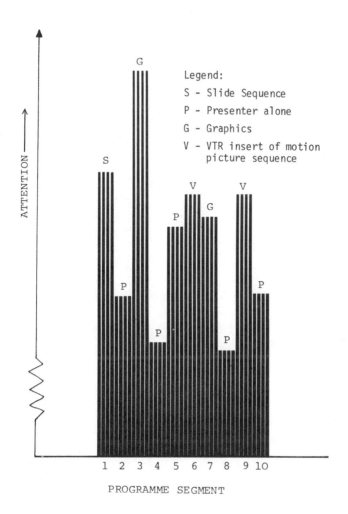

Figure 1. *Plot of attention vs programme segment in an ETV programme*

dropped to zero except for a short burst for a few seconds. The onset of a motion picture sequence produced a high viewing rate until the presenter appeared again. Such behaviour is not unexpected; it underscores our intention to refine methods of instructional design so that attention is maintained even if visually uninteresting material must be presented. (Preliminary results suggest that a 'talking head' will be watched more if the shot is not held constant but, for example, switched from one camera to another or from a long shot to a close up.) Less readily explained is the fact that Figure 2 shows that the presenter was watched fairly consistently during the first half of the programme. It may be linked to audio cues.

A similar cumulative record has been made of a person 'watching' an ETV programme. The audio was 'on' throughout and the programme attended to only 20 per cent of the time. For this viewer it was little more than a radio programme. If many people yield a similar record it would show a need to revise the programme.

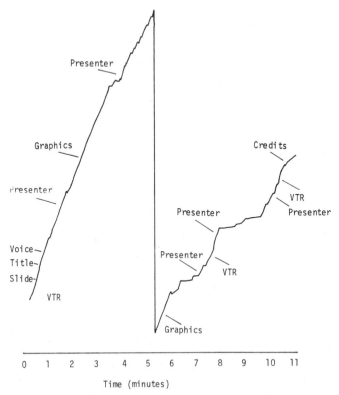

Figure 2. *How one person viewed the TV programme 'Forest Fires'*

Production Techniques

Inspection of cumulative records reveals frequent cue effects. To illustrate, non-viewing persons responded after hearing such phrases as: 'next year the forest may not be there'; 'sometimes forest rangers set fires'; '. . . out of control'; 'advantages of controlled fires'; and also after a pause in the audio track. Future research will investigate the interaction between attention to audio and video channels.

It is commonly assumed that motion pictures and television can maintain viewers' arousal and interest to some desired level by changing the stimulus frequently (by cutting from one shot to another and using montages of several shots to assemble a larger view). Figure 3 shows the relative effects of the different techniques used in these three versions. The low resolution display of the TV screen limits the amount of information that can be presented before attention diminishes. Perhaps this analytic tool can help us determine the cutting rate that maintains an acceptable level of attention to the visual display. Armed with laboratory-mediated feedback a highly developed programming strategy might be identified, one which integrates a variety of techniques for singling out details, making transitions, showing transformations of systems, etc.

Using this feedback controlled instructional design procedure, the producer of educational TV should be able to learn how to produce effective programmes more readily than without it. Concordia University's Graduate Programme in Educational Technology includes courses in the production and evaluation of ETV materials.

It is anticipated that this procedure will be used by students of ETV to develop relevant skills. In principle it could be used to analyze other instructional materials.

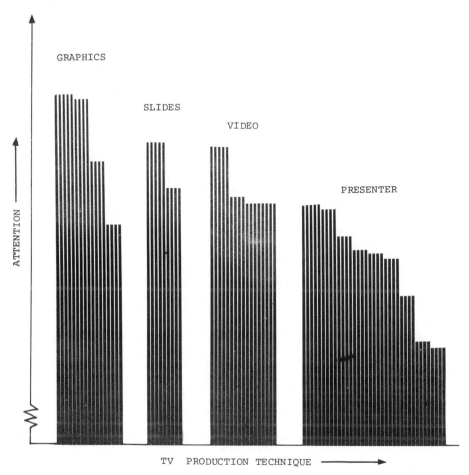

Figure 3. *Plot of attention vs production technique used in two ETV programmes*

Other Instructional Materials

We are beginning to use conjugate analysis as a means to determine the best pacing to use in slide/tape presentations. In addition it can detect slides which are not especially interesting to viewers or, conversely, slides which induce much viewing.

The technique can be adapted to the analysis of textual material provided the latter can be presented under experimentally defined conditions (eg as a sequence of slides, or using a TV camera which scans the material). We plan to design studies to determine its effectiveness in this area.

Viewing and Learning

Many investigators have reaffirmed and elaborated the basic notion that people can recall *some* information presented by a TV programme. Typically there is considerable variance in the level of individual student achievement. To what extent can these individual differences be explained by differences in attention to the precise segments of the programme which contain the information needed? If the viewer does not attend to information pertinent to post-viewing test items then that could explain why his score is lower than it otherwise might have been. Current research is investigating this question.

Conclusion

Instructional design practice does not always meet the minimum standards assumed by writers of texts on the subject. But even the latter rely frequently on one-shot analysis of the overall effectiveness of relatively large-scale instructional products (albeit with revision and retesting). Such input-output analysis provides no insight into the cybernetics of cognition and learning. It does not even suggest what would happen if different decisions had been made, eg about production techniques. It is really a static model of a continuing dynamic equilibrium process which we wish to regulate. Nor does it allow the scriptwriter *qua* instructional designer readily to develop knowledge of how to design instructional TV. We conclude that more and tighter feedback loops are needed to improve instructional design and instruction especially that which involves TV. Further we have outlined an attempt to conduct basic and applied research on the instructional design process as applied to ETV. This appears to be useful not only to improve instructional design theory directly but also to help trainees or practitioners to develop knowledge pertinent to the task of instructional design and evaluation, knowledge not readily attainable without experiencing the feedback processes provided.

References

Landa, L N (1962) The cybernetic approach to educational theory. *Voprosy Filosofii,* **16**, 9, pp 75-87. Moscow. (Translated)
Lindsley, O E (1962) A behavioural measure of television viewing. *Journal of Advertising Research,* **2**, pp 1-12.
Shears, A E (1978) *A Study of Relative Effectiveness of Various Production Techniques Using Conjugate Analysis Apparatus.* MA thesis, Concordia University, Canada.

Acknowledgement

Both the assistance of Arthur Shears and the assistance of a grant from the Quebec Minister of Education's Programme de Formation des Chercheurs et d'Action Concertée are gratefully acknowledged.

1.4 Creativity and Control - Neglected Factors within Self-Instruction Programme Design

Alexander Romiszowski
International Telecommunications Union, Brazil
and Barbara Atherton
South Thames College and Bayer (UK) Ltd

Abstract: Taking Self-Instruction to mean a teaching/learning process planned to meet certain objectives, where execution of the plan depends on the learner rather than the teacher, and the mode can be either individual (eg programmed instruction) or group (eg simulation and gaming), the potential variety and application of Self-Instruction — SI — is immense.

However, we find only a few such plans have been applied on a large scale, most not realizing their early promise. Stereotyped procedures and tools and models are being applied to situations for which they were never designed and they are all leading to non-achievement of desired results, rejection and resistance.

By analysis of a series of case studies from both education and training the authors illustrate that success is often a function of the levels of creativity in development of the plan and the levels of managerial skill in its execution. Techniques are suggested for the development of these largely neglected factors within educational technology projects.

Satisfactory performance in any job involves three aspects: knowing *when* to do it, knowing *how* to do it and *doing* it.

Introduction

The last 20 years have seen the appearance of countless new plans for individualized instruction. The structure of these plans (as well as their nomenclature) shows a considerable amount of overlap, the majority illustrating distinct hereditary links with programmed instruction.

However, in general the initial promise of SI plans has not been fully realized in practice. Many successful plans can be seen at a local level, but the various mini-innovations are a long way from becoming an integral part of the on-going teaching/learning system. They remain highly susceptible to changes in staffing, attitudes and policy, or 'deteriorate with 'institutionalization' as noted by Romiszowski (1968, 1977), Miller (1976) and Schoen (1976a and b).

Observation of plans from both education and training has led the authors to identify an imbalance in the emphasis that educational technologists tend to place on the development of innovative instructional plans. The emphasis is generally very much on the *how* to do it, very much less on the *when* to do it and still less on the *doing* it aspects of the job. As a result of neglecting the *when* aspect, schemes get launched which are inadequately designed for the prevailing conditions in which they must function. As a result of neglecting the *doing* it aspect, schemes which are reasonably well designed in the first instance, run into operational problems later which the system can neither cope with nor adjust to.

In order to attend to the *when* aspect a considerable amount of creative problem solving is called for on the part of the instructional designer. In order to attend to the *doing* aspect attention must be paid to the development of effective monitoring and control systems, which will rapidly indicate any divergence and deterioration in system outputs and will feed back this information, transforming it into corrective actions.

Thus the two aspects of **creativity** and **control** are seen as two important yet often neglected factors in instructional design.

The International Dictionary of Education (Kogan Page, 1977) defines Technology as 'the creative application of science to industrial (or other practical) purposes'. Our technology, however, has developed in the eyes of some observers an image which suggests the antithesis of creativity. Hamblin (1974) sees the Educational Technology approach as inevitably leading to stereotyped 'mass production' solutions, whereas more often than not education and training require a 'unit production' approach. Whilst correct in identifying the type of approach required, he is wrong in denying that educational technologists adopt a 'unit production' approach which adapts basic tools and techniques to the precise requirements of each problem being tackled. For example the Mathetics approach is a very detailed, yet very flexible, application of a few basic principles to the solution of a host of instructional design problems (Gilbert, 1962). There is nothing of a 'mass production' nature about this technique — each new problem gives rise to a unique solution, even if the steps of the decision process are essentially the same — and this is just one of many tools and techniques now available in the educational technologist's tool box.

The Systems Approach as Promoter of Creativity

One can conceive of the systems approach, in any of its applications, as composed of five main activities:

1 Defining the problem — to identify what one wishes to achieve.
2 Analyzing the problem — to generate and compare alternative means of achieving the objectives.
3 Developing the most appropriate or realistic of the means identified — the 'optimal solution'.
4 Implementing the solution — and observing the results.
5 Evaluating these results — and feeding back this information in order to revise or improve the solution where necessary.

So where does the creativity lie? Principally in the second of these five activities — the analysis of the problem and the generation of *alternative* solutions. These alternatives may be original or stereotyped; there may be many alternatives generated or few. In order to efficiently search for and generate viable yet original alternatives, the instructional designer must get accustomed to performing the 'anasynthesis' type of thinking described by Silvern (1965, 1972). He will not separate the processes of analysis and synthesis. He will think ahead to consider the implications of alternatives and he will have to make many conceptual 'jumps'.

Let us illustrate the 'jumps' by reference to the task that faces a training manager whenever someone brings in a 'training problem'.

He will have to take 'macro' level decisions concerning the problem as a whole. Is training really the best solution, do we have the resources to develop the training required, will we be able to implement, control and evaluate the training system effectively, etc? Then he (or one of his staff) will have to make many 'micro' level decisions in terms of instructional strategies, tactics, media etc.

Creative Problem Solving at the 'Macro' Level

Romiszowski (1978, 1979) has constructed an analysis schema for performance problems. We call it a schema because that is what it is intended to be — an

interrelation of the many aspects that might be 'behind' any given performance
problem (see Figure 1).

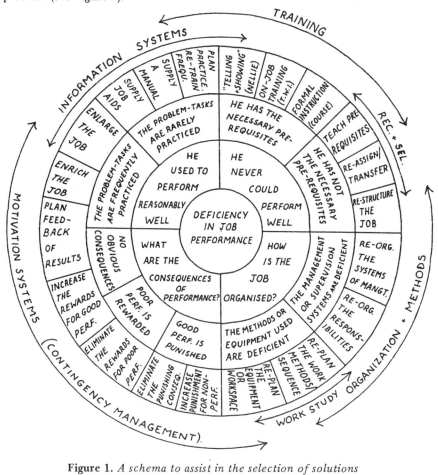

Figure 1. *A schema to assist in the selection of solutions
to performance problems (Romiszowski, A J 1978-1979)*

The schema is not necessarily complete. As any conceptual schema it is subject
to constant adaptation as new phenomena or new information are encountered.
However, we believe it will be easier for the reader to adapt a schema as presented
here than to adapt a semi-algorithmic presentation (eg Mager, 1970) which carries
with it the connotation (as do all algorithms) that every problem has a unique and
predictable solution.

Furthermore, the schema emphasizes the flexibility and the overlap that exists
in the process of selecting a solution. No sequential steps of analysis are implied.
Rather, the reader is encouraged to think 'systemically' of all the factors in relation
to all the others. Theoretically, almost any combination of almost any of the 20
types of solution listed in the outer rim of our circle could be selected as a specific
'total' solution to a specific complex, multi-faceted performance problem. In
practice, some of these solutions are mutually exclusive, so the sum total of viable
alternative choices is considerably less than the theoretical total number of possible
combinations (640,000) but would still remain in the thousands.

Finally, the schema emphasizes the importance of a multi-disciplinary approach and the prerequisite of effective horizontal communication and co-operation in the organization, so as not to artificially restrict the choices of solution open to us. Figure 1 emphasizes this point, by indicating the six types of support services which might exist in a typical large organization and which might be concerned with developing certain types of solution to performance problems. Quite clearly, any combination of these six types of intervention might be quite a viable 'total' solution to a given problem — this gives us a total variety of 63 different combinations of department (or 63 different possible structures for the team which is to solve the problem). Any lack of horizontal co-operation will severely limit this variety. It is not uncommon to meet instances in reality where this variety is limited to *one* — for example, the problem is first brought to the notice of the Training Department so you can be quite sure that a purely training solution will be produced.

Yet, if there is one thing which renders 'systemic thinking' impossible it is the compartmentalization of one's problem-solving schemas into 'watertight compartments'.

Creative Problem Solving at the 'Micro' Level

One can measure the creativity of a specific design by the success and the originality with which the basic principles have been adapted to the particular requirements of the problem. We will illustrate this point by reference to one set of 'basic principles' — those of Programmed Instruction. Biran (1972) outlined the application and limitations of programmed self-instruction. In the table following, we seek not to promote PI, but to illustrate how it is possible, with the *creative* application of the basic principles of PI to produce successful solutions to a variety of problems.

The examples mentioned serve to illustrate the richness possible in the adaptation of just one basic model of instruction; there are many other models which will be more appropriate in certain circumstances. We suggest that these other models, just as programmed instruction, may be creatively modified to the specific needs and characteristics of each project and should not be applied in a mechanistic, stereotyped manner. The danger of stereotyped, unthinking application of a given solution is ever present. One must never forget the purpose for which the model was originally designed and the environment it was designed to operate within.

Controlling the Design Process

Reverting to the 'macro' viewpoint, let us consider the factors which might promote or inhibit creativity in the instruction design process. Most importantly, we must create the working conditions that will promote, rather than kill, creativity.

This will require attention to the organizational structure of the instructional design teams. One should keep in mind the heuristic nature of the process, in avoiding any semblance of a linear, 'production line' approach to instructional design. The analyst, to be creative, must modify his basic approach and tools of analysis to suit the problem. He will only be able to do this if he 'follows through' to the synthesis stages. Thus, as soon as the project is too big to be a 'one-man-show', some form of integrated project team work should be planned which will enable all team members to maintain a global image of the project, even though they may specialize for a time in the details of one stage.

The working methods of the team will also require attention. An unstructured 'design by committee' approach is neither effective nor efficient. However, group work is often more productive from the viewpoint of creativity than individual effort. Organized group activities of the 'brainstorming' variety can be very useful

Limitations of programmed self-instruction (From Biran, 1972)	Some creative solutions which have overcome the limitations
Unsuitability: For teaching manual skills. (Dexterity or high speed.)	'Programmed simulators' (Wheatcroft, 1973; Romiszowski, 1968, 1974). See also the 'RITT' system.
For poor readers. (Young children or adults in industry.)	'RITT' system of paced audio-programming in industrial training (Agar, 1962). Language Master (Leedham and Unwin, 1971). Audio Tutorial (Postlewaite, 1972).
For open-ended subject matter. (Management, literature, etc.)	Programmed group instruction (BOAC management training). Structural communication (Hodgson, 1974).
When the exact needs and objectives of the target audience are unknown. (Orientation, reference, revision or learning.)	Information mapping (Horn, 1968, 1973).
When the content is subject to frequent changes, or the methods of work vary.	'Learner cue sheets' (Le Hunte, Learning Systems Ltd).
When the learners have other study habits.	Oral group response to OHP programme (Blake, UNESCO, 1975). Keller Plan for undergraduates (Keller, 1968, Keller and Sherman, 1974).

Table 1.

in promoting creative solutions. Several techniques for managing such activities specifically related to instructional design have been developed. Mager (1971) presents a technique for developing specific objectives from general aims in education by a type of brainstorming. The DACUM process (Design a curriculum), used by several Canadian organizations and educational institutions is another group-dynamics technique which organizes the process of generating and sequencing instructional objectives. (Adams, 1972, Sinnett, 1974.)

The Role of the Environment

The immediate working environment of the instructional design teams is important. Creativity, like any other behaviour, is likely to occur more often if it is reinforced. Attention should be given to the provision of reinforcement for original ideas. One obvious aspect is to ensure that new ideas, even if on face value appearing unrealistic, do get followed up in a systematic manner. The creation of a 'research and development' atmosphere with time devoted to following up novel ideas and to attempting to generalize the lessons learnt from these experiences, should pay off. However, this time should be controlled within reasonable limits, as the main project objectives must also be achieved on schedule.

The organizational structure of the wider environment in which the design team works also requires attention. We have already illustrated how the lack of horizontal communication and co-operation in an organization can severely limit the variety of alternative solutions that can be considered in practice. If the wider environment discourages the adoption of the 'wider system' viewpoint by the analyst, he will very soon adapt to the situation and simply do what the situation 'obviously' calls for. Any creativity in his approach will rapidly be stifled. Constraints must not be considered as barriers to innovation, but as potentially flexible factors within the wider system, requiring an equally creative approach in terms of their effect on the design and execution of the plan.

Finally, no amount of creativity and control in the design process of a plan will ensure its successful implementation and adoption unless the environment in which the plan must operate is appropriate to the needs of the plan and its users. Within the Infant/Primary and Lower Secondary sectors of the educational system we find widespread use of the SI plan concept. Here, the approach to both curriculum content and school organization have enabled an atmosphere and environment conducive to such development.

In our experience, the organizational requirements and environmental implications of such plans are continually underestimated and uncatered for, with the Avon County Resources for Learning Development Unit (Waterhouse) providing a welcome exception. Unless attention is paid not only to the organization of learning spaces (eg Smith, 1974) but also to the development of study-routes, record-keeping systems and control factors, the plan will not be able to feed back the information required to ensure that operational problems can be corrected in time to allow for the successful continuation of the plan.

Controlling the Long Term Execution of the Plan

In setting up a management system for a course, we have a (theoretical) choice between a strictly 'line management' approach in which decisions are centralized, which involves the receiving and execution of orders from above, or a 'project management' approach in which all concerned in the execution are kept fully informed of all project objectives, progress and problems, often being called on to assist with the decision-making process.

The former approach seems to be implied by certain pre-programmed instructional plans and is an aspect which has not gone down well with the teaching profession as a whole. Such an approach has more chance of success in a striclty 'training' situation, particularly if the instruction is to be carried out by para-professionals (Romiszowski and Machado, 1978). However, in general education, even using para-professional 'animators' as opposed to fully trained teachers, the chances of long term success are very slight (Romiszowski and Paster, 1977).

It has continually been our experience that unless teachers are actively involved with the design of a plan and receive in-service training and on-site guidance, the chances of success are limited. Furthermore, as the human elements in any instructional system are subject to change this training/guidance/involvement is an on-going process. This has serious implications for commercially produced or externally developed project material, as evidenced by the evaluation of the Humanities Project (Ruddock, 1976), and indications are that insufficient emphasis is placed on this aspect of management at both pre- and in-service training levels.

Thus the second alternative of 'project management' seems to be the more promising of the two, both in education and in training, but particularly so in formal education. The team teaching movement was one attempt to bring such an approach into the classroom. However, just getting together and 'teaching by committee' has no more chance of success than has 'design by committee'. Once again, one needs to operate as a group, but in a highly structured manner and in an environment which allows suffucient time and resources for the essential on-going planning, monitoring and maintenance of the system.

Each teacher acts as a control system (apart from his other functions). As such he must not only know and understand the objectives of the plan but have a commitment to the achievement of these objectives. This commitment will only be fully realized if, as innovation theory indicates (Havelock, 1973), the potential strategy is understood to be related directly to the needs of the learning situation by the implementing teachers.

Requirements for success	therefore	Teachers/trainers require
A sense of direction	⟶	To know and understand the objectives (identify achievements)
Commitment to achieve the objectives	⟶	To accept the concept of SI and to believe in its potential
Empathy with the medium/method	⟶	To understand the scope and the limitations of SI systems
Ability to perceive the medium from no of perspectives	⟶	To have a conceptual map (schema) of the plan adopted
Skill in the use of basic tools or procedures	⟶	To be able to operate within all the aspects of the system
Ability to recognize discord	⟶	To develop skills of analysis and evaluation of results
Flexibility in approach	⟶	To be prepared and able to change methods/modify approach
Adequate resources	⟶	To have time and resources to control and evaluate progress

Table 2.

In self-instructional systems, each learner also becomes part of the control system, and as such must also be aware not only of the individual elements of the system but also the relationship between the systems elements. We get closer to the cybernetic ideal of the 'self-correcting' system the more 'micro' the scale at which feedback control takes place. However, learners and teachers will need to be taught and persuaded to play their part in the control system. They will have to be well informed and to act objectively and creatively, in making control decisions. This implies a range of considerations that should be taken into account in planning their in-service training/guidance.

To take the case of the implementation of a partly self-instructional system, at least the requirements set out in Table 2 should be considered.

Conclusion

Whilst the above does not appear new in content, the implications in terms of emphasis on requirements will, we believe, go some way to ensuring that creativity and control are no longer neglected factors within SI programme design.

References

Adams, R E (1972) *DACUM Approach to Curriculum, Learning and Evaluation in Occupational Training.* Nova Scotia New State Corporation, Yarmouth.
Affarsekonomi, 10. (In Swedish.) Also, Swedish training system breaks the language barrier. *Industrial Training International.* UK, September 1966.
Agar (1962) Instruction of industrial workers by tape recorders.
Biran, L (1972) The role and limitations of programmed instruction. In Romiszowski, A J (ed)

APLET Yearbook of Educational and Instructional Technology 1972/3. Kogan Page, London.

Gilbert, T F (1962) Mathetics: the technology of education. *Journal of Mathetics,* 1 and 2. (Reprinted in UK by Recall.)

Hamblin, A C (1974) *The Evaluation and Control of Training.* McGraw-Hill, UK.

Havelock, R G (1973) Planning for innovation — through dissemination and utilization of knowledge. *Crusk.* Institute for Social Research, University of Michigan.

Hodgson, A M (1974) Structural communication in practice. In Romiszowski, A J (ed) *Yearbook of Educational and Instructional Technology 1974/5.* Kogan Page, London.

Horn, R E *et al* (1968) Information mapping for learning and reference. *Information Resources Inc.* Massachusetts.

Horn, R E (1973) Introduction to information mapping. *Information Resources Inc.* Lexington, Massachusetts.

Keller, F S (1968) Goodbye Teacher. *Journal of Applied Behavioural Analysis.* 1. USA

Keller, F S and Sherman, J G (1974) *Keller Plan Handbook.* W A Benjamin, California.

Leedham, J and Unwin, D (1971) *Programmed Learning in the Schools* (3rd edition). Longman, UK.

Le Hunte, R G J (unpublished) Training technology in practice. A collection of summary papers. *Inbucon Learning Systems Ltd.* Harrow, Middlesex.

Mager, R F (1971) *Goal Analysis.* Fearon, USA.

Mager, R F and Pipe, P (1970) *Analyzing Performance Problems.* Fearon, USA.

Miller, R L (1976) Individualized instruction in mathematics: a review of research. *Mathematics Teacher.* USA.

Page, G T and Thomas, J B (1977) *International Dictionary of Education.* Kogan Page, London.

Postlethwait, S N *et al* (1972) *The Audio-Tutorial Approach to Learning* (3rd edition). Burgess Publishing Co, USA.

Romiszowski, A J (1968) Programmed instruction in engineering and technical subjects. *Engineering.* London.

Romiszowski, A J (1974) *The Selection and Use of Instructional Media: A Systems Approach.* Kogan Page, London.

Romiszowski, A J (1977) *A Study of Individualised Systems for Mathematics Instruction at the Post Secondary Levels.* Doctoral Thesis. University of Loughborough Library, UK.

Romiszowski, A J (1978) Alguns Cuidados na applicação de Tecnologia Educacional en Grandes Projetos de Treinamento. (Some points to watch when applying educational technology in large scale training projects — Portuguese original.) Paper presented at the second conference of the ABTD (Brazilian Association of Training and Development, associated with the ASTD in the USA) in São Paulo, October 1978. Published in the proceedings.

Romiszowski, A J (1979) *Designing Instructional Systems.* Kogan Page, London.

Romiszowski, A J and Pastor, H V (1977) The in-service training of educational and para-educational staff in educational technology projects in Brazil. In *Aspects of Educational Technology,* XI. Kogan Page, London.

Romiszowski, A J and Machado, N (1978) Developing a large scale modularised training system for Brazilian telecommunications. In *Aspects of Educational Technology,* XII. Kogan Page, London.

Ruddock, J (1976) Dissemination of innovation: the humanities curriculum project. *Schools Council Working Paper,* 56. Evans/Methuen, London.

Schoen, H L (1976a) Self paced mathematics instruction: how effective has it been? *Arithmetic Teacher.* February, 1976.

Schoen, H L (1976b) Self paced mathematics instruction: how effective has it been in secondary and post-secondary school? *Mathematics Teacher.* May, 1976, USA.

Silvern, L (1965) The systems engineering of learning. A series of slide/sound presentations. Silvern Associates, USA.

Silvern, L (1972) *Systems Engineering Applied to Training.* Gulf Publishing Co, Houston, Texas.

Sinnett, W E (1974) The application of DACUM in retraining and post secondary curriculum development. Humber College of Applied Arts and Technology, Toronto.

Smith, P (1974) *Design of Learning Spaces.* Council for Educational Technology, London.

UNESCO (1975) *A Systems Approach to Teaching and Learning Procedures.* UNESCO Press, Paris.

Waterhouse, P *A Handbook of Classroom Management for Independent Learning.* Avon County Resources for Learning Development Unit, Bristol.

Wheatcroft, E (1973) *Simulators for Skill.* McGraw-Hill, UK.

1.5 A Competency-Based Approach to Course Development in Teacher Education

Elizabeth A Soremekun
Department of Educational Technology, University of Ife, Nigeria

Abstract: This paper describes the design, development and evaluation of a competency-based introductory undergraduate course in educational communication and technology by a team of instructional technologists.

Introduction

During the last few years a great deal of concern has been generated about skills development, particularly in developing countries, yet few courses at the university level would appear to have been designed around the development of such needed skills. The undergraduate students in Education at the University of Ife have been exposed to a relatively new approach to course design. A competency-based approach, according to Davies (1973), requires a thorough analysis of the task to be performed. Based upon this analysis, competencies or skills can then be identified and objectives specified and written.

This paper describes the design, development and evaluation of a competency-based course in Educational Communications and Technology for third-year students enrolled for the BSc/BA degree in Education. This course is taught as part of a broad based teacher preparation programme which all undergraduate students are required to take before completing their degree. During the last four years the course was taught with primarily an audio-visual focus to acquaint potential teachers with the use of audio-visual aids in classroom instruction. The course as presently designed, however, serves the dual function of meeting undergraduate teacher preparation requirements and introducing students to the field of educational communications and technology which is an area of specialization at the graduate level in the Faculty of Education.

Planning

A team of instructional technologists in the Department of Educational Technology were assigned the task of re-designing Education 303 (Educational Communications and Technology). The first effort was to reorganize the course in order to maximize efficiency and yet meet the specific needs of secondary schools. This planning stage covered a series of meetings, each meeting designed to focus on a particular aspect of the course.

One of the basic principles of a competency-based approach is to carefully and critically analyze the task to be performed (Davies, 1971). Davies identified three types of task analysis: topic analysis, job analysis and skills analysis. Topic analysis involves analyzing the intellectual task to be performed, ie understanding the theoretical basis of educational technology. Job analysis requires analyzing the physical or psycho-motor performance in carrying out the task, ie producing instructional materials. Skills analysis refers to analyzing the specific psycho-motor behaviour required to perform the job, ie layout design. The emphasis here is on how the job is carried out. It is only necessary if an intricate type of psycho-motor skill is required.

Our team commenced by specifying the competencies required by secondary school teachers in the area of educational communications and technology — job analysis. Specifying such competencies were based on the required skills for teachers (Figure 1) as assessed through administrative reports from secondary schools, the curriculum, observations during teaching practice, student population, the secondary school environment and available resources in secondary schools. It was necessary to

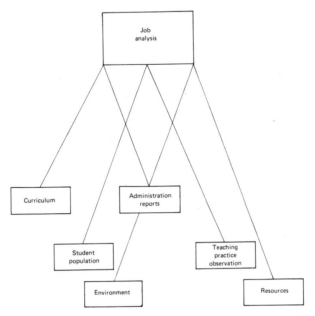

Figure 1. *Task analysis — job analysis*

concentrate on job analysis first in order to provide the necessary information for the second type of analysis we performed — topic analysis. Some instructional developers might prefer to start with topic analysis. However, the specific needs of the environmental setting in which teachers operate made job analysis a logical starting point. This is quite appropriate since there is no hard and fast rule concerning which type of analysis should come first.

Job analysis indicated several competencies for secondary teachers. They should be able to:

(a) plan their instruction incorporating the use of instructional materials;
(b) apply the general guidelines for the selection and utilization of instructional materials;
(c) design and produce various instructional materials;
(d) apply evaluation procedures to the instructional process.

Once having identified the required competencies for secondary school teachers, consideration was then given to the specific topics to be taught. These were further broken down into sub-topics. Those topics considered relevant to the required competencies were listed and arranged in a hierarchical order according to a logical sequence. This formed the basis for a course syllabus. Sub-topics were generated from the broad areas or categories specified. The following topic outline was produced:

Theoretical Basis of Educational Technology

☐ Technology in Education
☐ Learning Theory
☐ Communication Theory
☐ Perception

Curriculum and Instruction

☐ Educational Aims and Objectives
☐ Curriculum Objectives
☐ Instructional Systems
☐ Instructional Objectives
☐ Instructional Strategies

Utilization

☐ Introduction to Types of Media
☐ Characteristics of Media Types
☐ Selection and Utilization of Instructional Media

Evaluation

☐ Evaluation of Instructional Systems
☐ Evaluation of Instructional Materials

In refining each of the topics listed the specific task to be performed was the central focus as shown in the example given below on communications.

Topic: Communication Theory
Task: Concept of Noise
1 What is noise?
2 How does noise prevent effective communication?
3 What are some examples of noise?

A further analysis based on specific skills was deemed unnecessary since the required competencies for the job did not necessitate intricate psycho-motor skills. Sufficient attention was given to this under job analysis.

Organization

Re-designing the course to reflect a competency-based curriculum had certain implications for the way in which it is physically structured. The course had previously been taught by individual lecturers each presenting and organizing lectures as they wished. Greater emphasis is now placed on the attainment of specific skills and therefore all students must have a similar programme. A competency-based approach also meant greater emphasis on practical work since the course has a distinct psycho-motor component. Organizational considerations were based on (a) the nature of the task to be performed; (b) number of students; (c) number of staff available; (d) other resources (ie materials and equipment); (e) available space; (f) how much time could be allotted to the task; (g) time-table considerations.

Many of the above factors combined to influence the nature of the organizational pattern chosen. For example, (b), (c), (d) and (f) were the determining factors in deciding on large group instruction for lectures. The size of tutorial groups was influenced by (a), (e) and (g).

The basic pattern of organizational structure consisted of lectures, tutorials, individualized instruction, consultations and tours. All aspects of the course are designed to complement each other rather than duplicate effort.

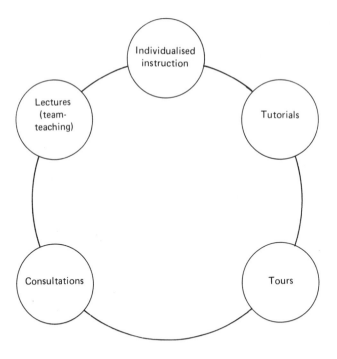

Figure 2. *Organizational pattern*

Lectures

A large group instructional mode is the basic pattern for the course. Lectures are held for two hours each week. This mode was also made necessary by the limited number of staff for teaching, the number of available classrooms, and the allocation of space as provided for in the university timetable. This pattern for lectures was also considered more practical since it could easily facilitate team-teaching. In the process of topic analysis, each lecturer identified those areas which they desired to teach. This approach prevented the duplication of resources and also freed lecturers to do more individualized work. One disadvantage, however, with the large group format is the degree of interaction which can take place during lectures. This kind of mode is predominantly teacher-dominated with little or no opportunity for student response. The objective of the lecture is to provide a basic theoretical understanding of the subject matter. Fifteen weeks of lectures were planned with each week devoted to a particular topic.

Tutorials

The objective of the tutorial is to help students apply theoretical constructs to practical situations. It is through these practical sessions that students gain experience in the design and production of instructional materials, and the operation of audio-visual equipment. Tutorials were organized in such a way as to give students several options within a single day and between days (see Figure 3). Six hours of lab or practical work were offered Monday to Thursday with three separate groups (A, B, C) operating simultaneously at any one hour. Group C handled the 'block hour' students (those wishing to take two hours at a time).

This meant that a student could finish the two hour tutorial requirement in one day; or take one hour on alternate days (eg Monday 10-11; Wednesday 9-10). To cater for 300 students, twelve lab hours had to be offered for each student to have fulfilled one hour of lab. This entailed providing 24 lab hours per week for the completion of the two hour requirement. Maximum flexibility was given with this arrangement for the student to meet timetable scheduling for other courses. Groups A and B taught lesson one for the first two days, and lesson two for the last two days. Group C taught lesson one and two each day.

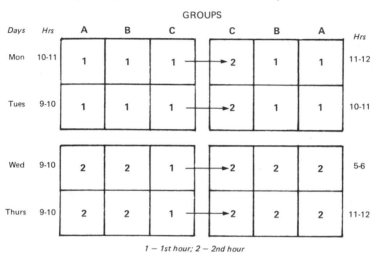

1 — 1st hour; 2 — 2nd hour

Figure 3. *Tutorial schedule*

The size of tutorial classes varied depending upon the particular commitments of students in other courses. This made some classes larger than others, even within a particular group. Groups A and B were designed to be larger than Group C with the former having an average class size of approximately 35 and Group C with approximately 10. The size of the latter group was aimed to facilitate 'block hour' teaching. The same instructional team responsible for the lectures also handled tutorials.

Individualized Instruction

The individualized mode of instruction was built into the course to enable those students, who wished, to do additional work on their own or to carry out the assignment at a time and place convenient to themselves. To facilitate this mode of instruction, labs were kept open throughout the day so that the facility might be available for student use. Group C had a predominantly individualized mode of instruction since the student/teacher ratio was more favourable for this kind of approach.

Consultation

Students were aware during the course of the semester that they were free to consult with lecturers over course material. Such contact was designed to increase understanding through student/teacher questions, probing, and analysis. Invariably these were held during office hours, but also prior to or after regular lab hours. A number of concerns arose during consultations. These normally centered around the following: (a) clarification of assignments, (b) expected performance, (c) progress in course, and (d) personal difficulties affecting coursework.

Tours

Five tours were arranged during the semester to familiarize students with those resources in the university related to the course which could be of assistance to them as professionals. The places visited included the library, language laboratory, computer centre, photographic/cinematographic sections and the closed-circuit television studio complex. Depending upon the size of the facility, large or small group tours were arranged.

A primary factor in the organizational pattern adopted was the specified competencies to be attained. The structure also saved time for the instructional staff and provided maximum flexibility for both staff and students. This kind of multifarious design made it necessary to have activities co-ordinated.

Course Management

During the initial planning stage it was decided that a co-ordinator was necessary to handle the administrative functions. The extent to which this is efficiently done has direct implications for the smooth running of the course. The co-ordinator played a role in three fundamental areas: planning, implementation and evaluation. During the planning stage the co-ordinator was responsible for calling meetings and making sure given assignments were carried out especially as these facilitated further action towards the development of the course. The course outline had to be compiled and resource materials were required for practical work. The co-ordinator's responsibility was to ensure that the department acquired the necessary resources and in sufficient numbers. Tours were also arranged to the respective facilities, giving time, date and number of students expected.

The major responsibility during the implementation of the course was enrolment of students into lab groups. A central enrolment register was kept and students later subdivided into groups as shown in Figure 2. This type of registration made record keeping for lab assignments and projects easier. Another important function was the co-ordination of examination questions. An examination meeting was held to discuss priority areas within which questions should be drawn. The ultimate guide for such questions, however, remained the objectives stated at the beginning of the course.

A fundamental assumption of a competency-based approach is the continuous assessment of students' progress. The University of Ife has adopted the semester system which makes the continuous assessment approach even more important. The co-ordinator was responsible for drawing up an evaluation chart indicating areas in which students would be assessed. Once posted, students were able to use this chart to check their progress on all assignments. Additional responsibilities of the co-ordinator concerning evaluation will also be discussed under the section on evaluation.

Evaluation

Evaluation was designed to be an integral part of the course. Several types of evaluation were planned. Formative evaluation took the form of (a) continuous assessment of students' work, and (b) continuous assessment of course content by the teaching staff. Summative evaluation consisted of the students' evaluation of the overall course and the instructors, and the students' final examination.

Equal emphasis in the course was placed on practical work and theory. Fifty per cent of the students' grade was, therefore, derived from projects completed and the remaining 50 per cent from their examination scores. A maximum number of points were assigned to each project thus allowing a student to amass a total of 50 points for all projects. A mid-semester objective examination was given to provide feedback on the theoretical aspect of the course and to acquaint students with a different examination format which would be a regular feature of the course.

As part of the team teaching approach it was agreed that lecturers would evaluate each other's lectures. Feedback was immediate, ie provided to the lecturer immediately he was finished with the lecture. This enabled any necessary adjustments to be made prior to the next lecture. Compiling evaluation results from lectures presented over a period of one month, the statistics show that based on a rating scale of 1 - 5:

(a) the organization, pacing and sequence of lectures received an average rating of 4.25 or very good;
(b) lecturers rated each other's presentation and delivery of material as average (3.63);
(c) audience participation, response and control received an average rating of 3.08;
(d) attendance at lectures was usually above average or more than one half of the class.

In addition to this type of evaluation, the instructional team met frequently to reassess the relevance of topics and lab work and to make revisions and modifications where necessary.

The overall assessment of students' progress was done both in practical work and in an examination format. Psycho-motor skills dealing with the use of equipment were tested during the final week of the semester. Competencies had to be demonstrated in the operation of a wide range of audio-visual equipment. The students were also required to complete final projects which demonstrated the application of their own subject area and knowledge gained in the course towards the development of an instructional sequence. An approach of this nature enables the student to integrate his knowledge. Another form of summative evaluation of students' work was the final examination given at the end of the semester. This took the form of a comprehensive essay composition lasting for a period of two hours. The examination was based on the assumption that students should have obtained competencies in the areas of curriculum and instruction, selection, utilization and evaluation. Examination questions were therefore drawn from these broad areas. Examination results indicated that 99.1 per cent of the students attained the specified competencies. Finally, students were asked to give their assessment of the course and the instructors. They were asked to evaluate the course in three areas: course design, course content and instruction. Two hundred students completed the evaluation form.

Course Design

The primary consideration in the design of the course was the competencies to be acquired. The students' feedback on this area was, therefore, deemed relevant in terms of the outcome as perceived by them for the future organization of the course. The results are as indicated in Table 1, showing that the majority of students (80 per cent) thought that the organization of the course was satisfactory and that the various alternatives provided for practical work should be continued. The rating on organization tended to be from satisfactory to very good indicating a favourable attitude in general. Students also tended to favour continuing existing alternatives for practical work or increasing the number.

Question	No Responding	Per cent
1 The overall organization of the course, ie lectures and practicals was:		
Very good	40	20
Satisfactory	160	80
Unsatisfactory	0	0
2 The various alternatives for lab hours should be:		
Continued	160	80
Discontinued	0	0
Increased	35	17.5
Decreased	5	2.5
N = 200		

Table 1. *Course design*

Question	No Responding	Per cent
1 The content of the course was:		
Adequate	200	100
Inadequate	0	0
2 Lecture topics were adequately covered:		
Yes	185	92.5
No	15	7.5
3 Lecture handouts were relevant to topics:		
Yes	200	100
No	0	0
4 Practicals helped me to acquire useful skills:		
Yes	200	100
No	0	0
5 The guided tours were:		
Very interesting	20	10
Interesting	170	85
Not of much value	10	5
N = 200		

Table 2. *Course content*

Course Content

The content for the course was derived from an analysis of the tasks to be performed by teachers when they were actually in the classroom. It was of interest, therefore, to find out if after taking the course pre-service teachers thought the content had been sufficient to provide the competencies stated in the objectives. The results are summarized in Table 2, indicating that students were satisfied with the content of the course and thought they had gained useful skills. A number of supplementary handouts were given to provide more in-depth knowledge concerning the topic covered and as a source of future reference. All students considered the handouts relevant. Another supplementary and enrichment exercise was the guided tour. Eighty-five per cent considered these interesting, 10 per cent very interesting and 5 per cent thought they were not of much value.

Instruction

Team teaching is not a novel idea, but it was the first time the approach had been used in this course. The students had been exposed to team teaching in other courses so it presented no special problem *per se*. The objective in evaluating this area was to find out their views on the overall instruction, as demonstrated in Table 3.

Question	No Responding	Per cent
1 Lecturers were enthusiastic about their work:		
Yes	200	100
No	0	0
2 Lecturers were generally helpful:		
Yes	200	100
No	0	0
3 How would you rate the instruction provided in the course:		
Excellent	0	0
Very good	95	47.5
Good	95	47.5
Fair	10	5
Poor	0	0
N = 200		

Table 3. *Instruction*

The majority of students (95 per cent) thought that the instruction provided in the course was good/very good and that lecturers were helpful and enthusiastic about their work.

An overall analysis from the student evaluation is that the organizational structure, content and implementation of the course were well received. Evaluation results in general suggest that the course could be offered again in the 1979/80 academic session with a similar format. Consideration would, however, have to be given to students' suggestions for improving the course as well as those problems experienced by the instructional team during the implementation stage.

Summary

This article has dealt with the use of a competency-based approach in developing an undergraduate course for teacher education in educational technology. Competencies were specified after analyzing the tasks secondary school teachers perform or should perform in the area of educational technology. Task analysis involved job and topic analysis with specific skills being identified and associated with the job to be performed. Various organizational patterns emerged based upon the objectives of the course. These included the use of large, small and normal classroom size groups, individualized instruction, consultations and guided tours. Team teaching facilitated a great deal of flexibility for the instructional staff. Not only could lectures and tutorials be comfortably handled, but more time was allowed for individual consultation with students. A large course of this nature, catering for approximately 300 students and being taught by three people, had to be co-ordinated to ensure some degree of standardization. The course management was done by a member of the instructional team who carried out required functions during the planning, implementation and evaluation stages. Evaluation of the course took several forms. Formative evaluation was done through the continuous assessment of (a) students' work and (b) the course content. Summative evaluation consisted of the final examination and the evaluation of the overall course by the students. Evaluation results revealed that students were satisfied with the course and thought they had gained useful skills by taking it.

It will be of interest to compare examination results from year-to-year, to see if the original high standard — with 99.1 per cent of students attaining the specified competencies — is maintained.

References

Davies, I K (1973) *Competency Based Learning: Technology, Management and Design.* McGraw-Hill, New York.

Rowntree, D (1974) *Educational Technology in Curriculum Development.* Harper & Row, London.

Soremekun, E A (1979) The role of educational technology in achieving national objectives in selected Nigerian universities. Unpublished doctoral dissertation, University of Indiana, Bloomington.

Worthen, B R and Sanders, J R (1973) *Educational Evaluation: Theory and Practice.* Jones, Ohio.

1.6 How do Students Use Lecture Handouts?

Mark Trueman and James Hartley
University of Keele

Abstract: Previous research has shown that the design of a lecture handout can markedly affect students' note-taking practices, and that note-taking is related to recall (Hartley and Davies, 1978). This article reports an investigation which has examined how students use the notes they have taken or the handouts with which they have been provided.

There has been very little research on how students use lecture handouts. The little that has been done has tended to focus on test or examination scores rather than on how students use handouts during and after lectures. In this paper, we concentrate on these latter issues. We have examined how students at Keele used a set of three handouts in a series of six related lectures.

These handouts were of a particular and rather rare kind. In booklet form, they presented on the right-hand pages a complete summary of the main points of the lectures with all the slides and blackboard diagrams. Space for note-taking was provided on the left-hand pages, and this fact was indicated to the students. Key words were omitted from the text (on average two per page) and blanks were left for the students to complete during the lectures.

The six lectures covered four topics within the area of motivation. The first handout (10 pages long) covered topic one. The second handout (13 pages long) covered topic two, and the third handout (seven pages long) covered topics three and four. The lecturer spent most of his time on topic one (two-and-a-half lectures) and least on topics three and four (half a lecture).

Our observations have focused on seven questions. These questions, and their answers, form the body of this report.

Question one: How Did Students Use These Handouts During the Lectures

The handout for topic one was available at the beginning of the first lecture, that for topic two at the beginning of the third lecture, and that for topics three and four at the beginning of the sixth (last) lecture.

Approximately 50 students attended the lectures. 15 of these were interviewed on how they used these handouts. The overall picture that emerged was as follows:

- ☐ All of the students had the appropriate handout before them at the beginning of the lecture.
- ☐ Half of the students ignored them at this time; half glanced through them; none managed to read them all through before the lecture started.
- ☐ All the students followed the lecturer through the handout as he gave his verbal exposition. Two-thirds of them read about a paragraph ahead, listened to what he said, checked to see how well it was covered in the handout, and made additional notes if appropriate. The remaining one-third paid more attention to the lecturer than to the handout, but kept an eye on the handout to see when the next blank space was coming up.
- ☐ None of the students reviewed their notes or handouts before they left the lecture theatre at the end of the lecture. Two-thirds of the students had lectures immediately following the psychology ones.
- ☐ None of the students read the handouts in their own time between the lectures.

Question two: Where Did Students Put Their Notes on the Handout?

Previous research has indicated that the provision of handouts remarkably cuts down student note-taking activities. This study replicates these findings in that, on average, students added only 113 further words per lecture.

These notes were distributed as follows:

- ☐ 43 per cent of the words were placed on the left-hand blank pages.
- ☐ 24 per cent were incorporated into the text.
- ☐ 15 per cent were annotations to the diagrams.
- ☐ 18 per cent were not made on the handout at all, but on separate notepaper provided by the students.
- ☐ Women students took slightly more notes than men, and incorporated them more into the text than did the men, but these differences were not significant.
- ☐ All the students assumed that they had filled in the blanks correctly. Analysis showed, however, that with 31 blanks available there was a 5 per cent error rate.

Question three: What Reasons Did the Students Give for Making Their Notes?

The 15 students were interviewed in detail about the individual notes they had made in the lectures. The results obtained are summarized in Tables 1 and 2.

These tables show an attention to detail rather than a broad concern with the main points of the lecture. Some students, however, were concerned with this latter issue. Of the 35 instances of notes categorized as headings or summary notes, 14 of these were titles which broke up the body of the text, and the remainder were brief summaries recorded on the blank page of the handout. One of the students who used this procedure commented, 'I'm simplifying, I'm making it easier for myself'. He added afterwards, somewhat doubtfully, 'Only time will tell'.

Type of notation and definition	No of notes	Percentage of total
Elaboration of points made in the handout	169	39
Examples of general points	86	20
Notes referring to points made by lecturer not mentioned in the handout	53	12
Definition of words or concepts	46	11
Summary/headings	35	8
Questions	22	5
Notes referring to points made by lecturer which conclude a section of the handout	10	2
References	10	2

Table 1. *Reasons for making particular notes given by students (i) text*

Type of notation	No of notes	Percentage of total
Annotation-labelling of diagrams	103	55
Elaboration of diagram	30	16
Conclusion for diagram (what does it show?)	21	11
Copied diagram from blackboard	17	9
Title for diagram	14	7
Reference for diagram	4	2

Table 2. *Reasons for making particular notes given by students (ii) diagrams*

Question four: What Did Students Think of the Handouts?

Previous research has suggested that students like lecture handouts — whatever their style! In this study, the findings were as follows:

☐ All the students said that they liked the handouts.
☐ 14 of them indicated that the blanks helped them to attend more to the lecture. (Two students asked for more blanks, two found them annoying.)
☐ 13 felt that the amount of detail was about right, but two students would have preferred more skeletal handouts.
☐ 12 liked the alternate blank side for notes, but the remainder felt that it was unnecessary or wasteful.
☐ 11 thought that the provision of blank pages was best for note-taking but three would have preferred the space to be more integrated into the text.

☐ 11 indicated that they intended to use the space at a later date for their own notes which would be made from private reading, or for revision.

The students generally saw two main advantages in the provision of handouts. First of all, they said that the handouts helped their understanding, indicated the direction the lecture would take, and reduced the note-taking load. Secondly, the the handouts led to more accurate communication (eg of facts and references) and the students felt that this would aid subsequent recall and revision.

Question five: How Did Different Features of the Handouts Affect Subsequent Recall?

Thirty students (14 men and 16 women) were tested without warning on their recall of the lecture content one week after the motivation lectures. The questions asked were related to the handout text, the blanks, the diagrams, and to points made by the lecturer which were not mentioned in the handout.

The percentage of correct answers per question type (with the number of questions in parentheses) is as follows:

Text	(3)	48 per cent correct
Blanks	(3)	69 per cent correct
Diagrams	(2)	59 per cent correct
Extra	(1)	40 per cent correct

There were no significant sex differences. These results suggest that the students are better at answering questions related to the blanks than to the other kinds of question. These results are in line with previous research.

Question six: How Did Students Use Their Notes and Handouts for Examination Purposes?

All the students were tested at the end of the academic year on their knowledge of motivation and six other topic areas in psychology. The paper was of the short-answer type: three compulsory questions on each topic had to be answered in two hours.

Twenty-two students completed a questionnaire concerning their revision for this examination. By asking questions on other topics as well as on motivation, we were able to assess indirectly the role of the motivation handouts in the revision process. The relevant data are as follows:

☐ When students had skeletal handouts for one topic (learning) and detailed handouts for another (motivation), they preferred the detailed handouts.

☐ Although the students claimed to divide their revision time equally between the seven topics, they found it necessary to read textbooks to a greater extent to support their revision from topics without handouts (seven students) or topics with skeletal handouts (13 students). (For the detailed handouts, the figure was five students.)

☐ When asked to name the three topics they found the hardest to revise and the three topics they found the easiest, motivation was reported to be a difficult topic to revise (fifth out of the seven). Nonetheless seven students said that motivation was easy. All of these students said that it was the provision of the detailed handouts that made the topic easy to revise.

☐ On being specifically asked how they used the motivation handouts for revision, 16 students said that they just re-read their notes and handouts, three made condensed versions of their notes, and three said that they hardly used their notes at all. Their average examination scores on the motivation section (out of 15) were 7.8, 8.8 and 4.5 respectively.

☐ In the examination as a whole the two lowest scoring topics (out of seven) were taught without the aid of handouts, and two of the four highest scoring topics were taught with detailed or skeletal handouts. It is not really possible to relate the handouts to examination performance more closely than this, however, because of the varying nature of the topics, the questions, the markers, etc.

Question seven: What Do Students Do With Their Handouts and Notes After the Lectures and the Examinations?

Fifteen students who had taken the motivation course a year before the present students were interviewed to see what they had done with their notes and handouts since that date. The results were as follows:

☐ All these students had used their notes for the end-of-year examination.

☐ Five of them had looked at their handouts and notes following the examination 'for interest', and one of them had lent them out to a friend. The remainder had not looked at them since the examination.

☐ Ten students indicated that they would probably look at the notes again, seven of them said they would use them for finals, and the other three said that they would probably look at them again for interest.

☐ Thirteen had their notes readily at hand, usually kept in a specific file. Two were not certain where their notes were, but knew they were filed somewhere. As one said, 'Somewhere in one of three places, I hope'.

☐ Only two of the students had added extra notes to their handout since the lecture. One of these had done so after the examination.

Conclusions

The answers to the initial questions in this report indicated that students liked the handouts and found them useful for aiding comprehension and revision. Certain features of their design seemed to be important in this respect. However, most students made few notes on the handouts and most did not add to them after the lecture was over: the handouts were filed away until they were needed for revision and then the students relied on them heavily — to the exclusion of other materials.

These findings thus point to the advantages and disadvantages of detailed handouts, and instructors will have to decide whether the initial advantages are outweighed by the final costs in their particular situation. In the present case, the lecturer still continues to use his handouts because he feels that students appreciate them and they present material which is not easily available in current textbooks. As he puts it: 'My main reasons for using the handouts are first, to make it easier for students to follow lectures; second, to present details without the need for lengthy dictation (eg of definitions, references); third, to reduce note-taking which presumably interferes with attention; fourth, to present all the diagrams used in the lectures, since it takes time to copy a graph or drawing and the point being made is easily lost.'

Finally, we must observe here that different kinds of handout lead to different kinds of outcome. So instructors using lecture handouts need to determine in advance not only what they themselves want to do but also what they want their students to do — during and after lectures.

References

Most of the previous research on handouts and note-taking is summarized in:

Hartley, J and Davies, I K (1978) Note-taking: a critical review. *Programmed Learning & Educational Technology,* **15,** 3, pp 207-224.

Research published since includes:

Collingwood, V and Hughes, D C (1978) Effects of three types of university lecture notes on student achievement. *Journal of Educational Psychology,* **70,** 2, pp 175-179.
Locke, E A (1978) An empirical study of lecture note-taking among college students. *Journal of Educational Research,* **71,** 2, pp 93-99.
Powers, S M and Powers, W (1978) Instruction-prepared notes and achievement in introductory psychology. *Journal of Experimental Education,* **47,** 1, pp 37-41.
Thomas, G S (1978) Use of student notes and lecture summaries as study guides for recall. *Journal of Educational Research,* **71,** 6, pp 316-319.

An interesting and related paper is:

Elton, L R B (1970) The use of duplicated lecture notes and self-tests in university teaching. In Bajpai, A C and Leedham, J (eds) *Aspects of Educational Technology,* **IV.** Pitman, London.

Acknowledgements

We are indebted to David Chantrey who allowed us to study his handouts, to Alan Branthwaite for his contributions to this study and to the students who participated. The research was supported by the Social Science Research Council.

Workshop Report
1.7 The Evaluation of Educational Projects and Programmes

C A Hawkins
Rijksuniversiteit Utrecht, The Netherlands

A background paper on 'An Evaluation Strategy based on pragmatic eclecticism' (Hawkins, 1979) forms the basis of this workshop. It reviews currently available theoretical models and practice, and draws upon these consciously and selectively to promote a strategy that, without redundancy, is directed towards the following goals.

1 The evaluation is considered relevant, fair and sensitive by all the parties concerned.
2 The recommendations made are likely to be implemented and accepted by all the parties concerned.

The participants all receive the background paper before the session takes place, so that they have an opportunity to assess the relevance of the approach for their own situation, and are in a position to contribute to the proceedings. The workshop commences with a short introduction and description of involvement with evaluation by all participants and the workshop leader, and then proceeds along the lines summarized below.

A Critical Review of Models and Definitions of Evaluation

The workshop commenced with a discussion of the range of perceptions and practices of evaluation at the present time, centred on the following discussion points.

1 Who requests the service of an evaluator, and why?
2 Who forms the audience to whom the evaluation study is directed?

As a result of the range of views and interests which these questions provoke, the various conceptions of evaluation can be put into context. The following six approaches are raised for consideration.

1 Evaluation as *measurement*
   This view will influence the work of evaluators who base their methodology on psychometrics and educational research.
2 Evaluation as *professional judgement*
   This is the conception implied by the evaluative strategies of a team of HMIs, a CNAA subject panel, or in the USA a college 'accreditation' team. The evaluators are experts in the field under consideration.
3 Evaluation as an assessment of *congruence between performance and objectives*
   This formulation derives from Tyler's curriculum model (1951), and also finds application, particularly in its formative aspects, in mastery learning, Keller plan and competency based education. More flexible and sensitive versions of *congruence* and *discrepancy* approaches can be found in the work of Scriven (1974) and Stake (1967).
4 An evolvement of this approach which distances itself further from the Tyler model can be described in evaluation as *curriculum development*.
5 The approach that Stufflebeam (1971) has proposed can be summarized as *evaluation to provide information for decision-makers*.
6 Stufflebeam's approach (1971) was intended to be a reaction to the definitions preceding his, but it is in fact not far from the first of these — evaluation as *measurement*. A further reaction to this approach has resulted in more subjective evaluation styles, which can be summarized in Parlett and Hamilton's phrase *'evaluation as illumination'* (1976).

The following classification of evaluation models (after House, 1978) is then presented for discussion.

Model	Proponent	Audience	Methodology
systems-analysis	Fielden	sponsors, administrators	cost-analysis
behavioural objectives	Tyler Popham	administrators, psychologists	achievement tests
decision-making	Stufflebeam Alkin	decision-makers, especially administrators	surveys, questionnaires, interviews
accreditation	CNAA	administrators	criteria, review by panel
goal-free	Scriven	consumers	bias-control logical analysis
transaction	Stake, MacDonald Parlett, Hamilton, Kluiter	consumers	case studies, interviews, observations

Table 1. *Classification of evaluation models*

It will be noted that, in general, moving down the table, the more democratic is the audience, the more subjective is the methodology, and the greater is the emphasis on 'interpret and understand' rather than 'predict and measure'. Two further classifications are also considered.

Popham's Classification (Popham, 1975)

1 Goal attainment models
2 Judgemental models emphasizing intrinsic criteria
3 Judgemental models emphasizing extrinsic criteria
4 Decision-facilitation models

MacDonald's Classification (MacDonald, 1973)

1 Bureaucratic evaluation
2 Autocratic evaluation
3 Democratic evaluation

Further socio-political considerations, which have a bearing on an evaluator's role and status can be illustrated by a classification of educational ideologies developed by Williams (1961). He relates each ideology to the social position and educational policy of its adherents, as in the following table.

Ideology	Social position	Educational policies
Liberal/Conservative	Aristocratic	Non-vocational The 'educated man'
Bourgeois	Merchant, Professional classes	Elitist Education as access to privileged positions
Democratic	Radical reformers	Expansionist, 'education for all'
Populist/proletarian	Working classes/ subordinate groups	Student relevance, choice, participation

Table 2. *Classification of educational ideologies (Williams, 1961)*

Such a tabulation makes it evident that an evaluator must be sensitive to the educational environment in which he is working, must be ready to acknowledge a multiplicity of co-existing ideologies as well as interest groups, and appreciate that the form and style of a successful evaluation will be determined by these factors and not the personal taste of the evaluator.

A summary discussion is centred on the question: Why are evaluation reports so frequently not attended to? Three reasons frequently put forward, according to the selective perceptions of the evaluative reviewer are (a) poor methodology and design; (b) neglect of the interests of some involved parties; and (c) excessively long, over-rigorous and technical reports which arrive too late.

A Proposed Evaluation Strategy

Although reference is made from time-to-time to hybrid models of evaluation, there have been few attempts to put together a full range of evaluative strategies in a cohesive whole. The underlying aims of the strategy that have been given at the commencement of this report can best be met by an evaluator whose profile can be described as that of a 'critical friend' to the project or programme under study, and whose strategy has the following features.

1 Preliminary assessment of the expressed issues and the organizational features of the project and its setting.
2 Identification or establishment of an evaluation committee which can act as a change agent.
3 Assessment of information already available.
4 A continuous search for discrepancies in intent, expectations and implementation.
5 A concurrent assessment of the accompanying acknowledgement of the need for and readiness to change.
6 Invention of methods of assessment that may be available and appropriate.
7 Design of the evaluation, based on a balance of factors such as efficiency, acceptability, validity and reliability of procedures, in the light of points 1 to 6.
8 Implementation and analysis.
9 Issues to be raised brought forward for discussion at an early informal stage, by as many groups as can be involved, so that suggestions can be negotiated and machinery for change established.
10 A speedy, short, sensitive evaluative report.

The Case Study

After discussion of the strategy, a case study is presented. This is designed to exemplify the discrepancies between previously expressed and implied issues, the expectations, perceptions and activities of students and teachers, and an assessment of the limited scope for immediate change that is typically encountered. An evaluation plan is made by all the participants working in pairs, and then the proposals are presented to the group in turn and discussed as a whole. With a longer version of the workshop, participants then discuss and propose strategies for situations requiring evaluation in situations in which they themselves are involved.

References

Hawkins, C A (1979) *An Evaluation Strategy Based on Pragmatic Eclecticism.* O & O van O, RU Utrecht.
House, E R (1978) Assumptions underlying evaluation models. *Educational Researcher,* 7, 3, pp 4-12.
MacDonald, B (1976) Evaluation and the control of education. *Schools Council Research Studies Curriculum Evaluation Today: Trends and Implications.* Macmillan, Basingstoke.
Parlett, M and Hamilton D (1976) Evaluation as illumination: a new approach to the study of innovatory programmes. In *Schools Council Research Studies Curriculum Evaluation Today: Trends and Implications.* Macmillan, Basingstoke.
Popham, W J (1975) *Educational Evaluation.* Prentice Hall, Englewood Cliffs, NJ.
Scriven, M (1974) Prose and cons about goal-free evaluation. In Popham, W J (ed) *Evaluation in Education.* McCutham, Berkeley.
Stake, R E (1967) The countenance of educational evaluation. *Teachers College Record,* 68, pp 523-40.
Stufflebeam, D L et al (1971) *Educational Evaluation and Decision Making.* F E Peacock, Itasca, Illinois.
Williams, R (1961) *The Long Revolution.* Chatto and Windus, London.

Section 2:
Resource-based Learning
(Including Distance Education)

2.0 Introduction

ETIC '79 Tracks

All three papers in this Section — Holmberg (2.1), Megarry (2.2), Noble (2.3) — appeared in Track 3, 'Learning Environment, Practice and Presentation Techniques', at ETIC '79.

Categories and Special Interests

All four contributions here — the workshop by Green, B (2.4) as well as the papers — belonged, naturally enough, in the 'Resource-Based Learning (Res)' category at Sheffield, with Megarry also in the 'Media design (MeDes)' category.

The tertiary education interest, coded 'Tert' which appears in Section 1 is continued very strongly by all four contributors in Section 2.

Links with Other Sections

Readers with a particular interest in Section 2 are also likely to be interested in the following contributions from *Section 4:* Rowntree (4.3), Evans (4.4), Wilkinson (4.5).

2.1 Distance Study in Educational Theory and Practice

Börje Holmberg
Fernuniversitat, West Germany

Abstract: The paper presents recent analyses of the relation of distance education to generally accepted principles of learning and teaching. A conceptual framework for practice in distance study through application of educational technology is introduced.

What is Distance Study?

Distance study is learning supported by 'those teaching methods in which because of the physical separateness of learners and teachers, the interactive, as well as the preactive phase of teaching, is conducted through print, mechanical, or electronic devices'.[1]

The following would seem to be three universally accepted characteristics of distance study.

1 Typical of the whole of distance study is that it is based on *non-contiguous communication,* ie 'the learner is at a distance from the teacher for much, most, or even all of the time during the teaching-learning process'.[2]

2 A *pre-produced course,* as *self-instructional* as possible, printed and/or consisting of presentations brought about by other media than print (audio or video-tapes, radio or TV programmes etc), guides the study.

3 Organized non-contiguous *two-way communication* is a constitutive element of distance study. It is in most cases principally brought about by assignments for submission for the students to solve and answer and for the tutors to comment on (in writing or on audio-tape), but freer forms of communication also occur.

Further, it would seem to be worth mentioning that, whereas on one hand distance study expressly serves the *individual* learner, the course development required and the organization making the non-contiguous teaching possible often give it a character of *mass communication* for the reason that large numbers of students make distance study economical.

Theoretical Approaches

In 1962 Childs first expressed his regret that so far little research in distance study had been done and later added: 'someone would perform a very great service indeed if he would undertake in a very serious and thoughtful way to relate the generally accepted principles of learning to the process of teaching through correspondence study.'[3]

The challenge contained in the second observation was recently taken up by Bååth, who has analyzed some modern teaching models (those of Skinner, Rothkopf, Ausubel, Bruner, Roger and Gagné and the so-called Structural

---

1 This is Moore's definition of what he calls 'telemathic teaching'. (Moore (1975) p 5.)
2 Sims (1977) p 4.
3 Childs (1971) p 118.

Communication model) with a view to finding out to what extent they are applicable to distance study.

The following were the results of Bååth's study:

☐ All the models investigated are applicable to distance study.
☐ Some of them (Skinner, Gagné, Rothkopf, Ausubel, Structural Communication) seem particularly adaptable to distance study in its fairly strictly structured form.
☐ Bruner's more open model and even Roger's model can be applied to distance study though not without special measures.
☐ Demands on distance study which should inspire new developments can be inferred from the models studied.[4]

Thus the methods of distance study are applicable to several competing theories. That this is so is evident also from the study made by Hilgard and Bower in their chapter on Theory of Instruction.[5]

Naturally, in spite of this it is possible to describe some learning theories as more compatible with distance study than others. Personally in this context I would refer to Nuthall and Snook's *rational model* with its view of students as 'rational agents' and its creed that 'Learning . . . should not be a process to which the student is subjected but an activity which he performs',[6] and further to two new theoretical works by Lehner developing, on the basis of Popper's philosophy, a so-called genetic teaching strategy aiming at problem-solving learning. Lehner regards all learning as problem-solving in that it consists of constructing hypotheses or theories and trying these out. In the sense of Popper's 'Conjectures and Refutations' the rejection of a false hypothesis in favour of a better one is seen as progress in learning. Causing students to follow the development of theories and research inclusive of the steps that have been found wrong is a method of introducing them to a subject and to critical and autonomous thinking.[7]

The relation between learning theory and teaching theory is rather indirect. The theories of distance study so far developed have only to a limited extent been able to provide prescriptive rules. If we accept that the task of scholarship is, on the one hand, theoretical, to bring about explanation, and on the other hand, practical, to provide for application or technology,[8] we can allow ourselves the statement that — unlike the situation referred to by Childs — a few steps have by now been taken in the field of distance study.

A process model and a cybernetic model of interest have been created by Delling[9] and Graff[10] respectively.[11] Moore has developed a theory of independent study, classifying educational programmes on the two dimensions distance and autonomy,[12] and has made an empirical study of the hypothesis that autonomous persons are particularly attracted to distant methods of learning and teaching, which was, on the whole, confirmed.[13]

A theoretical approach by Peters explains the characteristics of distance study as a result of this being an industrialized type of teaching and learning primarily made possible by technical media.[14] Peters points to rationalization, division of labour,

4 Bååth (1978).
5 Hilgard and Bower (1975) pp 608-609.
6 Nuthall and Snook (1973) p 67.
7 Lehner (1978a), Lehner (1978b).
8 Cf Popper (1972a) p 49.
9 Delling (1971).
10 Graff (1970).
11 I am summarizing these models in my German paper 'Fernstudiendidaktik als wissenschaftliches Fach'.
12 Moore (1977) p 32-33.
13 Moore (1976). The Dissertation Abstracts (1976, p 3344a) provide a summary.
14 Peters (1967), Peters (1973); the second of these, which is in English, provides a good summary of some of the most important points made by Peters.

mass production, mechanization, automation, planning, organization, controlling and checking etc in a systematic comparison with industrial work. Prescriptive principles are deducible from his work, but it is probably above all to be seen as an attempt to mark a clear line of division between distance study and face-to-face methods. His analysis provides a number of valuable observations and his book of 1973 particularly makes most inspiring reading.

Like those mentioned, and others, I have given some thought to what distance study implies and what practical conclusions can be drawn from such considerations. In this context I have developed a theory of *distance study as a kind of guided didactic conversation.* Distance study is self-study, but the student is not alone; he benefits from a course and from interaction with tutors and a supporting organization. The indirect presentation of study matter and the direct written or telephone interaction between the student and the tutor and others belonging to the supporting organization provide the instruments of conversation. The conversation is thus both real and simulated. The simulated conversation is not only what Lewis calls internalized conversation caused by a study of a text ('As we mull things over quietly and in solitude, we are actually holding a conversation with ourselves'),[15] but is a relationship between the course developers and the students created by an easily readable and reasonably colloquial style of presentation and the personal atmosphere of the course, superficially characterized by, for instance, the author(s) referring to himself/herself/themselves as *I* or *we* respectively and the students being spoken to as *you* ('I recommend that you . . .'). Questions and replies, suggestions and references to problems known to the students belong here. This style of presentation stimulates activity and implies reasoning, discussing *pro et contra,* referring to the student's previous experience and thus avoiding omissions in chains of thought. Revision tasks and self-checking exercises also belong to the simulated conversation. The contents are structured verbally and/or by typographical means. This is a prescriptive theory in that it suggests procedures expected to be effective in facilitating learning. It is now being empirically investigated as such. However, the theory is also an attempt to explain what the phenomenon distance study is, considering its particular position as a kind of support of self-study.[16] It constitutes the background of the prescriptive systems concept that I attempted to develop in my book of 1977.

The Practice of Distance Study

Distance study has been applied with considerable success for about 100 years, until the last few decades in the form of traditional correspondence study. The advent of educational technology strongly influenced its character, however. In a couple of systems, descriptions and handbooks the following components (among others) have been expressly analyzed, which makes this influence evident: goals and objectives of study, target-group analysis, contents, structure, organization, choice of media, two-way communication, course creation, evaluation, revision.[17]

Private correspondence schools (Pitman, International Correspondence Schools, Rustin, Hermods etc) and American Universities were pioneers in the field and are still extremely important. The most highly developed distance study leading to degrees seems to be provided by the Open University in Britain, which has a number of followers in Europe and elsewhere. (Fernuniversität in West Germany,

15 Lewis (1975) p 69.
16 Cf Holmberg (1960) p 18.
17 See eg *Brevkursproduksjon* Holmberg (1977) and Wedemeyer (1978).

UNED in Spain, Everyman's University in Israel etc.) Different from these but no less interesting are the activities of, for instance, the University of Mid-America, the University of Wisconsin Extension, the University of South Africa, the Centre National de Télé-Enseignement in France, the University of Athabasca in Canada and the extension departments of Australian, Canadian and US universities.

Typical of all these institutions is that their application of distance study agrees with the three main characteristics referred to at the beginning of this paper and that correspondence study in its written form remains the most widely applied and most essential approach.

From what has been said so far it is evident that there is some experience of what can be achieved by distance education. However, there is also much prejudice about the assumed limits of the range of activity of distance study. Let us for practical reasons consider the usefulness of distance study in the three domains of study objectives analyzed by Bloom *et al* (1964).

In the *cognitive* domain, which concerns the acquisition of intellectual knowledge, the effectiveness of distance study is seldom challenged. It is well known by now that here distance study is at least as effective as any other form of teaching and learning.[18]

Some *psycho-motor* objectives, ie skills like surgery or the capacity to handle dangerous chemicals, machinery etc, do not lend themselves to distance study, whereas other skills do (drawing and typewriting for instance). In some technical subjects the use of laboratory kits has proved very advantageous and has eliminated the need for much residential laboratory work.

In the *affective* domain, which is concerned with emotions and attitudes, it would seem to be evident that non-contiguous communication has less power to influence students than face-to-face meetings. The question is to what extent and in what areas *should* distance education be subjected to emotional influence.

The typical distance student is an adult with a number of social responsibilities and commitments. I would submit that adult distance students are automatically provided with the kind of general socialization acquired by adults in their normal social life, through their family, job and the company they keep, and that in planning distance study at the university level we are entitled to limit our socialization efforts to what academic life, study, research and 'professional socialization' require.

A specific *academic socialization* effect is no doubt expected of any serious study. This is concerned with the methods for unprejudiced search for truth, the use and recognition of sources of knowledge, critical scrutiny of theories and arguments and similar habits and approaches. There is every reason to assume that academic socialization is adequately catered for by distance study.[19]

From one aspect, distance study would seem to have special socialization potentials in this so-called academic sphere. What I have in mind is the training in *autonomous study*. We seem to have reason to assume that our students' work on their own is a habit-forming experience which develops independence.

What we must look further into — if there is any substance in our claim that independence and autonomy are typical of distance study — is how students themselves can influence or even independently decide not only *how* they are to study but also *what*, the latter by selecting their own learning objectives. Will it be possible to provide a wide range of study opportunities with clearly defined and declared study objectives for each small unit and make a completely free choice of such units available to students in individual combinations? Constructive approaches

18 Childs (1965) and Granholm (1971) provide ample evidence of this. 'One thing of which we may be certain is that correspondence study does an excellent job of subject matter instruction' (Childs (1965) p 8). Cf also Childs (1971b) pp 245-248.
19 Cf Holmberg (1976).

engaging the students in the selection of study objectives have been developed both by Potvin and by Ljoså and Sandvold. Potvin 'denies the institution and the tutor the right to prescribe what the learner should learn and how he is to learn it.'[20]

It is possible, though seldom practised, to provide an extensive battery of assignments, from among which students are encouraged to select those that they find particularly interesting or that coincide with their specific study objectives. This could be one way to bring about the student autonomy that has been discussed above. If students were to select their own study objectives, on the basis of this selection could concentrate on the corresponding parts of the course and were offered assignments related to the parts chosen or even alternative assignments within their chosen study areas, then the autonomous student would be provided with more appropriate study opportunities than distance education is normally capable of offering.

References

Ausubel, D P (1968) *Educational Psychology: a Cognitive View.* Holt, Rinehart & Winston, New York.

Bååth, J A (1978) *Korrespondensundervisningen i ljuset av ett antal samtida undervisningsmodeller.* Lund, Lunds Universitets Pedagogiska Institution.

Bloom, B S *et al* (1964) A Taxonomy of Educational Objectives: Cognitive Domain. Mackay.

Brevkursproduksjon i lys av systemtenkning (1975). NKS, Oslo.

Childs, G B (1965) Research in the correspondence instruction field. 7th ICCE Proceedings, KKI, Stockholm.

Childs, G B (1971a) Problems of teaching by correspondence. In Mackenzie, O and Christenson, E L *The Changing World of Correspondence Study.* Pennsylvania State University Press, University Park, Pennsylvania.

Childs, G B (1971b) Recent research developments in correspondence instruction. In Mackenzie, O and Christenson, E L *The Changing World of Correspondence Study.* Pennsylvania State University Press, University Park, Pennsylvania.

Delling, R M (1971) Grunzüge einer Wissenschaft von Fernstudium. In *Epistolodidaktika* (1971) 1, pp 14-20.

Egan, K (1972) Structural communication – a new contribution to pedagogy. In *Programmed Learning and Educational Technology* 9, 2, pp 63-72.

Graff, K (1970) *Voraussetzungen erfolgreichen Fernstudiums am Beispiel des schwedischen Fernstudiensystems.* Lüdke, Hamburg.

Hilgard, E R and Bower, G H (1975) *Theories of Learning.* Fourth edition. Prentice Hall, Englewood Cliffs, NJ.

Holmberg, B (1960) On the methods of teaching by correspondence. Lunds universitets årsskrift NF. Avd 1, **54**, 2. Gleerup, Lund.

Holmberg, B (1976) Academic socialisation and distance study. In *Epistolodidaktika* (1976) 1, pp 17-25.

Holmberg, B (1977) *Distance Education – a Survey and Bibliography.* Kogan Page, London.

Holmberg, B (1978) *Fernstudiendidaktik als wissenschaftliches Fach.* Fernuniversität (ZIFF), Hagen.

Lehner, H (1978a) Begriff und Bedeutung der genetischen Lerhstrategie in lerntheoretischer und kritisch-rationalistischer Sicht. Dissertation. Heidelberg. Dissertation, so far unpublished.

Lehner, H (1978b) Die Steuerung von Lernprozessen auf der Grundlage einer kognitiven Lerntheorie. A ZIFF project report. Fernuniversität, Hagen.

Lewis, B N (1975) Conversational man. In *Teaching at a Distance,* 2, pp 68-70.

Ljoså, E and Sandvold K E (1976) *The Students' Freedom of Choice Within the Didactical Structure of a Correspondence Course.* EHSC workshop document. Paris.

Moore, M G (1975) *Cognitive Style and Telemathic (Distance) Teaching.* ICCE Newsletter, 5, 4, pp 3-10.

Moore, M G (1975) Cognitive style and telemathic (distance) teaching. *ICCE Newsletter,* independence and attitudes to independent study among adult learners who use correspondence independent study and self directed independent study. The University of Wisconsin (dissertation), Madison.

20. Potvin (1976) p 30.

Moore, M G (1977) A model of independent study. In *Epistolodidaktika* (1977) 1, pp 6-37.

Nuthall, G and Snook, J (1973) Contemporary models of teaching. In Travers, R M W (ed) *Second Handbook of Research on Teaching.* Rand McNally, Chicago.

Peters, O (1967) Das Fernstudium an Universitäten und Hochschulen. Didaktische Struktur und vergleichende Interpretation: ein Beitrag zur Theorie der Fernlehre. Beltz, Weinheim.

Peters, O (1971) Theoretical aspects of correspondence instruction. In Mackenzie, O and Christensen, E L (eds) *The Changing World of Correspondence Study.* Pennsylvania State University Press, University Park, Pennsylvania.

Peters, O (1973) Die didaktische Struktur des Fernunterrichts. Untersuchgungen zu einer industrialisierten Form des Lehrens und Lernens. *Tübinger Beiträge zum Fernstudium,* 7. Beltz, Weinheim.

Popper, K (1972a) Naturgesetze und theoretische Systeme. In Albert, H (ed) *Theorie und Realität.* Mohr, Tübingen.

Popper, K (1972b) *Conjectures and Refutations. The Growth of Scientific Knowledge.* Routledge & Kegan Paul, London and Henley.

Potvin, D F (1976) An analysis of the andragogical approach to the didactics of distance education. In *The System of Distance Education,* 2 (10th ICCE Proceedings), pp 27-30. Liber, Malmö.

Sims, R S (1977) An inquiry into correspondence educating processes. Policies, principles and practices in correspondence education systems worldwide. (Unpublished ICCE–Unesco Report).

Wedemeyer, C A (1978) Learning through Technology. ZIFF-Papiere 26. Fernuniversität, Hagen.

2.2 Home Environment and Learning — Educational Technology at a Distance

Jacquetta Megarry
Jordanhill College of Education, Glasgow

Abstract: Distance teaching in the field of educational technology was pioneered by Jordanhill College when it set up its Diploma in Educational Technology course in 1975. This paper reports the findings of a small-scale study to discover the effect of the home learning environment on the way in which different components of the modules are used, and to see what problems students experienced.

Description of the Course

The subject of this paper is the CNAA-validated Diploma in Educational Technology which is offered by Jordanhill College of Education. The course lasts for two years and is taken part-time by teachers and lecturers who are in post. It depends on distance learning techniques for approximately one third of the formal study time (175 hours out of a total of 475 hours). The theoretical part of the course covers both theoretical aspects of educational technology[1] (180 hours) and

1 Defined, for the purposes of the course, as 'the application of scientific method and techniques to the design, implementation and evaluation of courses, with the aim of making the processes of learning more effective and efficient'.

management studies (100 hours), and it is here that nearly all the distance learning takes place. The practical parts of the course (production skills: 195 hours) are almost entirely covered in college sessions, though there is an independent learning element.

These time totals refer to planned study time (distance learning materials) or to teaching contact time (in-college sessions). The 475 hours total is distributed unevenly between the two years of the course, three-quarters (355 hours) occurring during the first year. The second year is devoted mainly to two major assignments which develop skills of analysis, application and synthesis and a curriculum project which provides a major opportunity for application of educational technology to a part of the course member's own teaching commitment. Assessment of all three of these is externally moderated; there is no final examination and award of the Diploma is based entirely on the results of continuous assessment.

Throughout the first year, the course is organized around overlapping cyclic patterns of four weeks, which take 12 weeks to complete. A typical cycle starts with an in-college weekend, with 10 hours teaching contact time providing a mixture of theoretical sessions, practical workshops and small group work at which base modules are given out for the next four weeks. The following weekend will include a short seminar on the subject of the assessable exercise based on the module, and during the next four weeks course members will complete the exercise (as well as the next three base modules). The third in-college weekend will include a short seminar to follow up the exercise, which has by then been marked.

Each week's work, which is focused on a 'module', is supposed to take about five hours. A typical module consists of a spiral-bound booklet, containing 40-100 typewritten pages of structured learning materials, often supported by audio-visual components (one or more audio-cassettes and/or a filmstrip). Where audio-visual materials are used, they generally form an integral part of the module, though their role varies from enrichment/enhancement to 'human interest' to surrogate first-hand experience.

The modules are designed to promote active learning in a number of ways, including the use of 'activities'; these are short tasks which ask for written responses from the students. For example, students might be asked to respond to an argument or question, to comment on selected frames from a filmstrip or to list problems encountered on a tape. Responses to activities are written on self-copying paper and the copy is posted back to the course team, who can then give individual guidance on request. Comments on the activities are provided at the back of the booklet. Occasionally students are asked to record their answers on the blank part of a cassette and return this (either as an evaluation activity, or as the response to an exercise).

Brief History

Applications are currently being received for the fifth intake to the Jordanhill DipEdTech course, though the results presented in this paper relate to the fourth intake. Since the first, in 1975, a number of changes, both major and minor, have occurred in the duration, content, methods, assessment, evaluation, organization, materials and status of the course. The course originally lasted for only four terms, and for some of the in-college sessions, co-operation of the employing authorities was required to release course members for attendance. It has been extended by stages to six full terms, and rearranged so that release is required only by one or two more distant course members (eg for travelling time and for attendance in periods which are holidays only in Scotland). There have also been changes in content, partly reflecting the changing face of educational technology and our image of it; for example, the attention devoted to resource centres has gradually been reduced, and that devoted to computers in education has progressively increased. Changes in methods and assessment techniques have also occurred; for example, the use of independent learning in the practical skills has gradually increased and become more sophisticated, to help cater for individual differences of pace and very varied initial levels of competence. Also, of the six exercises set on the content of the base modules, course members must now pass three *specified* exercises (on objectives, curriculum methods, and assessment and evaluation) and any two others, rather than *any* five out of seven as in previous years. A special feature of our course is its high commitment to evaluation procedures; this used to be embodied in the person of Carol Hewitt, whose role in the course was initially almost entirely that of evaluator, though circumstances later required her to contribute as author and lecturer in addition. Sadly, she has left for a different department, and evaluation responsibility is now more devolved throughout the course team; this has increased the blurring of roles (between that of tutor, teacher, author and evaluator).

The organization of the course has also changed, both to take account of other changes (time-table constraints and the extension of the course) and in response to student requests (eg to have a seminar *before* an exercise as well as after). In addition, as a result of demand from other institutions, the decision was taken in summer 1977 to put our course materials on sale. This was partly forced on us by requests for sample copies, which it was uneconomic to meet free of charge, but which it seemed churlish to refuse altogether. As a result, in the period October 1977 to January 1979 we have sold approximately 1,600 printed booklets.

Slides originally formed the visual component of the audio-visual materials issued with the print booklets. Cost factors (both production costs and manpower costs in labelling, sorting and packaging thousands of slides into sets) led us to change over from slides to half-frame filmstrips in the summer of 1978. Bulk processing, like long print-runs, militates against easy revision of modules and is therefore a mixed blessing. Likewise, validation by the Council for National Academic Awards (in 1977) has enhanced the status of the Diploma, and presumably its marketability as a qualification, but also makes major revisions more difficult.

There is a general expectation of a substantial drop-out rate from long courses involving distance learning of any kind. However, despite the heavy work loads which course members have to carry, the conflicting pressures imposed by their family commitments and their jobs, and the great distances from which some of them travel, drop-out has remained surprisingly modest for a course of this kind (Table 1):

Course	Number Enrolled	Number Withdrawn
1975-76	17	3 [1]
1976-78	13	0
1977-79	19	2 [2]
1978-80	21	1 (+1?)

Table 1. *Enrolment and drop-out since inception of Jordanhill DipEdTech course*

Past course members have been drawn from a wide variety of backgrounds including schools (mainly secondary but some from primary schools and schools for the handicapped, maladjusted and young offenders) and colleges (mainly further education, but also universities, colleges of education, polytechnics and

1 one of these was at start of course.
2 one of these caused by death.

central institutions). A sprinkling of others, from libraries, curriculum development centres and training agencies, have provided welcome additional ingredients. The geographical scatter has been considerable, including members from Eire, England (mostly the North) and all over Scotland. Incidentally, the proportion of women has been low throughout; we have had only four female course members out of 70.

The Investigation

A previous paper described the course in more detail, and explained the evaluation procedures used (Butts and Megarry, 1977). One of the problems identified was the relative inaccessibility of the base modules to evaluation procedures. Unlike the college sessions, we could not observe them, and the information provided by our normal techniques was becoming increasingly skeletal. Another problem was our general ignorance of the conditions under which the base modules are studied. Without knowing more about the way in which course members use the materials, it is difficult to improve their structure, organization or teaching effectiveness.

Some clues to the effect of the learning environment were provided by a request to course members to talk their way through a module on audio-cassette and send it to us. These cassette 'talk-throughs' provided some fascinating glimpses of the way course members used the modules and the constraints they were under (Megarry, 1977). However, as a method of data collection, it was unsuitable other than for stimulating ideas; it was time-consuming, both for course members to provide the information and for us to process it. The material was also difficult to condense and only four students (out of a total of 13) responded to our invitation in the first place.

In January 1979, therefore, I issued a questionnaire in two parts: the second part related to the base modules just being studied and was a part of our routine evaluation activity. The first part consisted of 17 questions aimed at finding out more about the conditions under which course members study base modules, and also what more general problems they might experience with the course. Course members appeared to take the questionnaire seriously: there was a very encouraging response rate of 100 per cent, and the average (self-reported) time spent on filling in the questionnaire was just over an hour. This excellent response may be in part a result of the lower demands made on current course members' 'evaluation patience' than in previous years. The results of this questionnaire form the basis of this paper.

Results

Because of pressure on space, only some of the questions and their responses are reproduced in this section; the original numbering has been preserved, however. Selected spontaneous comments are also given where relevant. Full results are available from the author.

1 **Where do you usually study DipEdTech materials (eg living room at home, library, school/college)?**
At home: 18 (including 4 who mentioned 'at college' occasionally); Mainly at college: 1

2 **Is it difficult for you to find a convenient and quiet place to use the materials?**
Yes: 6, No: 13

Comments
(a) Being married without children and with a wife who is also a student makes this relatively easy.
(c) Four children do tend to disturb one's tranquility. At least one child is seeking some form of attention.

(d) Almost impossible. Have become used to studying with some 'background' noise.

(g) At home, children and other demands on time make it nearly impossible to study. I already work late one night per week and tutor one other, so feel guilty about staying out any more than necessary since the EdTech course already demands about a weekend per month.

5 Does listening to/viewing the audio-visual materials cause you any problems?

Yes: 2, No: 15, No reply: 2

Comments
(b) Having a-v material included in material to be studied at home seemed an unusual idea to me at first, but now I prefer to have some a-v material in each unit.

(e) I find that they add to the quality of the material.

(h) Sometimes have to replay it several times to understand full meaning.

(i) Livens up the presentation.

(l) In fact quite the reverse. They compete better than the booklets for my attention.

6 How long at a 'sitting' do you normally study for (eg three hours in a block, bursts of half-an-hour)?

(answers varied enormously, as below)

Comments
(e) Two to six hours at one sitting with 10-minute breaks about every two hours to get the blood circulating.

(j) More often bursts of half-an-hour — one hour, but longer sittings of up to three hours normally to complete exercises.

(o) Difficult to answer — rarely can I work without interruption.

(q) I tend to do a whole or a half module at a time.

7 Do you usually start and stop study at the beginning and end of a sub-section?

Yes: 14, No: 5

Comments
(d) Rarely take more than three sessions to complete unit — usually break in middle on completion of an activity.

(e) Usually — but depends entirely on 'outside interference'.

(f) I like to gather all the information from the section, work through the response sheets and then think over the material.

(g) I normally stop when interrupted and mark (or find later) where I finished.

8 Are the modules subdivided into convenient sub-sections, given the constraints of study at home?

Yes: 19, No: 0

Comments
(d) I never find a problem of stopping midstream and restarting.

(e) Can be fitted into a school period of 35 minutes — convenient.

(f) Since I prefer to work in longer 'spurts', the length of the sub-section is immaterial to me.

9 Do the modules persistently tend to take longer than the advertised 5 hours?

Yes: 12, No: 7

Comments
(b) It's not the modules which take up the time, but the responses.

(c) No, but exercises do.

(e) It varies — Unit 1 took me long because of its difficult ideas — many of the others
I managed in less time due to having been familiar with the basics of some of the content.

(f) Exercises tend to take a bit longer. A first draft can usually be completed in the
time, but invariably improvements can be made.

(i) It may be that I tend to be a slow worker — I do, however, find the time well spent.

(k) Yes, you bet!

(m) No, not quite persistently.

10 How do you save time if a module is taking too long (eg read only parts, skim-read, omit activities)?

(Strategies varied, but the following are representative):

Comments

(e) I generally go through all of them, though I was bored stiff with the Programmed
Learning — for the first time I didn't do all the activities — and haven't forwarded them.

(f) I usually plough through all of it by devoting more time to it.

(g) Skim-read and omit activities — but try to do everything if possible.

(m) I don't — I take whatever time is necessary to finish properly. This is a reflection
of the fact that I have felt all the units so far have had something valuable to impart.
I would not hesitate to skip irrelevant material.

(n) Plough on!

(q) No — school work usually suffers if anything at all has to go by.

(r) Up till now, I have persisted with the module until completed.

11 Do you ever show DipEdTech materials to your family/friends/colleagues?

Yes: 14, No: 5

Comments (Mentioned wives (4 times) and colleagues (7 times). For example:)

(a) Only occasionally but useful for Computer Education Study Group.

(b) My wife (also a teacher) is interested and helpful.

(f) I have shown the materials to my colleagues and they are very impressed by its
quality and production.

(g) Yes, mainly colleagues.

(k) To my wife — but very little and only when I think she can add to my learning or
understanding — she is a teacher.

(l) I sometimes give an appropriate module to a colleague to study at home, eg
librarian, audio-visual technician or other Principal Teacher/AHT.

(m) My wife lends support, ideas, information — useful when sometimes cut off
physically from discussion with tutors, etc.

12 Do you have a regular time of day and day of the week when you work on DipEdTech materials?

Yes: 5, No: 10, No reply: 4

Comments

(b) Mainly weekends — occasionally during week.

(f) This depends on circumstances — I lay certain times aside but don't always use them.

(g) No — my own timetable of commitments is forever changing.

(i) I know I should, but I don't.

(l) Combination of when I feel like it and 'deadlines'.

(p) I don't — but I'm hoping to.

13 Do you let several modules pile up and then 'have a blitz'?

Never: 5, Occasionally: 10, Often: 4

Comments
(a) I try not to but at present have a 'blitzkrieg' situation, having fallen behind with several modules uncompleted.
(g) Often — a bad habit I have never been able to break.
(j) Never — so far, I have found the pace of the course as intimated. Provided time is allotted, it can be taken in its stride.
(k) Never — I'm too busy to afford the time for a blitz.
(l) Occasionally/often — I have an old house which I am renovating. I must devote time to it. This can cause a pile up of all my work, school and DipEdTech.
(n) Occasionally — I tend to let things go for a week after a weekend in college which results in me being late but I always catch up. I tended to work like this as a student but I'm trying to break it.

14 How do you tackle feedback activities?

As you go along: 17, In a block after reading the module: 2

Comments
(d) I do activities as I go, sometimes re-reading the section. I check answers where available on completion of units.
(e) I tend to skim read the section up to and including the feedback activity, then read carefully and tackle the activity.
(g) I work through the response sheets after each section — complete the module and then make reference to the answers.
(k) As I go along. I find it *productive* to do so. No, productive is the wrong word — I should say increases self-confidence and motivation.

15 Do the conditions of home study make it difficult to cope with the Assessment Exercises (as distinct from the modules) in the time suggested?

Yes: 11, No: 8
(Two comments emphasized that it was not the 'conditions of home study' but the exercises themselves — see comments (h) and (n) below)

Comments
(a) My difficulty is getting 'mass undisturbed time' (MUT), since I find I need to think through the exercise, plan it, revise or re-locate data and information needed, etc. To maintain a train of thought takes at least two or three hours, which is difficult to find in terms of MUT.
(e) I find I take much longer to do these than the time suggested. Conditions of home study make it particularly difficult to concentrate.
(f) The assessment exercises generally drive me back to re-examine modules which I have not read carefully enough.
(h) It is difficult and time-consuming (always takes more time for the exercises but I wouldn't say the reason was the conditions of home study). If the assessment exercises weren't difficult there wouldn't really be much point in them!
(i) I would feel dissatisfied about submitting what I have achieved in five hours. I usually feel it is not of the proper standard without a bit more work.
(k) They often take longer and require table and chair as opposed to the comfort of an armchair!
(n) The 'conditions of home study' have nothing to do with it! I just don't find I can do them in the prescribed time. Not that I mind — every time I finish an exercise I realise I wouldn't have anything like the grasp of the principles involved if I hadn't had to do the exercise.
(p) Lack of concentration and discussion opportunities.

16 If you were to study the same material in an institutional setting (eg a carrel in the College Library), how do you think this would affect:
  (1) your learning from the materials;
  (2) your enjoyment of the materials;
  (3) the likelihood of transferring/applying the ideas to your own school/college?

	increase*	decrease	no effect*
Your learning from the materials	8½	4	6½
Your enjoyment of the materials	4	7	8
The likelihood of transferring/applying the ideas to your own school/college	4	2	13

* one student ticked both

Comments
(e) I like to take a walk around the house to mull over a point, escape, take a breather, etc as the mood takes me. Institutions close early — my 'best' work is done between 10.00 and 12.00 pm.
(f) With the varying strains of a teaching day, working at home allows you flexibility to work when able to. I don't think units would lose validity in another setting.
(h) I enjoy being able to (say) make coffee, move around the study, etc.
(j) I hate being closed in — remnants of attack of acute claustrophobia in the past.
In any case, this would mean almost the same as extra in-service days/half days spent in college — and ensuing divorce.

17 Please assign ranks to the difficulties you find in getting the most out of the course:

	Average Rank	Ranked Rank
Length of time since last period of formal study	4.69	6
Pressure of normal work	1.6	1
Conflicts over allocation of time at home between Diploma work/family life	2.8	2
Finding a quiet area for study	5.1	7
Natural study pace fairly slow	4.1	3
Obtaining audio-visual equipment	5.5	8
Obtaining additional books, journals, etc	4.3	4
Others	4.67	5

Discussion

The results reveal vividly the human picture behind the easily-stated problems of distance learning. Commentary in this section follows the order of presentation in the Results section.

That nearly all course members studied at home was not surprising, though (unquoted) comments indicated that pressures on peace and quiet drove five course members to study at college at least occasionally (eg during children's school holidays). The fact that no one mentioned studying at school perhaps suggests the absence of suitable conditions and their generally earlier closing time relative to colleges, rather than indicating the absence of a need for an alternative to home study for school teachers. Certainly one third of respondents reported difficulty in finding a convenient, quiet place for study. Comment (g) on question 2 reminds us that apparent solutions (eg going to a public library) could exact their own price in tension over family commitments.

The use of audio-visual materials seems to be no more problematic than print. (The two who reported difficulties were referring to early problems over half-frame filmstrip viewers which have now been resolved.) Comments suggest that audio-visual materials may compete more successfully than print for attention; this may be one factor in Engel's finding that students overwhelmingly prefer to use audio-visual material in their own homes rather than on campus (Engel, 1976). McDonald and Knights (1979:48) report a minority of students who listened to audio-tapes while doing other things, especially driving and ironing. This questionnaire did not explicitly ask about this, but the tenor of the spontaneous comments suggests that our course members did not. Finally, there is no support for the idea that any of our students, like some of those at the Open University (Mason, 1979:31), find they cannot learn from audio-visual materials.

Questions 6 - 8 were prompted by reading an article based on Open University experience (Mason, 1978) which suggested that the OU study unit (10 - 12 hours) was too long. Mason put forward an alternative unit christened a 'Jewel' (1½ to 2 hours' work, 5 Jewels = 1 course unit). Reading this made me wonder if our own modules ought to be further sub-divided, but the answers do not support this idea. Perhaps this reflects our allegedly lower study target (five hours rather than 10 hours a week, but see also responses to question 9). The general impression from comments on question 6 - 8 is that the length of a study sitting is surprisingly great, especially for assessment exercises. It varies enormously, however, often as a result of factors not under the course members' control. Certainly, a large majority were able to start and stop at the end of a sub-section and those who could not were thwarted more by external interruption than by the lack of convenient breaks in the material. Several did not see the idea of stopping and starting 'midstream' as problematic.

Two-thirds of course members found that the modules persistently took longer than the billed 'five hours'. Comments emphasized that this was particularly true of the exercises. It is difficult to know how concerned we should be about this. Routine evaluation data from previous modules and previous courses shows that there is no close relationship between the apparent length of a module (in pages of text, minutes of audio-tape or numbers of frames in a filmstrip) and the time course members *say* they spend on them. To some extent our statement of 'intended study time five hours' has a normative effect (ie, the shorter modules seem to be studied in greater depth, the longer ones read more quickly). Since the exercises are assessable, some students will perhaps always spend longer than we intend. Nevertheless, the comments on question 9 do give the course team food for thought and we are currently reflecting what action (if any) we should take. Certainly, the answers to question 10 show a certain reluctance to cut corners; the two main strategies were to skip activities and to skim-read.

More than two-thirds of the course members showed our materials to colleagues, families and friends (seven mentioned 'colleagues' and four 'wives' explicitly). McDonald and Knights (1979:49) found that this was more likely in the case of material on audio-tape but our course members' comments do not repeat this finding. This probably partly reflects the different status of tapes in our course than in theirs; though tapes are by no means confined merely to enrichment as a role, they form an integral part of the print-based module and not *vice versa*. Printed booklets are also much easier to pass round, browse through, etc.

Comments on questions 12 and 13 were illuminating about course members' study techniques. Two-thirds did not have a regular study time, and some clearly regretted this. A majority let modules pile up 'occasionally', and four 'often'; the latter mostly regarded this as a bad habit but felt unable to break it. The activities were almost universally tackled (as intended) in passing and the comments on activities seemed to be used appropriately. (Inspection of the response sheets posted to us tends to confirm this impression.)

Problems were experienced by a majority with respect to assessment exercises; as noted earlier, these were even more demanding of 'Mass Undisturbed Time' than the modules themselves. Several course members answered 'No' because they felt that the conditions of home study were less of a problem than the inherent difficulties of the exercises themselves. As with excess time spent on the modules, it is difficult to know (a) whether course members would ever stick to a suggested time limit (since further polishing would always be possible) or (b) whether we should, as a result of these responses, cut our requirements or the total number of assessment exercises.

A mixed picture emerges on the hypothetical comparison with institution-based (as opposed to home-based) study of these materials. Course members were most likely to think that this would either increase or have no effect on their learning, that it would decrease or have no effect on their enjoyment and (a large majority) that it would have no effect on the likelihood of transfer.

Finally, a rather clear picture of the course members' difficulties emerged from their responses to question 17. (Strictly speaking, neither the averaging of ranks nor the subsequent ranking of the average ranks assigned is statistically defensible as we have no evidence that the ranks form a stronger than ordinal scale. Nevertheless, the data as presented is more conveniently digestible than the pooled raw ranks.) Overall, the pressure of normal work is the most significant difficulty encountered by a clear margin (12 ranked this '1') with conflicts over allocation of time at home coming second overall (four gave this top rank). A slow natural study pace was ranked third with problems of obtaining additional sources ranked nearly as high; these were followed by a range of other difficulties we had not suggested for ranking; six course members wrote in problems. The only ones they gave high ranks to were 'little time to practise skills acquired in school situation' (1) and 'illness' (2). The lapse of time since last period of formal study followed very closely, with problems of finding a quiet place to study and getting a-v equipment ranked lowest.

The overall impression that comes through is one of highly motivated teachers studying under conditions which range from suitable to extremely difficult. It is one which module authors and the course team will have to keep clearly in mind in the future.

References

Butts, D and Megarry, J (1977) Teaching educational technology at a distance. In Hills and Gilbert (1977) *Aspects of Educational Technology,* **XI,** pp 268-273. Kogan Page, London.
Engel, C E (1976) Audio tape programmes for individual study. *Research in Science Education,* 6, pp 7-14.
Hills, P and Gilbert, J (1977) *Aspects of Educational Technology II.* Kogan Page, London.
McDonald, R and Knights, S (1979) Learning from tapes: the experience of home-based students. *Programmed Learning and Educational Technology,* **XI,** Kogan Page, London.
Mason, J H (1978) The concept of a jewel or why course units are too coarse a unit. *Teaching at a Distance,* 12, pp 72-73.
Mason, J H (1979) Which medium, which message? *Visual Education,* February 1979, pp 29-33.
Megarry, J (1977) Teaching at a distance: the long arm of Jordanhill. *Times Educational Supplement (Scotland).* (22 4 77)

Workshop Report
Home Environment and Learning — Educational Technology at a Distance

Rapporteur: **Jim Hills,** *Coventry Technical College*

For the workshop following her paper, Jacquetta Megarry displayed a wide variety of course materials and workshop participants spent the first 15 minutes browsing through the documents.

A brief description of how the course was operated by the Jordanhill team was given and the problems of learning in the home environment were highlighted.

Support materials in the form of audio-cassettes and filmstrip were explained and examples were shown and discussed. The two main areas covered by these materials were (a) accountability and (b) the learning environment.

Further explanation of the choice of media took place followed by an open discussion of the problems outlined by the speaker. The main issues raised in the open discussion centred on such items as (a) tape commentary styles; (b) size of booklet and other paper-based learning materials; (c) choice of the medium for instruction; (d) the role of the face-to-face contact in the effectiveness of the course; (e) the low drop-out rate and its explanation. While these items were not necessarily the ones expected in connection with the problems of the home environment, they appeared to be uppermost in the minds of the workshop participants.

Miss Megarry gave very satisfactory answers to questions raised but reminded the workshop participants that she was presenting on behalf of a team who operate this course. The workshop participants responded well to the various comments and generally found the workshop to be a very useful follow-up to Miss Megarry's paper.

2.3 Providing Environments for Resource-Based Learning in Colleges of Further Education

Pat Noble
Garnett College of Education, London

Abstract: The paper reviews the scope for resource-based learning (RBL) in further education in terms of recent responses to users and to external agencies such as the Business Education Council and the Training Services Agency. It describes ways in which the aims and needs of user groups are being met, considers the readiness of further education teachers to exploit

RBL, and raises issues underlying the readiness of institutions and library resource centres to provide adequate learning environments.

In terms of curriculum development, the findings seem to show a situation of 'unstable congruence'.

Colleges and Their Students

A college of further education is provided by a local education authority to offer post-statutory education for students from 16 years of age. At 15 - 16, students may be linking schoolwork with some hours at a local college. From 16 - 19, they may be selecting courses to boost their competence in literacy, numeracy and life skills, with some hope of eventual employment, or of access to more advanced, formal courses. Equally at that age, they might be on day- or block-release from employment or studying full-time for their academic, craft, professional or vocational future. Many adults attend during the day or in the evenings for short courses and for weekly sessions, even for pre-retirement preparation. On formal, examinable courses, students tend to be taught intensively, under pressure of time constraints.

This paper concerns itself with colleges with less than 30 per cent advanced work and thus excludes colleges of higher education and technology and all polytechnics. There are some 600 colleges engaged in non-advanced further education.

Learning Resources Used with the Students

Despite the relatively low proportion of trained teachers in further education, there appears to be some measure of consensus about preferred learning resources. A time-honoured pattern emerged in an unpublished survey of about 200 teachers in further education. The findings appeared confirmed by a subsequent observational study in classrooms and in discussions with students and their lecturers. Textbooks were the most frequently reported source of stored knowledge but student access to texts could not be assumed to betoken individualized study, as most teachers averred that textbooks needed to be explained in class. They were not at all sure that students knew what was important in them. There was a consensual ranking by teachers who not only used texts, but also had in common the use they made of other resources.

The widespread use of handouts may reflect a number of factors. In some subjects, no satisfactory text exists, especially where the nature of technical and statutory changes necessitates updating. Moreover, it appears that teachers do not seem at all sure whether students can organize their own notes — they certainly feel that classes need handouts for reference. Worksheets are a normal part of teaching in practical subjects such as accountancy where classwork is often initiated by specially devised problems and cases, and in remedial levels of basic subjects. The worksheet itself rarely carries information but may guide students in using texts as books of reference; students often annotate the sheets, thus creating a store of worked examples. Rarely do handouts or worksheets refer students to further sources of information; rarely are full and adequate library references given even in academic and professional courses. Students probably receive an unwritten message from their lecturers that the knowledge provided is sufficient for their purposes.

Objective tests form part of course assessments in craft and vocational courses; there is some indication that their use in coursework may induce students to adopt a style of learning that suffices for the tests (Marton and Säljö, 1976). There are apparently many courses in the colleges where the library books play no direct part in the process of student-learning; their contents may well be mediated by lecturers and 'republished' as handouts, tailored to the course needs of busy, task-oriented students. The adequacy of the handout, as a knowledge-base for students, warrants some attention especially as lecturers admit that their students use college libraries less than they should; how far they themselves connive at such disregard for the library, and how far they see themselves as effective in fostering library and user education, are also issues warranting attention.

Students were reported to have access to pre-recorded material across a range of courses — secretarial, GCE and professional; no distinction was made between audio- and video-recordings. It is likely that much of the accessible material was used in the playback areas of library resource centres. Other forms of learning materials are shown to be a minority interest; this may in part reflect the lack of training amongst lecturers in further education, as on in-service courses considerable interest is engendered. Learning package design and evaluation is a possible special study in the third year of the BEd (CNAA) at Garnett College. Teachers lack neither knowledge nor, it seems, the equipment to provide students with access to stored knowledge.

Resource-Based Learning (RBL)

Resource-based learning may be identified when students are given access to stored knowledge as considered above; competence to learn from book and non-book media is one facet of the self-organized learner (Harri-Augstein, 1976), a facet that is largely undervalued in classrooms. Learning materials are merely adjuncts to most courses in further education, yet teachers agree that students should be able to do private study in college, although students on craft and vocational preparation courses are least likely to be seen to need time for private study. Of teachers on these lower level courses, 41 per cent of 54 denied the need for private study compared with 13 per cent of 116 teachers on academic, professional or technical courses (X^2 = 16.7 p< 0.001). Moreover, teachers are by no means sure that students should be given time to work on their own in classrooms. Yet at every level in further education, there exist reports of courses where RBL has been integrated into courses for classwork, for private study, and to form part of the normal demand for essays and reports for assessment purposes. Most such reports have been published by lecturers concerned to improve the quality of learning; they usually find that students work harder than with conventional courses and that time is won to give attention to individuals, but that for the least competent students, there is a less full, albeit more thorough coverage of the syllabus.

Three kinds of RBL environments are offered in colleges of further education: the *workshop or departmental centre* for practical, remedial or vocational work, the *linked study scheme* which incorporates some element of resource-based distance learning and the *library resource-centre*, using predominantly commercially produced materials.

Workshops and Departmental Centres

Workshops and departmental centres are more or less appropriately equipped learning spaces usually set out with the intention of encouraging individual or small group study, a high measure of personal success and a high level of purposeful activity for students. Communication workshops have been developed for students starting on courses (Davison, 1974); learning materials have been assembled and developed to help improve 'life skills' including the process of seeking work, coping with communication on the job and in non-work time. Materials are also offered to help improve basic literacy and numeracy, though the latter tends to become a specialized workshop activity in its own right. Materials may be provided to help develop competence for academic and professional courses. Typically, the resource bank is on open access, with teachers on duty to help, diagnose and 'tutor' students; to encourage this informal approach, the rooms tend to be furnished with grouped tables, individual study booths, cabinets, cupboards and trolleys of books, educational games and worksheets. Teachers seem able to develop and adapt materials to meet the needs of different course levels.

Teachers running such workshops would rarely designate themselves educational technologists, yet they assemble learning materials for a target population, and route students through the resource bank by use of both test results and intuition. They evaluate learning outcomes in terms of performance criteria, students' confidence, and their attitudes towards the learning process. In the numeracy workshop at Bradford College, computer-managed learning is used to route students through materials in the light of survey test results (Sands, 1977). Reprographic and audio-visual support services and the long arm of a sympathetic librarian can contribute substantially to the quality of learning; rarely however does an LEA provide the clerical hours that would free lecturers to develop and generate materials in response to emerging needs of current students. Self-access systems create a need for skills that figure in the training of clerks and library assistants rather than of teachers.

Workshops with self-access systems are not confined to the remedial levels of further education. For an intensive course for GCE 'A'-level Economics, two teachers sought to provide a learning system that would meet the needs of students with very different prior knowledge of both economics and mathematics, with different times available for study and for an inevitably staggered enrolment period (Negus, 1976). An externally prescribed syllabus provided a collection of topics or themes, only some of which required strict sequencing. Learning packages were created to include some basic information, reference to book and non-book sources, extracts from official publications, self-assessment questions, numerical exercises and discussion topics. None of these materials was new to economics teaching at this level; what was striking was the willingness of the lecturers to give students access to stored knowledge for private study, to give them command over their own learning and to provide course time so that the RBL was integral to coursework. Pacing was provided by weekly tutorial assessments; it was found that student note-taking needed supervision as selection and organization now depended on these skills.

Students were not wholly prepared for such a shift of responsibility. They were reported to have undertaken more reading and essay writing than in previous years; as a group, their examination results were not significantly different from other years' grades. The staff decided to develop the course in the light of experience, to provide space for guided discussion groups and for viewing educational video-tapes. They seemed convinced that the quality of the learning environment had been improved by the new system.

A rather similar idea was evolved by a young teacher for full-time and day-release students studying 'commodities' sold by retailers. Teachers and students have difficulty in locating and assembling information about raw materials and their processing, manufacturing procedures, product quality, durability and suitability for a customer's intended purpose. A resource centre was devised as a departmental workshop in which materials, samples, trade literature and accumulated project work from previous courses constituted the data bank. Explanatory audio-tapes were devised to talk students through inspection and observation exercises. The workshop not only involved time and energy from the innovator, but space, equipment and finance within the department (van Berlo, 1978).

A workshop for learning engineering processes and the writing of technical reports, integrating practical and theoretical study, have contributed to the education of engineering technicians. Some of the introductory work in these areas is covered in GCE courses in technology and design, so the lecturer in further education is faced with students having varied prior knowledge, and thus needing individualized provision. A workshop resource centre was created for students on block-release attendance, where they would be able to see progress in their self-access learning, and augment the available workshop time where necessary. Here, too, learning packages were created listing learning objectives, tasks, materials and available resources. As practical tasks were involved, a record-of-work chart was displayed to pace and schedule practicals; the students were free to intermix tests at the workbench with reference work, theory, and consultation with the teacher and with other students. Study booths for preparing the technical report were provided. 'Support facilities' included workshop technicians who assembled and issued the practical kits, and book and non-book resource materials housed on open access in the workshop; the library collaborated a system of long-term loans to ensure an adequate supply of reference material. Not only did students seem to value the system but the teacher also found considerable job satisfaction in the shift from formal exposition to progress chasing, advising and tutoring (McKeown, 1977).

Each account shows how the learning environment is gradually brought into congruence with the intentions of the learning system; each innovator seems to find a challenge in coping with the recurrent issues of storage and retrieval, pacing systems and support services. Accounts tend to be written in the early stages before the mass of learning materials 'goes critical' and the system capitalizes on the earlier effort. Business activities rooms being developed to implement the simulated and problem-solving course intentions of the Business Education Council will probably face similar developmental stages.

Linked Study Schemes

Linked study incorporates elements of correspondence courses, using stored knowledge in packaged form; for some adults, this is a preferred mode of study regardless of available taught courses in local colleges. Nonetheless, the lone learner may from time-to-time need guidance, the opportunity to pose questions and develop arguments, and a chance to evaluate evidence as presented by others; equally, students may need access to the specialist resources of a college library. By offering linked courses, colleges can provide environments supportive to the resource-based learner, with only marginal impact on the organization of its existing courses and procedures.

There is a long tradition of home study in the field of professional education especially for accountancy; a number of colleges now integrate learning materials and correspondence tuition from the self-financing colleges with tutorial and classwork in face-to-face sessions when previous study units can be reviewed, advanced preparation can be made for the next phase of home study, recent developments in subjects can be reviewed together with specially difficult topics, and examination questions can be attempted and reviewed. Linked courses are usually geared to the materials of one college; experience shows that diverse preparatory materials can be accommodated. One college offers a learning by appointment scheme that can be linked to a home study course (Davies, 1977, Appendix 4).

Moray College of Further Education is one of four institutions offering resource-based courses combining home study of college-produced learning materials with face-to-face tuition for National Certificates in Business Studies and Public Administration for the Scottish Business Education Council. Such courses, termed Private Study, are intended for students over 20 for whom the journey to college for normal class attendance proves unreasonable. Numbers are as yet small; younger students would be eligible if employers gave full day-release for home study and for short full-time blocks. Technician Education Council/CET experience in devising analogous collaborative materials for 'external' students is reported in Coffey (1978).

In 1975, a small scale experiment was proposed by Fred Flower to discover the effects of introducing RBL techniques of the Open University into colleges of further education. He proposed a locally generated scheme based on a single college or group of colleges, possibly harnessing correspondence materials. He drew encouragement from experience in his own college in offering audio-cassettes for revision and for a GCE course combining reading, written assignments, taped lectures and tutorials (Flower, 1975). The consortium now exists linking four colleges, and learning materials for GCE subjects from the National Extension College. The power-house of experience in this field is Barnet College of Further Education where the staff have now written a manual for local colleges; it reviews the administration, tutoring and student support systems that need to be organized (Barnet CFE, 1978). Both the NEC and Garnett College are interested in helping lecturers to develop the tutorial skills that become so important in 'Flexistudy'. Barnet is now monitoring the progress of its 200 students and a number of other colleges are showing active interest in the scheme described in Davies (1977, Appendices 1 and 3), and now supported by a development officer funded by The Council for Educational Technology.

Library Resource Centres

A college may concentrate its provision in a library resource centre; with, say, 1,500 full-time equivalent students, DES standards of recommended provision would perhaps yield 90 - 100 study places — or about 6 per cent provision. If 45 per cent of students were in full-time attendance, 10 per cent library study in their curriculum takes 68 places; 15 per cent of library-based RBL would need 101 places, quite apart from any demands by part-time students. Most colleges would have difficulty meeting this level of demand and would need to designate other rooms for RBL, perhaps developing a pattern of workshops and departmental centres. Few colleges can easily provide congenial accommodation for tutorials or ready access to telephones for supervising home-based students. Space and facilities are roughly congruent with *current* demands on them; a period of mismatch and territorial reallocation would be involved in any general curriculum development of RBL.

Time to search is one cost incurred in harnessing commercially produced materials as learning resources; academic and technical time is needed for schemes that seek to generate new materials, hence some of the collaborative proposals described. Access to any developing resource bank becomes important to teachers who seek to integrate the materials into concurrent courses; Bradford College seems to offer some solutions by allocating adjacent class-rooms for associated teaching, and internally seconding staff to the workshops. It is difficult to derive from published accounts the time commitment and skills represented by innovatory schemes.

For some teachers, the management of RBL provides considerable job satisfaction; others, less willing to provide students with access to stored knowledge, doubt student competence to sustain individualized study, to organize their own notes, to check their own answers or to seek information from libraries. The following propositions were presented to lecturers in colleges:

> Students should be able to do private study in college and help each other in class. They can put together a rational argument by themselves and can be expected to work outside class. They do take private study time seriously and shape up well if set a project on their own.

Those giving fullest endorsement were teaching on GCE courses (N=16); those giving least endorsement to the six statements were on ONC/D courses and the lecturers on TEC courses were intermediate. The differences were statistically significant (Kruskal Wallis one way ANOVA for ranked scores H=75.73 df=2 p< 0.001). Certainly, environments for RBL do not find full support in colleges of further education even today.

After a conference on library resource centres at the Further Education Staff College, Blagdon, in 1976, a Vice-Principal was reported as saying, 'I remain to be convinced that any of these systems will enable us to do more with less resources than the traditional arrangements properly used with economical numbers. And I certainly cannot see individualized learning replacing whole courses with the types of students which are the mainstay of most technical colleges' (Further Education Staff College, 1976). Yet support for RBL approaches was offered by the Technician Education Council (1974) when it stated, 'colleges are encouraged to develop informal approaches to teaching, and to allocate to the student time for self-instruction, the organization of his work and assimilation of what has been taught' (p 21). It is to be hoped that the experience of early innovators can smooth the path of later adopters.

References

Barnet College of Further Education (1978) Flexistudy: a manual for local colleges. National Extension College Reports, 2, 4. Cambridge.

Berlo, van G (1978) Commodities studies within the retail and distributive courses: a case study of the establishment of a resource centre. Diploma in Further Education Report. Garnett College, London.

Coffey, J (1978) Development of an open learning system in further education. Council for Educational Technology Working Paper 15. London.

Davies, T C (1977) Open learning for mature students. Council for Educational Technology Working Paper 14. London.

Davison, D (1974) Craft of communication. Contact, 2, 27, pp 16-17.

Flower, F D (1975) A further education college looks at the Open University. Teaching at a Distance, 2, pp 20-25.

Further Education Staff College (1976) College libraries and resource centres. Coombe Lodge Report, 9, 11. Coombe Lodge, Blagdon, near Bristol.

Harri-Augstein, E S (1976) How to become a self-organized learner. Centre for the Study of Human Learning. Brunel University.

McKeown, S (1977) A comparison of the attitudes of a group of telecommunication technician students towards traditional teaching methods and RBL techniques. Garnett College Special Study, BEd (CNAA).

Marton, F and Säljö, R (1976) On qualitative differences in learning. British Journal of Educational Psychology, 46, 1, pp 4-11.

Negus, P (1976) Individualized learning and economics. Economics, 12, 54, pp 91-96.

Sands, T (1977) The development of a mathematics workshop. Continuing Maths Project News, 4, pp 4-5. University of Sussex.

Technician Education Council (1974) Policy Statement, June.

2.4 Flexistudy — Further Education College-Based Distance Learning with Face-to-Face Tutorials

Brian Green
Barnet College, Hertfordshire

Flexistudy as described by Mr Green is a system which provides students with a correspondence course text and the services of a college lecturer to act as a correspondence tutor. Course assignments are sent to the tutor for marking. The student attends college for occasional tutorials, as well as having telephone access to the tutor.

The system is a response to a series of problems common to conventional part-time classes. Typically, these fail to provide for:

Students who are unable or unwilling to attend at a fixed time on a regular basis. These include shift-workers, mobile workers, the disabled, etc; students who wish to start their course in the middle of a session; students who want a minority interest course, where student numbers are below minimum class size.

What the student requires is the opportunity to study independently, yet to be provided with access to all the resources he requires — text, tutorials, counselling, media resources, library, examination boards, social contact, etc. These resources are largely available at most colleges of further education. The main obstacle to the success of any open learning scheme is the time and expense involved in producing suitable course materials.

Barnet College found that National Extension College materials provided a solution to this problem. The courses are well proven and quite attractively produced covering a wide range of subjects at 'O' and 'A' level.

In September 1977, 'Flexistudy' was launched at Barnet College in 28 subjects. By December 1977, there were 90 course enrolments in 22 subjects. Enrolments have now (April 1979) reached 340.

Most Flexistudy courses provide for 10 - 15 assignments for marking by the tutor and 10 face-to-face tutorials arranged at the mutual convenience of tutor and students. B Holmberg (1977) identifies five areas in which such face-to-face sessions are considered valuable:

1 Securing cognitive learning by discussion and application of the knowledge acquired to themes brought up in direct contacts with tutors and fellow students.
2 Practising psycho-motor skills in laboratories and under similar conditions; also verbal skills are trained through personal communication.
3 Understanding the communication process and human behaviours.
4 Acquiring attitudes and habits of value for the study, such as critical approaches, checking information and sources, openness to new ways of thinking.
5 Mutual inspiration and stimulation of fellow students.

To these I would add the following:

6 Establishing a personal relationship between student and tutor, reducing

the 'loneliness of the long distance learner'.

7 Familiarizing the student with college resources (library, media resources, counselling and careers services, etc).

8 Encouraging the completion of written assignments and keeping up the momentum of study.

The nature and size of the tutorial is determined by the needs and levels of the students. However, the purpose of the tutorial is not to imitate the conventional lesson and thereby double a course designed to teach on its own, but to deal with problems and to encourage the student to develop the independent study skills necessary both for Flexistudy and subsequent learning projects.

National Extension College courses take the form of printed text, with diagrams and illustrations. Some courses are linked with television series which form an integral part of the course. Flexistudy students have found the video-cassette facilities in the college's resources centre invaluable. Tutors are invited to recommend audio-visual materials from the college's collection to students in the same way as additional reading. The media-resources department of the college, collaborating with Flexistudy tutors, is also producing material designed specifically to support NEC courses. These materials will be available both for use in the college resources centre and, where the medium allows, on loan to the student.

Other colleges are encouraged to adopt and adapt Flexistudy for their own use. There are already five establishments operating Flexistudy schemes. By next year there will probably be 14 centres. How should colleges evaluate Flexistudy with a view to adopting it?

Rowntree (1974) derives 12 key questions from H D Brickell's work on appraising other people's innovations. Let us examine these questions with reference to Flexistudy.

1 *How suitable?* This will vary. Each establishment should carry out its own research.

2 *How effective?* Initial indications show that both drop-out rate and exam results on Flexistudy compare favourably with conventional correspondence and part-time courses.

3 *How big?* There are no restrictions on size.

4 *How complete?* The NEC courses are complete in themselves, although the possibilities and scope of audio-visual support material grows with the number of schemes in operation.

5 *How complex?* Being self-contained, the courses are easy to operate. Record keeping by tutors is essential.

6 *How flexible?* The courses are rigidly structured, but tutors can 'edit' units and vary the assignments to suit individual students.

7 *How different?* The scheme offers students, previously unable or unwilling to come to classes, an alternative method of learning. The Flexistudy individualized learning approach leads to an 'unfreezing' of previous teaching practices and experimentation with new methods throughout the college.

8 *How repeatable?* Experience shows that the scheme can be successfully repeated elsewhere.

9 *How compatible?* No existing classes have been closed as a result of Flexistudy. Students enquiring about Flexistudy are urged to join part-time classes where possible.

10 *How ready?* The course material is available. It can be started at short notice.

11 *How testable?* We are operating a two-year pilot project. Nothing (except students' goodwill) would be lost if the scheme were abandoned.

12 *How expensive?* The scheme is self-financing. Tutor and administration costs and course books are included in the fee charged to the student (£22 for a course with 10 tutorials). However, the scheme must be subsidized if it is

to become accessible to a wider section of society especially in inner city areas.

Flexistudy can be used to make educational opportunity available to those for whom we fail to provide at present. However, any use of the scheme to cut conventional classes must be resisted if we are to offer the public a real choice of learning situations.

References

Holmberg, Börje (1977) *Distance Education.* Kogan Page, London.
Rowntree, Derek (1974) *Educational Technology in Curriculum Development.* Harper & Row.

Section 3:
Media Design

3.0 Introduction

ETIC '79 Tracks

Of the two papers in this Section, Moakley's account of the CCTV Phoenix Arising from the Ashes at San Francisco (3.1) was presented at ETIC '79 in Track 1, 'Self-Instructional Programmes in Practice'. The other paper, Hartley and Trueman (3.2) featured in Track 3, 'Learning Environment, Practice and Presentation Techniques'.

Categories and Special Interests

This Section title corresponds exactly with one of the Conference categories, both papers and all four workshops being coded 'MeDes' at Sheffield.

The interest in tertiary education ('Tert') evident in the first two Sections is continued in Section 3 by Moakley, Hartley and Trueman, and Pettman (3.4). Belsey and Wellington (3.3), on the other hand, are firmly concerned with schools and were in the 'Primary and Secondary Education (PriSec)' category at ETIC '79.

A wide range of both educational and training interests is covered by Webb — with Hudson, Cooper, Mills, Corfield and Clarke — in their extra long-running workshop (3.5).

Links with Other Sections

Readers with a particular interest in Section 3 are also likely to be interested in the following contributions from other sections:

Section 6: Scholl (6.2).
Section 7: Moakley (7.2), Symes (7.3).
Section 8: Bryce and Stewart (8.1).
Section 10: Lawless (10.1).

3.1 The Television Phoenix at San Francisco State University

Francis X Moakley
Audio Visual Center, San Francisco State University

Abstract: In 1958, San Francisco State University was one of the first US colleges to receive Ford Foundation money to use television to 'improve teaching'. In less than three years the project money was gone and television was in decline. Little was done to change the approach to television in the curriculum until the early 1970s. Utilizing newer technology, renewal of old systems and a curriculum analysis system, the re-birth of television-based technology on the San Francisco State Campus has been the story of the Phoenix rising from the ashes. The paper traces the history and development of the present system with an emphasis on multiple uses of cable systems; organizational changes brought about by such a system; development and use of commercial sources of material; student and faculty production centres; and budget considerations.

San Francisco State University is an urban institution with a student enrolment of approximately 25,000. Located in the south-western corner of one of the most diverse and cosmopolitan of American cities, it has a long tradition of innovation with media.

In 1922 Anna Dorris, later to help found and become the President of America's first national media association, started the department of Visual Instruction at SFSU. On her retirement in 1948, an Audio-Visual Center had been established that continues to the present day. With these few elements of history and tradition as background we can see that a climate for media use and innovation was part of the San Francisco State scene.

In 1956, a time of great hope and promise for educational television, President Paul Leonard pointed the University in a new direction when he successfully obtained Ford Foundation support for an educational television (ETV) project that was one of the first of its kind in America. Funding was for two years and four courses were developed, presented and evaluated. Three of the four courses were evaluated to be superior to the same content taught in a conventional classroom manner. At the end of the experiment, there was no state support to build on what had been a successful beginning.

Reasons for this failure of continued support need to be examined for this was the first major use of television on the campus. First, there was no general faculty support for the project. It had been conceived at the top and was sent down to the faculty. It was also perceived by many as a direct threat to faculty jobs. The quality of production was high, but still not high enough to compete with the commercial offerings that the experimental work was being compared to. Last, there was no attempt during the development and execution of the project to create conditions that would allow gains achieved to become the base on which to build.

Another major development outside the ETV project was the design and building of an academic programme in broadcasting. The department was initially envisaged as a center that would create a new broadcasting man, one who was more of a thinker and policy-maker than technician. ETV was looked on as a service, not an academic enterprise.

Media centers were receiving support at this time that was broad-based and allowed ETV to survive. In 1956, the Media Policy Statement, Staffing and Budget formulas were proposed and accepted. In many of the state universities the ETV function come under the Director of the Audio-Visual Center and become a service center within AV.

At San Francisco State things were different. At the conclusion of the Ford Foundation grant and the development of a Broadcast department, ETV was subsumed by Audio-Visual. The association was brief. Almost immediately, a study was made of ETV and recommendations were made and carried out to establish a separate ETV identity so that a faculty that had a need for video service could deal directly without going through Audio-Visual. The ETV Director also felt that the service should concentrate on production and not on distribution of media on campus. That was to be left to AV. To support ETV's declared mission, the only equipment support was through the academic broadcast programme, ETV became a user of such space on a priority below instruction. Furthermore, ETV was required to 'rent' the facility to pay for staff time and wear and tear on equipment when it used the academic production space.

Co-operating with the broadcast facility on campus, ETV was able to produce a Semantics course with Dr Hayakawa. This course was kinescoped, re-played many times on campus and put into national syndication. Work was completed with commercial and public broadcast channels in the City and many video programmes were obtained and played back on a scheduled basis.

On the surface, the future seemed bright for ETV at San Francisco. This was deceptive. There was a call by the State legislature to develop a comprehensive plan for ETV in California. None was forthcoming and in 1971/1972 the state responded by reducing ETV budget support across the state university system by 50 per cent. There was a need to develop a faculty rights and responsibilities policy for the system. This was not done.

In 1968, with the assistance of federal funds, the University took delivery of six portable video recorder units containing camera, record and playback systems. ETV policy for the use of this equipment required an operator for use. The popularity of such equipment created an enormous financial burden for educational television. The portable equipment, although not up to broadcast standards, had an enormous effect in changing faculty attitudes. Prior to the portapak, productions were done in a studio that, at the least, had to be awe-inspiring. For much of the 1960s the academic television teaching plant at San Francisco was larger, if not better equipped, than any of the major networks, west of the Mississippi. For a faculty, to walk into such a facility was an experiment in incidental intimidation. The use of portable equipment was not frightening or intimidating. In 1971, when budget cuts forced changes, ETV loaned out the PVTR equipment as it could no longer support the small format service. It was at this moment in media history at San Francisco State that the television phoenix began its rise from the ashes of budget defeat.

In 1971, when funding cuts forced the ETV programme to distribute the six portable video recorders to 'heavy users', the Audio-Visual Center received one of these units. It was an instant success. The unit began slowly and was up to a use factor of 10 hours a day within a matter of months. A course in television production with portable television was developed around the one system. But more than the pragmatic value, the unit served as a stimulus to thinking about television by AVC staff and faculty. We knew the increased demand for media production and distribution was becoming a strain on our limited resources. The portable video recorder was viewed as a present and future solution to low-cost production requiring motion. We felt the distribution problem could be costly if we were required to buy playback units for many classrooms. Since two of our AVC rooms were connected to the existing 12 channel campus cable system, we decided to study the possibilities inherent in our own system and the state of the art of cable systems development. After several months of research and cable systems installation training for two AVC technicians, we developed a plan for remodelling and expanding the older system. Concurrently with the re-examination of television by the AVC, ETV was continuing to suffer budgetarily. The California Legislature, in 1972, stated that television would stay at reduced funding until proposals for increased efficiencies in television utilization would be forthcoming. Portable television recorders were beginning to come into the inventory of media centers everywhere. The AVC moved to commit 'audio-visual' dollars in 1972-1973 by buying four units. In the first year, they were used 36 out of every 40 hours they were available. The Audio-Visual Center also changed faculty access to the portable equipment. Under ETV each use of a unit had to have an operator. No operator, no equipment. AV changed this by training faculty in a series of workshops and then directly checking out the equipment to them. No operator was required. Additionally, units were made available on weekends creating a seven-day-a-week service. The programme proved popular with the faculty and the units available for use increased to 16. Other equipment and services followed — all portable. 1974 saw the addition of special effects generators. This allowed for multiple camera production with crew. In 1975, we designed and built a three camera system with special effects and audio mixer. This unit gave the Center mobile studio capability for the first time. Since we expanded the production capability of our users, the next development was to build an editing system for post-production work. Two such stations were completed by the end of 1975. In 1976 we were asked by faculty to provide large video image capability in colour. We responded by purchasing an Advent teleprojector and then built a transport system that made what was designed to be an immobile fixture change and become a campus resource. In 1977, we obtained our first colour units and designed and operated remote head end equipment. In 1978 and 1979 we are increasing our colour capability and retiring, as they wear out, our black and white systems.

Sustained faculty interest and demand have allowed us to obtain administrative support for funding. Funding sources have included Federal as well as State monies. Equipment has been obtained from new and replacement fund sources. Staff ingenuity has allowed us to create systems by unique combinations of existing hardware. A preventive maintenance programme that checks all equipment after every use has allowed us to operate with a great deal of reliability.

Proud as the Center is of its accomplishments in building a non-broadcast television service, it is in the area of cable that we see the greatest potential for future service to the university. The vision has been shared by the faculty. In 1975, a survey was conducted among the faculty that strongly endorsed direct distribution of media to classrooms. This survey coincided with the Center's own research on the newer cable technologies. The initial cable proposed in the early 1960s had a severe limitation on channel capacity. For the center to adopt this system would severely limit present and future needs. An alternative plan to the existing system was proposed by the Audio-Visual Center and accepted by the university administration. This new plan would remove the existing cable technology and replace it with a system with far greater channel capacity. Center technical personnel were responsible for the installation of the new equipment. Monies that would have been used for labour costs, should the older system be retained, were diverted to capital investment to complete the system. Much ancillary equipment was provided by a sister institution that decided on still another method of video development.

The installation of cable, amplifiers, etc was scheduled in increments. By September 1977, the system had increased the number of rooms wired for cable services three times over what the previous system provided. During the past two years the total of wired instructional spaces has increased to almost 300.

The cable system has several unique elements in its design. On a philosophical basis it is planned that the system be evolutionary, responding to those areas of the campus that desire it most. Schools have the flexibility to indicate their priority from a range of services. No grand plan requires conformity. One result of this philosophy was the determination by the School of Business to obtain stock market quotes as a primary signal while the School of Behavioral and Social Sciences felt the need for a television version of the Reuters News Service. Programming and service requests are by faculty choice.

One must know what is available before one can ask for services. To that extent, it is important to review what technical options are available to a user. First, the system can carry 35 channels of information simultaneously. The system can be re-configured to carry 105 channels should the need arise and can configure sub-systems within the campus system for use by separate schools. Such re-work could allow each school to handle 35 channels for its own needs. The 'head en l' for this system is in the Audio-Visual Center. Three film chains, three video-cassette players, ½-inch tape-players, 8mm projectors, automatic character generator, and in 1979 videodisc portable data modems, and a remote broadcast station comprise programme origination. Reception by the faculty is on both personal and university-owned receivers. Twisted-pair wiring complements coaxial cable at tap sites to provide two-way communication to facilitate service requests. A film and video library of over 2,000 titles and a choice from 40 video sources are available to the faculty. Utilization figures from the reception sources on campus have increased four fold in the past year. We distribute programmes on the cable, on demand, over 70 hours a week.

We feel the system as now conceived, will handle our perceived needs in the immediate future. We still do not think that we have used all of the potential of the system. We are particularly pleased that our faculty are showing their acceptance and support by their increasing use of the system. We are glad to see the Phoenix rising.

References

Broadband telecommunications at San Francisco State University, 1979-1980.

Layer, Harold A (1978) A broadband system for higher education. *Educational and Industrial Television,* Dec, 1978.

Pulvers, Martin R (1976) A history of closed and open circuit educational television at San Francisco State University. Masters Thesis. San Francisco.

3.2 Some Observations on Producing and Measuring Readable Writing

James Hartley and Mark Trueman
Department of Psychology, University of Keele

Abstract: The layout of a piece of technical prose was redesigned and the wording of the text re-written with the aim of making it more readable. Readers estimated the comparative ease of reading sentences and paragraphs from the original and the revised versions, and the different versions were subjected to various tests of readability.

The paper describes the procedures used to simplify layout and text. Particular attention is drawn to the fact that different measures produce different results and the implications of this for future work.

This paper describes (i) how we re-wrote a piece of technical text to make it easier to understand, and (ii) how we attempted to measure our success at this task. The purpose of the paper is to chart the difficulties in which we found ourselves. Our aim is to make the task easier for others who may wish to follow our path.

Redesigning Technical Prose

There are numerous guidelines on how to produce readable writing, but unfortunately they are not consistent. Klare (unpublished), for example, reported wide areas of disagreement in the 156 suggestions that he found in 15 books (five of which were written for writers in general and 10 for technical writers).

Furthermore, most of the available guidelines do not take into account typographic design considerations. An exception here, of course, is the book by Hartley (1978). The general procedures currently advocated by Hartley for redesigning text can be listed under three headings:

1 *Textual*
- ☐ Use the active voice.
- ☐ Use simpler wording.
- ☐ Either shorten sentences, or expand them into two or three simpler sentences.
- ☐ Divide long paragraphs into short ones.
- ☐ Number and list actions and procedures (and put them in temporal sequence).
- ☐ When in difficulty think of how you would explain to a friend what you are trying to write. Write this down. Polish it.

2 *Typographical*
- ☐ Decide on the printed line-length and typesize. Type the text with a matching number of characters per line.
- ☐ Use units of line-feed in proportion to separate out and to group units of text. (Eg separate headings from the text by using half a line-space below the heading and one line-space above it: separate paragraphs from each other by half a line-space: start new sentences on a new line.)
- ☐ Set the text unjustified (ie with equal word spacing and ragged right-hand margin — as in normal typescript).
- ☐ End each line at a sensible place syntactically (eg at the ends of clauses). Avoid word breaks (hyphenation) at line ends.

☐ End each page at a sensible place (eg do not have the first line of a new paragraph as the last line of the page).
☐ Use bold lower-case type (not capitals) for main headings.

3 *Procedural*

☐ Leave each revised draft for at least 12 hours.
☐ Revise and simplify revised drafts.
☐ Do not look back at the original text (except afterwards to check on ambiguities or points of meaning).
☐ Ask colleagues to help simplify the revised draft (either by simplifying it themselves, or by pointing out where they might expect difficulties to occur).
☐ Repeat as often as time allows.

The procedural aspects of these guidelines are only suggestions but they are particularly important. Problem words and phrases in one version seem to appear in two or three revisions before they finally disappear. There never seems to be a final solution.

To see how these guidelines work in practice, readers are now invited to compare Figures 1 and 2. These figures present the first page in its original and revised form from a document containing four pages of text. As noted above, the text in Figure 2 can still be improved.

Measuring the Readability of Technical Writing

In this section of this paper we wish to describe the procedures that we used to assess the effectiveness of our changes to this illustrated piece of text and to comment on what we found.

In brief, we carried out four enquiries:

1 We applied 10 readability measures to three sections of the original and the revised document.
Most readability measures use two variables to measure the difficulty of a piece of prose: the average sentence length (in words) and the average number of syllables in the words. The way readability measures combine these measures varies (see Klare, 1963, 1974-5), but these two measures provide an objective count of two key features of text difficulty.
2 We applied one version of the cloze technique (Taylor, 1953) to the same three sections of text.
This technique involves preparing versions of the text with every nth word omitted (eg every seventh). Readers are then asked to supply the missing words. The words supplied by the reader can be scored as exact hits or misses (ie the same as those used by the original writer) or they can be scored more freely (by allowing acceptable synonyms).
3 We asked sixth-formers to rate the readability of:
(a) 'spaced' versus 'solid' paragraphs from the text;
(b) revised versus original paragraphs from the text;
(c) revised versus original sentences from the text.
4 We asked fifth-formers to circle on the revised text those words, phrases, sentences or paragraphs that they thought other people like themselves would find difficult to understand.

Because of space limitations, the detailed results of these four enquiries cannot be presented here. However, the data are available from the authors on request.

BELL SYSTEM PRACTICES
AT&TCo Standard

INSULATING RUBBER BLANKET DESCRIPTION, MAINTENANCE, AND INSPECTION

1. GENERAL

1.01   The care, maintenance, and inspection of the insulating rubber blankets are described in this section.

1.02   This section is reissued to delete reference to the KS-16302 cleaner which has been superseded by the B cleaning fluid (AT-8236).

1.03   Insulating blankets are for use as a temporary insulating wrapping on poles which may come in contact with power lines during construction work. The blanket is also for use as an insulating mat on which a workman must stand while operating external derrick controls for a derrick being used in the vicinity of power lines. The use of insulating blankets is described in Section 621-205-010.

1.04   The insulating qualities of blankets are reduced when they become wet. For this reason, insulating blankets shall not be used during periods of rain or to cover pockets of water on the ground.

1.05   The insulating blanket is **not** a substitute for insulating gloves. Insulating gloves shall always be worn in conjunction with the use of the blanket.

1.06   When using an insulating blanket as a mat, care must be taken not to place it directly on sharp gravel, glass, or other sharp objects which will cause cuts. Either sweep the area to remove such objects or place boards to protect the blanket.

BELL SYSTEM PRACTICES
AT&T Co Standard

INSULATING RUBBER BLANKETS

Description, Maintenance and Inspection

1.0   **General**

1.1   This section describes the care, maintenance and inspection of insulating rubber blankets.

1.2   This section is re-issued to delete reference to the KS-13602 cleaner; this has been superseded by the B cleaning fluid (AT-8236).

1.3   Insulating blankets are used to provide temporary insulation around poles that might come into contact with power lines during construction work.
The blankets are also used as insulation mats for workmen to stand on when they are operating the external controls of a derrick near power lines.
The use of insulating blankets is described in Section 621-205-010.

1.4   The insulating quality of the blanket is reduced when it gets wet.
For this reason do not use insulating blankets to cover pools of water on the ground, or when it is raining.

1.5   An insulating blanket is **not** a substitute for insulating gloves.
Always wear insulating gloves when using an insulating blanket.

1.6   When using the blanket as a mat take care not to place it directly on sharp gravel, glass or other sharp objects which might damage it.
Either sweep the area to remove such objects, or put down boards to protect the blanket.

Figure 1
Part of the original text

Figure 2
A revised version of text

(Figures reproduced by courtesy of Bell Telephone Company)

In brief:

1 The 10 readability measures produced conflicting results. The results varied according to which measure was being used, and different measures produced different results with the different sections of the text. The most consistent measures were obtained from the formula based on polysyllabic words (ie three or more syllables) and sentence length.

2 The cloze procedure that we used (deleting every fifth word) produced similarly inconsistent results: two of the revised sections were apparently easier than their originals, but not the third.

3 The sixth-formers:
   (a) rated the 'spaced' paragraphs more readable than the 'solid' ones but only when they contained *more* than two sentences;
   (b) rated every revised paragraph more readable than its original counterpart; and
   (c) rated 20 out of 24 revised sentences to be more readable than their original counterparts.

4 The fifth-formers did not circle much but what they did circle was most informative. They pin-pointed words, phrases, and even sentences which could profit from further revision.

Conclusions

In this paper we looked at procedures designed to make text easier to understand, and we examined different ways of assessing the difficulty of text. Our aim was to look at quick, crude and obvious methods, with the idea of seeing how useful they were for writers of technical materials.

Our conclusions are as follows:

1 The application of the procedures that we suggest in the first section of this paper does lead to text which is judged easier to understand.

2 Readability measures have a number of faults. Their virtues are, however, that they are objective, and that they can be applied quickly without the need to resort to other readers.

Different measures present different results, so 'grade-levels' need to be taken with a pinch of salt. Nonetheless, a readability measure can indicate whether one piece of text is easier than another. For technical prose we would recommend the use of Gunning's FOG or McLaughlin's SMOG index (see Klare, 1974-5) on the grounds of ease of calculation.

3 However, we found it more valuable to ask users of the text to make comparisons between 'before and after' versions — either of the total text, or selected paragraphs and/or sentences.

Our findings suggest that it may be more informative to collect sentence data but it is perhaps more tedious to do this than to collect paragraph data. It is worth remembering that the more participants one can use in this judgement process the more reliance one can place upon the results.

4 Finally, we found that a quick, easy and helpful method of assessing the readability of technical prose was to ask users to indicate where they thought other similar users might find points of difficulty. This is the procedure we recommend.

References

Hartley, J (1978) *Designing Instructional Text*. Kogan Page, London; Nichols, New York.
Klare, G R (unpublished) Some suggestions for clear writing found in fifteen source books. Paper available from the author, Department of Psychology, Ohio University, Athens, Ohio.

Klare, G R (1963) *The Measurement of Readability.* Iowa State University Press, Ames, Iowa.
Klare, G R (1974-5) Assessing readability. In *Reading Research Quarterly,* X, 1, pp 62-102.
Taylor, W L (1953) Cloze procedure: a new tool for measuring readability. *Journalism Quarterly,* 30, pp 415-433.

Useful further reading

Davies, A (1973) *Printed Media and the Reader.* Units 8 and 9 of Post-Experience Course 261. Open University, Milton Keynes.
Kincaid, J P and Gamble, C G (1977) Ease of comprehension of standard and readable automobile insurance policies as a function of reading ability. *Journal of Reading Behavior,* IX, 1, pp 85-87.
Klare, G R, Sinaiko, H W and Stolurow, L M (1972) The cloze procedure: a convenient readability test for training materials and translations. *International Review of Applied Psychology,* 21, 2, pp 203-208.
McLaughlin, G H (1974) Temptations of the Flesch. *Instructional Science,* 2, 4, pp 367-383.
Stokes, A (1978) The reliability of readability formulae. *Journal of Research in Reading,* 1, 1, pp 21-34.
Wright, P (1977) Presenting technical information: a survey of research findings. *Instructional Science,* 6, pp 93-134.

Acknowledgements

We are indebted to pupils and teachers at the Regis School, Wolverhampton, Holy Trinity School, Crawley, and Clough Hall School, Kidsgrove, who assisted with our enquiries.

Appendix

How to Calculate the Gunning FOG Index

- ☐ Take a sample of 100 words.
- ☐ Calculate the average number of words in those sentences within the 100 words.
- ☐ Count the number of words with three or more syllables.
- ☐ Add the average number of words per sentence to the total number of words with three or more syllables.
- ☐ Multiply the result by 0.4.
- ☐ The result is the reading grade level.
- ☐ Add five to get an approximate British age-level.

How to Calculate the McLaughlin SMOG Index

- ☐ Take a sample of 30 sentences.
- ☐ Count the number of words with three or more syllables.
- ☐ Find the square root of this number.
- ☐ Add three.
- ☐ The result is the SMOG grade level.
- ☐ Add five to get an approximate British age-level.

nb The SMOG grade level should be higher than the FOG grade level, as the former is based on a 100 per cent comprehension criterion and the latter on 50 per cent. (See Klare, 1974-5, p 80.)

Footnote
Patricia Wright has suggested (personal communication) that it might be better to ask users to mark sections of the text that they think people 'less able than themselves' or 'younger than themselves' would find difficult. In this way the onus of admitting a personal difficulty in comprehension would be further reduced.

Workshop Report
Producing and Measuring Readable Writing

James Hartley and Mark Trueman
University of Keele

This workshop might have been better entitled 'rules for re-spacing technical text' as more time was spent on discussing and trying out such rules than on discussing procedures for simplifying the language of text.

The spacing of text can be considered from both a vertical and a horizontal point of view (Hartley, 1978). We, however, focused most attention directly on horizontal spacing. Our aim was to see if *simple* rules of procedure could be developed for computer-assisted printing which would increase the proportion of lines in text which would start or end with a syntactic unit. (The rationale for doing this was discussed by Hartley, 1978.)

Three sets of rules were provided and members of the workshop were asked to apply them to any of the conference abstracts. The aim was to see what difficulties would arise from their application.

The rules — in order of complexity — were:

1.1 Take the first line of text and consider the last word. If this word is *followed* by any punctuation mark, accept this line and consider the next one.

1.2 Take the first line of text and consider the last word. If this word is *preceded* by any punctuation mark, stop the line at the punctuation mark, and carry over this last word to form the first word of the next line. Then apply rules 1.1 and 1.2 to the next line (whose text might have to be re-arranged or 'shunted on' — to fit in with the column width).

1.3 If there are no punctuation marks before or after the last word, accept the line, and consider the next one.

2.1 In this version rules 1.1, 1.2 and 1.3 apply except that all new sentences within each paragraph begin on a new line, irrespective of where they start in the original text.

3.1 If the last word is not preceded by any punctuation mark but it is one from the following list of words, then carry this word over to start the next line.

a	*for*	*under*	*beneath*	*before*	*the*	*to*
over	*above*	*after*	*of*	*in*	*beside*	*around*

3.2 If the last word is not preceded by any punctuation mark but forms one of the following pairs of words, then carry over the pair of words to start the next line.

of a	*in a*	*besides a*	*around a*
for a	*under a*	*beneath a*	*before a*
to a	*over a*	*above a*	*after a*
of the	*in the*	*besides the*	*around the*
for the	*under the*	*beneath the*	*before the*
to the	*over the*	*above the*	*after the*

Three assumptions were also made:

1 Separate paragraphs by a line space without indentation.
2 Set text unjustified (ie with equal word spacing and ragged right margin as in normal typescript).
3 Avoid hyphenation in single words or between pairs of words (eg audio-visual at line endings.

The workshop members found most difficulty with rules 3.1 and 3.2 and many queries arose and additional combinations were suggested. In terms of simplicity, it seemed that rules 1.1, 1.2 and 1.3 were possible but it was felt that 1.3 would lead to a very ragged text if narrow column widths were used, or if there were a large number of short sentences.

Reference

Hartley, J (1978) Space and structure in instructional text. Paper presented to the NATO Conference on Processing Visual Information. September 1978. Het Vennenbos, Holland. (Copies available from the author on request.)

Workshop Report
3.3 Songs and Slides in the Teaching of English as a Foreign Language

Mrs V R Belsey and Miss Jane Wellington
Devon

The workshop was designed to show how songs and slides can be successfully married to the teaching of correct pronunciation, intonation and grammatical patterns of English for foreign students. Songs and slides can also lead the way to the development of Western narrative skills and methods of presentation often taken for granted by Europeans.

The authors discussed the relationship between language and music. They played the melody of Elgar's *Enigma Variations* to show how the melody line falls at the point of greatest accentuation. A tape-slide version of *Mr Monday* had been used to teach English intonation, and the speakers played a before-and-after tape of a student who spent 45 minutes working on the song in a laboratory.

Folk songs can be used extensively to teach various aspects of pronunciation. The song is presented in tape-slide mode, followed by discussion of the structures and pronunciation points, written work and laboratory work.

Songs are selected for themes as well as for grammatical and pronunciation points. They are divided into (a) folk themes; (b) comic themes; (c) changing chorus and repetition songs; (d) modern theme folk songs.

Some songs (eg *Dry Bones*) have been used for ESP purposes and even adapted to describe technical machinery ('the big end's connected to the camshaft'). This material is used as about 20 per cent to 25 per cent of total teaching material, usually the last lesson of the morning.

In some cases, students have made their own visual material to accompany songs, and even their own worksheets for use by other classes.

In using folk themes to teach EFL, the speakers hoped to give foreign students who come to Britain confidence in their own traditions and an appreciation of simple songs and stories wherever they may be found.

Workshop Report
3.4 Establishing a CCTV System

L Pettman
Dorset Institute of Higher Education

This case study is concerned with the main features that determined the development of a closed circuit television (CCTV) system for a new building, built in 1977 to accommodate the Dorset Institute of Higher Education at Wallisdown, Poole.

The Wallisdown site of the Institute operate courses in Business and Professional Studies, Management, Tourism, Catering and Hotel Administration and Arts and Social Sciences, from HND to Degree level. A seven storey building houses the majority of teaching rooms, a purpose built CCTV studio and control room.

A year before the building work was completed discussions took place to decide on the functions of the CCTV system. It was decided the first priority was to develop a reliable video 'off-air' recording and replay system. The replay system should be designed to enable the lecturer in the classroom to have independent control of the video-tape during replay. A cable system, centred on the control room of the CCTV studio, was built into the teaching block building and now extends to 42 classrooms. A cable system operating on video signal was chosen rather than a number of mobile trolley-borne VCRs as experiences elsewhere had shown that a classroom-located VCR was subject to unserviceability through staff and student mishandling.

Cable systems normally require some audio communication between classroom and control centre to allow the lecturer to request a technician to operate the master VCR to replay the tape. This need was overcome by modifying the classroom monitor with a push button switch which, when operated by the lecturer, automatically activates the master VCR to start. The time delay between operating the modified button control and obtaining a replay picture on the monitor is no more than five seconds. No extra cabling is required for this system as the control voltage is transmitted via the video cable braiding.

The 'off-air' recording system is also modified to provide control to six record players (also used for the replay service). Each replay machine can be programmed seven days ahead by using four time clocks modified to control five outlets. Each time clock will switch on and switch off each master recorder to an accuracy of 15 seconds.

Having designed the type of replay system we required, which was proven before we moved to the new building, decisions were taken to provide those resources necessary to record in-house events on tape. I avoid the phrase 'making our own television programmes' as it was necessary in terms of both human and material resources to find the most cost-effective means to meet our needs for internally produced television. The most cost-effective 'in-house' television is the recording of role play and the subsequent replay for analysis. Not only is this activity less costly in time than scripted programme making but the evaluation of the effectiveness of television in teaching is more direct and assessable.

A television crew as such were not employed. Role play recording was achieved by using Institute technicians employed within a Teaching Resources Centre organization. The Teaching Resources Centre controls all media production and audio-visual aid services. This centre is operated in parallel with a Learning Resources Centre based on a library complex.

The priority use of the CCTV system was therefore, first to provide a reliable replay system (a video-tape, as a teaching aid, can only be as effective if students and staff can use it), and second to produce tape of role play activity. The CCTV control room was designed to meet these two functions. The production control desk was designed to be operated by one person, aided by one camera-man in the studio and occasionally with a floor manager. The studio was equipped with two CCTV 2300 three tube plumbicon cameras; one camera was modified to be operated by remote control from the control room. The control desk is equipped with five monitors, (on-line, camera one and two, caption and effects). The production panel gives cut, fade, wipe and matt mode functions.

Directly above the production panel were placed the editing control and a six channel audio control. Two Edit/Record VCRs were located on each side of the operator. This compact control desk design is far removed from the traditional layout that provides grouped controls for each specialist in a production team. Our need was to reduce those concerned in the CCTV activity to a minimum and in addition to avoid creating a television production aura around the television studio. The attempt has been made to make the CCTV facility available to any member of staff to use the studio as a CCTV classroom. The full utilization of the system can only be effective if staff regard the studio as simply a specialist classroom or indeed as they would a laboratory where students undertake activity with specialist equipment.

Subsequently we have produced a number of scripted television programmes for our own courses and external users. The design of the control room has proved to accommodate the additional personnel required for programme production. The replay and production equipment in the studio and control room is based on the U-matic format. The reliability and record/replay quality of the Sony U-matic together with the 2850 Sony Editors has been good and has proved to be a good choice for base standard equipment.

Workshop Report
3.5 Better Tape-Slide Programmes for the Amateur

F J Webb, *Harwell Education Centre*
E Hudson, *Sheffield City Polytechnic*
N Cooper, *Sheffield City Polytechnic*
J T Mills, *Athelstan Middle School, Sheffield*
G Corfield, *Sheffield City Polytechnic*
J Clarke, *Dundee College of Education*

The purpose of this workshop, directed by Mr Webb, was to show that simple programmes, produced with simple resources and minimal expense, can be attractive and effective teaching aids.

The Script

Mr E Hudson described the systematic approach employed at Sheffield Polytechnic to produce effective tape-slides to achieve student success. The aims and objectives must be clearly written down, as in any form of programmed learning, and the principal teaching points listed. The target population must be identified and a logical scheme of evaluation and revision of the material laid down. It must be decided whether a 'presentation' or a 'programme' is appropriate; the former presents information for the student to absorb, the latter involves the student in an integrated learning process, including instruction, activity and assessment.

Having laid down the objectives the scriptwriter must then construct his programme from both words and pictures. He can write the words first, or sketch the pictures first and then write words to describe them. Best of all, he can write down the words and sketch the pictures together; at any point he can concentrate on the verbal or visual aspect. The verbal content must be concise and clear, but not too formal; it should sound like a conversation — simple words, short sentences. The visual content should also be simple — one slide, one idea.

The Artwork

Any educational tape-slide programme requires some artwork, if only a title slide. A wide range of 'instant art' material is now available to produce attractive and effective artwork with the application of the minimum of artistic talent. Remember, 'one slide — one idea'; if your picture conveys one idea to the student you have succeeded.

Cartridge paper is cheap, but coloured board is more substantial and has a smoother surface. Printed papers such as Pantone are expensive, but provide hundreds of different colours. White paper should be avoided as a background: it dazzles the student. Black is much better: it shows up colours well, and incidentally is easily corrected. Use bright colours sparingly, for emphasis; background colours should be restful, even drab.

A4 is a convenient size, but demands neat artwork, especially for projection on a large screen. A very simple technique is to employ stick-on shapes, stick-on tapes, cut-out magazine illustrations, coloured overlays, patterns and patches. Alterations and corrections are easy; the appearance of the picture can be judged before sticking anything down.

Dry transfer lettering is available in a great variety of sizes and styles, and in a number of colours. Several rules should be observed:

(a) Lettering should not be too small, nor too large. 6mm high is about right for A4 artwork (twice the height of typescript).
(b) Not too much lettering; IBM limit their computer displays of instructional text to six lines.
(c) Use capitals and lower case letters for maximum legibility, not capitals alone.
(d) Text displayed must agree with the spoken commentary, but not to duplicate it.
(e) If text is not to be read, it should be clearly *illegible* — gibberish lettering is available.
(f) Use simple typefaces, not fancy ones.

The Photography

Any 35mm camera can be used for making slides from artwork, but a single lens reflex is by far the best. It obviates parallex corrections — what you see is what the camera takes. To photograph A4 artwork you need a close-up lens, an extension tube, or best of all a macro lens. Mr N Cooper described the simple form of copying stand used at Sheffield Polytechnic. An enlarger might be modified as a substitute. It must be rigid enough to avoid camera-shake and allow accurate focusing; the camera back must be accurately parallel to the artwork.

Daylight can be used for illumination, preferably diffused sunlight. Then ordinary daylight type colour film can be used. With artificial light, even illumination is essential — two or four lamps equidistant from the artwork, at approximately $45°$ to the lens axis. Take care not to throw shadows over the artwork. There is no need to bake the artwork under a battery of photofloods; four 60 or 100 watt bulbs are adequate. Of course you must use artificial light type colour film, or the correct filter.

All lenses produce the sharpest picture when stopped down to f/8 or smaller. This also increases the depth of focus — which is quite small at these short distances. To calculate the exposure you can use several methods. An incident light meter placed at the centre of the artwork will measure the illumination. You could point your exposure meter at a sheet of white card placed on the copying stand, and increase the exposure indicated by a factor two or four depending on the tone of the artwork. Or you could keep some average coloured picture as a reference and point your exposure meter at this. Experience will quickly enable you to achieve consistent acceptable pictures.

It is highly desirable to mount all slides in plastic mounts, between glass. This avoids damage to the film, dust, scratches, finger marks; it reduces the chance of the slide jamming in the projector and eliminates buckling of the film in the heat of the projector lamp with consequent loss of focus.

Recording the Commentary

Mr J T Mills demonstrated simple recording techniques capable of producing acceptable results. A cassette recorder with automatic recording level is the easiest to use, and is really the only option when recording 'on location' — out of doors or down a coal mine. However, in the studio an open reel machine is to be preferred; the recording quality is far higher, and editing the tape becomes a simple process. Editing not only facilitates the assembly of a tape from different sources, but also greatly reduces the strain of a recording session; a mistake can just be cut out later.

To edit a tape you need a splicing block, a razor blade and a reel of splicing tape. To find the exact place to cut the tape, play the tape and stop it as near as possible to the fault. Then, turning the spools backward and forward by hand, locate the precise position for the cut — an accuracy of 5mm is easily possible. Mark this position on the back of the tape with a wax pencil. Then make a similar mark at the end of the piece of tape to be removed. To make a joint, locate the tape in the splicing block, magnetic surface down, cut the tape square (a diagonal cut is theoretically better, but more difficult), remove the unwanted length of tape with a second cut, butt the two ends together in the splicing block and join them with a piece of splicing tape 15 - 20mm long.

The acoustics of the recording room make all the difference between a pleasing recording and an unsatisfactory one. A bedroom at the back of the house, with the curtains drawn, can be quiet and fairly dead. Failing this a reasonably soundproof enclosure can be improvised by hiding your head in an armchair and covering yourself with a thick blanket. Whatever your recording set-up, always record a minute of ambient silence in case you need to add pauses at the editing stage — blank tape will not match.

The Single Projector

A single projector provides the simplest means of showing a tape-slide programme. A teacher can change slides by following a script, or an individual student can follow audible cues. Many types of automatic slide projector are available, taking inaudible signals for slide advance from the tape. These range from the simple Philips unit for use with an open reel recorder, to units of varying complexity, some with built-in cassette decks and amplification, and self-contained projectors with rear projection screens, such as the Singer Caramate. Many of these units provide facilities for recording the inaudible control pulses on the tape or cassette.

Any single projector programme presents discrete images separated by black intervals. This is excellent for displaying separate pieces of information, but not for presenting a logical argument — even something as ordinary as the consecutive steps in a simple sum. If a logical argument must be presented by a series of slides, there must be continuity from one slide to the next, and the student must have no doubt what each separate slide is intended to convey — the fresh information must be arrowed or emphasized. He must never find himself hunting to find out what has been added to the previous slide.

A second drawback of the black interval is contrast. Bright slides alternating with the darkness of a well blacked-out room quickly daze the students. Keep the contrast down by employing dark backgrounds with the minimum of bright areas. For small back projection screens viewed in subdued lighting this question of excessive contrast is less serious.

Apart from these two limitations, a single projector programme has advantages over dual projector programmes. It is simpler and requires fewer slides. There is no correlation between successive slides, so there is no need to consider registration or to avoid unfortunate conjunctions between successive images.

Dual Projectors

Using two projectors with the appropriate control equipment permits fading from one image to another at varying rates, or superimposing one image on another. Dr G Corfield listed the following applications of this lap-dissolve technique in the field of science teaching:

(a) Building up tabulated data, diagrams, equations.
(b) Detailed examination of data by highlighting points of interest, eg figures in tables, positions in diagrams, adding captions and arrows.
(c) Simple animation, such as the addition and replacement of sections of diagrams and models.

(d) Simulated movement of models, of particular interest to chemists, eg
the rotation or vibration of particular groups in a complex molecule.

(e) Progress of experimental chemical reactions by a sequence of repeated
shots of the same piece of apparatus as the reaction proceeds.

The advantages and disadvantages are the opposite of a single projector
programme. Successive images are strongly correlated, so there is no problem in
presenting a most complex argument. But great care is needed in the preparation,
photography and projection of diagrams and models in exact registration.

Teaching with Tape-Slides

If a tape-slide programme is to be effective as a teaching programme, rather than
a straightforward presentation, just as much thought must be given to the learning
situation and to the accompanying materials as to the audio-visual aspects.
Mr J Clarke described how these various aspects were integrated into a coherent
teaching scheme at Dundee College of Education. The visual material must be
consistently attractive, to maintain student motivation after the novelty of the
medium has worn off. The student's good intentions must not be frustrated by the
unavailability of materials or equipment at whatever time he requires them, or
by breakdown of the equipment, by delay in assessing progress, or by lack of
tutoring as and when necessary.

Audio-visual material for individual instruction must always be accompanied by
written material. A typical workbook would contain:

(a) A list of objectives in behavioural terms.

(b) A list of the topics covered by the programme.

(c) A companion set of exercises, diagrams, graphs, definitions, through which
the student works as the tape-slide programme proceeds.

(d) A transcript of the commentary for revision purposes, or to enable the
student to synchronize tape and slides at any intermediate point in the
programme.

(e) A post test.

Section 4:
The Development of Learning Packages

4.0 Introduction

ETIC '79 Tracks

The first three papers in this Section — Anderson (4.1), Le Hunte (4.2), Rowntree (4.3) — are from Track 3, 'Learning Environment, Practice and Presentation Techniques'. They are followed by two Track 2, 'Learning Design', contributions from Evans (4.4) and Wilkinson (4.5).

Categories and Special Interests

The why, when and how to developing learning packages inevitably involve decisions on learning strategies and tactics. Small wonder then that all five papers in this Section, together with Bray's workshop (4.6), were coded 'Strats' at Sheffield. The equally obvious link with resource-based learning made 'Res' a natural further coding for Rowntree, Evans, and Wilkinson.

Learning packages have found wide applications. This is demonstrated by the fact that Anderson's paper has a military setting ('Mil') while Wilkinson's is from tertiary education ('Tert') and both Le Hunte and Bray are concerned with industrial applications ('Ind').

Links with Other Sections

Readers with a particular interest in Section 4 are also likely to be interested in the contributions in Section 1.

4.1 The Design, Development and Assessment of a Learning Programme for Part-Time Adult Education

E W Anderson
University of Newcastle-upon-Tyne

Abstract: Following the adoption of objective-based training in the Royal Navy (RN) in the late 1960s, it was necessary for the Royal Naval Reserve (RNR) training courses to be redesigned on similar lines. The design of the first and only complete programme (a six-year course for the Degaussing branch) was commenced in 1969 and completed in 1978. The new programme was formally adopted with a workshop at the Royal Naval School of Educational Training and Technology in February 1979. It is intended to describe the development of the programme and to examine its relevance to other areas of part-time adult education.

The Course

Degaussing, which involves the measurement of a ship's magnetic field so that this can be effectively compensated, rendering the ship less likely to be destroyed by magnetic mines, is the one branch of RNR training not duplicated in the RN. The RN also has a commitment to Degaussing through the NATO Alliance, but it is not in a position to take over Degaussing for a variety of reasons.

Previous Degaussing training was largely built up by trial and error as new techniques were introduced, and two major difficulties could be identified:

(a) Trainees could be promoted to positions of control in a practical situation through passing a purely theoretical examination.
(b) Training during the year in RNR Divisions and annual training at the Admiralty Degaussing Establishment (ADGE) were virtually unco-ordinated.

The Royal Naval Reserve

This brings into focus the problems of the RNR training situation which must be understood if the possible transfer of techniques to other courses is to be seen in context.

The RNR is a largely volunteer force with the sea-training side spread among 11 Divisions, widely scattered between Dundee and Southampton. Each Division runs two drill evenings a week for training and all active members must attend at least one of these. In addition, there is a commitment to two weeks' full-time training annually and there may be occasional training weekends. Training in Divisions, allowing for holiday periods, ceremonial and other activities, amounts to 35 sessions of two hours each, giving 70 hours a year.

The major characteristics of the learning environment can be summarized: training is part-time and largely limited to evenings; attendance may be irregular and interest factors are vital; expert instruction is often lacking while resources, financial and otherwise, are limited; the flow of new entries is uncertain and their academic standards vary; trainees are widely scattered and in small groups, and the trainee wastage rate can be high; with small classes there are also validation problems; furthermore training is directed to a long-term rather than an immediate objective; finally, there are 'community events' which interrupt training.

It must be stressed, however, that Degaussing is different in one respect from much of the normal RNR training. As it is almost entirely shore-based, the mis-match between the training and the operational level is comparatively small.

Since training methods in the RN formed the original basis for the Degaussing course design, it is also relevant to consider briefly the major differences between the two environments: the RN is less concerned with 'interest factors' as trainees are committed to a certain length of service, and other motivating factors, such as pay, exist; skills learned are applied without the time lapse characteristic of RNR training; furthermore the RN is a 'total institution' and thus affects all aspects of life including training; resources, including expert instruction, are more readily available in the RN and course design, validation, etc is more easily formalized and achieved owing to the finance available and the numbers involved.

Therefore, it can be concluded that the RNR is attempting to teach many of the same areas of knowledge and skill found in the RN to regular service standards in an environment with far more constraints. Thus, the methods of training adopted in the RN need to be adapted to take account of the RNR situation, particularly with regard to environmental constraints and target populations.

The Model

To accommodate the RNR situation, the basic RN model (Figure 1) needs to be modified in several ways. There is little mis-match between the operational and training level and therefore the job analysis can be combined. Thus, only one set of objectives need be stated and these can be validated at the same level.

Since the RNR is a volunteer service with recruitment problems, personnel selection is not related specifically to the job, the only criterion being the level of pass in the entry test. Given a suitable result in this, a new entry who so wishes may train in the Degaussing branch and there is no other element of trainee selection.

With major variations between the learning environments of RNR Divisions, the organization of training has local external constraints inbuilt. For example, those Divisions which are ashore have a firm base for installing the Range instruments; those which are afloat do not. Similarly there are wide variations in the number and quality of instructional staff and therefore the course execution will vary. Furthermore, since the number of trainees involved in any one year is likely to be small, the 'whole man' aspect must also be considered during this element.

While there will be on-job training, there will be no operational criterion test, and external assessment will result from work at an operational Range. The outline of the modified model can then be constructed giving a core of four main elements: analysis, objectives, course design, and assessment. Other details can be added to produce a final model which represents more closely the requirements of the RNR (Figure 2), with particular regard to the Degaussing course.

Analysis

Before the detailed analysis could commence, it was necessary to write the Outline Operational Performance Standard (OOPS), an outline given in broad terms. This should cover the whole subject and include all relevant major items. It therefore precludes any premature involvement in detail but allows initial discussion with supervisors and master learners on the framework. Once it has been agreed, the OOPS then forms one guide for the analysis. To produce the OOPS the following sources were consulted: (i) the existing syllabus; (ii) the training staff of the ADGE,

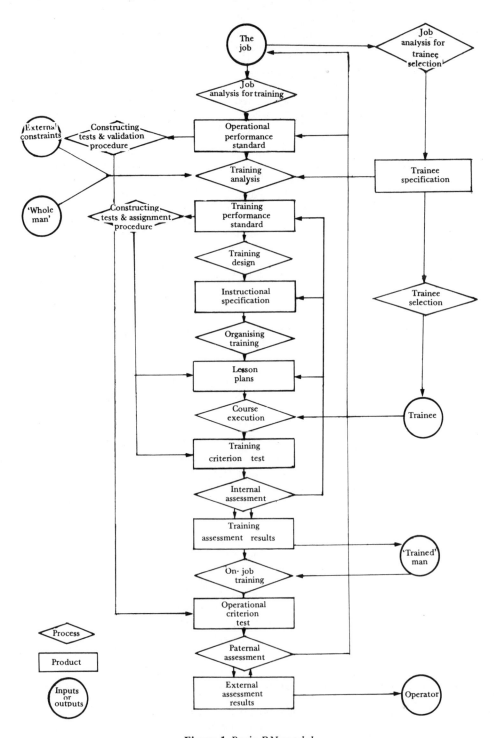

Figure 1 *Basic RN model*

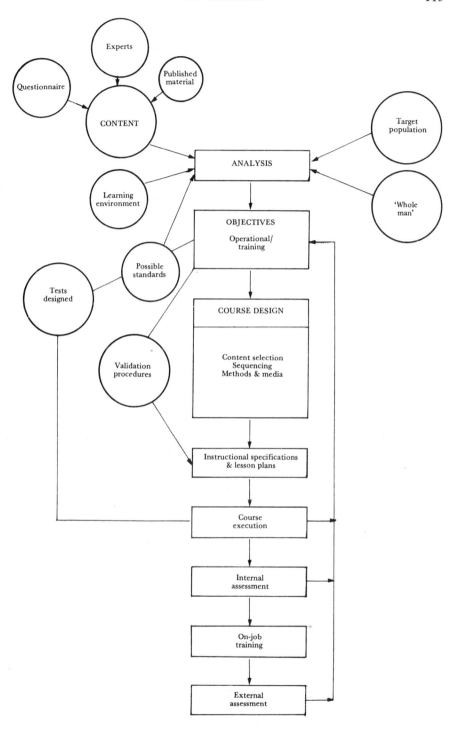

Figure 2 *Final RNR model*

Fort Rowner, Gosport; (iii) questionnaire replies; (iv) master learners and trainees.

As a result, the syllabus was restructured so that it became possible to complete all the theoretical background preparation at RNR Divisions and the annual two weeks' training at the ADGE could be devoted almost exclusively to practical operations. Clearly such a major revision affected the required pre-entry knowledge level demanded, the possible standards expected, and the course examinations together with other aspects concerning the target population.

Using the OOPS as a basis, an analysis of the operational aspects of the course was made. The results were checked against handouts and discussed with master performers so that the task descriptions could be checked and finalized.

Objectives

The full statement of objectives for a course is known as the Performance Standard and there would normally be two of these: one at the operational level (OPS), and the other derived from it, at the training level (TPS). The first describes the performance in the real life situation, for example in a ship, while the second consists of those objectives which can be learned in the training situation. The difference between the two represents the training which must take place on the job, through experience. Therefore, training objectives tend to be proximate whereas operational objectives are ultimate. The main constraints which limit the completion of the OPS in training are costs and time, and they therefore constitute a management decision.

While the OPS and the TPS are usually quite distinct in the RN, this is less so in the case of the RNR Degaussing course. The truly operational level would be achieved at the standard Loop Range, but in fact for the annual training the simulated range at the ADGE, Fort Rowner, is used. Thus, the course assessment which also governs advancement takes place under less than operational conditions, although the mis-match is comparatively small. However, few Divisions possess effective simulated ranges and therefore the training objectives are concerned basically with theory, possibly using certain pieces of the actual equipment. It might be argued that since the course is designed to produce effective performance only, theory objectives are not strictly relevant. However, it must be remembered that theoretical work contributes towards motivation. Therefore a balanced programme to hold the attention of high calibre trainees is essential.

To allow maximum flexibility in training and ease of decision-making when considering priorities, it was requested that the objectives be classified. There are many criteria which might be used in this context, but it was decided that the following were the most significant: (i) relationship to the final performance under operational conditions; (ii) level of expertise in practical skills; (iii) amount of supervision required; (iv) detailed relationship of theoretical skills to the final performance; (v) significance in the overall Degaussing training programme.

With each objective scaled according to such criteria, it should be possible to assess its relevance as the training need and situation changes.

Design

The training objectives, representing the final performance were then put into sequence and analyzed into their constituent enabling objectives. This was facilitated in certain cases by the fact that synthesis had previously occurred to produce the objectives, but again it was necessary to check the level and ensure that all the enabling objectives were of a similar complexity. Each was constructed using the same three-part framework, with a statement of performance, conditions, and implicit or explicit standards.

The enabling objectives for the practical aspects of the training fall into a natural sequence, but those for the theoretical basis were examined closely. On checking with matrix and network analysis diagrams it was found that a clearer progression of associations resulted when the magnetics and electrics topics were separated. By plotting associations in a matrix, it was possible to see where gaps occurred and then to rearrange the enabling objectives so that a virtually continuous series of associations resulted. By constructing a network, those enabling objectives which needed to be completed before others could be commenced were more easily identified. These two techniques are of course worthy of detailed study in their own right. The lesson specifications containing this data were completed by the addition of criterion tests and suggested visual aids. Assessment sheets were also written for the practical aspects.

While many of the methods discussed provide suitable means of communication for different parts of the course, the lesson was selected for its basis. For small groups in which maximum participation is expected but learning must occur over a limited time period, neither the lecture nor the discussion is satisfactory. The major disadvantage of the lesson in this context concerns the variation of entry level, since progress is likely to take place at the rate of the slowest learner. Therefore, to help overcome this, much of the material was programmed in different forms and in fact all the material was carefully structured. As a result, in certain Divisions, where no qualified instructor was available, the course could be used on an independent study basis.

The lesson plans were designed with five main sections and a list of lesson details. In section one the equipment and aids needed for all parts of the lesson are tabulated. These would include items specially designed for the course, such as vugraphs together with apparatus readily available in the Divisions. Sections two and four consist essentially of a self-administered pre-test and post-test respectively. The answers are given on the reverse of the plan, those referring to section two at the top and those to section four at the bottom. Both sets of answers are printed upside down so that they can be viewed separately by folding back either the upper or the lower part of the sheet. Thus it is possible to complete the initial revision questions and check on the solutions without inadvertently seeing the answers to section four.

Section three is subdivided into three parts: (i) the instructor; (ii) the main body of the lesson; (iii) the consolidation. For each of the relevant keywords, subject matter and visual aids are listed in appropriate order. Any special details, problems, or interesting results are noted in section five. Apart from the programmed material and vugraphs, other aids including work cards, slides, a CCTV tape and standard 8mm films were specially designed for the course.

Assessment

The initial validation of the entire course was made by the instructors at the ADGE and also by the Degaussing experts in the RNR. Having been a major source of information during the analysis stage, they were asked to check that the material they had supplied had been satisfactorily included. This was a somewhat cursory examination and a more detailed procedure was followed at the Tyne and London Divisions of the RNR where precise notes were kept on all aspects of the course and trainee progress throughout its first year of operation. Furthermore, the opinions of both instructors and trainees were canvassed and recorded during this process.

With the programmed aspects of the course, a more formal and rigid approach to validation could be adopted. However, limitations of the RNR learning environment militate against detailed validation. The problems of small numbers, irregular attendance, and a range of ability might be mentioned, particularly as these tend to apply generally throughout part-time adult education. Clearly, with probably a maximum of six trainees in the year it is impossible to produce separate groups. Furthermore, if a control group were required the matching would prove very difficult as there would be little on which to assess ability. Even if such an experiment were established and were considered valid, the practical implementation could hardly survive the probable irregularity of attendance. If cost effectiveness and the necessity to introduce courses reasonably quickly is also considered, it may be realized that a modified method of valuation is required. The procedure adopted has proved easy and quick to administer within the constraints of the RNR situation and is considered to have general validity in part-time adult education.

The procedure differs in a number of ways from more standard practice. It is an individual rather than a group exercise. Also, the tutor is active, monitoring the advancement of each student through each frame. By using progress charts each difficulty is recorded while it is fresh, and possible remedies may be immediately apparent. Furthermore, the comments may range more widely than merely an 'incorrect' response, and frames which do not demand a response can also be analyzed. Finally, with such careful monitoring and recording, the validation can be completed more accurately if several sessions are necessary. A measure of internal assessment is maintained continuously throughout the course by the criterion tests given for each enabling objective.

At a lower level, more detailed internal assessment was made through the questions provided with each lesson plan. These could be used for self-assessment or for class tests and in the latter case it was found that the process was facilitated by using the overhead projector and Cosford Responders.

So far, final examination results have shown clearly that Divisions adopting the course have shown a marked improvement. Furthermore, requests for training have trebled. To provide external assessment, a feedback system has been prepared. Apart from regular meetings and the exchange of records, this involves the provision of task books which can be used to monitor on-job training. The package is completed with (i) a data list; (ii) an explanation of usage; (iii) a list of necessary aids.

Conclusions

The effectiveness of this programme has been demonstrated in the RNR and it is the model, with suitable modifications for subject matter, for the other courses being designed with that service. With further alterations in response to the different environments, it has also been used for the construction of other courses in part-time adult education. These range from DES short programmes to WEA courses. They each present their own problems of analysis, design and assessment. The use of a systems approach in the development of such courses yields benefits for the effective structuring of learning at every stage.

4.2 Training Design for Manager Skills

R J Le Hunte
Inbucon Learning Systems

Abstract: The paper reports the application of training design principles to analyze manager performance requirements and to design instruction and performance development schemes.

Introduction

In industry and commerce there are well-established practices of training design — methods to analyze what is required for a job or tasks to be performed, and to design training schemes that meet the requirement. We can cite the use of the TWI (Training Within Industry) approach of job breakdown and job instruction since the 1940s, the skills analysis method in the 1950s, and the development of programmed learning and educational technology in the past two decades.

One feature that all these developments have in common is that their application has been confined in the main to the training of 'operators' — machinists, assembly line operatives, clerks, shop assistants. At supervisory and management levels there has been no equivalent development. While there is a great deal of material around to assist the training of managers, the analysis process, to identify needs and to design training to meet those needs, has largely been by-passed.

This paper outlines an approach to designing management training that has been applied successfully in a number of companies. In the context of the theme of this conference, it is an approach which follows the basic disciplines underpinning programmed learning and educational technology. The following sections describe the type of training scheme that can be produced, the process of designing such a scheme, and the reasons why this approach succeeds.

The End Product

If we wish to train managers in a particular task or skill we make the reasonable assumption that it is possible to define the task, and that it is also possible to express the task definition in simple, practical 'how to do it' terms, as a manager's *job aid.*

It is common practice to provide job aids for operators, maintainers and technicians, so why not adopt a similar practice for managers? To help a manager perform a particular task successfully we can provide guidance in:

- the way to approach the task (attitude);
- where he should be trying to get to (performance objectives);
- what to do to get there;
- how to do it;
- how to check whether he is progressing in the right direction.

The key requirement of the job aid is that it should advocate a simple, practical approach to successful task performance. If the method is elaborate or time consuming it is unlikely that a busy manager will use it.

An example of a panel from a job aid on 'How to Negotiate' is shown in Figure 1. This provides guidance in the key initial step of planning outcomes prior to conducting negotiations. There are some nine panels in the total job aid, each

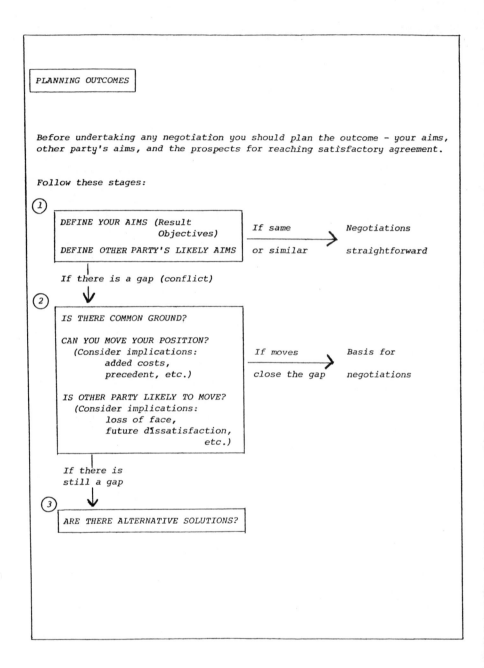

Figure 1. *Panel from a job aid on how to negotiate*

| ACTIVITY 3 | PLANNING OUTCOMES |

It is necessary to install a new piece of plant in a particular section (estimated installation time 6 hours). The Production Manager cannot afford to lose production time, and makes a request that the plant is installed next Sunday, outside production hours.

Plant installation engineers have worked for the past six weekends, and have categorically stated that they are not prepared to work a seventh. The Production Manager arranges a short meeting to negotiate a solution. Acting in his role, follow the stages opposite to plan outcomes.

| MANAGER AIM |
| ENGINEERS' AIM |

| COMMON GROUND |
| MANAGER MOVE |
| ENGINEERS' MOVE |

| ALTERNATIVE SOLUTION |

Figure 2. *One activity from a training module on how to negotiate*

dealing with a specific behaviour, action or performance check in the task of negotiating.

The job aid is a reference guide for job application, and for a training module on how to perform the task. The training module is designed as a sequence of *learner activities*. For example, the four-and-a-half hour module on 'How to Negotiate' includes eight activities, and one of these activities (on Planning Outcomes) is shown in Figure 2.

Activities are varied, and can include: questionnaires (to appraise own attitude or style); job actions (to start putting it into practice); individual or paired learning exercises; syndicate exercises; case studies; roleplays; presentations; projects.

In some cases, job aid panels are deliberately left incomplete and training activities are included in the module to generate details for the panels. So managers contribute to the job aid and start to develop a sense of ownership.

A complete set of job aid panels and activities is issued to each learner at the start of the training module. The trainer, or senior line manager running the module, also has a separate 'Trainer Guide'. This comprises a series of Unit Sheets, like the one shown in Figure 3 for instruction in planning outcomes prior to negotiating.

The Trainer Guide includes a Unit Sheet for each activity showing:

(a) how to lead up to the activity;
(b) how to monitor the activity;
(c) how to review the activity.

Points of reference to the job aid and to flip charts or transparencies, are stated on the Unit Sheet. The intention is to provide the trainer with a complete kit to run the training module, so that he need do no original preparation work.

To summarize, we have described three components of a training module for training in a management task:

(a) job aid (a 'how to do it' guide);
(b) sequence of learner activities;
(c) trainer guide (how to handle each activity).

The emphasis is on total participation throughout. The trainer provides a short input (no lectures) to each activity in turn, followed by reviews.

The Design Process

Assuming that the needs of managers in a company have been identified, in terms of a set of management tasks (eg how to negotiate; how to coach; how to make the organization work for you) the stages of training design in each task can be summarized as follows:

☐ Establish terminal behaviours.
☐ Determine entry level.
☐ Prepare a module plan.
☐ Draw up a detailed task definition and write the job aid.
☐ Design module activities.
☐ Prepare detailed Trainer Guide, or alternative form of input and control.
☐ Test, by running the module and revising it.

This is a simplification because the design process is not a series of neat discrete steps but a succession of approximations. The first five stages all overlap. The one stage which always comes right at the end, when the module design has been buttoned up, is preparation of the 'Trainer Guide'.

The stages listed describe a common, basic approach to training design, irrespective of whether we are concerned with management training or operative

UNIT 3	PLANNING OUTCOMES	Est. 30 mins

INFORM   *   It pays to plan negotiations in advance - this brings us back to your favourite subject - RESULT OBJECTIVES

      *   Define aims   - results you want   *Flip 6*
                   results other party wants

         Assess prospects for closing the gap
         Plan alternative solution

      *   Spelt out in three stages on page 6 of job aid.   *Job Aid*
         Talk through stages on page 6

ACTIVITY 3   Ask group to complete Activity 3, page 7 of job aid   *Job Aid*
                working in pairs - acting as Manager to plan
                outcomes of 'negotiations'.

                As they start the activity comment:

                    - assume that normal production hours are the
                      same as in your plant

REVIEW   *   Ask one pair for answers, writing up each statement
         on flip.   *FLIP*
         Ask 'is this a basis for successful negotiations?'

      *   Ask other pairs for any differences
         (Possible answers shown on next page of Trainer
          Guide)

      *   Be precise in definitions of aims (required results)

      *   Need alternative solutions - this decreases risk of
         stalemate

      *   Invite reactions to merit of planning outcomes this
         way

      *   Comment - people play 'games' over major negotiations
         by publicising an aim far more extreme than what they
         hope to achieve (40°/$_{o}$ wage demand). Then they can be
         seen to be making concessions during the actual
         negotiations.

     Managers will be able to:

      *   recognise the range and types of dealings in which
         they have to 'negotiate'

      *   work to both immediate and longer term goals in
         approaching any negotiations

      *   identify the steps in planning possible outcomes
         of negotiations, and preparing

      *   recognise ways of influencing people

      *   conduct negotiations, and assess performance against
         a set of effective performance characteristics

      *   recognise the influence of organisation climate
         and style on negotiating prospects.

Figure 3. *Trainer guide — one unit sheet from a training module*

training. The following notes indicate how these stages are applied for training managers.

Establish Terminal Behaviours

If you read a book or attend a course on behavioural objectives, you will find that most of the examples relate to clear cut, observable tasks. Most management tasks, incorporating interpersonal skills and higher level cognitive skills, are not so straightforward. It may require several drafts to arrive at a reasonably precise set of terminal behaviours.

For example, this is an attempt at defining terminal behaviours for a training module on 'How to Negotiate' for production managers (developing from a first draft — 'Managers will be able to prepare and conduct negotiations').

Determine Entry Level

You need to consider both starting ability and commitment by answering these questions about the target population:

☐ To what extent *do* they perform this task already?
☐ To what extent *can* they perform this task?
☐ To what extent *do they want to* perform this task?

Prepare a Module Plan

At this stage the purpose is to decide the sequence of activities through the module. Sometimes this can only be done after the task has been defined in detail (next stage). A module plan for 'How to Negotiate' is shown in Figure 4.

Often, a module plan can also include pre-work activities and post-training (application) activities.

Draw Up a Detailed Task Definition

DESIGN MODULE ACTIVITIES
These two stages are the most tricky ones. If you are analyzing an operative task you can observe the skilled performer and record what he does. In the case of a management task there are a number of problems:

☐ How do you decide who is a skilled performer?
☐ A lot of what he does goes on inside his head.
☐ The timespan for the whole task may be a long one, and the separate parts of the task may be undertaken at different times.

One apparent advantage is that for any management task there is a great deal of available written material (eg there are many books dealing with the task of motivating people). But this resource poses the biggest problem of all as most of the available material deals with the theory of management and not with management practice. You need to apply rigorous behavioural disciplines to translate such material into 'doing' terms — the usual effect is to reduce the material into a very small proportion of its original volume (sometimes nil).

A similar point applies to the selection, or design, of activities. Often a number of case studies, or games, may exist. But most of the time you should regard these as a 'second best' choice only — your first intention should be to design an actual job action as the activity. Only consider a case study when a job action is not practicable. For example, if you want to instruct managers to plan coaching assignments you could give them a case study of a coaching need, and ask them to develop plans. On the other hand, if you get them to prepare plans for actual needs of their subordinates they have something they can take back to their jobs and apply immediately.

MODULE – HOW TO NEGOTIATE	
UNITS	**ACTIVITIES**
1. Types of negotiation	Individual exercise to identify different negotiations they undertake.
2. Immediate and longer terms goals	Group discussion of case study showing different outcomes of negotiation
3. Planning outcomes	Paired exercise to plan outcomes for a given case
4. Preparation	Group discussion of preparation needed for a particular case
5. How to Influence People	Syndicate exercise to provide practical examples of each type of influencing tactic
6. Characteristics of Negotiations	Group discussion of common failings in relation to each characteristic
7. Conducting Negotiations	Roleplays, in syndicates
8. The Successful Negotiator	Group exercise to pinpoint differences between average and good negotiators.

Figure 4. *How to negotiate*

Prepare Detailed Training Guide

If you follow the learner-based discipline of this approach to prepare learner activities and learner jobs aids first, it is then relatively easy to write the Trainer Guide. All you need is a single sheet for each activity, showing lead in points, activity, and key review points. Any visual aids should also be prepared.

The First Stage

In the design process described to date, the starting point is an identified set of management tasks to meet training needs.

There is a vital initial stage, in order to decide what tasks to include. This is to identify the performance objectives for the jobs in question — not training objectives — in precise terms. If the training is intended for existing, rather than newly appointed, managers this first stage needs to be extended:

1 What are the performance objectives for the jobs in question?
2 What are the performance shortfalls of managers in post?
3 What are the reasons for these shortfalls?

This performance analysis enables you to pinpoint specific improvements and development needs.

Why This Approach Succeeds

This approach is successful for a number of reasons.

1 It is geared to improvement in job performance. The starting point is to establish required performance, and performance shortfalls, and the training is tailored to meeting job performance goals.
2 The basic approach is to analyze the problem, then to design a solution. This contrasts with the more usual practice in management training, of latching on to ready made solutions, irrespective of problems.
3 The whole emphasis is on management practice, not on theories of management.
4 The learner receives sets of professionally designed job aids. They bear little resemblance to the more traditional course handouts summarizing what the lecturer said.
5 Every training module is built around a series of learner activities (job actions whenever practicable) with minimum input. This is a complete break from the more traditional approach of lectures with case studies.
6 One of the aims of each module is to build commitment to job application since a training session will not in itself achieve a sustained behaviour change. We design each module to lead to a recognized and accepted job activity.
7 This style of training module can be conducted by a line manager, as effectively as a trainer. The design, with short inputs, minimizes the need for 'trainer' skills. In fact the scheme yields the best results when it is conducted by a line manager with his management team.
8 There is a high degree of flexibility, and adaptability, in the method. Modules and part modules can be run as off-job training sessions or on-job coaching sessions. The design approach allows for ready adaptation to alternative modes of instruction. For example, a module can easily be converted from trainer administration to self-instruction. The basic design, to the point of preparing a job aid and defining activities, is identical for both modes. Instead of a trainer guide, self-use instructions can be inserted before each activity, plus activity answers.

The purpose and strength of this approach, in relation to much of what purports to be management training, is best summed up by the remark of one line manager in a company with a long record of management training: 'This new scheme is not training at all. What you have done is to provide managers with the opportunity, and the means, to improve their performance'.

4.3 Developing a Self-Instructional Course on How to Develop Self-Instructional Courses!

Derek Rowntree
The Open University

Abstract: The paper describes the origins and development of an Open University course intended for teachers in higher education who wish to produce self-instructional materials for their students. How did the course team come together? How did they decide on an overall form and structure for the course, and on what its aims, objectives and content should be? What did the completed course look like? How has it been received by its users? How can it be developed and made accessible to all who might seek benefit from it?

Historical Origins

Eight years ago, at this conference in 1971, I mentioned that we in the Institute of Educational Technology (IET) were regularly being asked why we did not practise what we preach and produce an Open University course on educational technology (Rowntree, 1971). At last I am able to report some activity in that area. Early in 1976 I was asked to get together and chair a course team from within IET. Its task was to be the development of a self-instructional packaged course for teachers in post-secondary education. And the subject? How to develop self-instructional packaged courses!

Our immediate client was the Open University Consultancy Service (now re-named the Open University Centre for International Co-operation and Services). Their chief concern is in advising and assisting other countries (eg Pakistan and Venezuela) in setting up their own distance learning institutions. The Consultancy Service had identified a need for a course that could be used by the staff of such new institutions in order to develop the necessary skills and knowledge. Such a course, once produced (and translated) would be made available to individuals working alone, or to groups (with or without live tuition), in colleges and universities around the world.

Getting Under Way

I began consulting individuals about what content might go into the course and who would be the best people to have on the team. By and large, I encountered considerable doubts as to whether the proposed course was even feasible. (Some of us will remember similar doubts in the 1960s as to whether programme-writing could be taught by a programme). Also, colleagues were generally more vociferous about what should be left out of the course, and what pitfalls to avoid, rather than about what should go into the course and how it should be treated. Furthermore, most indicated that they would prefer a clearer idea of what the course might look like before deciding whether they could offer to contribute! Hence it became necessary to draft a framework for the course and to outline possible content and treatment.

From the start, we had the idea of a course in three stages. The first stage was to introduce the reader[1] to the idea of self-instruction and to the key role played in course development by 'evaluation and improvement'. The second stage was to get him (or her) writing a self-instructional 'lesson' (say, one to two hours' worth of teaching) under our guidance. The third stage was to guide the reader in planning a complete course.

Aims and Objectives

We were also easily agreed on the overall aim of the course. Originally we had been asked to aim at 'improving the educational technology skills' of teachers in distance education. However, we felt that while such teachers might not readily jump at the chance of becoming better educational technologists, they would accept the possibility of becoming better *teachers* — at least in the self-instructional area. So that became our aim: to help the reader teach better than he/she otherwise would have done — especially via self-instructional materials. (I must confess that we found no problem in avoiding all use of the slogan 'educational technology'!) Although the aim was very general, it did make clear that our intention was practical — our reader was to become more capable in teaching through self-instruction, not in writing reports or speaking more knowledgeably about such teaching.

All the same, so general an aim could have been translated into specific objectives in a variety of different ways. Members of the course team did indeed draft different sets of objectives. So many, that, taken all together they would scarcely have been achievable in a two-year MA course, let alone within the time-span we were aiming at — between 120 and 180 hours of study time (about the equivalent of 12 OU course units). We were also aware that some of the suggested objectives were ones we had not achieved ourselves — which could only mean that they were not essential to good self-instructional teaching! Anyway, we pruned the suggestions until we were left with eight major objectives, presented to the reader as follows:

'. . . we expect you to enhance your abilities in all of the following areas:
1 Articulating aims and objectives for any course you propose to produce.
2 Identifying the prerequisite skills and knowledge you are assuming of students for your course and deciding how to select from applicants.
3 Selecting content for your course and organizing it into a 'learnable' sequence of lessons or units or modules.
4 Identifying the teaching media available for your course and determining the role each is to play.
5 Structuring each self-instructional lesson/unit/module so as to enable your students to learn most effectively.
6 Designing assessment tests or methods that give a true indication of what each student has learned from your course as a whole and from individual lessons/units/modules.
7 Evaluating your self-instructional course by critical analysis and by trying it out on students, and thus identifying its effects and effectiveness.
8 Improving your course in the light of evaluation.'

1   Writing a course about writing a course offered scope for many levels of confusion among the course team. For example if someone talked of 'the students' was he talking of 'our' students or our students' students? So we decided to call our students 'readers' and use 'students' only for the people *their* courses could be prepared for. The problems multiplied when we found ourselves writing two lessons on quite a different subject for inclusion within this course!

But how were we to approach those objectives, and the many 'component' objectives contained in each? In what order? And what could we usefully tell the reader and have him/her do in order to reach them? In fact, we could describe our approach, using 'ed-tech' jargon, as 'spiral curriculum with a touch of backward chaining'. The curriculum is 'spiral' in that all of the concepts implied in the list of objectives above (eg content-selection, learnable structure, evaluation) are introduced early in Stage I, the reader is given further and more intensive practice with them in Stage II, and he works on them yet again, but in a context that calls for new interpretations, in Stage III. The 'backward chaining' can be seen in the fact that instead of introducing our readers to planning a course as a whole, then to writing individual 'lessons', and then to evaluating the material produced (which is how they will ultimately do the job), we decided to take them through it in reverse order.

Stage I of the Course

Stage I introduces our readers to criteria and procedures by which self-instructional materials can be analyzed and evaluated. We do so by getting the reader to carry out a critical analysis (using a simple check-list) on a short lesson that *we* have written. Needless to say, our specimen lesson contains every fault of self-instruction writing known to the course team — plus (also needless to say) one or two that we did not know we were including! After having our reader examine the lesson several times, each time with more explicit clues from us as to what he should be looking out for (and thus, we hope, spotting yet more errors each time) we show him a copy of the lesson on which we have indicated, and written our comments on, the various faults.

We then give the reader guidance on correcting the faults and ask him to produce a revised version. But we make it clear that this too will have weaknesses, perhaps ones that will only show up when the material is tried out by the people for whom it was intended — the students. So we introduce him to the techniques of developmental testing and the final exercise in Stage I is for our reader to try out his improved version of the lesson on a sample of 'guinea-pig' students, and produce a final version in the light of that experience.

So Stage I impresses the reader with a sense of the possibility of improving teaching materials. It also gives him a language of analysis and the basis of a methodology for evaluation.

How We Use Our Media

Perhaps I should say a word or two here about the teaching media we use in the course. The chief medium is *print* — words and pictures — presented on the pages of booklets. We include some audio-tape material in the section of the course where we are talking about the selection of media. We also, in the same section, include a variety of objects (eg metal fracture specimens, circular slide rule, lens) to show how practical work can be provided for in a self-instructional package. And we include some filmstrips.

But we have included no 'moving picture' media (films or video-tapes), although we discuss the omission within the course itself. In general, it arises out of our understanding that most potential readers will be teaching with 'little media' rather than big, and our belief that the basic principles of self-instructional communication can, in any case, be amply demonstrated with little media (especially print and, perhaps, audio-tapes) leaving the reader reasonably capable of generalizing to any other media he may have access to. The only other medium we use extensively is *practical work* — in that much of the course is concerned with guiding the reader through the experience of writing self-instructional materials and trying them out on students.

As you will have gathered, the course expects much activity from the reader. In this, as in several other respects, it is meant as a model for the kind of course he/she might be expected to produce. The booklets that make up the text are structured in the usual Open University fashion (what I have called 'tutorial in print'), which clearly derives from programmed learning. That is, instead of presenting pages and pages of unbroken prose for the reader to 'read, learn and inwardly digest', we pause frequently to ask questions or set activities. These may draw the reader's attention to important points, get him to offer examples of his own, give him practice with the principles being discussed, and so on. And, of course, we provide him with feedback (eg a specimen answer) against which to evaluate his own response.

Stage II

Stage II presented us with certain problems in the above respect. Here, you will remember, our intention was to have the reader write a self-instructional lesson. Now, if one were tutoring such people face-to-face, and if one felt capable of dealing with their subject-matter, one would naturally say, 'Write and evaluate a lesson on a topic of your own choice'. We might have structured Stage II like that. After first taking the reader through the principles of planning, writing, presenting, assessing and evaluating a lesson, using 'tutorial-in-print' exercises based on examples from a variety of subject-matter, we might have then said, 'Now do it for a topic of your own choice'. In fact, we decided that this would have been to leave the reader working in the dark. At the time when he most needed help, while grappling with the task that brought him to the course for help in the first place, we would have been leaving him without feedback.

So we decided that the reader should be working on a topic of *our* choice. That way, when we got him, for example, to 'analyze the literature' on the topic, we would know what literature he would be analyzing because we would have provided it. More importantly, we would be able to analyze the same literature and let him compare his findings with ours. Again when we discussed, say, objectives and then got him to produce a set of objectives for the topic, we would be able to show him ours for the same topic.

Clearly, if our readers were to be motivated to play along with us, the choice of topic was crucial. It would have to be of wide appeal (both to our readers and to their potential try-out students), capable of being taught at a reasonably high level (eg in terms of Bloom's taxonomy) in between one and two hours, not possessed of too obvious a content or teaching structure, allowing of a variety of teaching strategies to be applied to it, and accessible, without disproportionate investment of time, to readers whether from arts or science backgrounds. After discarding many possibilities, we settled on *A Balanced Diet* as a suitable topic.

Hence, Stage II presents the reader with a 'source wallet' containing materials on nutrition (eg chapters from textbooks, journal articles, daily diet diaries) and guides him through the processes of planning, writing and evaluating a lesson based on this material. We also wrote a version of the lesson ourselves. This is included in Stage II, within a sealed envelope, so that the reader can enjoy the ultimate in feedback — comparing his completed lesson with ours and, if he tries both out on students, perhaps finding that his is the more effective!

Stage III

Stage III offers a different kind of experience, in at least three ways. First of all, we expect the reader to be working now on his *own* subject matter. So we cannot give him examples related to that subject or specific feedback in the activities we ask him to carry out. Only the reader, and his colleagues and students, can appraise what he produces. Secondly, we expect him to be planning a *course* rather than an individual lesson. And we stress throughout that, while Stage III builds on his experience of lesson preparation, producing a course is more complex than producing a string of disconnected lessons, eg the greater the variety of content covered is likely to demand a greater variety of teaching media, and what a student has learned from a course may not be assessable simply by adding together what he has learned from each separate lesson. Thirdly, we are much more *open* (less prescriptive) about how to develop self-instructional teaching.

A few words more about that last point. In Stages I and II we preach the fairly standard 'systematic approach' (eg Rowntree, 1974) that starts from the defining of aims and objectives. This we did because we are convinced that such an approach can be relied on to result in competent, effective teaching materials. And we wanted our readers to have an early experience of success. But we admit at the beginning of Stage III that not all producers of effective teaching materials stick rigorously to that approach. We do not ourselves, and did not even in producing this course. But we still do see it (or more precisely our experience of programmed learning in which it developed) as providing us with an unconscious but invaluable discipline while pursuing the flexible, idiosyncratic approaches of our more recent years. We hope to have given our readers some grounding in this discipline in Stage II.

So, moving into Stage III, we lead the reader into making decisions about the content of a course, about structuring a course, selection of media, assessment strategy, and course evaluation. But this time we expose him to a variety of viewpoints and alternative approaches (eg planning a course on the basis of content rather than objectives). If the reader prefers to stick to the approach of Stage II, with or without his personal amendments, he is welcome to do so; but we invite him to find out his own best way.

Where Do We Go From Here?

The course as a whole gave us what we had been awaiting for years: the chance to 'codify our experience'. Writing the course gave me and my colleagues the incentive to make public and general a whole lot of ideas that had hitherto been used in giving private and particular advice on other academics' materials but had never been made available for such people to apply it on their own.

We know that much good teaching has gone into the course. But it is too early to say how much good learning will come out of it. So far, the course has not been used by the 'target' reader — an academic working through the material alone or with one or two colleagues no more expert than he. It has been used by groups working in a classroom with tutors from the OU Centre for International Co-operation and Services. In that context, the material has been found very stimulating and much approved of by 'readers'. Though, not surprisingly, while they were interested in discussing how we wrote *A Balanced Diet* lesson, most preferred to write lessons on their own topics rather than on ours. Also they felt that Stages I and II were enough for them, not least because they saw themselves as 'lesson-writers', with the overall course structure planned for them by someone else. How far such reactions are peculiar to these students, or are the product of the situation, time pressures, or the interests of the tutors, we cannot tell. We are not alarmed, however, that different readers may choose to use the package in different ways. A resource with any richness and creative ambiguity will inevitably allow a multiplicity of interpretations — enabling readers to make what they will of it (rather than merely to accept or reject what they are given). Nevertheless, many improvements have been made to the course in the light of developmental testing. More will follow. The comments of our readers are usually insightful in that they come from 'students' who are also experienced teachers!

My latest concern is with how to offer this material to college teachers in the UK. For instance, I wonder if we have here the basis for an OU 'continuing education' course on *Developing Resource-based Courses*. This would run over 32 weeks of part-time study. At least half of that time would be spent by students in planning, writing and testing their own materials with guidance from our correspondence tutors. Conceivably our tutors might even enable their students in different colleges to collaborate in curriculum development. But how many teachers would sign up for such a course? Would it seem too time-consuming? Would the acquisition of new skills and OU certification for them (and for existing ones) prove sufficient motivation? Who would pay the fees? Could the course be self-financing? Are there institutions which would share in its production and operation? Or would we be better advised to dismantle our grand design and offer instead a series of shorter courses (eg, on writing a lesson, or on evaluating a course)? Perhaps we should even forget about distance learning, in this instance, and run the courses as face-to-face workshops at the Open University or even in the colleges of our students? In the next few weeks I hope to establish positive and workable answers to questions such as these — and to return to report on progress before another eight years have slipped by.

References

Rowntree, D (1971) 'Course production', pp 64-75. In Packham, D *et al* (eds) *Aspects of Educational Technology*, V. Pitman, London.
Rowntree, D (1974) *Educational Technology in Curriculum Development*. Harper & Row, London.

4.4 Packaging a Workshop

L F Evans
The City University, London

Abstract: The design and development of a training programme for academic and administrative staff on 'The Conduct of Meetings in Universities' led to the production of a number of exercises which were initially highly dependent on the skills of the programme director when used in a workshop.

The need to provide training in more than one location led to an analysis and redesign of some exercises, and the development of a method of 'training trainers' in their use.

The paper includes examples of the original exercises, the feedback methods used in their analysis, the modifications made and the 'training for trainers' scheme.

The 'Conduct of Meetings in Universities' project, which generated as its training component 'Meetings Workshop', has been described elsewhere (see references). In the initial plan of the scheme, it was envisaged that this training component would be used extensively in institutions of Higher Education, and the design of training materials was oriented toward their use in situations outside the originating staff and institution.

CENTRE FOR EDUCATIONAL TECHNOLOGY
THE CITY UNIVERSITY

Meetings Workshop
Evaluation of Course

Please complete this form, in order to assist in the evaluation of this course, and to use the information in planning future activities.

Ring round the response which most nearly corresponds to your opinion, using the scale +3 to -3 given, 0 indicating "no opinion", and inserting further comment in the space provided.

Session	Interest							Usefulness							Effectiveness						
	+3	+2	+1	0	-1	-2	-3	+3	+2	+1	0	-1	-2	-3	+3	+2	+1	0	-1	-2	-3

Further comments on session

Session	Interest							Usefulness							Effectiveness						
	+3	+2	+1	0	-1	-2	-3	+3	+2	+1	0	-1	-2	-3	+3	+2	+1	0	-1	-2	-3

Further comments on session

Session	Interest							Usefulness							Effectiveness						
	+3	+2	+1	0	-1	-2	-3	+3	+2	+1	0	-1	-2	-3	+3	+2	+1	0	-1	-2	-3

Further comments on session

Session	Interest							Usefulness							Effectiveness						
	+3	+2	+1	0	-1	-2	-3	+3	+2	+1	0	-1	-2	-3	+3	+2	+1	0	-1	-2	-3

Further comments on session

	Interest							Usefulness							Effectiveness						
	+3	+2	+1	0	-1	-2	-3	+3	+2	+1	0	-1	-2	-3	+3	+2	+1	0	-1	-2	-3
The Course as a whole																					
Comments on Course Organisation																					
Comments on "ambience" i.e. rooms, facilities, meals, accommodation.																					
Any other comments or suggestions																					

Figure 1. Response form on workshop operation

In order to ensure that the workshop operation was evaluated and that feedback from this evaluation was available immediately for development and improvement of subsequent workshops, a response form (Figure 1) was designed and subsequently used throughout the life of the scheme to date.

Using the feedback from this form, and from the concluding evaluation session in each workshop, the overall pattern of the event, and the detail and operation of a number of exercises, were modified. To give an indication of the extent of this overall modification, the programmes of the original workshop and of the current workshop, and the original and current version of one exercise are shown in Figure 2.

In planning for the provision of the workshop outside the City University Centre for Educational Technology, two main problems were identified: first, those exercises which were highly 'director independent'; second, the knowledge and skill requisite for the workshop director. In dealing with the first of these problems, the initial step was to codify and record as accurately as possible the instructions and commentary provided by the workshop director during the operation of the exercise, and to develop this into a form comprehensible and acceptable to staff who would be involved in directing the exercise. In some cases, there was a significant interaction between this and the knowledge and skills of a director. To take one specific example, the 'Chairman' exercise is run in a 'snowball' fashion; the mechanics of its operation are readily understood and carried out up to the point of the 'full workshop' stage. At this stage, it is necessary that the director acts effectively in the role of chairman of a large meeting, is able to draw out learning points from this behaviour, and is able to analyze and summarize the process and relate it to models of meetings in academic institutions. Implicit in this, therefore, is one of the requisite skills of a potential workshop director. In addition to this chairman-like skill, since this is the first major activity an 'aura' of confident background knowledge of institutions of higher education, and the meetings which take place in them, is necessary to ensure an appropriate initial climate in the workshop.

Figure 3 lists the instructions given to staff taking over the operation of this exercise, and an 'incoming' staff member's operating notes. This example has been chosen to indicate the approach which was used in initiating staff into the operation of individual exercises.

The training pattern which was developed to enable new staff eventually to take over the direction of the entire workshop involved: first, an initial discussion with the present director aimed at identifying knowledge and skills of the newcomer and attempting to determine whether there was an appropriate background to continue in training; next, attendance at a standard workshop as a participant, with an additional task of observing and noting impressions of the operation of each of the exercises and attending the post-workshop debriefing with the present staff. This was followed by the study of instructions such as those illustrated earlier, and attendance at a pre-workshop staff briefing.

During the first workshop at which the newcomer acts as a staff member, he will be responsible for the running of one exercise, usually either The Secretary's Job or Committee Simulation, since these are the most highly-structured and the least director-dependent. During the whole of the workshop, the newcomer is involved in supporting activity during all the exercises, eg distributing working papers, monitoring group progress, collaborating in video-recording. Following this experience and the post-workshop staff debriefing, there is further discussion with the current director and an agreement to undertake the responsibility for the direction of most of the exercises. If this, which can be somewhat of an ordeal, is survived the penultimate step in takeover will be for the newcomer entirely to direct the next workshop, with the current director present as adjunct, ball boy, or long stop. Following this, the 'incoming' director undertakes entire responsibility for the next workshop.

THE CITY UNIVERSITY

ST JOHN STREET   LONDON LCIV 4PB   01-253 4399

CENTRE FOR EDUCATIONAL TECHNOLOGY

"MEETINGS WORKSHOP"   24-26 September 1973

Programme

Monday 24-9-73

09.30-10.00	Arrival and registration	A241 A
10.00-10.15	Introduction and briefing	A241 A
10.20-11.15	Introduction to simulation exercises	A241 G
11.15-11.30	Coffee	A241 A
11.30-12.45	Exercise I	A241 A/G
12.45-13.30	Luncheon	Level 6 Refectory
13.45-15.00	Exercise II V.T.R.	A241 A/G
15.00-15.30	Tea. Notes on Exercise II.	A241 A
15.30-17.30	Exercise II Play-back and discussion	A241 A/G
18.00-19.30	Sherry and Dinner	
20.00-21.30	Exercise III	A241 A/G

Tuesday 25-9-73

10.00-11.15	Personality and Behaviour I.	A241 G
11.15-11.30	Coffee	A241 A
11.30-12.45	"Senate in Action" exercise Phase I	A241 A
13.00-14.00	Luncheon	Level 6 Refectory
14.00-15.15	Personality and Behaviour II.	A241 G
15.15-15.30	Tea	A241 A
15.30-17.30	"Senate in Action" exercise Phase II	A241 A
19.00-20.30	Course Dinner	Finsbury Hall

Wednesday 26-9-73

Time	Activity	Location
10.00-10.45	The Chairman's Role	A241 A
10.45-11.00	Coffee	A241 A
11.00-12.30	Exercise "Choosing a Tutor" I.	A241 A/G
12.45-13.45	Luncheon	Level 6 Refectory
13.45-15.15	Exercise "Choosing a Tutor" II.	A241 A/G
15.15-15.30	Tea	A241 A
15.30-16.00	Exercise concluded	A241 A/G
16.00-17.00	Evaluation review	A241 A

THE CITY UNIVERSITY

Northampton Square London EC1V 0HB

telephone:01-253 4399 telex:263896

Centre for Educational Technology

Head of the Centre L F Evans

"Meetings Workshop"   PROGRAMME   14-16 February 1979

Wednesday, 14 February

Time	Activity		Location
12.00-12.30	Reception		Refectory L.6 PDR
12.45-13.45	Luncheon		Refectory L.6 PDR
14.00-14.10	Introduction to Workshop		A537C
14.10-15.30	Exercise I	"Chairman"	A537C
15.30-15.50	Tea		A537 Foyer
16.00-18.00	Exercise II	"Secretary"	A537C
18.30-19.30	Supper		Refectory L.6 PDR
19.30-21.00	Exercise III	Committee Simulation	A537C & B
21.00-21.15	Seminar briefing and Senate papers		A537C

Thursday, 15 February

09.30-09.55	"Senate In Action"	Briefing	A537C
09.55-10.40	"Senate In Action"	Video	A537C
10.40-11.00	Coffee		A537 Foyer
11.00-12.15	"Senate In Action"	Groups	A537C
12.30-13.30	Luncheon		Refectory L.6 PDR
13.45-15.00	"Senate In Action"	Plenary	A537C
15.00-15.20	Tea		A537 Foyer
15.20-16.30	Seminar		A537C
16.30-17.15	"Choosing a Tutor"	Briefing	A537C
18.00-19.00	Supper		Refectory L.6 PDR

Friday, 16 February

09.00-09.20	"Choosing a Tutor"	Final briefing	A537C
09.20-10.00	"Choosing a Tutor"	Meetings	A537C & B + Studio
10.05-10.20	"Choosing a Tutor"	Groups briefing	A537C
10.20-10.40	Coffee		A537 Foyer
10.40-12.00	"Choosing a Tutor"	Video review	A537C
12.00-13.30	Luncheon		Refectory L.6 PDR
13.30-14.15	"Choosing a Tutor"	Groups	A537C
14.15-15.00	"Choosing a Tutor"	Plenary	A537C
	Tea available		A537 Foyer
15.00-16.00	Consolidation and evaluation review		A537C

Figure 2. *Original and current exercises and programmes given to participants*

ORIGINAL

SOME CHAIRMANLIKE BEHAVIOUR

a   b   c

1. Checks the appropriateness of the seating arrangement. ___ ___ ___ *
2. Starts the meeting on time. ___ ___ ___
3. Sets an appropriate tone. ___ ___ ___
4. Keeps the purpose of the meeting and of each discussion clearly before the members. ___ ___ ___
5. Ensures that any decisions made are clearly stated as such. ___ ___ ___
6. Ensures that any decisions made are properly recorded. ___ ___ ___
7. Facilitates contributions from reticent people. ___ ___ ___
8. Keeps participants aware of how the meeting is proceeding. ___ ___ ___
9. Keeps the line of argument clear: identifies and inhibits irrelevancies. ___ ___ ___
10. Gives all parties to an argument an opportunity to present their case. ___ ___ ___
11. Remains in control of processes and procedures, avoiding alignment with any "party". ___ ___ ___
12. Paces the meeting to meet the needs of the members. ___ ___ ___
13. Is properly briefed, agenda and papers "marked up" if necessary. ___ ___ ___
14. ___ ___ ___
15. ___ ___ ___

*Please rate each item on a ·1,2,3,4,5 scale:

   5 = most important for good chairmanship
   1 = not important
or 0 = not applicable, irrelevant.

Write your responses in column (a).

Do not write in lines 14 and 15 or columns (b) and (c) until requested.

TARGET TIME 5 minutes

Current

SOME CHAIRMANLIKE BEHAVIOUR

a   b   c

1. Checks the appropriateness of the seating arrangement. ___ ___ ___ *
2. Starts the meeting on time. ___ ___ ___
3. Sets an appropriate tone. ___ ___ ___
4. Keeps the purpose of the meeting and of each discussion clearly before the members. ___ ___ ___
5. Ensures that any decisions made are clearly stated as such. ___ ___ ___
6. Ensures that any decisions made are properly recorded. ___ ___ ___
7. Facilitates contributions from reticent people. ___ ___ ___
8. Keeps participants aware of how the meeting is proceeding. ___ ___ ___
9. Keeps the line of argument clear: identifies and inhibits irrelevancies. ___ ___ ___
10. Gives all parties to an argument an opportunity to present their case. ___ ___ ___
11. Remains in control of processes and procedures, avoiding alignment with any "party". ___ ___ ___
12. Paces the meeting to meet the needs of the members. ___ ___ ___
13. Is properly briefed, agenda and papers "marked up" if necessary. ___ ___ ___
14. ___ ___ ___
15. ___ ___ ___

*Please rate each item on a ·1,2,3,4,5 scale:

   5 = most important for good chairmanship
   1 = not important
or 0 = not applicable, irrelevant.

Write your responses in column (a).

Do not write in lines 14 and 15 or columns (b) and (c) until requested.

TARGET TIME 5 minutes

Figure 2. (continued)

```
    Tutors'              CHAIRMANLIKE BEHAVIOUR
    Instructions         ──────────────────────


See separate sheet for equipment and preparation.



1.  Distribute worksheet
    Reiterate orally the instructions displayed
    Give the word "go"
    Start timer and prowl to check on progress
    If all have completed inside target time, stop and
     proceed to next stage


2.  Display group instructions
    Reiterate orally
    Form groups - minimum of 3 participants, maximum of 7
    Start the groups working
    Start timer

    At 12 minutes, remind all of time limit and, if monitoring
     shows that more time will be needed, announce a 5-minute
     time extension.


3.  At 20 minutes, check that all the groups have recorded
     group-agreed ratings, written additional item, and
     displayed group ratings on grid.
    Settle workshop back into plenary form, identify items
     in which major disparities of rating occur, and lead
     discussion on those items.
    Should any item have a uniformly low rating, as may
     sometimes happen,- particularly "recording of decisions"
     and seat arrangements - cajole the plenary into recognising
     the Chairman's ultimate responsibility here.
    Try to reach a consensus rating for each item, then display
     and discuss the items produced by the groups;  usually these
     can be subjected to some composite treatment and reduced to
     two or three.


4.  At conclusion, display model of this type of meeting, and
     draw the analogy between this and many university meeting
     structures.
    Indicate the time aspects of each state of the process and
     emphasise the significant improvement in understanding and
     agreement which results from discussion, although this is
     time-consuming.
```

Figure 3. *Operating instruction for chairman exercise*

2. Introduction to first exercise Chairman like Behaviour

There are two important people in meetings the Chairman and Secretary.

We shall spend most of the morning looking at what these two do. For this first exercise we have taken 13 actions of a chairman out of the many 100's of items of behaviour displayed by a Chairman

Go through points on the flip-chart

> Read each statement carefully, then mark in column (a) your personal rating using any number between
> 1: LOW IMPORTANCE
> 5: MOST IMPORTANT
> 0: IRRELEVANT
> DO NOT GRADE   Target time: 4 minutes

CHAIRMA LIKE BEHAVIOUR

Handout exercises Chairmanlike Behaviour

←Display flip-chart 2

10
15

Introduction to phase 2 of Chairman exercise:
Most of you have now finished and committed your own view: You are now asked to reach a group agreement to come to a consensus view. The instruction is to discuss with group and agree group rating and then _devise_ two more chairmanlike activities which you think should be rated 4/5. You have 15 minutes in which to do this.

Note It is important that participants complete the Ex.
—declare if necessary, an injury time bonus of 5 mins to write their own chairmanlike behaviour and another 5 mins if necessary. This is to draw contrast between individual activity (4mins) and group work (up to 25 mins)

In last 5 mins give out acetate sheet for activity 14 and ask them to fill in flip chart 3

40

Move round course to check on progress   5

Divide group into 4's on basis of who is sitting next to each other

Prepare flip chart 3 or display if prep'd (see page 5)

Distribute acetate sheet and pens of different colour   25

Figure 3. (continued)

From this process it will be recognized that packaging and transfer involves an empirical amalgam of educational technology and 'sitting by Nellie'. The process has been successfully operated in the handing over of the workshop to other universities and polytechnics in Britain, and to two universities and the Royal Military College of Canada in North America and, in a rather more tenuous form in which the later stages were adapted into an extensive correspondence to effect a handover, to the University of Otago in New Zealand.

The information contained in the preceding description was communicated to a group of some 70 participants during the conference. This information was supplemented with additional hand-out examples of staff instructions and the identification of the major problems experienced in the packaging and transfer of each exercise. The less definable attributes of the director in terms of personality and behaviour were also discussed. One participant raised the problem of the creation of climate within the workshop and the relationship of that climate to the purpose of the workshop. The presenter expressed the view that in cases where some behavioural and attitudinal change was a major purpose of the workshop, the creation of an initial uncertainty in the context of a generally supportive climate was the most effective, whereas in the case where skills acquisition and application was a primary purpose, a climate of certainty and highly-structured support had proved most effective.

The presenter would like to use this opportunity of expressing his appreciation of the useful feedback comment which was produced during the discussion.

References

Have Senate — will travel (1978). In *Aspects of Educational Technology*, **XII**. Kogan Page, London.
Issues in staff development (October, 1975). *The Conduct of Meetings*, pp 103 *et seq.* SDU/UTMU, London.

4.5 Peer Instruction in Learning Packages

G M Wilkinson
Ulster Polytechnic

Abstract: It is recognized that self-instructional materials require a varying amount of tutorial support in proportion to their inherent imperfections. Immediate availability of the tutor to compensate for these imperfections is not always possible and it has been observed that students very often turn to their peers for help and guidance.

In a basic self-instructional audio-visual workshop with tutor support (involving mainly psycho-motor and cognitive objectives), students were paired and an estimate was made of the extent to which each student learnt by each mode. A sample of students was interviewed and a questionnaire was given to all 92 students.

If, as appears to be the case, peer-instruction makes a significant contribution to the learning, it should be possible to incorporate it into instructional materials in a formalized rather than *ad hoc* way.

Research literature has been located and examined to obtain guidelines as to how this technique can be incorporated in learning packages.

Multi-Mode Learning

In self-instructional packages it often appears that the ultimate goal is to design
learning situations in which the learner can learn in isolation. Is such a goal always
realistic and feasible? Observations of learners operating in such systems
(Wilkinson, 1976) suggest that they often become bored and restless unless
motivation and self-discipline are high. While this can be attributed to imperfections
in the instructional materials, perhaps there is an even more fundamental reason
related to the general characteristics of learners.

Learning with and from other people is a natural mode of learning and to ignore
it is to miss a dimension providing stimulation, encouragement and reassurance
among other factors. Traditionally, this dimension has been partly provided by
tutor/learner contact and some would consider this as the optimum mode of
learning. If, however, we are to preserve some of the inherent benefits of
self-instruction such as self-pacing and also wish to retain the dimension of
interaction with a tutor, we are immediately involved in the costly procedure of
open access to tutors.

Realistically, if human contacts are to be provided in a self-instructional
situation, one has to turn to a less costly and more readily available resource than
open access to tutors, ie the learner's peers.

Students as Teachers

Goldschmid (1976) suggests that students are one of the most under-used teaching
resources in higher education. Beach (1974) has suggested that the small interactive
human group has come into its own and that we have begun to realize something
of its power and potential; as a result, he asserts that we need to know more about
how students learn from each other.

One of the key elements in the Personalized System of Instruction (Ruskin,
R S and Ruskin, R L, 1977) is the 'proctor'; usually a more senior student who
has already mastered the learning tasks. Proctors permit repeated testing, immediate
scoring, tutoring and an enhancement of the personal/social aspect of the learning
process. Tosti (1973) suggests that a growing number of instructors are using
students who are presently enrolled in the class as proctors because it eliminates
the requirement for obtaining outside personnel. In *Learning Cells*, Goldschmid
and Goldschmid (1976) indicate that students can work successfully in pairs, in
which they alternate asking and answering questions on commonly read materials;
this suggests that students can facilitate the learning of other students without
necessarily having totally mastered the content.

Peer-Instruction in a Self-Instructional Workshop

Observation of student 'learning' techniques in an audio-visual workshop would
indicate that despite the provision of self-instructional materials and the
availability of tutors, on occasions, students consulted their peers with regard to
their learning tasks. Why this should be so would seem to be an interesting topic
for investigation. The workshop was set up to provide instruction in the operation
of basic hardware and the production of allied software. Each student had a
worksheet for each technique which specified the tasks but which also included
questions to promote understanding of processes and application of knowledge
through simple fault-finding problems.

Self-Instructional Materials

To facilitate self-instruction, each technique had a step-by-step programme with
allied operational manuals, advertising literature, technical data and in some cases,

video-tapes. To compensate for imperfections in these materials, on most occasions, tutors were available. In practice, the tutors tried to redirect students to parts of the self-instructional materials and to exemplify the materials rather than offer separate instruction.

Assessment of the work took place concurrently with the tutor signing a worksheet related to each group of tasks when they were completed satisfactorily. Due to lack of tutor time, these assessments were often reduced to sampling.

Rosenbaum (1973) points out that most self-instructional materials have a basic weakness; they lack adequate supervision. Students are often incapable of supervising their own work because, for example, of over-familiarity with it; indeed if left to their own devices, the students may not be aware that they have made errors. The teacher has just so much real time to interact with the students and it is not enough, hence the interest in peers as teachers.

Investigation of Peer-Instruction

To facilitate the investigation of the extent and purposes of peer-instruction, students were paired according to their own choosing and asked to work together; however, to ensure active participation by both members of the dyad, assessment was on an individual basis. With the first group of students, enquiries were made as to how they learnt from each other and this information was used to help in the construction of a questionnaire. The questionnaire was tried out on a second group and was slightly modified. Over a year, the questionnaire was given to all the remaining students (N=89) using the workshop. The students varied from young teachers in training to mature nurses in a Health Visitor's Course.

Questions Posed in the Questionnaire

The questions asked for information in relation to three modes of learning:

(a) learning from self-instructional packages;
(b) learning from tutors;
(c) learning from fellow course members.

Within each learning task, the students were asked to estimate by percentage how much they had learnt by each mode. Most used and preferred to use all three modes of learning. It was surprising that on average 34 per cent of the learning was estimated to have been facilitated by peer-interaction. While this percentage was probably boosted by the imperfections of the self-instructional materials and lack of immediate access to the tutors, peer-interaction would still appear to be a significant mode of learning which cannot be ignored in the design of certain learning situations. However, to utilize peer-instruction, one needs to know why and how it occurs.

Further, as might have been expected the data suggested that the blends of modes of learning differed from one individual to another; perhaps indicating that all three modes should be incorporated into individualized learning systems.

The Self-Instructional Packages Related to Tutor and Peer-Teaching

Since the workshop was primarily designed as self-instructional, questions were posed to ascertain why learning took place from tutors and peers rather than from the packages. Some students suggested that the tutor provided reassurance, was quicker and easier to learn from, clarified points of uncertainty and provided additional information. While some thought the tutor was more motivating and flexible, others believed that the self-instructional materials gave them independence and as much time as they wanted on any one task.

Apparently peers explained in everyday simple words and thought the way a learner would. Reassurance came because 'two heads were better than one' and other people saw and did things differently, thus providing new perspectives in a learning situation. Some students suggested that they learnt from observing others and questioning why; while others suggested that they learnt from the mistakes of others. It was interesting that in some cases, the tasks were shared; one reading the instructions and the other doing. The roles were then reversed. Some students pointed out that peer consultation could be quicker than self-instruction and were prepared to gamble on this.

In peer-teaching, can peers teach only when they know how to perform the tasks? It was interesting that 72 per cent of the students thought that peers could teach without having mastered the tasks totally; they could help to interpret the self-instructional materials and attempts could be observed and mistakes identified jointly. In particular, the opportunity to discuss the tasks seemed to be much appreciated because others saw the tasks in a different light. These comments need to be contrasted with some definitions of peer-tutoring which assume mastery by the peer teachers. AECT (1977) states that 'Peer-tutoring is done by other learners who have already met the learning objectives; peer tutors do not provide basic instruction but rather help learners in conjunction with other instructional materials.'

Imperfections in the Self-Instructional Materials

It was recognized that the students would turn to tutors and peers if the self-instructional materials were imperfect. From the questionnaire, it was suggested that there should be an increased use of labelled diagrams with less technical jargon and more severe editing of information. About 56 per cent of the students thought the materials were sometimes boring to use but only 30 per cent thought this self-instructional process was too dehumanized. During use of the materials, 52 per cent did not study the materials systematically and fully. Again, 67 per cent did not always understand the materials and 42 per cent felt they were not confident enough to depend on the materials alone. While using the materials, 68 per cent felt they would have welcomed opportunities to discuss points with another person.

While, obviously, the self-instructional materials should be improved upon, there is a limit to this. There is sufficient evidence here to place less confidence in the self-instructional materials as they stand and more on attempting to integrate peer-teaching into the learning system.

Time Spent on Peer-Teaching

Is the time spent by a student in teaching another student wasted as far as the student doing the teaching is concerned? Here 93 per cent of the students believed that they learnt through teaching. The words 'reinforcement' and 'consolidation' were the most popular reasons given for this. Some students believed that peers posed questions and answers they might not have thought of and others thought the process of teaching engendered confidence and helped to organize what was learnt. The process of verbalization appeared to encourage the students to think things out fully.

As one student succinctly put it, 'It helped me to categorize and structure my own knowledge — a more logical order ensured'. That a student should explain what he has learnt to another student could be a viable learning activity, particularly in the latter stages of learning involving consolidation and integration.

The Interaction of the Three Modes of Learning

Over all the learning tasks, students estimated that they learnt 49 per cent from the self-instructional materials, 17 per cent from tutors and 34 per cent from colleagues. The majority of students believed that all three modes of learning were essential — as one student put it, 'One can follow instructions, discuss them with fellow course members and check doubts with tutors'. Using all the modes appeared to promote confidence in the thoroughness and accuracy of the learning. In some cases, students expressed a dislike of self-instruction and preferred tutor or peer-teaching but certain students preferred the independence of self-instruction. Some students pointed out that it was difficult to reconcile an environment for self-instruction with the inevitable noise and disturbance of tutor and peer-teaching.

Integrating Peer-Teaching Into Learning Situations

Peer-teaching can take place formally and informally. Pascal (1974) describes a number of formal ways it can be used and he concludes that it is necessary for the instructor to devise activities to facilitate the peer-teaching of the students. It would appear that peer-teaching could be structured into learning situations through initial suggestion, either by the tutor or in the self-instructional materials. At appropriate points in the learning process a student could be asked to:

(a) discuss procedures with a peer;
(b) have his work checked by a peer;
(c) answer questions put by a peer and ask for his comments on the answers.

Conclusion

Learning is a complex process; to design learning situations only in terms of a particular mode of learning is to exclude specific advantages that accrue from the other modes. It would appear that learning from peers has distinctive contributions in maintaining the momentum of the learning process and in the appraisal and consolidation of what has been learnt.

References

AECT (1977) *Educational Technology. Definition and Glossary of Terms,* 1. AECT.
Beach, L R (1974) Self-directed student groups and college learning. *Higher Education,* 3. pp 187-200.
Goldschmid, B and Goldschmid, M L (1976) Peer-teaching in higher education: a review. *Higher Education,* 5, pp 9-33.
Pascal, C E (1974) Undergraduates as teachers. *Improving College and University Teaching,* 22, 22, pp 109-110 (Spring 1974).
Rosenbaum, P S (1973) Peer mediated instruction. Teachers' College Press, Columbia University, New York.
Ruskin, R S and Ruskin, R L (1977) Personalised instruction and its relation to other instructional systems. *Educational Technology,* September.
Tosti, D (1973) Peer-proctor in individualised programs. *Educational Technology,* August.
Wilkinson, G M (1976) Towards an effective utilisation of learning packages in institutes of higher education. In Clarke, J and Leedham, J (eds) *Aspects of Educational Technology,* X. Kogan Page, London.

4.6 Self-Instruction for Hotel and Catering Skills

L M Bray
The George Brown College of Applied Arts and Technology, Toronto

The hospitality industry is one of Canada's fastest growing job markets, but finding trained people to fill these jobs is a perennial problem. College curricula are often unable to keep pace with industry's needs, while industry lacks the time and expertise to train employees on the job. A recent survey estimated that a mere 10 per cent of all hospitality industry employees had received any formal training.

In 1973, the George Brown College of Applied Arts and Technology (one of Canada's major centres for hotel and catering training) proposed that a co-operative system of training be established between industry and technical colleges. The basis of this system would be a series of standardized training materials, flexible enough for use in both locations. A Canada Manpower Training Improvement Plan grant provided the funding and the Hospitality Training Resource Project began in 1975.

Since then, 42 self-instructional training packages have been developed, covering all skills required for chef and waiter training, plus dishwashing, sanitation, and safety. Each package covers theory, plus step-by-step instruction for practical tasks, illustrated by colour slides on microfiche. Pre- and post-tests are built into each package, as well as skills checklists to be completed by the trainee's instructor or supervisor.

The development procedure for the training packages involved a fair amount of trial and error at the beginning. We started by assembling all task lists and DACUM charts already produced by other provinces, and by the Canadian Federation of Chefs de Cuisine, and combining them to produce a master list of package titles and contents.

Initially, package writing was to be shared amongst four colleges in Ontario. However, this approach soon proved to be impractical as the colleges were hundreds of miles apart, thereby making it impossible for writers to meet regularly to discuss content and format. Hence, we had to start all over again, and set up a central course development team at George Brown. This group of 15 people included chefs and *maitres d'hotel* recruited directly from industry, recent graduates from the George Brown chef programme, photographers, a graphics artist, editors, typists and various technical experts hired on a short-term basis. In addition, we had the help of a Quality Control Committee of instructors from the College, who met with us each week to approve our draft material.

Once the 'script' was approved, we photographed each step of instruction to provide the learner with his own 'live' demonstration and a visual standard with which to compare his efforts. We had not proceeded very far, however, before it became evident that we were going to accumulate a massive number of slides — far too many for convenient use or storage. After investigating a number of visual media, we chose colour microfiche — a very new process and one with great potential for self-instructional learning.

After the photography stage came more editing and further Quality Control meetings until we were finally pleased with the results. The workbooks were then typed on word-processing equipment, ready to go to press. Captions were typeset for each slide, and slides and captions numbered and laid out in sequence for microfiche processing by Bell & Howell Ltd. Our project evolved, in fact, into a mini-publishing company, encompassing everything from original writing to final typesetting.

On the average, it took about 16 weeks to develop each package with three or four packages under development at once. Each package averaged 135 pages with 250 slides on colour microfiche.

Field testing of two packages was carried out during the development phase but large-scale testing of the entire system will start later this year when we will examine different applications of the packages in both colleges and industry.

In technical colleges, the packages are ideally suited for an individualized-learning, modular course, operated on a continuous intake-exit basis. However, the materials can also be used as additional individual learning resources, or for group instruction (by using the microfiche reader as a slide projector). This last example will be especially applicable to the more remote technical colleges who may lack the facilities, equipment, or food products to carry out advanced or specialized chef- and waiter-training.

In industry, where labour turnover is high and training time is limited, modular self-paced materials will be especially useful. However, management commitment to training is essential and practice under supervision is still essential, even if the training materials are largely self-instructional.

Finally, we hope that the 42 packages developed thus far will create a bank of information which could be recombined in different ways to create tailor-made courses. We will also be investigating the applications of this training system outside Canada — especially in developing countries. Although the packages are written in English, the colour microfiche provide visual instruction that would easily be supplemented by audio-tapes in other languages.

Package development has now been completed and orders are being taken within Canada and internationally. Further information and price lists can be obtained from The Dean, Food Technology Division, George Brown College of Applied Arts and Technology, PO Box 1015, Station B, Toronto M5T 279, Ontario, Canada.

Section 5:
Applications in Primary and Secondary Education

5.0 Introduction

ETIC '79 Tracks

The four papers in this Section divide equally between Tracks 1 and 2. Banks *et al* (5.1) and Daly (5.2) were presented at Sheffield in Track 1, 'Self-Instructional Programmes in Practice', while Sakamoto (5.3) and Harris and Watts (5.4) made their presentations in Track 2, 'Learning Design'.

Categories and Special Interests

Obviously, each of the papers in this Section and also the workshops linked to the papers by Banks *et al* and by Harris and Watts, were coded 'PriSec' ('Primary and Secondary Education') at ETIC '79.

Daly and Harris/Watts were also coded 'Strats', for 'Strategies and Presentation of Learning'. The Harris/Watts paper and workshop were additionally coded 'Eval' for 'Evaluation' because of their special concern with this aspect of learning design.

Links with Other Sections

Readers with a particular interest in Section 5 are also likely to be interested in the following contributions from other sections:

Section 1: Ellington *et al* (1.1).
Section 3: Belsey and Wellington (3.3).
Section 8: Shaw (8.3).

5.1 The Development of the Kent Mathematics Project

B Banks, A J Larcombe and A Tourret
West Kent Teachers' Centre, Tunbridge Wells

Abstract: The scheme was started in 1965 with experimental work on programmed learning. The trial printed and taped programmes were reinforced with worksheet material and a short group course was tried out with two school groups. Extended into nine other schools, the scheme expanded and by late 1970 was being used in nearly 60 Kent schools of all types catering for 9 to 16 year old children. The scheme was officially adopted in 1970 and by 1977/78 was used in over 100 schools by about 30,000 pupils and 500 teachers. The KMP team members by then had increased to 6.2 and the material bank was able to cope with all abilities.

In the design of material, acceptable programmed learning techniques were used and the material bank and learning model met all educational technology requirements including total self-evaluating procedures in three main areas, (a) the classroom, (b) the teachers and (c) the material-bank. Evaluation procedures used regular teachers' meetings at three Kent Teachers' Centres over 10 years, school visits by KMP team members and a validation conference in 1976 with nearly 70 experienced KMP teachers.

Early Development

The history of the innovation and early development of KMP — Kent Mathematics Project — can be traced through APL and APLET International Conference papers from 1967 to 1971.

In its early days, KMP was almost diametrically opposed to the attitudes of the leaders of mathematics education in this country. Discovery and investigational approaches in Primary schools and modular environmental mathematics in Secondary schools for non-examination pupils were being encouraged and only token attention was paid to PL in teachers' training courses. PL theory and practice seemed incompatible with current learning philosophies. However, in 1962, two major investigations were carried out at Ridgewaye School, Southborough, Kent, comparing lock-step class teaching with programmes designed by the same teacher and they showed PL to be superior in test results, retention and student attitude. Indeed, the early trials at Ridgewaye School were so encouraging that there was no choice but to reconcile PL practice with current educational ideas about mathematics learning. The most startling characteristic of the trials was the motivational aspect and it was compelling to seek to harness this motivation to concept-development up to 5th form work. Many other work-card schemes have reported similar motivation but most have been modular, unconnected and not aimed at higher school mathematics.

Main Development

KMP evolved into innovative areas along novel lines. Teachers' conventional roles were challenged, more students were accepting and enjoying workloads and showing surprising integrity over learning independently. A new assessment system emerged and promised to be superior to formal examinations and it was certain that children were developing an unusual richness in mathematics concept-building from resource-material. Each stage of concept-formation became entry behaviour for the next stage, which in its turn had a retention-testing function for the previous stage, and students were not allowed to proceed without mastery at each stage. This means that each student's mathematics learning world was a successful one and the difference between students was in the heights of concept-development attained, and these heights were assessable.

The KMP assessment system was based on the design and evolution of a material bank into a framework of hierarchies of concept-building. In order to identify the difficulty of a task, it was categorized into a mathematics level and allotted a level-score. The mean of a group of learning-tasks could therefore be the basis of an assessment procedure related to concept-building in topic areas.

The massive objective of 'mathematics learning for all abilities of children between nine and 16 years' governed both the levels and topic areas, and the material-bank was intended to contain resources for introductory Primary work, learning for very backward children in Middle and Secondary schools and examination topics in CSE and 'O' level syllabuses.

As the scheme developed, all material was subjected to try-out procedures which were concerned with success in the classroom. Parameters inspected were in terms of the learning-task itself, its objectives, manageability, test and position in the structured concept hierarchy. When first designed, early tasks were positioned from an intuitive decision based on experience, but when related tasks appeared later, earlier tasks had to be moved up or down to accommodate them. Also, towards the end of KMP development, some tasks, not vital in concept-development, were moved because teachers had found them too easy or difficult in their existing positions. All tasks are now positioned after long-term try-out (15 years) on a large number of students (27,000 in 1976), so their level-scores can be assumed to be reliable and objective.

An extension of the system was an identification of presentation for fast, medium and slow pupils. Since the framework of concept-building was designed as a hierarchy in maths topics, it was possible that a particular concept could be encountered by a bright child at an early age, a less able child much later and a backward pupil at an even older age. Clearly, different presentations concerned with verbiage, learning-gradient and reinforcement were required for some topics and where appropriate, separate presentations were designed and made available. These aspects of the material were also subjected to try-out and validation.

In 1974, Schools Council sponsored a two-year project (MA 1105) for very slow learners, attached to KMP and aimed to plug the material-bank with tasks for Secondary pupils with reading and/or learning difficulties. Material was coded 'L' for 'low-level learners'.

The Concept Hierarchy

KMP uses eight mathematical levels for concept development between nine and 16 years (with an 'overflow' level 9). Level 1 contains material dealing with concepts believed to be appropriate to *average* nine year-olds and Level 8 is what would be expected at 'O' level. It works out that a level is roughly one year's maths development for pupils of *above average* ability so that children starting KMP at 9 years and successfully working through one level per year should reach Grade A standard at 'O' level at 16 years. Some exceptional children could start at eight years and attain this standard at 15 years or less, whereas the unfortunate backward children involved in the Schools Council Project would be unlikely to reach Level 4 by the end of their 5th year, having delayed their start until Secondary stage. Figure 1 shows how age and ability match KMP levels.

The term 'concept' is used so loosely in educational circles that the KMP interpretation of it needs definition. Very simply, we use the word for mathematical topics or sub-topics such as 'number', 'area', 'graphs', 'constructions', 'angles' and so on, so that we can structure a hierarchy in terms of mathematical development that every teacher can understand. Of all authorities in the educational technology world, Susan Markle was the most helpful in selecting a definition of practical use.

Concepts are developed along lines of tasks on a network and although these lines interweave in conceptual terms (the 'constructions' and 'triangles' lines, the 'matrices' and 'transformations' lines, for instance), a proper analysis showing all interweaving lines would be unreadable. However, a rough idea of the KMP hierarchy can be obtained by the position in the network of the Pythagoras 2 task in Level 5. This assumes understanding of area and requires the pupils to calculate squares and square roots, all developed earlier in lower levels. Also, the pupils have been introduced to Pythagoras through a concrete stage involving constructing, cutting out and fitting together triangles.

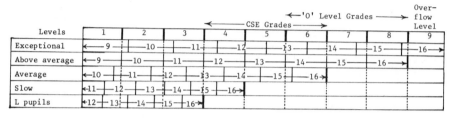

Figure 1.

(The numbers from 9 to 16 represent ages *at the end* of the academic year).
'Exceptional' means outstanding ability in mathematics and ability to learn fast.
'Average' is not related to the normal distribution curve, but is intended to mean the 'unexceptional' in cleverness or backwardness and is a common term used and known by all teachers. Not all average pupils complete Level 6 at 16 years.
'Slow' means a need for simple language, diagrammatic descriptions, a shallow learning gradient and much consolidation at each stage.
'L' pupils are the subjects of the Schools Council Project for very slow learners.

Findings

The table in Figure 1 is the result of about 15 years' investigation into concept-building in KMP. It exposes many significant weaknesses in mathematics lock-step learning by class-teaching. These weaknesses lie in the following assumptions and practices, common in most schools, especially Secondary.

(a) Chronologically-Based Courses

Although we all know that failure in mathematics at any point can be disastrous, when any school designs mathematics courses based on 'first year', 'second year' (and so on) syllabuses, it is a prescription for failure for a large percentage of students. Even in a closely setted group. KMP has always found a wide disparity between the fastest and slowest pupils and a wide difference in the rate at which different topics are mastered. In class-teaching there will always be a balance between a percentage of slow pupils who founder, and its inverse percentage of fast pupils who waste time free-wheeling, not necessarily in mathematics as a general subject, but in different topics such as Number, Geometry and Algebra. Exposure to such courses is not fair to students.

(b) Environmental Mathematics

There seems to be a persistent belief that environmental mathematics is motivational for young pupils and older non-examination students. Of course, everyday examples are necessary to build concepts which should be developed from the known to the unknown and should form part of the learning strategy of any task wherever possible, but a total submersion of concept building into environmental mathematics is full of dangers. First, concept development in a given module or assignment is extremely difficult to identify and record and is nearly always indeterminant for young children. Structured concept building is therefore practically impossible and gaps are not filled.

Second, non-examination students in Secondary schools are usually those not considered able to obtain a CSE Grade 5. Since CSE objectives claim to cater for pupils above the 40th percentile, it means that about 40 per cent of our school population will require special attention. According to KMP findings shown in Figure 1, CSE Grade 5 goes down to the end of KMP Level 3, where the concepts are still at a fairly low level. Any calculation or mathematical concept, if embedded in environmental material, should therefore be at a fairly low level in order that the pupil can do the work, and any mis-matching of the pupil's level with that required by the task will only cause failure and distress. Current marketed material seems to have missed this point and KMP finds that success in concept-building is in itself motivating and should be the first consideration in designing material and courses.

(c) Minimum Standards For All

Many Secondary schools expect minimum standards in formal maths topics for all students before transfer. Figure 1 shows that a percentage of children will not be capable of reaching certain standards related to chronological age, so the effect of any 'leaving test' is to guarantee a certain number of failed pupils before they enter the Secondary school. Also, all pupils in the Primary or Middle school will have been subjected to a syllabus in which a standard test has defined the objectives and this is not necessarily appropriate for all children and tends to be restrictive.

Examinations

(a) Objectives

There is an incompatibility between formal examination objectives and KMP philosophy and practice. Quite explicitly, one CSE Board's objectives define Grades in terms of excellence for Grade 1 and 'confusion' and 'defeat' for Grade 5. Although the objectives are designed as criteria based on an nth-hand version of Bloom's Taxonomy, I understand that papers are nevertheless marked as percentages and Grade boundaries determined from the normal distribution curve. 'O' level Board literature is not as explicit but mark boundaries for Grades imply a similar situation. The implication of all examinations and Board syllabuses is that a school should subject its students to a course in mathematics and test them at the end to find out who was successful and to what extent and who failed the course. KMP philosophy and practice is that students should embark on a personalized course of concept-development, each step being checked by tests and consolidated before advance. Students therefore advance only if they are successful and 'confusion' and 'defeat' are avoided at all costs. Despite incompatibilities, KMP has been used to prepare successfully students for 'O' level Board examinations. A Mode 2 with London Universities Examinations Board is in its third experimental year and several schools have entered candidates for other Boards' Mode 1 examinations. KMP has obtained varied success (some of which is outstanding), but detailed results are not possible to report in this paper. Usually, the Board syllabus is compared with KMP material, and group-learning is arranged where required for missing topics, examinology and practice with past papers.

(b) Constraints

Rich concept development is affected by constraints which are created by teachers' attitudes to examinations. One should not be surprised that a blanket acceptance that only examinations count smothers ideal learning. There is no doubt that the development of psycho-motor skills, ingenuity, long-term persistence, problem-solving and inventiveness are laudable objectives in Bloom's non-cognitive domains and can be included in mathematics learning with great benefit to the student. Also, there are numerous topics such as the Fibonnacci series and Golden Ratio and investigations into special interests, as suggested by Edith Biggs, which generate exciting work. However, because it is impossible or very difficult to set examination questions on such topics or work, Board syllabuses do not include them and tend to be uniformly uninspiring. Teachers follow syllabuses slavishly because they say they cannot spare time from examination preparation. Mode 3 examinations, because they permit release from syllabus constraints have been tried by some KMP schools, but apart from the first two Ridgewaye CSE examinations in 1972 and 1973, have not been encouraging, mainly because the Board has insisted on using the examination as the reference unit, despite the KMP maths level-scoring assessment procedure being more objective than a one-off examination.

Material Design

Early published programmes and their association with teaching machines certainly caused concern amongst teachers and the later term 'educational technology' did nothing to allay fears that Big Brother was taking over. In fact, there was a rightful objection to all early programmes on educational grounds. Too many were designed by psychologists or those with no deep involvement in the classroom and there seemed to be a male preoccupation with gadgetry that flooded the market with machines with only a few demonstration programmes. Oddly, teachers were not involved to any great extent and it is not surprising that PL, as it was introduced, offended much that was current educational philosophy. Skinner's fixed-path programmes and discovery learning were poles apart and Crowder's branching technique, although providing different paths, was equally objectionable because the paths were few and still fixed. In any case, teachers are not readily convinced by 'them' above, especially psychologists, and only a few were curious enough to investigate PL. Of these, still fewer were willing to face up to the work and rigour of learning esoteric PL practice and developing and validating programmes properly.

The problem was one of extracting from PL all the effective aspects which would be acceptable to teachers and rejecting those which were not. Thus, KMP retained behavioural objectives, strategy-planning, KR, try-out and validation, but rejected formal prompting, all material being in the printed word, a total rul-eg approach and all references to PL and educational technology. KMP has proved that communication through diagrams can be successful, eg-rul approaches effective and taped programmes highly efficient. It has also been found that uniqueness amongst children has been underestimated and that personality differences can affect learning from different presentations.

Evaluation and Validation

In 1974, it was encouraging to read in the Commonwealth Secretariat study, 'New Media in Education in the Commonwealth', that KMP and nearly all the 20 summarized conclusions were in agreement. 'The only real purpose of evaluating a project is to enable modifications and improvements to take place' fitted perfectly into KMP procedures, and 'Evaluation for its own sake is a profitless exercise' gave a salutary answer to the esoteric preoccupation with project evaluation at national level. KMP was firm in its attitude that accountability should be concerned with each student and that all other accountabilities fall naturally into place.

As the project expanded, six identifiable components emerged and came under scrutiny. All interacted with each other and constant modification through feedback refined the scheme to its present successful state. The KMP team, catalystic rather than authoritarian, has not dictated development but has steered the scheme through its evolution, and I am sure that one of the success factors in KMP has been the extent to which teachers have been involved in decision-making and feel KMP is their own scheme. The six components are: (i) the teacher, (ii) the system, (iii) the student, (iv) the material, (v) the KMP team, (vi) meetings and courses.

The material has received special attention. Since 1972, newly-designed tasks have been first tried out on a few students, modified, sent out to at least six try-out schools and reports from students and teachers collected. Further modifications were applied and the material was then sent to all appropriate KMP schools. In 1976, the bulk of the material bank was validated at a conference of nearly 70 experienced teachers from Primary, Middle and Secondary schools. The teachers were asked to assess each task in terms of 80/80 success, that is, whether a task, in their opinion, achieved 80 per cent success with 80 per cent of the pupils and if not, how it could be modified to reach this criterion, or whether it should be discarded. All comments were recorded and a further criterion was set because there was disagreement about some of the tasks. Another 80 per cent had to be included so that tasks were accepted if they met an 80/80/80 criterion, that is, that 80 per cent of the teachers agreed that a particular task achieved 80 per cent success with 80 per cent of the students.

KMP, as an educational technology model, has certainly exposed surprising inadequacies in current school practices and, in many instances, has shown the way to significant improvement.

References

Banks, B (1967) *Problems and Methods in Programmed Learning,* 1, p 21.

Banks, B (1968) In Dunn, W R and Holroyd, C (eds) *Aspects of Educational Technology,* II, p 221. Methuen, London.

Banks, B (1969) In Mann, A P and Brunstrom, C P (eds) *Aspects of Educational Technology* III, p 175. Pitman, London.

Banks, B (1970) In Bajpai, A C and Leedham, J F (eds) *Aspects of Educational Technology,* IV, p 502. Pitman, London.

Bloom, B (1956) Taxonomy of educational objectives. *Cognitive Domain.* Longmans Green, London.

CEDO Research Team (1974) *New Media in Education in the Commonwealth,* p 287. Nobles the Printers, Southampton.

Gilligan, J, Hazelton, W and Kaye, W (1971) In Packham, A, Cleary, A and Mayes, T (eds) *Aspects of Educational Technology V,* p 161. Pitman, London.

Larcombe, A J *Special Education: Forward Trends,* 4, 2, p 12.

Markle, Susan Meyer (1969) *Good Frames and Bad,* 2nd edition, p 179. John Wiley, London.

Workshop Report
The Kent Mathematics Project

B Banks, A J Larcombe, A Tourret

After presentation of the above paper, this workshop provided an opportunity for informal questioning and discussion about the classroom operation of the KMP material bank system and the aspects of the KMP material which have been influenced by principles of educational technology.

Particular interest was shown in the ways that KMP has sought to tackle many of the problems related to teaching mathematics to pupils across a wide ability range:

1 The flexibility provided by the material bank, which enables teachers to select personalized courses for each pupil, whatever his or her ability. The discussion centred around the use of a concept network to aid the teachers' selection of tasks.
2 The freedom and ease with which the pupils are able to move from material with a gentle learning gradient to material with a steeper learning gradient was highlighted.
3 The use of mastery tests for both diagnostic and evaluative purposes was discussed. Reference to the continuous assessment potential within the KMP hierarchy was of particular interest. An outline of the current uses of KMP in conjunction with a wide variety of syllabus requirements and examination modes was given.
4 The potential for continuity in mathematics for pupils changing from Primary Schools using KMP to Secondary Schools also using KMP was an aspect which also aroused interest.

Other aspects covered in the discussion were: the nature and use of the KMP material for slow learners in secondary schools; remedial use of the material bank; achievement motivation; in-service education of teachers; success of KMP when used by non-specialist mathematics teachers; the teacher's role when using KMP; encouraging a creative input from specialist mathematics teachers; dissemination of KMP; publication schedule and costing.

Apart from the discussion and questioning, delegates were given an opportunity to handle KMP published material.

5.2 Can Keller Plan Work in Schools?

D W Daly
Scottish Council for Educational Technology

Abstract: Keller Plan is an independent learning system which originated in higher education in America in the early 1960s. The system was first used in the UK in the early 1970s in higher education and more recently it has been used in schools in this country. The purpose of this paper is to examine the changes to the Plan which have been made since its original formulation nearly 20 years ago to its present use in schools in the UK. The paper also considers the implications for schools in the 1980s if an independent learning system such as Keller Plan were to be widely used.

It is assumed that the reader is familiar with the original formulation of Keller Plan, a full description of which is given in the paper by Keller (1968).

Keller Plan in Schools in the UK in the 1970s

Keller Plan has been used in schools and colleges of further education in this country for more than four years and further details on its use in these sectors of education can be found in case studies described elsewhere (Daly and Robertson, 1978). Although the Plan has been used in a number of subject areas in these sectors of education, most of the teachers use it in physics and chemistry. It should also be made clear that the generalizations in this section on the use of the Plan in schools are based on the practical experience of the teachers involved in its use and are not the results of a closely controlled educational research experiment.

When Keller Plan was used in schools, a number of modifications were made to Keller's original formulation and these are described under the headings of the five features.

Self-Pacing

Many of the teachers found that complete self-pacing of a pupil's study in a subject had to be restricted in practice. First, the existence of external and end of term examinations created difficulties in the implementation of a self-paced system. These examinations covered a fixed syllabus and were taken by pupils on a fixed date and teachers felt that they had a duty to their pupils to try to ensure that any individual pupil's pace was fast enough to enable him to cover enough of the syllabus to have a chance of passing the examination. Target dates were introduced by the teachers to give pupils a rough idea of the number of units they should have completed by a given date, if they intended to complete in time all of the units covered by a particular examination. The target dates gave guidance to the pupils and helped the teachers to identify those pupils who were falling behind schedule.

A second difficulty concerning self-pacing was the motivation, responsibility and maturity of the pupils involved in the Keller Plan course.

In some cases the Plan was used in mixed ability classes of 13 to 14 year-old pupils. Some of these pupils were taking the subject being taught by Keller Plan to fit in with their parents' wishes or as a requirement of the school curriculum. Such pupils were sometimes poorly motivated and, for some, the freedom to work at their own pace could mean the freedom not to work at all. In these circumstances, teachers felt that they had a responsibility to attempt to impose a minimum acceptable rate of study.

A third problem of self-pacing was concerned with whether all or only some of the staff of a school subject department were using Keller Plan. Some of the teachers who used the Plan were the only teachers in their department who were doing so. Within the present school framework it is quite likely that a class of pupils will move from one teacher to another at the end of an academic year. Thus, a class of pupils all at different stages in a Keller Plan course could be handed on from one teacher who was implementing the Plan to another teacher using traditional methods. This would be an unsatisfactory situation from the point of view of both teachers and pupils. In these circumstances complete self-pacing for pupils would increase the variation in their achievement at the end of a year and so would exacerbate the difficulties of transfer to a teacher who was not implementing the Plan.

Thus, although students were given some freedom to determine the pace at which they worked, the extent of this freedom was limited and teachers did try to impose a minimum acceptable rate of study.

Mastery

The teachers felt that the term 'mastery' had to be clarified. If by mastery was meant achievement of all of the objectives of a unit, most of the teachers did not require mastery of their pupils.

The first difficulty to be considered here is the relationship between self-pacing and mastery. If mastery is to be required of all pupils, it is unreasonable to expect them to demonstrate mastery on a time schedule decided by the teacher. Thus, if the teacher departs from the self-pacing feature of the Plan as originally described by Keller, he must also accept less than 100 per cent mastery by his pupils.

A second reason for departing from the 100 per cent mastery requirement is that in external examinations a pass mark of 50 per cent or less is usually set and it would be unreasonable and impractical for a teacher to set a 90 per cent or 100 per cent mastery requirement in unit tests, when pupils are working within a tight time schedule towards an examination in which a much lower level of performance is acceptable.

A third reason is that teachers found that mastery of some important objectives was necessary since the skills thereby acquired were necessary prerequisites for future work. With other objectives which were simply ends in themselves, less than 100 per cent mastery was acceptable.

A fourth difficulty is concerned with the problem of covering in a fairly brief unit test all of the stated objectives of the unit. In practice, teachers found that sometimes their tests did not cover all of the objectives of a unit. This was related to the fact that with a large class of pupils and with no proctors available to help him to mark tests, the teacher had to limit the number of tests and the length of each test.

Thus, although 100 per cent mastery of a unit's objectives was accepted by the teachers as the ideal requirement for pupil progress to a subsequent unit, in many cases teachers were prepared to accept a lower level of performance by pupils in unit tests.

Lectures as Motivation

Most of the teachers used lectures infrequently and found that they could be very useful in motivating pupils.

However, in some Keller Plan schemes lectures and demonstrations were not optional and they did provide pupils with critical information.

Some teachers used lectures for revision purposes when all the pupils in a class had completed the unit connected with the lecture. Teachers also used demonstration lectures for revision when they felt that an experiment was too dangerous or costly for pupils to perform individually.

Stress upon the Written Word

Teachers did rely heavily on the written word in their units although films, tape/slide and other media had been used satisfactorily.

Use of Proctors

None of the teachers had used proctors to mark unit tests. In Keller's original scheme in higher education, proctors were undergraduates chosen for their previous mastery of the course. In a school setting, a proctor would be an older pupil who had successfully completed the Keller Plan course in an earlier year.

Apart from a number of practical and political difficulties related to the use of pupil proctors, it is fair to say that the teachers who implemented the Plan would probably have been unhappy to delegate the responsibility for marking tests to senior pupils.

The use of proctors was central to Keller's original ideas and a ratio of 10 students to one proctor was advocated. Some of the teachers who implemented Keller Plan had to work with a class of 20 pupils. Thus, some teachers had to fulfil the role of proctor with double the number of pupils originally recommended; the role of graduate assistant — supervising laboratory work, keeping records and helping in the overall management of the course; and the role of instructor — selecting study material and writing units, constructing tests and examinations, and evaluating each student's progress.

Clearly this placed a very heavy burden on teachers, to some extent impaired the effectiveness of the system and represented a major departure from Keller's original ideas.

It is clear from the above discussion that the schemes being implemented by teachers cannot accurately be described as Keller Plan according to the original description.

Keller Plan in Schools in the UK in the 1980s

The fact that the Plan was extensively modified when it was used in schools is hardly surprising and is certainly no criticism of the teachers concerned. The differences between a new university in Brazil in the early 1960s and a comprehensive school in Scotland in the late 1970s is very great in time, distance and educational context.

However, a distinction should be drawn between those modifications to the Plan which teachers wished to make and those modifications which were forced on teachers as a result of the constraints imposed by the institutional framework of the school. Educational technologists are concerned to promote the idea of individualizing learning in schools so it is important to consider the necessary changes in school structure and the problems which might result if a system such as Keller Plan were to be used more widely in its original form in the 1980s.

Self-Pacing

It was seen in the last section that the existence of an external or end-of-term examination on a fixed date as the major assessment of pupils on a course made genuine self-pacing impossible. It may well be that there will be pressure from parents, employers, institutions of further and higher education and from teachers themselves to allow some kind of final examination or certification to continue in the 1980s.

In these circumstances, if pupils are to be allowed to work at their own pace any final examination should be taken by different pupils on different dates, soon after each individual pupil finishes the course. It is not fair to the pupil who finishes early to expect him to take the final examination some considerable time later when all pupils have finished the course, since this will involve him in considerable revision which will be unnecessary for the slower finishers.

The alternative to a series of final examinations taken by pupils on different dates would be some form of continuous assessment. In Keller's original scheme, 25 per cent of a student's course grade was based on an end of term examination covering the term's work, sat by all students at the same time. The remaining 75 per cent of the grade was based on the number of units successfully completed during the term. Thus, a combination of the two different kinds of assessment is possible. In any event, it is clear that teachers must adopt new assessment techniques to allow a self-paced system to operate satisfactorily.

Another genuine difficulty in self-pacing at school level is the extent to which pupils may be given responsibility for their own learning.

Many of the teachers had decided to use Keller Plan because they felt that it was inherently valuable to encourage pupils to take more responsibility for their own learning. However, at present society takes much of this responsibility by obliging pupils up to the age of 16 years to attend school and to take certain subjects. In these circumstances, should teachers be expected to motivate pupils and attempt to impose a minimum acceptable rate of study?

If genuine self-pacing is to be allowed, can pupils be given the freedom not to work at all? These are philosophical questions for society to answer but there will be real practical problems in implementing a genuinely self-paced system in schools if answers cannot be found.

One possible solution in the 1980s might be an expansion of facilities for continuing education once pupils leave school. Part of the teacher's desire to help the poorly motivated pupil is connected to his feeling that the pupil's opportunities for learning in later life are limited. If the pupil had greater opportunities to learn in later life the teacher (and society) might be prepared to give him greater responsibility for his own learning at school.

It seems clear from the earlier discussion that it is highly desirable for all of the staff of a subject department in a school to be involved in implementing a self-paced system. There are, of course, a number of institutional and social problems connected with genuine self-pacing which have implications for the whole school organization across different subjects.

A much more flexible time-tabling system would be required which would allow pupils to control the amount of time which they spent on different subjects. Pupils would still require access to teachers (or proctors) for tutoring, test marking, and occasional lectures and teachers could make themselves available at advertised times for these purposes.

At present the social unit for a pupil in school is likely to be his year group. In a self-paced system used in a mixed ability setting it is likely that the year group would break up and a pupil's social unit could become other pupils of different ages at the same level of achievement in a subject. While it is likely that the resulting organizational problems could be solved, the desirability of such a change from a social point of view is open to debate. There may be social rather than educational advantages for the weaker pupil in being carried along at the faster average rate of the class in the present teaching system.

Mastery

If genuine self-pacing were allowed and a sufficient number of proctors were available, it would be possible to overcome most of the difficulties discussed earlier and to expect 100 per cent mastery by pupils in unit tests. If practical problems still remained, it would be possible to resort to the concept of 'probable' mastery defined by Stace (1975).

The one remaining difficulty would be the relatively low pass mark of 50 per cent or less which is usually set in external examinations. In our examination system at present, time is held constant (ie most pupils of the same age sit an examination at the same time) and pupil achievement varies. Within a self-paced system it would be possible to hold achievement constant (ie mastery is required of all pupils) and let time vary. Thus an examination pass might be awarded only if a pupil achieved all of the objectives of the course at the final examination. If this were to be considered an impossibly high standard of performance for pupils to achieve, it would still be necessary for examining boards to give a very clear indication to teachers and pupils of the criterion of acceptable performance for different grades of pass. If this were done in terms of clearly specified objectives, pupils and teachers would be able to determine the mastery requirements in relevant course units. Of course if some form of continuous assessment were used, such problems would not arise.

Lectures as Motivation

This feature of Keller Plan could be implemented without difficulty by teachers if they chose to do so.

Stress Upon the Written Word

It is unlikely that any institutional constraints would prevent teachers from relying on the written word if they wished to do so.

Use of Proctors

Donovan (1976) has remarked in a higher education context that 'you may as well not use Keller Plan if you don't use student proctors'. The use of school pupils to tutor other pupils would cause serious problems at present. It is against regulations for a teacher without a professional teaching qualification to teach pupils in a state school and it might be difficult to draw a distinction between teaching and tutoring. It seems that in the foreseeable future the introduction of pupil proctors would be unacceptable to the teaching profession. Even if this problem could be overcome, it might be difficult to find time for senior pupils to be released from their own studies to undertake the duties of proctors. The question of rewards (financial or other) for the services of proctors would also have to be considered.

In the absence of pupil proctors, an increase in qualified teaching staff would seem to be the only solution to this problem.

There would be implications for schools which are not mentioned under the five features above if Keller Plan were to be widely used. The arrangement of space in the school would have to be changed to provide rooms in which pupils could work on their own on different course units. Arrangements for the storage and use of books, laboratory equipment and other resources would have to be carefully planned.

Another important consideration for schools would be costs. It has already been mentioned that an increase in the number of teachers would be required if pupil proctors were not available. All of the teachers who had used Keller Plan found that if one ignores the cost of the teacher's time in writing the units their courses did not cost any more to run than traditional courses. However, it would not be possible to ignore the costs of unit production and evaluation for a widespread implementation of Keller Plan in a number of subjects.

Teachers who have implemented the Plan so far, have found they had to cope with a heavy administrative burden of keeping records on pupils' performance and progress. It is possible in the 1980s that micro-computers could be introduced into schools to give teachers some assistance with this task. It might also be possible to use micro-computers for test production, marking and analysis.

Conclusion

From the discussion above, it is clear that Keller Plan can work in schools but at present only in modified form. If the Plan were to be used widely in its original form in schools in the 1980s there would have to be radical changes in teaching and assessment methods; in school organization and layout; in the financing of education; in the attitudes to education of pupils, teachers, parents, employers and others.

It is most unlikely that such changes will take place rapidly enough to allow the widespread use of Keller Plan to become a practical proposition at least in the early 1980s.

The use of the Plan in schools is at an early stage of development and much further work remains to be done to determine its value and appropriateness for individual pupils, teachers, subject areas and schools. Further development work should be carried out with better funding and the imposition of fewer institutional constraints so that the necessary radical changes can be initiated.

It is the task of the educational technologist to influence not only teachers but also educational policy makers so that teachers' efforts to implement such schemes as Keller Plan are not hindered by a rigid institutional framework, designed for the teaching methods of previous decades.

Keller Plan can work in schools, but has society the will to let it work?

References

Daly, D W and Robertson, S M (eds) (1978) *Keller Plan in the Classroom.* Scottish Council for Educational Technology.

Donovan, W F (1976) *Remarks in Self-Paced Study Bulletin 4.* Institute for Educational Technology, University of Surrey.

Keller, F S (1968) Goodbye Teacher... *Journal of Applied Behavioural Analysis,* 1, pp 79-89.

Stace, B (1975) *Remarks in Self-Paced Study Bulletin 3.* Institute for Educational Technology, University of Surrey.

5.3 Instructional Design by the COMET Method

T Sakamoto
Tokyo Institute of Technology

Abstract: COMET is a method of designing instructional plans by optimal combination of child, objectives, methods and teacher's behavior. The first step is to identify the smallest possible units of learning and to analyze the learning materials. By selecting a number of elements from the analyzed materials and considering their rearrangement into different groups, it is possible to formulate various combinations giving a variety of instructional packages. The COMET method discriminates between the relevant and the irrelevant dimensions in applying concept learning to the instructional process.

What is Comet?

The *Comet* method is one of the methods for instructional design which were developed in the Sakamoto Laboratory for Educational Technology, Tokyo Institute of Technology. Four components of classroom teaching, Child (C), Objective (O), Method (ME), and Teacher (T) are integrated to decide the optimal plan for classroom teaching.

In terms of the child, the characteristics of children, particularly their errors and distractions are considered. As for the educational goals, instructional contents and terminal behaviors or items for their evaluation are variable factors. As concerns the methods, the flows of teaching, types of teaching, modes of teaching, instructional media and so on are the objects to be considered. Concerning the teacher, teaching behaviors such as presenting, response arousing, response control, giving, diagnosing, etc are combined.

The Instructional Design Procedure by Comet

Figure 1 shows an example of a behavior matrix for science education. The behavioral objectives are written as concrete sentences composed of a combination of contents and terminal behaviors. The goals corresponding to each number in the matrix are written out as in these examples:

⑧ to find out through measurement that in case the length, size and material of conductor varies, the current strengths is different under the same voltage.

㉗ to infer that in metal wire electric current is in proportion to voltage and the reciprocal of the proportion constant is electrical resistance, and so on.

Contents		I. Knowledge			II. Skill						III. Thinking					IV. Attitude			
		1. indicate	2. express	3. discover	1. prepare	2. operate	3. gather	4. measure	5. present	6. apply	1. hypothesize	2. classify	3. infer	4. summary	5. evaluate	1. cooperate	2. show	3. demand	4. like
A: EVENT	a. Ammeter																		
	b. Voltmeter																		
	c. Dry Cell (Power Source)																		
	d. Slide Rheostat																		
	e. Oscilloscope																		
B: SIGN	a. Ⓐ [mA] [A]																		
	b. Ⓥ [V]																		
	c. C																		
	d. [Ω] [KΩ]																		
	e.																		
C: PHENOMENON — Kirchhoff's Law	a.-g.---f.																		
C: PHENOMENON — Ohm's Law	g. Electric current flowing metal wire varies dependent upon the voltage strength between edges of the conductor		◎7																
	h. In case the length, size & material of conductor vary, the current strength is different under the same voltage			○8															
	i. In a conductor, electric current varies by voltage			○9															

	D: METHOD PROCEDURE		E: CONCEPT, PRINCIPLE, LAW
	Kirchhoff's Law	Ohm's Law	Ohm's Law
a. ---- e. ----- i. ----	Voltmeter is connected in parallel to circuit		
j.		Measure the electric current for the different length of wires (1, 1/2, 1/3) in varying voltage	
a. ---- b. -----			
c.			Strength of electric current flowing metal wire is in proportion to voltage between edges
d.			Gradient shown in graph is different dependent upon the difference of the length of metal wire
e.			In metal wire, electric current is in proportion to voltage, and the reciprocal of the proportion constant is called electric resistance
f. ----			

Circled markers: 16, 21, 27, 28, 29

Figure 1.
Content-terminal behavior = electric current and voltage

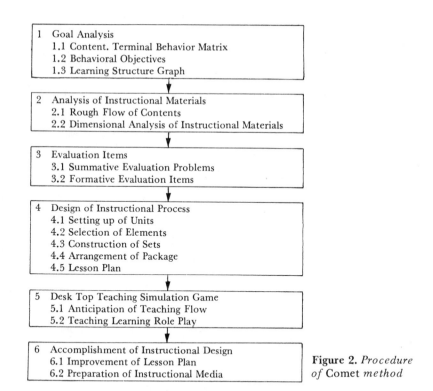

Figure 2. *Procedure of* Comet *method*

The categories in the matrix and the learning structure graph vary from one subject to another. Thus the goals can be distinctly grasped through goal analysis. Figure 2 shows the procedure of instructional design by *Comet* method.

Goal Analysis

In terms of goal analysis, there are three techniques.

(a) Preparing the content-terminal behavior matrix.
(b) Writing behavioral objectives on the basis of the matrix.
(c) Making out the learning structure graph which integrates the behavioral objectives.

Analysis of Instructional Materials

The core is the dimensional analysis of a topic using a matrix. This enables the development of instructional materials which reflect all the dimensions of the topic that learners are likely to explore.

Here, the instructional materials are regarded not as an instance and media but as information representing the structure of learning contents.

Thus, learners acquire the learning contents through extracting 'the information as connotation' on the basis of 'the information as cues' contained in the instance presented on instructional media and environment.

Figure 3 shows the structure of instructional materials from the viewpoint of dimensional analysis. Here, one of the characteristics is that errors should be clearly divided into wrong and distracted. Learning means not conducting wrong responses to negative values in relevant dimensions, overcoming the alteration of values in irrelevant dimensions and making correct responses to positive values in relevant dimensions.

A dimensional analysis table is useful for improving the content-terminal behaviour matrix, making evaluation items, elaborating the teaching sequence, and conducting instructional design.

The procedure of dimensional analysis is as shown in Figure 4. The terminology here is derived from concept learning research in experimental psychology. In applying the concepts of pure science to the actual teaching/learning process, it is very difficult to identify and differentiate between the relevant and irrelevant dimensions and their respective values.

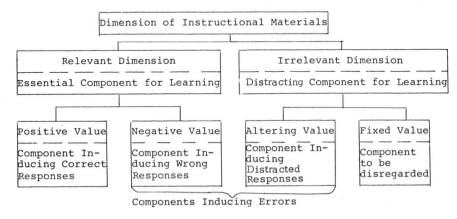

Figure 3. *Structure of dimension of instructional materials*

I. Sampling Instances	1. Select the contents to be main objectives 2. List up instances related to the contents 3. Classify the positive and negative instances representing contents
II. Determination of relevant dimension	1. Extract positive values in relevant dimension, i e the characteristics which are common to positive values, but uncommon to negative values 2. Extract negative values, i e the characteristics which are contained in some of negative instances, but not contained in positive instance at all 3. Name relevant dimensions which contain mutually contrasting positive and negative values in one dimension
III. Determination of irrelevant dimension	1. Extract, irrelevant dimension, i e the characteristics which contain traits common to both positive and negative instances in one dimension 2. Pick up several values to be altered 3. Fix difficult irrelevant dimensions for teaching-learning 4. Determine one value to be fixed
IV. Clarifying the structure of instructional materials	1. Making dimensional analysis table 2. Set concrete objectives in learning unit, which consist of overcoming irrelevant dimensions denying negative values and acquiring positive values in relevant dimensions

Figure 4. *Procedure for dimensional analysis of instructional materials*

Evaluation

Evaluation items are made on the basis of content-terminal behavior matrix and a dimensional analysis table. As the summative evaluation is concerned, behavioral objectives in content-terminal behavior matrix and the learning structure graph should be examined. Concrete contents for both summative and formative evaluation should be generally and summarily decided on the basis of a dimensional analysis table.

Design for Teaching Process

4.1 Setting up Units (Numbers refer to Figure 2)

This is about setting up the minimum units of learning activity. For example, the unit for learning Ohm's Law:

> Unit A; construct a suitable electric circuit in order to examine the relationship between current and voltage, measure the changes in current strength by altering voltage to different length of metal wire; induce Ohm's Law.
> Unit B; examine the relationship between electric resistance and several conditions such as length and amplitude of metal wire.
> Unit C; find out the change of the sum of electric resistance by way of connecting (parallel or series) and induce combined value of resistance.

4.2 Selection of Element

Each unit is composed of elements, some of which are of relevant dimensions and some of irrelevant ones as shown in Figure 5.

4.3 Construction of Sets

There are many spatial and temporal combinations of elements in each unit. For example, the inductive method consists of learning relevant dimensions first, and the discovery method consists of overcoming irrelevant dimensions from many instances at first.

Such a sequencing of elements produces sets which are the core of the teaching plan including instructional media, teaching strategy, and modes of learners' groups (Figure 6).

4.4 Package

Each unit has its own assembly of sets. A package is arranged by sequencing a set from each unit through several units. The combination of sets is theoretically the multiplication of number of sets in all units (Figure 7).

4.5 Lesson Plan

Flexible series of sets are expected to be arranged. In other words, each package would be hypothetically accomplished as an elaborated lesson plan whereby a division is effected into several blocks to be taught in each unit classroom hour.

Desk Top Teaching Simulation Game

Tentative lesson plans are realized in the form of a teaching simulation game. First, teachers or student teachers meet to discuss the learners' anticipated behavior in the teaching/learning process.

		Selection of elements for composing unit	
		relevant dimension	irrelevant dimension
OHM'S LAW	A ---- --- ---	(1) --- (2) --- (11) ---	① --- ② --- ⑤ ---
FACTORS ON RESISTANCE	B --- ----- ----	(10) --- (11) ---- -----	⑤ ⑥
	C ---	(16) ---	⑤

Figure 5. *Model of setting of unit and selection of elements*

Then one of them takes a teacher's role and others take learners' roles to play a teaching/learning simulation game according to the lesson plan. Paper models of some tools such as puppets of a teacher and learners, desks, chairs, TV, etc are used on a large piece of paper or board which is assumed to be a classroom or other instructional environment. The scenery is recorded by VTR and playback to improve teaching behaviors and teaching strategy and tactics at any time as required.

Applications of *Comet*

This is merely a brief summary of the *Comet* method. This sort of technology for instructional design should be useful for both pre-service and in-service teacher training as well as elaborated curriculum development by professional groups.

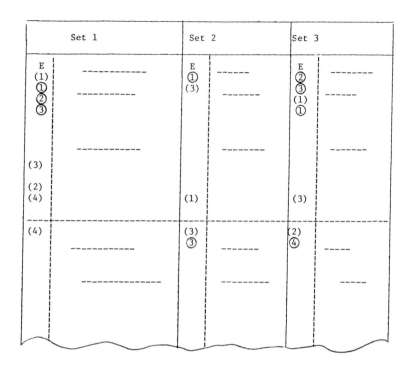

Figure 6. *Model of construction of set*

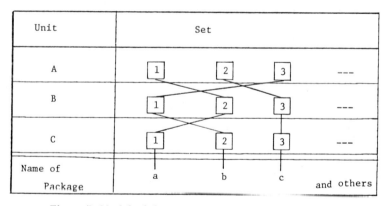

Figure 7. *Model of the package composed of sets in units*

5.4 Evaluation of the Schools Council Avon/Bath University Modular Courses in Technology Project

N D C Harris and P J Watts
University of Bath

Abstract: The Modular Courses in Technology, aimed at CSE and O-level, have been designed by teachers and are based on behavioural objectives, worksheets, pupil readers and experimental work. The paper considers the Illuminative Evaluation section of the overall evaluation prc gramme currently being carried out by the Science and Technology Education Centre of the University of Bath. The decision to include an illuminative component in the total evaluation is discussed. The methods used are examined, including the problems which have arisen. Particular emphasis is placed on obse:vation in classrooms, laboratories and workshops, and on informal interviews with teachers and pupils. Although this is a predominantly subjective approach, the information derived can be analyzed and compared with predetermined criteria and with information from the other parts of the evaluation programme.

Introduction

The *Guardian* newspaper ran a 'Why work in industry?' essay competition in 1977 and according to Harford Thomas (1977), who analyzed the entries, two out of three 15 to 19 year olds saw industry as 'ugly, dirty, dangerous, monotonous, repetitive, soul destroying, inhuman, underpaid and strike-bound'.

In response to demands by government and industry for an increase in technological awareness of children in our secondary schools, several schemes have been proposed or initiated over the past few years. These plans have had the declared aim of raising the level of technological consciousness of school leavers and encouraging them to be more favourably disposed towards industry. More specifically these schemes try to encourage children to consider a technologically based industrial career, either straight from school or after a period of further or higher education. One such scheme is the Avon/Bath University Modular Courses in Technology Project. (A similar parallel scheme was devised by a group of teachers in Hertfordshire and West London.)

The aims of the project are threefold:

1 to develop intellectual ability in a cognitive context;
2 to create individual interest in, and awareness of, the technological influence on society;
3 to develop practical technological skills.

In order to meet these aims a set of general objectives was drawn up.

The Avon/Bath University Project

This scheme was the result of a series of meetings organized in 1974 under the general guidance of Dr Ray Page of Bath University and Mr John Poole of Avon Science and Technology Centre. Teachers from local authorities around Bath were closely involved from the beginning and formed themselves into six groups, each given the responsibility for producing a specific programme, or module, of work. (Schools Council Newsletter, 1978.)

There were three core modules (compulsory) in the first year followed in the second year by two optional modules (from a choice of 11 which included those designed by the Herts/West London group), and a major project.

Avon/Bath University		Herts/West London
1 Energy		1 Acoustics
2 Problem Solving	Core	2 Electrical Applications
3 Material Science	Modules	3 Electronics
4 Optical Instruments		4 Instrumentation
5 Aerodynamics		5 Mechanisms
6 Electronics		6 Pneumatics
		7 Structures
		8 Technology and Man

Each module lasts for an average of 10 weeks with four periods of 35 minutes making a total time of 24 hours per module.

The Modular Courses are designed so that science, craft and technology/technical studies departments, or a combination of them can run the course. The courses are aimed at 'O' level and CSE Mode I/III (Grade 3 and above).

Resource Packages are provided for each module and consist of a Pupil Reader, Pupil Activity Sheets and a Teacher's Guide. There is also a back-up service provided by the Science and Technology Centres at Bath University and in Avon.

A total of 16 schools are currently acting as full trial units, 15 being within easy reach of Bath.

The Evaluation Programme

The evaluation programme currently running comprises three parts:

Cognitive Test
This has six sections of multiple-choice questions, each section covering a single module.
Attitude Test
Actual statements, made by several hundred fourth-formers about technologists, their work, the place of technology in the school curriculum, and attitudes towards industry form the basis of this test. (Page and Orr, 1978.)
Illuminative
An illuminative section was included to give an impressionistic viewpoint in addition to that of the classical statistical approach.

Information on Schools

Basic information about each school was entered on a form and included details such as: department(s) responsible for running the course; industrial experience (if any) of staff; option modules offered; number of GCE and CSE entrants expected.

Module Popularity

The popularity of the modules can be determined from Table 1. This information could be useful when deciding on the apparatus that should be stocked by the Science and Technology Centres and the quantity of resource packages to be produced.

Option Module	School																No of schools choosing option	Total no of pupils studying option
	A	B	C	D	E	F	G	H	I	J	K	L	M	N	O	P		
Electronics	*	*		*	*		*	*			*	*		*	*		10	487
Optical Instruments	*																1	31
Aeronautics				*			*				*						3	138
Mechanisms		*		*				*			*			*	*		6	318
Numbers studying modular courses	31	31		82	64		34	60			40	40		27	78			487

Notes (i) Table refers to Avon/Bath University Modules
  (ii) Figures correct at 20.1.79
  (iii) Blank column = school not yet visited

Table 1. *Module popularity*

Pupil Numbers

Table 2 shows the total pupil numbers in the trial schools visited. It is pertinent to note the 1978-79 figures for school M: unless 20 pupils opt for a course it is not permitted to run; in 1978 only 14 pupils opted for the Technology programme and it did not start.

Interviews — Staff

The initial interviews were wide ranging in order to obtain a broad picture. The interviews were recorded for transcribing later. The main areas discussed included:

(a) Internal and external support.
(b) Resource backing (finance and materials).
(c) Teaching philosophy and approach.
(d) Workload (staff and pupils).
(e) Time constraints.
(f) Level of pre-knowledge required of pupils (and staff).
(g) Reactions to individual modules.
(h) Suggestions for improvement.
(i) Course material comments.

Teachers are interviewed initially on a one-to-one basis and then as a group, where two or more teachers are involved with the course. The group interview has been particularly effective when querying how much support is forthcoming from the senior staff of a school. An individual is often reluctant to criticize the management policies of his school, but if he feels that he has support from his departmental colleagues then his reticence fades and a useful insight can be gained into how the school works.

Support

We discovered that the level of support from senior staff in schools ranged from excellent to indifferent: 'Excellent support from Head . . . He took me (Head of

School	No of Pupils on Course		Total on Course
	1977-78 (5th Year)	1978-79 (4th Year)	
A	27 (2G)	31	58
B	19	12 (2G)	31
C	17	14	31
D	55 (2G)	30	85
E	40	42 (2G)	82
F	28	36 (2G)	64
G	36 (6G)	17	53
H	16	18 (1G)	34
I	20	40 (1G)	60
J			
K			
L	23 (7G)	17	40
M	40	NIL	40
N	46	33	79
O	9	18	27
P	38 (2G)	40 (2G)	78
Totals	414 (19G)	348 (10G)	762

Notes (i) Table refers to Avon/Bath University Scheme
(ii) Figures correct at 20.1.79
(iii) Blank row = school not yet visited

Table 2. *Number of pupils studying modular courses in technology*

Department) and other staff on a trip to the Continent to see how they tackled technology over there'. 'Our Headmaster is, to put it kindly, rather neutral . . . we have to find our support where we can.'

Evidence exists that the County Careers Service in certain areas is not fully aware of the standards and aims of the course. Unlike the established and well-known courses which are recognized by parents and employers, a new course may be an unknown quantity to the Careers Service.

The support from the Innovators/Organizers was criticized by some teachers. A successful of exchange of ideas between schools was organized for March 1979 as a direct result of these reactions.

Resources

Several schools were very critical of the small amount of money available to them for implementing what can be an expensive course. The average capitation allowance was around £150 — this is seen to be inadequate when, for example, the recommended electronics kits are £50 *each*. The individual project component lists at one school averaged £3 per pupil and there were 36 pupils involved.

Teaching Philosophy and General Approach

Some teachers felt that the suggested teaching approach restricted them in their performance in class. One teacher was worried that the teaching approach forced teachers: '. . . to operate within very narrow limits — it does not allow for "opportunism" in the classroom'. Another teacher said: 'An interesting point comes up and we discuss its relevance, but by the end of the allocated time *(period)* I find that because of the diversion we haven't fully covered the laid down part of the syllabus.'

From these remarks it can be seen that some of the modules are over-loaded in spite of the fact that they were designed by experienced teachers. It could be argued that the pressure to finish the syllabus within the allocated time period is affecting the 'natural' style of certain teachers so that they perceive the course as too structured and constraining. However, it should be remembered that these were trial materials being used for the first or second time only.

Workload

This can be looked at from two angles: that of the teacher and that of the pupil. So far the majority of interviews have been with teachers.

There is evidence that unfamiliarity with the contents of some of the modules causes a lack of confidence amongst staff. Some have openly admitted that they have to spend considerable time at weekends and during vacation 'mugging-up' so that they can acquaint themselves with the subject matter. Virtually all teachers are in favour of In-Service Education of Teachers Courses based specifically on module syllabuses.

Worksheet/Laboratory Preparation

'The lack of readers meant that "X" had to spend considerable time making his own worksheets.' 'It produces a workload out of all proportion to its timetable allocation.'

Worksheets are part of the resource package. It is clear that these have not been received by some schools.

Problems Arising with Mathematics

Considerable criticism was levelled at the standard of mathematics shown by pupils. 'I find that those who do SMP are lacking in basics. The better pupils tend to do traditional maths.' (Maths Department teacher helping on the Technology programme.) 'They seem incapable of doing the simplest things like using ratios, fractions — they always divide smaller numbers into larger, irrespective. Some can't even use a ruler!'

These comments are just some of the many made about the level of maths of pupils on the technology course. Either SMP maths is not relevant to the Technology syllabuses or the Technology course is not designed to take advantage of the new mathematics syllabuses.

Opinion expressed by Pupils on Careers in Technological/Industrial Field

The small number of interviews carried out have raised two issues:

(a) a number of pupils do not like technology and industry for reasons similar to those given by the *Guardian* essayists;

(b) of the few girls interviewed, the majority were put off technology because it was seen as a course with heavy mathematical demands 'just like physics' rather than by its association with industry.

It is interesting to note, however, that when girls do opt for the Technology course they do extremely well, usually above average. The only GCE 'A' grades in one school went to the two girls in the group.

Assumed Knowledge Level of Pupils

Several schools in our trial programme have option policies which prevent the most able students from taking the Technology course. In these schools the new courses are seen as essentially 'craft' options and therefore only suitable for the least able; 'the physics rejects' was how one teacher described his class.

The effect of the incorrect selection policy on morale of both teachers and pupils can be imagined. In such schools the pupils are simply unable to cope with the level of learning and application required. This highlights a problem for curriculum designers who produce programmes that specify minimal ability — how can they ensure that the schools chosen as trial units will follow the guidelines? Innovators have little or no control on schools which are operating inappropriately as far as testing of programme material is concerned.

We have now added a further section to the common data form to indicate the option system operating. This appears to be important in determining whether or not the school is selecting, or offering the course to, pupils of the appropriate potential.

Conclusion

At the time of writing the evaluation programme has not progressed as far as was hoped because of events beyond our control. The majority of these could not have been predicted (eg severe weather, industrial disputes).

The initial teacher-and-pupil interviews should be completed soon. The views of employers will be sought to see how well holders of GCE or CSE Technology perform on apprenticeship or similar training schemes. A start has been made on follow-up studies of pupils who have either continued with full-time studies (school or further education) or entered industry. The views of school and college staff will be obtained on the performance of pupils who have used their GCE or CSE in Technology to enter courses at an advanced level. (There is already evidence that some colleges are willing to accept GCE or CSE Technology as an alternative to Physics or Engineering Science.)

As already indicated, option schemes can produce problems for both course designers and evaluators. If we accept that the main purpose of the trial programme is to establish whether the objectives of the course can be met by pupils who meet the recommended minimum level of competency, then how relevant is the data collected from schools where pupils do not meet this standard? It can be argued that if pupils from the latter schools fail to obtain at least a grade 3 CSE then the designers' decision to recommend minimum standards has been vindicated. On the other hand it might be said that if such pupils show improvement, however slight, in technological appreciation and understanding (in spite of their lower entry level) then the course has had the desired effect.

Obviously project directors, co-ordinators and evaluators have no control on decisions made in schools. Gross, Giacquinta and Bernstein (1971) state that a major obstacle to curriculum innovation is the '. . . existence of organizational arrangements . . . that . . . (are) incompatible with the innovation.' In view of the lack of uniformity in the option schemes of the trial schools it could be argued that trial schools should have been limited to those which see Technology as complementary to, rather than in competition with, traditional science subjects.

How far should the evaluator attempt to influence the decisions made in future years? Can the evaluation reports be written in a brief and concise form to be circulated to Headmasters and Advisers? The evaluation was technically required by the Schools Council. Are two different reports required? Readers of evaluation reports are not always trained interpreters of statistical data: ' . . . the value of experimental evaluation to different interest groups is limited by . . . the form in which its results are published.' (Munro, 1977). Hence, a more readable form of reporting is often desirable so that decision-makers who are not statisticians are kept fully informed. The report of our aspect of the work should highlight the feelings, attitudes and expectations of the staff and pupils who are using the course materials.

References

Gross, N, Giacquinta, J and Bernstein, M (1971) *Implementing Organizational Innovations,* p 199. Harper & Row, London.
Harper, R (1978) Modular courses in technology. *Schools Council Newsletter,* 27.
Munro, R G (1977) *Innovation: Success or Failure?* pp 20, 21. Hodder and Stoughton, London.
Page, R and Orr, M (1978) Attitudes to technology. *School Technology,* pp 14-15.
Page, R (1978) A modular 'O' level/CSE course in technology. *Studies in Design Education and Craft,* 10, 2, pp 91-99.
Thomas, H (1977) Why work in industry? 22 June 1977. The *Guardian.*

Workshop Report
School's Council Modular Courses in Technology

In order to give members of the Conference an opportunity to see the contents of the Modular Courses, the workshop was organized by Dr Harris and Mr Watts on a 'self-help' basis. The materials used in the modules (teacher's guide, pupil reader and worksheets) and some of the experimental work were available for inspection.

The following modules were available:

Energy, Problem Solving, Materials Technology, Electronics (two versions), Mechanisms, Pneumatics, Aeronautics, Optical Instruments, Instrumentation, Electrical Applications, Acoustics, Structures, Technology and Man.

Members of the workshop spent as much or as little time on each module as they wished. The two workshop leaders explained and elaborated as requested.

Section 6:
Applications in Tertiary Education

6.0 Introduction

ETIC '79 Tracks

The papers in this Section come from all three Tracks. Nunan (6.1), Scholl (6.2) and Wood (6.3) were presented in Track 1, 'Self-Instructional programmes in Practice'. Race (6.4) featured in Track 2, 'Learning Design'. Green, E E (6.5) and Hills/Moyes (6.6) were presented in Track 3, 'Learning Environment, Practice and Presentation Techniques'.

Categories and Special Interests

All six papers and McDonald's workshop (6.7) were coded 'Tert' for 'Tertiary Education'. Scholl also had a 'MeDes' coding, for 'Media Design' at Sheffield. Two of the papers, Wood and Green, E E, and also McDonald's workshop, were concerned with learning strategies and therefore were additionally coded 'Strats'.

Two other special interests also come through strongly in this Section. Nunan and Wood are particularly concerned with teacher training — and so had a 'TTr' coding at ETIC '79 — while Race and Hills and Moyes both have a special science teaching interest.

Links with Other Sections

Readers with a particular interest in Section 6 are also likely to be interested in the following contributions from other sections:

Section 1: Mitchell (1.1), Soremekun (1.5), Trueman and Hartley (1.6).
Section 2: Holmberg (2.1), Megarry (2.2), Noble (2.3), Green, B (2.4).
Section 3: Moakley (3.1), Hartley and Trueman (3.2), Pettman (3.4)
Section 4: Wilkinson (4.5).
Section 8: Cooper and Lockwood (8.2), Black (8.6).
Section 9: Scobbie and McAleese (9.3).
Section 10: Walsh (10.6).

6.1 Educational Technology for the Teacher Education Curriculum

E Nunan
Salisbury College of Advanced Education, South Australia

Abstract: All teachers know something about audio-visual aids; few teachers express the desire to know anything about educational technology. All teachers are interested in teaching methods; few teachers are motivated to investigate techniques of instructional design.

While teacher training institutions endorse the relevance of courses in educational technology there is little evidence of the application of such courses during student-teaching practice or internship periods. Further, in schools the practice of educational technology is limited to a few enthusiasts.

Yet it is not that the various items of hardware or software, the production techniques, or the methodological aspects inherent in the application of educational technology are regarded by teachers as useless — indeed, most teachers are acutely aware of the stimulus provided by visual materials and the instructional possibilities inherent in the media.

How are we to explain the perceived irrelevance of educational technology? Consumer resistance? Laziness? Inability to comprehend a body of new knowledge? Or is an explanation to be found in the rejection by teachers of the management ideology of educational technology? And what are the implications of this perceived irrelevance for the role of educational technology in the curriculum of teacher education?

For some time now I have been involved with the educational side of educational technology. At the level of specialist 'training' or indoctrination into the ideologies and beliefs of the professional practising educational technologist (whatever the current re-vamped image resulting from the last identity crisis[1]), I am often interested to the extent of watching the various fads and fashions reflected in the values portrayed by professional conferences and journals. A much more important and vital area, to me at least, is the educational aspect of informing classroom teachers of the supposed relevance of a field of study which purports to provide practical and theoretical information on 'the design, application, evaluation and development of systems, methods and materials to improve the process of human learning'.[2]

Given this impressive and encompassing definition, one imagines hordes of pre-service trainee teachers and practising teachers, ravenous for such information, flocking to courses in educational technology. One also expects to see restructured teacher-trainee courses in which the study and practice of educational technology form a substantial and central core of the training given to pre-service teacher trainees. Throughout the universities and other tertiary institutions which offer teacher training one also expects to come across recognition of the relevance of such a body of knowledge by finding specialist departments in the technology of education — just as one might find sections labelled the philosophy, sociology, psychology or history of education.

How do we (from the educational technologist's viewpoint) explain away the present lip-service paid to educational technology that is often encountered within teacher training institutions or the view of much of the traditional university establishment that educational technologists are 'latter-day oil prospectors of the academic world'?[3] How do we account for the apparent irrelevance of this subject to teachers (excepting the one or two committed enthusiasts within each school)?

In my experience, the answer is not to be found in supplying further and more extensive training in compulsory courses in educational technology or in short term schemes to instruct in programmed instruction, individualization, or the like. Instead, some understanding of this situation can be gained through investigating the ideological framework of educational technology.

Ideological analysis, which attempts to underline the meanings of the values inherent in a branch of knowledge, is particularly appropriate here — one has only to look at any of the standard texts to realize that educational technology is (apart from its hardware training aspects) being presented in an ideological fashion as an attitude or collection of values which are transferred into a special type of educational action. We find that educational technology implies a shift from a predominantly intuitive attitude to teaching and learning towards a more systemic and analytical approach. Rowntree,[4] for example, maintains that educational technology is essentially a 'rational problem-solving approach to education, a way of thinking sceptically and systematically about learning and teaching'. Further, in the *British Journal of Educational Technology*, Chadwick[5] contrasts the educational technology approach with the traditional approach, noting that 'to provide the validated and co-ordinated educational materials (in the various media softwares) required for optimal organization and operation of the educational environment, the process of production of materials must also be significantly different'.

The educational technology attitude (or approach) has two prime values, both of which are facets of a management ideology. First, the processes of teaching/learning, as viewed by those who wish to manage such processes, are dissociated from the skills derived from the craft knowledge and traditions of teaching. The second supportive and interactive value relates to the separation of conception from execution — the educational technologist, as an expert in design, threatens to control production (curriculum content), the instruments of production (the hardware and software within schools or groups of schools) and indirectly styles the manner in which content is presented (often inherent in the decisions made concerning production and the instruments of production).

The rejection of this management ideology by teachers is implicit rather than explicit and in practical terms rather than theoretical argument. A theoretical articulation of this rejection can be gleaned from talking with trainee teachers and teachers who have undertaken courses in educational technology — the source of apprehension towards educational technology resides in an understanding of the two management values through their experiences of educational technology.

From their viewpoint, what at present passes for educational technology is structured from the position of those who would wish to manage rather than those involved in performing either teaching or learning. Any teacher who uses mass-produced commercially prepared software, attempts to implement a local curriculum, or begins to carry out design and production, soon comes face-to-face with the management ideology. At its simplest and most pernicious level he is often discouraged by a school administration who are led to believe that such matters are the province of experts — and educational technologists have a vested interest in maintaining this attitude (often through technological 'mystification') as their very existence may be at stake.

At the professional level, the educational technologist attempts to support his management role by employing existing theoretical studies (in psychology, communications and education) in an attempt to instantly weld together a justificatory structure which possesses its own identity. Such an amalgam, as many critics note, is yet to provide significant guidance for the practical activities of teaching/learning or curriculum development/evaluation as carried out by teachers.

At the theoretical level, the values of the management ideology are carried by the twin pillars of educational technology — behaviourism (or neo-behaviourism) and the systemic (or often systematic) approach.

Both of these concepts are dependent upon a particular view of rational conduct, where it is assumed that rational action can be pre-planned before an event begins; the notion that rationality might reside in the choices that are made as the action unfolds is rejected. (At this point, we may recall that Rowntree's conception of educational technology hinges on the notion of 'rational'.) This philosophical position entails a separation of means from ends (execution from conception, or process from purpose). The notion of description in terms of praxis is, of course denied. The view of *rational* adopted by the educational technologist is, of course, essential for a managerial ideology (where control is outside those who execute the action). Although the theoretical level of justification is important to the educational technologist (and will probably become increasingly more so) it is not really the source of power for the group.

Power springs from *control over the instruments of production* — in a very real sense it is only after this control is gained and maintained that the influence can widen to design, application, evaluation and development of forms arising from technology. (Without this hardware control, educational technology becomes educational design, curriculum, or research and evaluation.)

This control of the instruments of production is quite unimportant where an educational technologist is especially contracted for design and production by some client. Here, educational technology is essentially practised as a technique towards some end defined by a client. However, in the case of the teacher, design, and to a lesser extent, production, form part of the creative processes of teaching.

Teaching cannot be equated with a performance or presentation before students — the decisions of what to teach, to whom, at what level, in which manner, using what form of assistance, cannot be separated from the actual classroom performance. The point that teachers make is that these decisions are highly contextual — that is, the answers to these questions depend upon the teacher himself, the ability mix of his students, the content of the lessons/learning modules and the technologies employed.

Planning or design is therefore an integral part of teaching — it is no wonder that teachers are suspicious of a subject which, due to its ideological overtones, threatens to remove this vital, creative and satisfying aspect of their work. Further, to many teachers the design models applied by educational technologists display a lack of understanding of the realities of the classroom floor. Many teachers contend that, in their experience, the processes of teaching/learning cannot be completely designed for or planned — and, to apply the word design or planning to matters outside the designer's control is absurd. As people involved with teaching/learning situations, teachers well realize that they cannot, nor would they wish to, control the learners in their classroom. To such teachers the very concept of learning involves uncertainty in the sense that the two-way processes between students and teacher are beyond total control — a learning/teaching design can, at best, only be a sketch of an intention which is often abandoned during the teaching/learning process. Thus, in a very real sense rational action in a classroom resides in the choices made as the action unfolds!

This does not mean that teachers are against planning or design — what they point out is that they are against a concept of design which is too operative or mechanistic to be useful in their work context. The challenge to develop a relevant educational technology for this area is all too apparent.

The issue of control over the instruments of production has yet to surface in the context of school based production. While an interested teacher is still able to implement his design in terms of ohp transparencies, colour slides, duplicated and photostat materials and perhaps CCTV or 8mm film, the matter of access and control is unimportant. Yet, with the development of specialist in-school personnel (either library based resource officers, key teachers in educational technology, or production officers), design, production, and access become a function of these positions — there is then an immediacy in the threat that a part of the creative aspect of teaching is to be managed for the teacher.

Is it little wonder then that teachers prefer to view media hardware and the associated materials as audio-visual aids — aids, of course, that are to assist, not control, the carrying out of educational events? The decisions of when, why, how and if to use such aids is within the professional ambit of the teacher — the managerial intent of present educational technology, on the other hand, places limits upon or structures the practices and procedures of teaching/learning in ways which circumvent such decisions.

To be of relevance to the teacher, educational technology must relate to the realities of the classroom floor as they are seen by those who work upon it — that is, a body of knowledge and technique must be derived from educational practices rather than the theoretical positions which justify an ideology.

Given this analysis, what can now be said concerning the place for educational technology in the curriculum of teacher education?[6]

At the theoretical level the challenge for a relevant educational technology must be met — this involves the development of an alternative educational technology which rejects exclusive commitment to the values inherent in the management ideology. On the practical level, it involves the demonstration and acting out of its theoretical level in terms of the curriculum and its implementation.

The guiding principle for such a curriculum in educational technology for teacher education is that the application of both technique and theoretical knowledge occurs within a given context and involves both the physical and philosophical traditions of the activities of teaching and learning as perceived by those involved in the activity.

However, to outline the application of this principle, it is useful to introduce two terms which can be used to describe and analyze the application of educational technology to the teaching/learning situation.

In a recent article[7] Roger Mansfield and I contend that for an alternative educational technology two types of precepts, operative and normative, are essential. Much of present educational technology can be viewed as an attempt to scientifically generate a set of operative precepts — rules of the type that state: 'to cause x to happen, you must do y'. The basis of this emphasis is contained in a belief of the application of explicit and rational processes to problems of human learning — the possession of knowledge about such precepts therefore justifies control over design. Educational technologists can prescribe 'y' for others as their specialist knowledge allows them to predict that 'x' will occur.

This ideological position structures a view of knowledge production, transmission and receivability. First, content is viewed in terms of list structures of hierarchical behaviours and the procedures in outlining such structures form an essential technique of educational technology. Second, the means for transmitting knowledge are prescribed in terms of message design, media selections which are consistent with 'presentation' stimuli and a careful sequencing of content in terms of hierarchical objectives. Finally, it is assumed that the packaged content is readily received by learners — the essence of instruction has been distilled into the materials through the deliberations of the first two stages.

An alternative educational technology is based upon a coming together of both operative and normative precepts; it is only when normative precepts are also present — for deciding whether to apply, reject or modify operative precepts — that the operative precepts can acquire a measure of validity. Here, normative is taken to mean concerned with the establishment of types and standards of behaviour, reflecting either activity-based traditions or philosophical stances. Thus, a judgement of what constitutes the best way of proceeding in a given educational situation rests in balancing a number of normative and operational considerations which are considered contextually – ie in terms of the specific situation in hand. Consequently, any successful application of normative precepts rests with a knowledge of practices and possible results of practices when applied to similar situations.

Now what can be said about the place for educational technology in the curriculum of teacher education? Perhaps a concrete example may assist in explaining the application of these ideas. As my experience relates to teaching educational technology at Salisbury College of Advanced Education (South Australia), for my examples I shall use the same levels of courses which are in operation there. What follows as course suggestions is not necessarily the content or intention of the present courses at Salisbury.

Educational technology is offered as a compulsory first year unit with optional studies at third and fourth year level within both the Diploma of Teaching and Bachelor of Education Awards – such courses are generally undertaken by pre-service trainee teachers. As well as this, Salisbury College of Advanced Education offers a one year full-time nationally accredited Graduate Diploma in Educational Technology undertaken by graduates (either University degree, basic teacher-education award, or equivalent) which has been developed to train educational technologists (or educational media specialists) from all parts of the community.

A course at the first year level (for non specialists) which is structured from the viewpoint of an alternative technology would look very much like an audio-visual aids familiarization course. The reason for this antiquated course structure which deals primarily with operative precepts (mostly related to equipment operation) is that students at this level lack the classroom experience necessary for an understanding of normative aspects. If possible, this course should mesh with other courses such as general methods or micro-teaching so that students might gain some appreciation of the contextual nature of decisions which are made in the classroom. Where production is attempted, this could well be done without reference to such things as behavioural objectives, media selection or evaluation – here, the emphasis is not so much on design but upon integrating production as an application of learned techniques within some real or simulated problem. At this level, educational technology is more the application of technology in education and directed towards methods and materials. It is to be hoped that at this level all aspiring teachers are provided with a range of skills which are relatively free from the theoretical aspects of design, evaluation, and systems thinking.

At third and fourth year levels there is clearly more scope for building upon such a foundation – however, such courses might well be described as curriculum development exercises. The course should be school-based to the extent of insisting that a number of productional possibilities be justified in terms of a specific teaching/learning climate and evaluative procedures applied to processes or materials after testing within a school. A feature of such a course would be the application of technology within a curriculum episode where justification of the various design, implementation and evaluation decisions is dependent upon both normative and operative precepts. For example, media selection and design might be argued for in terms of the demands of operative models (such as Tosti and Ball's) and competing normative precepts (that a particular curriculum has as a part of its internal structure as a particular view of learning). Such issues are often brought into the open when one considers the questions surrounding the evaluation/measurement of teaching/learning. However, the important point at this level is that educational technology is understood through attempting to deal with the practical problems that teachers face when attempting to implement or design (for internal consumption) curricula. The normative aspects arise naturally from a consideration of the best way to proceed in a given circumstance – the student now begins to get practice at balancing normative and operational considerations within specific boundaries.

At our last level of Graduate Diploma it is arguable whether students ought merely to receive the management ideology. Sociologically, the existence of a profession is dependent upon a form of indoctrination into the values of the profession. Yet, even at this level, given that many such students are to manage in an educational context (and not contract themselves to government, business, the military etc) I would support an analysis of the professional ideology as a part of the course. Thus, while any such course structure at this level might feature prescriptive and operative precepts derived from behaviourism, systems analysis, resource management, diffusion and innovation and the like, their application in something as complex as a school, group of schools, or education authority depends upon normative considerations, and, as Norman McKenzie[8] notes, how is educational technology to deal with questions of value?

The answer to this question, especially in a field such as education whose primary concern is values, is to admit such questions into our concerns, perhaps beginning with the most pressing need to acknowledge this in courses in educational technology for pre-service trainee teachers and teachers.

References

1 see, for example, McKenzie, N (1976) A crisis of identity. *British Journal of Educational Technology*, 7, 1, pp 4-6.
2 definition adopted by the Australian Society of Educational Technology.
3 Bonham, G W (1976) Educational media: a mixed bag. *Change*, 8, 3, pp 32-34.
4 Rowntree, D (1974) *Educational Technology in Curriculum Development*. Harper and Row, London.
5 Chadwick, C (1973) Educational technology: progress, prospects and comparisons. *British Journal of Educational Technology*, 4, 2, pp 80-94.
6 for another approach, see Collier, K G (1977) Educational technology and the curriculum of teacher education. *British Journal of Educational Technology*, 8, 1, pp 5-11.
7 Mansfield, R L and Nunan, E E (1978) Towards an alternative educational technology. *British Journal of Educational Technology*, 9, 3, pp 170-176.
8 McKenzie, N (1976) *British Journal of Educational Technology*, 7, 5.

6.2 Mediated Self-Instruction: Its History and Continuing Development at the University of Connecticut

P Scholl
University of Connecticut

Abstract: Mediated programming at the University of Connecticut was developed by Dr David Curl between 1962 and 1964. Black and white photographic prints with typewritten captions were developed into copy flats. The medium used was 2x2 slides supplemented by regular 8mm loop film. Color was used where it seemed important. No audio sound information was developed. These early programmes are now being replaced by programmes which use different mediums. Synchronized sound/slide presentations (with and without programme stop and synchronous reverse) are used, as are one page printed instruction sheets and audio-cassette information programmes. Some problems which have been encountered can be overcome. These include scheduling problems, student reluctance to learn alone and laboratory upkeep. Other problems, such as the high development costs and adequate time for criterion testing, require a philosophical mind set. The advantages outweigh the problems, however, and programmed instruction use will continue to expand at the University of Connecticut.

The Beginning

Over the last two decades, research into and discussions about the variables of programmed instruction have been far reaching. Should rules follow examples or vice versa? Is it best for a learner to construct an answer, choose an answer, think an answer or merely read an answer? These questions, among others, have been widely researched and the answers have not been clear cut. Even the value of behavioural objectives has not been universally accepted. In spite of the lack of significant research findings a practical example of programmed instruction has been quietly operating for the past 15 years in the Center for Instructional Media and Technology at the University of Connecticut.

Dr David Curl established the Mediated Self-Instruction Laboratory between 1962 and 1964 as a service to the University of Connecticut School of Education. His interest in, and expertise with, this type of instruction was a result of his need to teach photography to foreign students who had a minimal command of the English language. Combining the concepts of programming, sequenced pictures and visual cueing with teaching machines, Dr Curl arrived at a practical solution to his very real problem. The solution — Mediated Self-Instruction — was so successful it led to additional programmes and eventually to the programmes at the University of Connecticut.

Dr Curl's programming technique uses black and white photographs, cued by the application of colour, arrows, lines and enlargements of critical components. It uses printed verbal information when this is appropriate. Reproduced as 2x2 35mm slides, the pictorial-verbal material is presented by rear screen projection to minimize problems for the learners.

The Mediated Self-Instruction Laboratory at the University of Connecticut was established to teach students the operation of basic audio-visual equipment. It served as a model for two additional learning centers at the University. Faculty members from other departments within the University visited the CIMT laboratory for ideas. Their observations, combined with information available at professional meetings and from professional literature during the late 60s and early 70s, convinced them of the practical applications for mediated instruction.

Funds have, for a number of years, been available from various federal agencies to increase the effectiveness of instruction in science and health related areas. Many innovative programmes received this outside funding. With the staff from the Self-Instruction Laboratory acting as consultants, the Schools of Pharmacy and Nursing each established a Learning Center. Each school chose a different method of obtaining its programmed material, and each chose a different way of staffing its Center.

The Learning Center at the School of Pharmacy was established in one large room. Commercial carrels were purchased and comfortable chairs provided. Extra electrical capacity was provided to take care of the needs of both the presentation equipment and additional equipment which might be used at the learning stations such as microscopes, test equipment, etc.

The School of Pharmacy decided to purchase some basic programmes, but to make primary use of audio-taped lectures by the school's own faculty. Because the school has an extensive print library, the decision was made to operate the Learning Center with a part-time media professional and graduate assistants.

The School of Nursing Learning Center was constructed to much the same specifications. Commercial carrels, comfortable seating and acoustic control, including carpeting were provided. In addition, the Center has an area constructed and equipped to simulate a hospital room. Hospital beds and other items simulate the conditions under which the students will work when they start their practical experience in a hospital.

The School of Nursing was able to employ a full-time administrator for its Learning Center. The Media Specialist is a registered nurse who has graduate training in Media. Primary use is made of commercially prepared programme material. Nursing faculty members are expected to preview and recommend for purchase those mediated materials which directly relate to their area of instruction.

The Present

The operation of the Pharmacy Learning Center is supervised by a part-time professional who has a Master's Degree in Instructional Media. This person supervises the graduate assistants and provides the technical and administrative expertise needed to operate the Learning Center. Graduate assistants operate the check out system for audio-tapes and other programmed material which has been purchased. The Learning Center is capable of presenting all media formats.

Operating the School of Nursing Center involves reviewing commercial materials and adding acceptable programmes to the existing collection. Many of these are in the sound filmstrip format. However, the Center is capable of presenting sound-slides, motion pictures, film loops, and ¾-inch color video cassettes. The software in this collection dictates the hardware which must be available in the Center.

Most of the early programmes used in the Mediated Self-Instruction Laboratory have been replaced with new ones. However, a few of the original programmes have proved to be so basic, useful and valuable that they are still very much in use. The newer programmes teach the operation of late model standard audio-visual media hardware.

The principal clients for the Self-Instruction Laboratory are pre-service teacher training students in the University of Connecticut School of Education. Using the laboratory is an activity that produces indirect as well as direct learning. Variety of experience is therefore highly desirable. In the interests of variety and efficiency, recently developed programmes use different formats.

One well-used format is the sound/slide presentation. Directions are posted at all the learning stations and students quickly learn to operate the self-contained sound/slide presentation equipment. These programmes all incorporate a spoken *stop* command so students can halt the programme to complete a learning task which requires an extended period of time to complete.

The newest programmes are also sound/slide presentations, but the cassette equipment has digital control which provides a review feature. Students can reverse the programme and maintain synchronization of audio-track and slides.

While some of the programmes become more sophisticated, others become simpler. It became apparent, as a result of informal experimentation, that students could understand how to produce a thermal transparency using printed instructions. The mechanical operation is trivial. It is the knowledge of which writing materials produce the best images and which produce no image at all that is the important learning outcome. Printed directions and a prepared master are adequate for this purpose.

Another piece of equipment which requires only simple programme materials is the ubiquitous and widely used cassette recorder. A set of visual instructions showing how to load the programme cassette and an additional tape for practice purposes is sufficient to teach students about this piece of equipment.

A supervisor is always available to take care of the operational problems which inevitably arise in a laboratory. He helps students who may have a problem interpreting a programme, provides assistance in case of equipment malfunction and maintains a clean and orderly learning environment in the laboratory.

Mediated Self-Instruction does have some problems. It appears to be impossible to produce the perfect programme. No singe one; however much revised, has been able to meet all the individual differences found in a large population of students. In a laboratory which tries to teach students how to operate mechanical equipment, the naive student who has had very little or no contact with mechanical aids illustrates the problem. This student cannot operate without specific, detailed and flawless instructions. He or she becomes totally and absolutely dependent on the programme. The perfection required of a programme under these conditions seems to be beyond the comprehension of those who take mechanical things for granted.

Some students, on the other hand, think they have no need for the instruction being presented and therefore fail to read the printed directions. Some even fail to make any use whatsoever of the programme. As in all instructional enterprises, motivation plays a critical role.

It is difficult to incorporate the technique of fading into the short programme. Without cue reduction, some students become dependent on the programmes for their performance. As a practical matter, they must be actively encouraged to operate the equipment without the programme. When learning a criterion, students know they cannot use the programme to take the test. Knowing the examination criteria, they can test themselves.

Very few students like to learn completely by themselves. Although the laboratory is arranged so that students can work by themselves at each learning station, most prefer to learn with a friend. They want interaction with others who will help them interpret the directions and give them confidence. Most understand they must actually work with the equipment and therefore they alternate with their learning partner each time they use the programme.

The Future

The future of programmed instruction at the University of Connecticut will depend on a number of factors. Unfortunately, the primary factor will not be the effectiveness of the Laboratory and the Learning Centers but will be the amount of money available, and the commitment and availability of media and programming professionals.

US federal funds are becoming less available to educational institutions. The 1980s, according to demographic information, will be a time of declining enrolments in higher education and this will also lead to a decline in budgets. Money is, unquestionably, at the root of programme development. Creative time, production time, try-out time and revision time are all expensive, and an enormous amount of this time is required for the programming process. The investment can be justified if the programmes are basic to a curriculum or if they will be used by a large number of students over a long period of time. Techniques and information which change often and drastically will not be programmed unless very large numbers of students are involved.

Both the School of Pharmacy and the School of Nursing are approaching the end of grants that established and then maintained their programmes for the past five years. The validity of these programmes has been established beyond question. As, and when funds can be made available from various sources, these programmes will expand. Lacking additional funds, the programmes will be maintained at their present level because the faculty has become accustomed to having this type of learning opportunity available to their students.

At the Center for Instructional Media and Technology, the character of the work will change. Over the last couple of years, the pressure to operate the laboratory on an extended schedule for large numbers of students has been reduced. The lighter operating schedule allows more time for research. Research activities provide growth opportunities for the professional staff and also provide practical information to be shared with other schools and departments. New programmes are being developed for Instructional Media classes and the emphasis is on finding the most efficient programmes possible to help students learn mechanical operations and develop an intellectual understanding.

Efficiency does not necessarily dictate that the least expensive programmes will be produced and put into operation. The more expensive reversing programmes may require only one presentation for complete learning, whereas the non-reversing programmes may require more than one presentation for adequate learning. All the reversing programmes now in operation have digital counters to determine how often this feature is used under actual operating conditions. Records are being kept with a view to selecting the most efficient programme technique for each operation.

Mediated Self-Instruction at the University of Connecticut has been successful and is accepted by the faculty. It has been successful because it reliably facilitates the learning outcomes instructors expect. The Laboratory and Learning Centers will grow as funds are available. The staff of the Mediated Self-Instruction Laboratory in the Center for Instructional Media and Technology will continue to work to maintain its leadership in innovative mediated programming.

6.3 A Modular System of Self-Instruction in Educational Technology within a Course of Teacher Training

Alan Wood
Bolton College of Education (Technical)

Abstract: This paper describes the organization, application and implications of the rationale of educational technology within a course of teacher training. A comparison is made between the existing course and a course using the techniques of educational technology to teach the teacher trainees. Self-instructional modules incorporating flowcharts, algorithms and the management technique of network analysis were based upon a systematic analysis of the learning process and a setting of specific objectives for the tasks involved.

The Systems Approach to Learning

The problem of instruction can be treated as a systems concept, and a systematic approach has been developed among others, by CERI (1971), Edney (1972), Gane (1972), Gerlach and Ely (1971) and Romiszowski (1974). The process of education may be seen to require an engineering approach. While teachers do not normally think of themselves as engineers, what they do when they plan and carry out instruction is, in a sense, a type of engineering. In short, the teacher's task is to design and develop an educational environment within which students can learn efficiently.

From this point of view the various media, both non-projected or projected, should be examined in terms of the instructional functions they perform. The more functions a teacher can perform, the more adaptive he can be. A primary aim of the educational technology modules within the course of teacher training with which this report is concerned was, therefore, a systematic and practical study of the ways in which the modern media of communication could extend and improve teaching and learning. A secondary aim was to be effective but simple in methods of presentation for the areas to be covered by the studies. The need was to develop a design for an educational technology module which would specify, with minimum uncertainty, the objectives for the teacher trainees and would interrelate all facets of the system to achieve the objectives. It was thought that proven management techniques used in areas other than education could perhaps facilitate pre-planning and management of the proposed system by the tutors and the teacher trainees and reduce the possibility of uncertainty and error due to the sole reliance on verbal descriptions. More effective use of the audio-visual facilities could possibly be developed if such processes were systematically programmed into the instructional module. Hence, algorithms, networks and modified flow-charts were included in a *Student Task Book for Educational Technology*.

In the limited time allocated (periods of 50 minutes) for the educational technology workshop modules, continuous prose was not considered appropriate in outlining the rationale of educational technology or determining the student's needs or pre-knowledge in various areas and aspects of the subject. Consequently, algorithms were incorporated within the text relating to objectives, selection of media and use of the college library.

The advantages of the algorithm over using continuous prose are: (a) a saving in time, (b) the user is required to make a series of explicit decisions, usually of a binary nature (yes/no), about a limited series of discrete questions, (c) the user can reach a conclusion about a specific issue by making only the minimum necessary decisions. In the initial 'start' algorithm, feedback to tutors has been incorporated by asking the trainees to record their individual responses. By using this approach to instruction for teacher trainees it was anticipated that the alternative methods outlined and used in their training situation could be generalized to other situations and subject matter areas in which a teacher seeks to communicate with others. The technique of Network Analysis was utlized to show the logical pattern of the tasks to be carried out by trainees in the workshop sessions together with associated lectures. Networking of the educational technology course incorporated within teacher training enables tutors and trainees to view all aspects as a whole and not as individual compartments, each separate from the other. This rationalization points out the logical step sequence of a teaching pattern for tutors and pinpoints the immediate essentials required by trainees to establish a firm foundation to their own individual learning process.

Individual Instruction

Individualized and self-instructional methods were considered to be an integral part of the methods of learning by the trainees. An important premise to the fact that the trainees will perhaps only apply methods if they learned from them themselves was that student teachers will themselves become innovators.

Consequently, the Student Task Book was prepared with these objectives in view and was compiled so that each student could be given guide-lines as to the effective operation of equipment. This is an objective for all to achieve, but in view of the variety of disciplines taught by the students, ie Mathematics, Business Studies, Nursing, Engineering, Building, General Studies, the more general objective was for a student to participate in his own education in relation to his own subject matter area and to perceive alternative methods of communication. The needs of the individual were to be catered for within a group learning situation.

The questions that follow can be asked of any instructional system, to determine the degree to which the system pays attention to the needs of the individual student. They are applicable to the project described in this report. The answers expected of such an instructional system that is attentive to the needs of the individual student are given after each question.

(a)	Are written instructional objectives given to the student?	YES
(b)	Are all the students expected to achieve the same objective at the same time?	NO
(c)	Do all students use the same instructional materials?	NO
(d)	Are all students expected to follow the same procedure while in the classroom?	NO
(e)	Do all students work at each subject for the same amount of time?	NO
(f)	Do students spend most of their workshop time doing what everyone else is doing?	NO

The students are guided in the decision-making process. Despite his imperfect self-knowledge, a student knows more about himself than the tutor does. No teacher or educational technologist is an expert in all areas of teaching. Therefore, to come closest to selecting the most appropriate materials, procedures, times and objectives in a particular area with a particular population, the student himself must do a large part of the selecting. The questions that follow bear on this aspect of an individualized instruction system. Again, the answers given indicate how well the instructional system is individualized.

☐	May the student decide which materials he will use in trying to achieve an objective?	YES
☐	May the student decide which procedures he will follow in attempting to achieve an objective?	YES
☐	May the student decide how much time he will devote to an activity?	YES

The above statements are consistent with the philosophy espoused by the Learning Resources Unit of BCE(T) even within the constraints of a technologically intensive workshop module based upon effective operation of multi-media equipment.

While it might seem to some that educational technology and the casting of the teacher into a role as one who diagnoses and then directs a student to suitable learning resources forestalls a teacher's development as a teacher, it may be in practice that it will free the teacher's time to do things that the older system did not permit.

Outline of the Project

During the academic year 1976-77, 342 teacher trainees at BCE(T) were taught the concepts and principles of educational technology and the operation of various items of equipment. Approximately half the number of trainees were taught this module of training using a self-instructional package in book form, the remainder by the existing college method.

The aim of the project was to relate these two methods to the trainees' faculties (Arts or Science) and to their initial attitude to educational technology, also to compare, irrespective of faculty and attitude, the success of the self-instructional and existing methods.

All trainees were tested for initial attitude to educational technology prior to commencement of instruction. A pre-test was administered to determine trainees' pre-knowledge of the concepts and principles to be taught. No standardized tests were available with norms for this population. A questionnaire designed by Hartley (1971) to measure teachers' attitudes to new educational media, was utilized. The pre-test was compiled by the writer in conjunction with colleagues. The trainees were randomly assigned to faculty groups for instruction. The groups were then randomly assigned to treatments, either experimental or control. The treatment for the experimental group, which was the self-instructional package containing specific objectives for the instruction, was compiled by the writer. Due to absence, trainee numbers were reduced to 328. In the interests of good internal design these were further reduced by randomization to 288 for the purpose of the statistical design.

In a 2x2x2 factorial design Analysis of Variance the sample population was categorized into two groups, Arts and Sciences. Each trainee was ranked in accordance with his attitude rating — above-median *favourable,* and below-median *unfavourable.* Each faculty group was sub-divided and randomized into four further groups. Two groups from each section were instructed using the self-instructional methods and the remaining four groups, two from each Section, were instructed using the existing college method.

The pre-test was used as a post-test. Using post-test scores a factorial analysis of variance showed the first order methods by attitudes interaction to be significant at the 5 per cent level and the main effects of methods significant at the 1 per cent level. (Refer to Table 1.)

Source	Ss	df	V	F
Between Methods	22.2222	1		15.0099**
Between Faculties	7.3472	1		4.9626
Between Attitudes	12.5000	1		8.4430**
Methods x Faculties	0.0556	1		0.0375
Methods x Attitudes	10.1252	1		6.8390*
Faculties x Attitudes	1.3883	1		0.9380
Method x Faculties x Attitudes	1.1246	1		0.7596
Residual	414.5559	280	1.4805	
Totals	469.3195	287		

** $<$1% level   * $<$5% level

Total Scores

Arts		M1	M2
	F	161	149
	U	160	130

Science		M1	M2
	F	172	171
	U	170	133

	M1	M2
Ar	321	279
Sc	342	304

	M1	M2
F	333	320
U	330	263

	Ar	Sc
F	310	343
U	290	303

Each total is the sum of 72 scores

M1	663
M2	583

Ar	600
Sc	646

F	653
U	593

Overall total

1246

M1 — Experimental M2 — Control F — Favourable attitude U — unfavourable attitude

Table 1. *Analysis of variance of post-test scores*
(From: Lewis, 1968, p 115)

An analysis of covariance was carried out to determine the significance of differences between methods and between attitudes and methods using the pre- and post-test scores, the scores on the pre-test being used as the basis for adjustment.

A comparison between the self-instructional method and the existing course method showed overall mean gains which were highly significant for the former method for both Arts and Science trainees possessing an initial attitude unfavourable to new media.

Favourable attitudes toward new media as predictive of attainment ability although not significant denote the superiority of trainees in the above-median attitude range over those in the below-median attitude range. This superiority in performance was irrespective of faculty.

Design of the Project

Groups							
M1F		M2F		M1U		M2U	
x	y	x	y	x	y	x	y

M1 — Experimental (self-instructional module)
M2 — Control (existing course)
F — Favourable attitude to new media
U — Unfavourable attitude to new media
x — Pre-test score
y — Post-test score

Table 2.

The analysis shows the overall differences among the adjusted means to be significant at the 1 per cent level. (Refer to Table 3.) Comparing trainees who had unfavourable attitudes to media, taught by the existing methods (Group M2U) with the remaining groups, the former group is inferior in attainment. Those trainees with unfavourable attitudes to new media taught by the self-instructional method (Group M1U) are superior in achievement to all other groups.

Examining the differences between groups and applying a 't' test, the difference between the experimental group with unfavourable attitude to new media (M1U) and the control group with the same attitude (M2U) is significant at the 1 per cent level. For the groups with favourable attitudes there is no significant difference in attainment. The computed values of 't' are found to be as follows:

$$(M1F - M2F)t = 0.622 \qquad \text{Not significant}$$
$$(M1U - M2U)t = 3.893 \qquad \text{Significant (1 per cent level)}$$

This is possibly indicative that the technique of systematic instructional analysis is a prerequisite in order to develop meaningful self-instructional materials, and that active participation of the learner is required at all times throughout an instructional sequence in conjunction with highly specific and measurable objectives. It is accepted, however, that individualized instruction, by a variety of means and under varied conditions, is one important component of an instructional system though by no means the only one.

Conclusions

The implication of this project is that active self-directed learning, using management techniques and principles of educational technology, enhances learning for those with initial attitudes unfavourable to educational technology. There is no evidence of attitude change.

Source of Variation	df	Σx^2	Σxy	Σy^2	$\dfrac{\Sigma xy}{\Sigma x^2}$	df	$\Sigma y^2 - \dfrac{(\Sigma xy}{\Sigma x^2}$	Mean Square
Total	287	733.9862	215.3473	569.3195	—	286	506.1378	—
Within groups	284	724.9721	196.0137	524.4723	0.2796	283	471.4752	1.6659
Between groups	3					3	34.6626	11.5542*

$* <1\%$ level

Adjusted Group Means

Group	X mean	Deviation from overall mean (2.5069)	Deviation x Regression (0.2796)	Y mean	Adjusted Y mean
M1F	2.7083	0.2014	0.0563	4.6250	4.5687
M2F	2.5416	0.0347	0.0097	4.4444	4.4347
M1U	2.5555	0.0486	0.0135	4.5833	4.5698
M2U	2.2222	-0.2847	-0.0796	3.6527	3.7323

Analysis of Covariance

X	Y	
722	1246	overall sum
2.5069	4.3263	overall mean

Table 3. *Analysis of Covariance
(variation between and within groups) (From: Lewis, D G 1978, p 172)*

Students' personality and attitudes are of importance in teacher training. If modifications to attitudes and consequently, it is hoped, behaviour are important, knowledge of initial attitudes are necessary to determine the direction of any attitude change. The implications of the predictive value of attitude to educational technology and achievement require further investigation.

During the next decade teacher training will be undergoing a radical transformation. Many establishments have already joined forces with other institutions and many will be involved in searching re-appraisals of their accustomed work. There is need for further investigation in other areas of a teacher training course; into forms of instruction of a self-instructional nature using independent study techniques and resource based learning.

This does not imply that *all* teacher training should be based on self-instructional methods. The nature of educational technology implies the opposite, for educational technology is concerned with the systematic formulation of the aims and purposes of a teacher's work; the matching of his techniques to those aims and purposes and the subsequent gauging of the effectiveness of the techniques in achieving those aims. The end product for all students is the personalization of learning.

References

CERI (1971) *Educational Technology. The Design and Implementation of Learning Systems.*
Centre for Educational Research and Innovation. OECD. HMSO, London.
Edney, P J (1972) *A Systems Analysis of Training.* Pitman, London.
Gane, C (1972) *Managing the Training Function. Using Instructional Technology and Systems Concepts.* Allen and Unwin, London.
Gerlach, V S and Ely, D P (1971) *Teaching and Media. A Systematic Approach.* Prentice-Hall Inc., New Jersey.
Lewis, D G (1968) *Experimental Design in Education.* ULP, London.
Romiszowski, A J (1974) *The Selection and Use of Instructional Media. A Systems Approach.* Kogan Page, London.

6.4 An Objective Approach to Teaching Physical Chemistry

W P Race
Polytechnic of Wales

Abstract: This paper discusses the development, use and evaluation of an extended series of objective-based semi-programmed course units in physical chemistry subject areas. The design of the course takes into account such factors as the problems often experienced by students with English language difficulties, and the need to distinguish between important concepts and more descriptive background material. The paper describes the format chosen for structured handout material, the management of the course, visual aids used, student reaction to the course, and evaluation of its effectiveness. It is believed that a similar approach may be used with advantage over a wide spectrum of science and engineering courses.

Introduction

'Physical chemistry is the hardest part of the course' is often the sentiment expressed by science and engineering students. This is partly because it is a subject which demands understanding — memory alone is of little use. Also, it requires the ability to extend known concepts to unfamiliar situations — quite advanced problem-solving skills. The situation is further complicated by the need to place physical chemistry early in any science course as its concepts and methodology are essential to the understanding of so many parts of other scientific subject areas. Therefore, in higher education at universities and polytechnics alike, new students are subjected to the rigours of physical chemistry at an early stage and the opening statement all too often reflects such students' experience.

Chemical engineering courses at present attract many students from the oil-rich nations. For most of these students the first attempt at advanced study using the English language can present serious problems. The main danger is that these students are so preoccupied with taking down 'grammatically-correct' lecture notes that they have little time left to grasp the essentials of fundamental concepts.

Before trying to model a course structure to make physical chemistry more approachable for all students it is constructive to list some of the disadvantages of the traditional lecture and the use of 'straight' handouts (ie duplicated lecture notes).

Disadvantages of Lectures

- ☐ Students have little time to think; most energies are dissipated in writing.
- ☐ There is little 'remedial' opportunity if fundamental concepts early in the course are not grasped properly.
- ☐ Students may have little idea of exactly what performance is required of them in the context of each element of study.
- ☐ Descriptive and qualitative subject areas require excessive time, leaving less time for fundamental concepts which may be far more important.

Disadvantages of Lectures with Handouts

- ☐ If handouts are issued regularly (or in advance) the tendency is for students to skip lectures when under pressure (eg writing up laboratory work) as they can obtain a copy of the handouts from friends.
- ☐ Students can 'switch off' during lectures, as the basic need to take notes is absent.

Advantages of Lectures with Handouts

However, the *advantages* of using handouts (especially in fairly basic courses) are numerous, and include:

- ☐ Students with language problems are not spending all their energies trying to write, particularly in descriptive areas.
- ☐ Much more time can be organized into talking *about* material rather than simply *generating* it; more questioning, discussing and constructive argument can take place.

Bearing in mind the above factors, let us consider the following design objectives for a physical chemistry course (and many other similar courses). The course should aim:

- ☐ to cater for students with language problems;
- ☐ to incorporate elements of objective self-assessment and testing, so that at all stages students are aware of their standard;
- ☐ to develop a form of 'structured' handout, avoiding the disadvantages of 'straight' handouts;
- ☐ to include frequent revision activities, so that the need for 'pre-exam cramming' is almost eliminated;
- ☐ to develop course materials which can be used for students at different levels and from different subject areas, by varying the pace of instruction and the content and depth of exercises;
- ☐ to enhance the coherence of theoretical work with the corresponding laboratory course (see Race, 1978).

The following is a brief description of the development and use of a series of objective-based semi-programmed course units in physical chemistry subject areas (including thermo-dynamics, chemical kinetics, electro-chemistry, etc) where the author attempts to achieve as many as possible of the above objectives.

Structure of Course Units

Firstly, each syllabus area was broken down into study objectives (and a few areas that did not 'enable the student to do something' were discarded altogether!). The objectives were then grouped into relatively self-contained sets, which would be expected to take about three-quarters of an hour to teach. Then, based on each such set of objectives, a course was designed incorporating revision and practice exercises, to take about 55 minutes altogether to teach. Each course unit was based on a structured handout (of between three and six pages) with the following features:

☐ The list of between four and seven 'Unit Objectives' to explain clearly to the student what he should be able to do after coverage of the unit.
☐ Exposition of theory, including blank spaces or graph frames, for the student to copy in diagrams, equations, etc from OHP transparencies shown during the session.
☐ Blank spaces for students individually to write answers to 'elicitation' questions posed in class.
☐ Space for practice problems to consolidate the material learned.

The handouts are duplicated on one side of the paper only, leaving the other side blank for impromptu additions students may wish to make during the sessions. The layout is planned carefully so that (for example) a new page may begin by asking questions about the material learned on the previous page. Also, if elicitation questions are posed towards the foot of a page, the correct solutions are presented at the top of the next page. At the beginning of a unit, after the objectives are stated, there is often a brief set of questions to revise prerequisite concepts from previous units; this enhances continuity through the course.

Chemical Kinetics. Unit 3

Unit Objectives: after this Unit you should be able to:
(1) list 4 factors which affect the rates of reactions;
(2) indicate the likelihood of each factor affecting the rates of reactions in general;
(3) write a *rate equation* for a general reaction;
(4) explain what is meant by the *orders* of a reaction, and the *total order* of a reaction;
(5) define the *rate constant* of a reaction in terms of the rate equation;
(6) write the dimensions of the rate constant for reactions with the following total orders: 0, 1, 2, 3.

Introductory Revision
(a) List the titles of 5 methods for measuring reaction rates.

. . . .
. . . .

(b) List 5 difficulties which can be encountered in measuring rates.

. . . .
. . . .

Exercise
Write below 4 factors or parameters which you may expect to affect the rates of reactions, and after each factor describe how likely the factor is to affect the average reaction in terms of such words as 'usually, often, always, sometimes'.
(i) . . . .
(ii) . . . .
(iii) . . . .
(iv) . . . .

Figure 1. *The first page of a typical course unit,*
showing objectives, brief revision exercises and an 'elicitation' exercise

Management of the Course

A course unit handout is issued at the start of each lecture period. At the outset of the course, it is explained that if students miss a unit (except for certified illness!) the responsibility of 'catching up' is theirs and that a spare unit will not be provided. 'The essential part is what you do with the unit during the session, not the mere possession of the handout', the students are told.

Students are asked not to 'turn the page' until told to do so, so that the value of the recall questions is maximized (ie so that they do not cheat and scan the answers in advance). In fact, after a few units students are subconsciously arming themselves with the answers to possible questions and their learning is further enhanced.

At the start of each period, the objectives are scanned and students asked to indicate by a show of hands how many of the objectives may already be achievable for them. Towards the close of the period the objectives are returned to, and at this stage class members are usually asked to demonstrate their having achieved them.

Throughout the course it is emphasized that the units are designed so that each successive unit assumes, and depends on, the objectives of previous units having been attained.

After about six of the units have been covered, an assessment exercise is issued to the class (sometimes without warning). This consists of a completion-type script, usually of three to six pages. Often, the numbers of marks available for each question are indicated, so that students gain an appreciation of the relative degree of importance of different elements of subject matter. As the answered scripts are collected, each student is issued with a 'correct solutions' duplicate of the exercise, with answers written in, so he receives immediate feedback and has both questions and answers at his disposal while his memory of his own attempt to answer is fresh.

Often, each student is asked to guess what his percentage score is for the exercise, and write in his estimate. This process proves very useful for identifying those students who have difficulties they are not aware of (they guess over 20 per cent higher than they score). In practice most of the guesses are surprisingly accurate – perhaps for many students (once the 'inaccurate guessers' are found) there is little need to mark the tests!

Since the subject matter can be covered much more rapidly when students are not writing it all out, much more time is available for revision. Toward the end of each subject course it was found useful to alternate the form of revision session around the following:

☐ Collectively attempting 'old questions' in class, with lecturer guidance.
☐ Attempting 'old questions' independently in class for 30 minutes, exchanging scripts, then marking according to the type of detailed 'micro-marking' scheme that could be used for an examination. (Students often commented that they learned more about the relative importance of material elements from such marking experience than from attempting the questions.)
☐ Assessment exercises on specified groups of units (of the kind mentioned earlier).
☐ Quiz-games (an account of some of these is to be submitted to the 1979 SAGSET Conference).

Visual Aids

Physical chemistry includes many subject areas where graphs and diagrams provide very important illustrations of concepts and system behaviour. Some – like phase diagrams – are quite complex. Since the student is to insert this kind of information into the course units, it is worth considering how best to present the

---

Thermodynamics. Assessment Exercise: Units 9-12

Name . . . . Date . . . . Mark . . . .

/5   1. Write an expression for Δs accompanying a temperature change at constant volume.

/5   2. Write an expression for Δs accompanying an isothermal expansion process.

/10   3. Write a relationship between T, ΔG, ΔH and ΔS applying to constant T and P.

/5   4. Write an expression for ΔG accompanying the reversible isothermal expansion of an ideal gas.

/10   5. Write the Gibbs-Helmholtz equation.

/5   6. Write an expression for the entropy of mixing ideal gases.

/10   7. Write the Clapeyron equation.

/10   8. Write the Clausius-Clapeyron equation, in a form suitable for graphical treatment.

/10   9. Write the 'reaction isochore' in a form suitable for graphical treatment.

/10   10. Sketch below the forms of the graphs when each of these relationships is used, and indicate on each graph the value of the slope.

/10   11. Write the reaction isotherm.

/10   12. For an electrochemical cell, write expressions in terms of the cell emf for:
$\Delta G^{\ominus}$
$\Delta S^{\ominus}$
$\Delta H^{\ominus}$

Figure 2. *The first page of a typical assessment exercise*

information to him. It is easier to understand a complex diagram if the student sees it built up step by step. This can be done using a chalkboard. However, the use of OHP transparencies with several overlays proves most effective and versatile. This method has unique advantages for oral questioning, as (for example) an overlay displaying phase field identification labels can be suddenly removed from a phase diagram, and the class can be questioned about the missing labels. Care is taken to make the transparencies colourful, and often colour codes are used to aid classification of categories of information.

For one particular area of the syllabus, instead of using home-made transparencies, the professional expertise of a graphic designer was used, giving transparencies of high quality. Students were then asked whether the quality transparencies had improved the impact of the subject matter. Most thought the transparencies more memorable; all students indeed spent longer transcribing into their own units the transcriptions reflecting the neatness and balance of the transparencies. However, it is still quite possible that in the long run students find it more meaningful to emulate lecturer-drawn diagrams, rather than professionally drawn.

Evaluation of the Course

From the assessment exercises set at various stages it was clear that after a settling-in period of a few weeks students showed consistent performance standards, which improved as the course progressed. Because high-flyers were rewarded by percentage scores around 90, even they found sufficient incentive to improve, and it was not unusual to find one or two near-perfect answers to any exercise. More important, the extra time made available for revision and practice allowed remedial work with students finding particular difficulties.

Emphasis has been laid on the ability to achieve the objectives equating with the potential to excel in the examination at the end of the course. Examination results have been even better than expected, with very few students emerging from the course without at least a satisfactory understanding of the main principles. Lecturers taking some of the students up to two years later have commented on the soundness of the grasp of the basic work.

Questionnaires issued to different groups of students at various stages in the course were used to monitor student reaction to many aspects of the course content and methodology. There was 100 per cent response to the questionnaires, and the results were most encouraging. Many students asked boldly for other subjects on their courses to be converted to structured objective-based handouts.

The cost of producing a course in this form is quite low. All handout originals were typed out directly by the author, allowing precise attention to page layout and the size of spaces left for diagrams, equations, etc. The handouts were then replicated in batches of about 60, using offset lithograph equipment. The economic advantages of producing larger batches were rejected in favour of allowing modifications, amendments and additions to be incorporated on a yearly basis.

Adaptation to Meet Other Needs

It was found highly practicable to use many of the course units for other classes as follows:

(a) Advanced classes, eg final year honours degree students. Several units from the basic electro-chemistry course were used at speed to provide a crash revision course prior to advanced study units.

(b) 'Peripheral' studies. Since many groups of units were essentially complete within themselves they could be used for students whose courses contained a few physical chemistry topics.

In both cases the exercises and practice problems were tailored to the requirements of the students concerned.

Conclusions

The design and implementation of a course such as that described above does not depend on advanced or sophisticated concepts and methodology of educational technology. It depends on accurate diagnosis of the basic needs of the students, and on the use of an efficient system of course management. Although it may

The Polytechnic of Wales. Politechnig Cymru

QUESTIONNAIRE ON PHYSICAL CHEMISTRY COURSE

(Please return to Dr W P Race)

Introduction

The purpose of this survey is to evaluate reactions towards the methods used in the courses taught in Objective form, and to determine the best directions for extension and development of teaching in physical chemistry.

	Undecided	Yes	No
1. Did you find physical chemistry in the present course easier to understand than in your last physical chemistry course?	☐	☐	☐
2. Do you find that physical chemistry is easier to learn than other branches of chemistry?	☐	☐	☐
3. Do you find that physical chemistry is harder to learn than other subjects in general?	☐	☐	☐

4. Write below the subject you have enjoyed LEAST in the last year:

. . . .

5. State briefly WHY you disliked the above subject (replies treated in confidence!)

. . . .

6. Place the following branches of physical chemistry in 'order of preference' for each year of your course. Write '1' for the branch you like best, '2' next best, etc.

1st Year			*2nd Year*
Phase Equilibria	☐	☐	Electrochemistry
Thermodynamics	☐	☐	Chemical Kinetics
		☐	Colloid Chemistry
		☐	Thermodynamics: 3rd Law

7. Do you think the *practical* course was sufficiently related to the theory? . . . .

8. Briefly give reasons for your choice of 'best preference' in 6 above.

. . . .

9. Briefly give reasons for your 'worst preference' in 6 above.

. . . .

10. List in order of priority the contribution of the following aspects toward successful and enjoyable learning of physical chemistry. (Put '1' for highest).

☐ You like the subject anyway.

☐ Objectives help you pick out the important parts.

☐ Favourable atmosphere in class.

☐ Revision aided by objectives.

☐ Use of overhead projector rather than blackboard.

☐ Units designed so that you have not to write continuously.

☐ Units designed so that you do have some parts to fill in.

☐ Units designed with assessment exercises.

Questionnaire (continued)

11. Indicate how useful you found the following aspects of Unit design:	Very Useful	Quite Useful	Not Useful	No Comment
Blank 'reverse' pages for your own comments.				
Units Numbered.				
Bits left for you to complete in lectures.				
Revision exercises unexpectedly.				
Subjects divided into self-sufficient Units.				
Objectives presented for each Unit.				
More time left to talk about subjects instead of always writing.				

12. If you missed a Unit, how easy or difficult was it to 'catch up' satisfactorily?
☐ very difficult   ☐ quite difficult   ☐ quite easy   ☐ very easy

Figure 3. *First page of questionnaire on physical chemistry course units*

appear to take much time, it is an auto-catalytic process (a chemist's term for something that, once started, speeds itself up until it is complete) for two reasons. The motivation to continue is produced by the enthusiasm of the students and the improvement of their achievement. Once started it would be a 'let-down' to a class to return to 'traditional' teaching methods or materials.

This paper has not referred to the vast amount of published material from educationalists and psychologists relevant to teaching and learning methodology. This is not only because the reader of this volume is already surrounded by copious references to an ever-growing literature; it is better for anyone intending to design the 'optimum' course for his students to draw first from personal experience of the needs of the students and the factors concerned with the nature of the subject matter. The expertise behind published work is more valuable in the later stages of 'refining' rather than in the initiation stage. It is better to start a new venture, maintaining a careful watch for ways of improving it, than merely to ponder indefinitely on the best way to start!

At a time when too often educational technologists talk in a language alien to the practising educator this work is intended to be 'a report from the shop floor' which should encourage other ordinary teachers to 'throw off the shackles of tradition' and launch out into enhancing the effectiveness of the teaching areas they know. Educational technology is not a collection of audio-visual aids, or a list of theories about teaching and learning; it is a way of life which brings the ultimate in job-satisfaction to the dedicated teacher and helps students learn more easily, more enjoyably, and more effectively.

Reference

Race, W P (1978) *Aspects of Educational Technology* **XII**, Chapter 5, Paper 33. Kogan Page, London.

6.5 Making Large Group Instruction Effective: a Case Study

E E Green
Brigham Young University, Provo, Utah, USA

Abstract: Developing mass audience (1,000 or more) general education courses at the university level has historically been a difficult experience for the developer, instructor and student. With the pressure from administrative levels to be more cost-effective, attempts have been made at Brigham Young University to experiment with better teaching techniques to satisfy the requirements for a competency-based, interdisciplinary general education approach to a history course. This paper presents evaluation data showing how the basic problems associated with large group instruction can be solved. It reports data from a three-year experience in the development of Social Science 100 to show how adequate test writing, teacher assistant training, audio-visual lecture support, an organized syllabus, teacher evaluation and improvement techniques, supplementary and individualized instruction, and summative and formative evaluation reports all work together to solve most of the problems associated with large group instruction.

The paper also explains the innovative use of a computerized testing center in which the computer prepares examinations stratified according to various concepts, corrects papers and reports results immediately to students.

Introduction

Teachers, students and instructional developers alike become frustrated at the thought of the mass-audience general education courses springing up on college campuses. The developer is frustrated because of the scarcity of research concerning class size, the lack of development experience for audiences of 1,000 or more, and the bad reputation of large-group instruction. The subject matter expert is frustrated because he sees no way to survive with 1,000 or more students to instruct and inspire and a mere handful of teaching assistants to help him do it. It seems to him impossible under these circumstances to keep up with his professional reading and personal research. Then, too, students have complained for years that teachers of large classes cannot meet their needs. They have typically called for small-group or individualized instruction.

The only people who appear happy through all of this are administrators, who report the cost savings of handling 2,000 students with one full-time-equivalent.

Most of these frustrations, however, are caused by problems which have not been properly examined over the years. Typically, planners of large-audience classes attempt to carry on the lecture tradition, except that the lecturer may appear on a TV screen and speak with amplified voice. The result usually is that the lecturer's problems are also amplified. Few have analyzed the large-audience course and have adjusted its design to accommodate the needs of the increased number of students. Not many, for example, have paid much attention to developing an organized syllabus which would co-ordinate audio-visual material, assignments, tests, and other lecture information. Nor has there been much co-ordination of test items with rules, examples, practice, and feedback information.

This report will discuss an approach to one such course, showing how the basic problems associated with large-group instruction have been analyzed and solutions developed.

Developers with the McKay Institute at Brigham Young University have worked for a year and a half on a general education course, Social Science 100, which is competency-based and interdisciplinary. Social Science 100 attempts to relate aspects of American history, economics and political science into a meaningful educational experience. It is being taught by six professors, experts in their fields, who co-operate in organizing subject matter and delivering the lectures. The class, which averages over 1,000 students per session, meets in a large auditorium. Working together, the six instructors and members of the development team created an approach to effective large-group instruction.

Components of the Course

The approach to the development of Social Science 100 integrated several components: an organized syllabus, a teacher syllabus, an improved testing system, teacher assistant training, audio-visual support for the lectures, teacher evaluation, and evaluation reports. Each of these components is described below:

Student Syllabus

The student syllabus presents a detailed and clear outline of the entire course. It is divided into units (the large blocks of related information) and lectures. Preceding each unit is a simple essay which explains the main ideas to be presented in the lectures contained in that unit. This essay, which serves as an advanced organizer, gives the student a large view of the unit ahead.

Corresponding to each lecture is (i) a purpose statement, (ii) a detailed sentence outline, together with reproductions of the most important slides and space for the students to take notes, and (iii) supplementary readings. At the end of the syllabus is a packet containing study questions correlated with the lectures and text.

The student is encouraged to refer to the syllabus frequently, preferably before, during and after class. Before coming to the lecture he is encouraged to read the outlines and any supplementary readings associated with the lecture. During the lecture he follows the outline as he takes notes in the space provided. Because much of the lecture information appears in the syllabus, the amount of note-taking is minimal. After the lecture he can use the syllabus to review for exams and labs. Study questions and reading assignments help direct his attention to the most important ideas.

Developers went ahead with this format only after data collected on one experimental lecture showed that students preferred it. Further analyses of student attitudes show a similar positive response.

Teacher Syllabus

The teacher's syllabus contains the same items as the student syllabus but adds the test items associated with each lecture and other audio-visual material. This level of detail is extremely important because of the necessity of sending the course to the BYU-Hawaii campus, Ricks College (schools associated with the Brigham Young University system) as well as to Adult Continuing Education Centers located at convenient locations in areas remote from the main BYU campus. Since other instructors will be employing large-group instruction, specific detail must be given for the implementation of the lectures, testing system and all of the other support materials and methods given.

Enough structure is provided in the teacher's syllabus to enable the instructor to teach certain basic competencies which are required of all students in the general education programme for Social Science 100. It also allows him to prepare his own supplementary material and expand certain concepts based upon his own interests. He must, however, remember that he is teaching for certain items on the test which are considered essential that all students must possess after learning the course.

Testing

An analysis has been made of all the tests written by the instructors and recommendations have been made by means of a table of specifications indicating test items to be revised or deleted, and areas for which new test items must be written. This analysis of the test items helped reveal the correlation between the professor's exam questions and the lecture, text and lab information. Test data shows that improvements in test scores have been made from Fall to Winter semester. (See Figure 1)

Attempts have been made to co-ordinate the study questions in the student syllabus with the test items prepared for the test file, which is housed in a computerized testing center serving the entire University. Students are required to take tests in the Testing Center where exams are computer generated from files developed by the testing team. Immediate feedback is given to the student because of the rapidity of the computer-scores examinations.

The Testing Center reveals that about 90 per cent of the students taking the course now pass the general education competency exam in Social Science 100.

Teacher Assistant Training Programme

Because the class enrolment is so large — approximately 4,000 to 5,000 each year — it has been necessary to employ approximately 30 teaching assistants. These are advanced undergraduates or newly enrolled graduate students who work for 10 to 20 hours each week.

It was felt that these teaching assistants would be more successful if they were given some training beforehand, rather than being required to learn by experience, as is usually the case. Accordingly, at the beginning of each semester all teaching assistants were asked to participate in a half-day training programme, consisting of a two-hour slide-tape-workbook presentation followed by a discussion period. The training session offered information in the following areas: professionalism; becoming familiar with the course materials and methods; understanding the subject matter; developing proper attitudes toward the course and toward the students; developing better teaching techniques with regard to planning, presenting information at the students' level, giving adequate example and practice information to students, asking good questions; and, finally, suggestions for handling problem situations in class. Teaching assistants were encouraged to use the study questions to guide them in presenting content in their lab sessions.

After the initial two-hour presentation, weekly evaluations were performed in each of the Teacher Assistant (TA) sections so that further help could be given to those who were deficient in any one or more of the categories listed above. In effect, the evaluation then became not a summative or formative evaluation, but a 'needs assessment' through which the weaknesses of each TA were identified and appropriate action could be taken by the development team.

Audio-Visual Support

LECTURE SUPPORT

When the course was first taught, the six instructors delivered the lectures with little or no audio-visual support. Evaluations conducted by the teacher improvement team indicated a need for audio-visual support, which has resulted in the

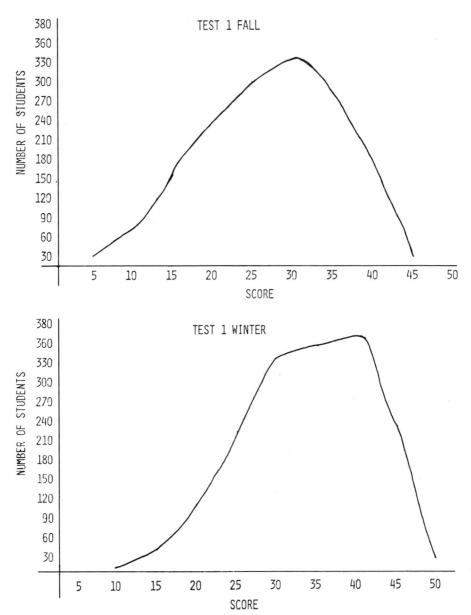

Figure 1. *Improvement in test scores from Fall to Winter semester*

development of over 2,000 slides and several film clips, slide/tape presentations and audio programmes. In order for these audio-visual aids to be used, modifications were necessary in the lecture hall. New projection equipment, lighting and a lectern were designed and are now being installed.

MOVIES
Every other week the class sponsors a full-length motion picture which corresponds with the period of history being discussed. This year, the following movies played

to capacity audiences: *1776; The Immigrants; Birth of a Nation; Free at Last; Money on the Land; Inherit the Wind; Grapes of Wrath; All Quiet on the Western Front; Patton.*

Teacher Evaluations

During the first two semesters, a team separate from the initial development team collected data on student responses to teacher effectiveness. After the data was collected the evaluators distributed summaries to each lecturer, together with suggestions for improvement. Further help was then provided by the development team. No more evaluations were thought necessary after the first two semesters because by this time the teachers had followed the recommendations and were performing well.

Summative and Formative Evaluations

The evaluation team has been responsible for summative evaluations reporting data from student questionnaires, annotated copies of syllabuses and weekly meetings with the team of subject matter experts in charge of this course. Formative evaluation data will be collected in the Fall of 1979 to report to the administration the effect of the course and account for the money spent.

Summary

Most of the problems associated with large-group instruction have been met and overcome through the integration of all the components listed above. This has been done notwithstanding the complexity of working with competency based instruction, a large group of faculty developers and instructors, the requirement to become cost-efficient and cost-effective, and the attempt to design an interdisciplinary course. Many problems still exist, of course, but after one-and-a-half years of development, we can safely say that evaluation data indicates that money spent thus far for development has been well spent. The initial negative feeling of instructors toward large group instruction has been tempered by the experience of the last year-and-a-half. Plans are being made to remodel the large auditorium to accommodate remote control capability by the instructor. There is also the possibility of rear screen projection, and better seating and lighting. After one more year of effort the administration will decide the final status of large-group instruction on the BYU campus. At present, however, instructors and the administration feel that large group instruction does have its place for undergraduate general education courses. It has at last been proved to be not only cost-efficient but also as cost-effective as small group instruction.

6.6 The Learning Environment in Chemistry: the Contribution of the Educational Techniques Subject Group of the Chemical Society

P J Hills
University of Surrey
R B Moyes
University of Hull

Abstract: The Educational Techniques Subject Group of the Chemical Society has about 1,000 members drawn from all sectors of education. In recent years it has attempted to improve the learning environment in Chemistry by developing resource centres and software for these centres. The Group has acted as a focus for the development of resource centres in a number of institutions and holds national meetings to discuss aspects of their growth. The Group has produced tape-book combinations in important areas of the subject and these have received general acclaim. In order to support resource centres, a resource bank of visual aids has been set up and a Media Exchange Scheme is in operation. For school teachers, a system of resource boxes is being developed which shows considerable promise. A catalogue of unpublished resource materials was published in 1974 and a new edition is under consideration. This paper discusses the detail of these schemes, their relative success, and their effect on the learning environment in chemistry.

Introduction

When the Royal Institute of Chemistry and the Chemical Society began the process of amalgamation in 1972, the activities of the Society were organized into a series of Boards and Divisions, including an Education and Training Board and an Education Division. Within each Division enthusiasts joined together to form subject groups with the aim of identifying specialists and interested members. The Education Division has three such subject groups, one concerned with curriculum, one with assessment and one with educational techniques. The Division has more than 4,000 members; the educational techniques subject group has just under 1,000 members. Of these, about 31 per cent are teachers in secondary education, 38 per cent are teachers in tertiary education and the remainder, including 16 per cent from overseas, belong to a wide variety of categories.

At the outset, the group had the good fortune to enlist as its first Chairman Professor L J Haynes of the Open University and he formulated the aims of the group as:

(a) to provide up-to-date information for teachers and trainers on the methods, techniques and materials available for chemical education;

(b) to originate new materials.

Both of these aims might be expected to affect the learning environment in chemistry.

The Bibliography

In pursuance of the first aim the Committee set out to provide a series of articles in the periodical *Chemistry in Britain* on aspects of educational technology. The first series contained 'Sources of sound and videotapes', 'Programmed Learning, how and where', and 'Lectures, seminars and tutorials' which appeared in 1972 and 1973. Later, in 1975 and 1976, articles on 'Audio-tapes' and on 'Film' appeared. Judged by the requests for reprints, these articles have been a substantial success, reflecting the considerable effort that had gone into their production. The aim in each was to produce a list of sources of material within the chosen technique and to discuss the usefulness of the material on offer. The result was often rather different, reflecting the personality of each author, but in general the anticipated aim was achieved.

Monographs

The group have tried to make sure that discussion meetings are not lost forever when the talking stops. A number of monographs originating in discussion meetings have been produced, both from meetings organized by the group, and from meetings organized by others, in which the group played a part. Such titles as: 'Alternatives to the Lecture in Chemistry'. 'Educational Techniques in the Teaching of Chemistry', and 'Independent Learning in Tertiary Science Education' will exemplify the range of interests. The second monograph arose from a symposium held at the British Association for the Advancement of Science meeting at the University of Surrey in 1975. The third monograph followed a request from the International Union of Pure and Applied Chemistry Education Committee to examine the use of educational technology in the training of teachers of chemistry.

Since the publication of the *Science Teacher Education Programme* (McGraw-Hill, 1974) it had been felt that a suitable follow-up would be a series of case studies on the use of educational techniques in the training of science teachers. Spurred by the interest of the British Committee for Chemical Education, the Educational Techniques Subject Group of the Chemical Society and the Association of University Chemistry Education Tutors set up a joint editorial committee to bring the idea to fruition.

The following have contributed to the monograph:

C R Sutton	Audio-recordings
J Harding, R J Hateley *et al*	Classroom-based student work
J E B McGarvey and I W Williams	Micro-teaching
M B Ormerod	Models
C V Platts	Non-projected materials (displays and exhibitions)
P Childs	Overhead projectors
G Lloyd	Resource packs and classroom simulation
I F Roberts and D B Thompson	Resources — an integrated approach based on crystals and their structures

This monograph does not claim a comprehensive coverage of the uses of educational technology in the training of science teachers. What it does aim to do is to provide a forum for science tutors and others to describe some of the educational techniques currently being used in the training of science teachers.

The Catalogue

The group attempted to catalogue unpublished teaching resource materials in chemistry and succeeded in listing nearly 300 items, a total which compares favourably with other catalogues, probably because no validation was attempted. The 1974 edition is now sold out but would, in any case, now be very much out of date. In considering a new edition the Group hopes to extend the scope of the catalogue into published materials, even if this only amounts to listing items in catalogues which may be relevant to the teaching of chemistry. There is also a mass of new material produced since 1974 which needs to be found and catalogued. Finally, there are problems of format, how the catalogue can be produced in a form which is readily and inexpensively updated.

Originating and Circulating Material

The remaining contributions of the group are concerned with originating new material, using its unique position in a learned society, with international experts available to it, and to circulating material to interested participants.

Chemistry Cassettes

When the Educational Techniques Group was formed in 1972, several members of the Committee had already had some considerable experience of using and producing audio-cassettes. They were convinced of the great potential value to education of this medium and they felt the Group would perform a useful service to chemical education by publishing a series of cassettes in which distinguished chemists would present authoritative accounts of aspects of chemistry, designed for use by undergraduate, and in some cases sixth-form, students.

The series was launched in March 1976 with the publication of three titles: *Heavy Metals as Contaminants of the Human Environment,* by Professor Derek Bryce-Smith (University of Reading); *Some Aspects of the Electrochemistry of Solutions,* by Professor Graham Hills (University of Southampton); and *Some Organic Reaction Pathways,* by Dr Peter Sykes (University of Cambridge). A two-cassette title: *Symmetry in Chemistry,* by Professor Sydney Kettle (University of East Anglia) followed in the November of that year. Then, in January 1978, two further titles appeared: *An Introduction to NMR Spectroscopy,* by Dr Bruce Gilbert and Professor Richard Norman (University of York) and *Some Reaction Pathways of Double Bonds,* by Dr Peter Sykes (University of Cambridge). Each cassette was accompanied by a detailed workbook containing diagrams, equations, spectra etc, additional copies of these being available for purchase for student use.

The response was rapid and gratifying and sales figures quickly demonstrated that there was a good market, both at home and overseas, for material of this kind. At the last count, cassettes had been sold in 27 countries. The responses from reviewers were very encouraging and although, of course, it could not be expected that there would be no criticisms, it is clear that reviewers were very favourably impressed with the series as a whole and with the style and content of individual titles. The General Editor maintains a file of all reviews received and group members are very welcome to consult this.

Financially the series has been very successful and has provided the Group with a vital source of additional income, without which it would not have been possible to carry out a number of projects.

The General Editor has, since the inception of the series, been Peter Groves of the University of Aston in Birmingham. He has also been Honorary Treasurer of the Group and his retirement from that position in April 1979 will allow him to devote more time to Chemistry cassettes.

The Educational Techniques Group is responsible for all aspects of editorial policy and for recording, cassette production and printing. Marketing is carried out for the Group by the Marketing Division of the Chemical Society.

The Group has plans for several new titles which will, it is hoped, appear over the coming months. Two further titles on reaction mechanisms by Dr Peter Sykes are now in production; scripts are being prepared for titles on structural inorganic chemistry, electrode processes, co-ordination chemistry and ion selective electrodes; several other topics are under discussion with potential authors. The General Editor is always willing to receive suggestions for new titles and to have comments from group members about the series as a whole or about individual titles. He would especially welcome hearing from school teachers with their suggestions for titles which would be useful for sixth-form studies.

Media Exchange Scheme

The Group has assembled a number of learning packages produced by groups in 12 different British Universities and Polytechnics. The packages make use of such formats as programmed texts, audio-tapes, slides, models and video-tapes, and are designed for the most part for use in teaching Chemistry to first year undergraduates. In all, some 95 titles are available.

Members interested in using such materials in the teaching of chemistry at tertiary level are invited to apply to have up to three of these packages at a time sent to them for a two-week inspection period, subject to an undertaking that the packages will not be copied in any way and that they will be returned undamaged within the specified period.

We are asking a fee of £5.00 (cheques payable to ETSG) to cover the cost of the scheme's catalogue of packages and postage on the materials. This will entitle members to a copy of the catalogue and a number of mailings of packages depending on postage costs. Should they then wish to inspect further packages we shall ask for a further contribution towards postage.

Co-operation resulting from the scheme could take several forms, such as purchase of materials or co-operation with the producer in the production of further material. In any event, further contact after the initial inspection is left to the parties concerned.

Resource Bank of Visual Aids

The aim of the scheme is to produce a set of low-cost B/W diagrams covering material in general chemistry, from which teachers can produce their own visual aids, eg OHP transparencies, 35mm slides, pupil handouts etc.

The material is intended to be of use to secondary teachers at sixth-form level and to tertiary teachers in colleges of higher and further education, colleges of education and introductory courses at university. The topics covered (see list below) are thus intended to provide a broad, basic coverage of general chemistry with the emphasis being on illustrating fundamental ideas. The diagrams will be produced in a format suitable for direct reproduction as OHP transparencies or handouts (A4 size), arranged by topic. Within each topic it is hoped to include both elementary and rather more advanced material, so that it is useful to a wide range of teachers in different institutions who can select and adapt material for their own situations. The diagrams are coded and numbered within topics so that further material can be added at a later date, and it is intended to include an index (with cross-references) and teaching notes. Copyright on the published material will be held by ETSG/CS but purchasers will be free to reproduce the diagrams for their own use in any format. If the first set of material is successful then it is hoped to produce more material to supplement and extend the Resource Bank.

The following topics will be included in the full set: Electro-chemistry, Kinetics and Mechanism, Atomic Structure, Phase Equilibria, Structure and Bonding, Periodicity, Main Group Elements, Stereo-chemistry, Carbon Chemistry,

Environmental Chemistry, Laboratory Techniques, Thermo-chemistry, Structure
Determination, Radio-chemistry, Structure of Solids, Properties of Gases, Polymers,
Surface Chemistry, Transition Metals, Industrial Chemistry, Analytical Chemistry.

The project is being co-ordinated by Dr Peter Childs (Thomond College of
Education, Limerick, Ireland) and Dr Chris Mason (Archbishop Tenison's Grammar
School, 55 Kennington Oval, London SE1 5SR). At present the work involves
collecting suitable material to illustrate each topic, and initially is concentrated
on the first 11 topics in the above list. It is envisaged that these may be produced
first as a half-set to test the reaction of teachers and the likely demand.
IUPAC/UNESCO has expressed some interest in supporting the project to provide
a number of subsidized sets for developing countries and the project is also
supported by a grant from the Chemical Society's Education Fund.

Resource Boxes

Teachers in schools, colleges and universities are now faced with a wide range of
materials in a variety of media. The concept of a resource box was developed by
the Group as something that could contain a variety of resources and information
on one topic area to make the teacher aware of the material available and help him
to make sensible choices.

The series of resource boxes, which began in 1977 with a box on Plastics, is
being extended into new areas. A 'Kinetics' resource box is nearing completion
and a number of further boxes are undergoing development.

Resource Centres

Many of our members put these ideas into effect through resource centres or
learning aids laboratories in their own institutions. A successful meeting was held
in Sheffield in 1976. The group has acted as a nucleus around which much
development has occurred, often through the leadership of the group's treasurer,
Mr P D Groves, who will be organizing a further meeting on resource centres under
the aegis of the group at the Autumn Meeting of the Chemical Society in
September 1979.

Conclusion

Since its inception the group has striven to improve the learning environment in
chemistry by the production of new teaching materials and by drawing the
attention of teachers of chemistry to the wide range of facilities and materials
available to them.

6.7 Teaching Adults in Higher Education

R J McDonald
Murdoch University, Perth, Western Australia

Mature students are now finding their way in ever-increasing numbers into universities, polytechnics and colleges — institutions which (with the exception of The Open University) were initially designed with the needs of 18-year-old school leavers in mind. Therefore it may be time to question whether the teaching methods appropriate to school leavers, and which often differ from those used at school, are appropriate for adults.

The purpose of the workshop was to enable participants to discuss ways in which teaching/learning strategies could be adopted or adapted to take into account the needs of mature students.

It is necessary not to approach any definition of 'Mature' too simplistically. The learning style of each student is affected by his or her previous educational and other experience. Some adult students may well be closer to the average school leaver in their approach than others. In the same way, some school leavers may exhibit a learning style which we have come to associate more closely with adult learners. Age alone can never be the determining factor, but in general we can say that as a person assumes more and more responsibility for his own life and leaves his school days further behind, his learning style also changes.

Differences Between Adults and School Leavers

Participants suggested that there are a number of ways in which mature students differ from school leavers which are relevant to teachers:

1 Mature students are more motivated than school leavers and are committed to their study for a particular purpose; this may make them less tolerant of material they consider to be irrelevant.
2 They have more life experience than school leavers (and are, after all, older) and this may affect their attitudes and make them very critical students.
3 They may initially have more difficulty than school leavers with study skills and with the 'language of study'.
4 Mature students are often much more anxious than school leavers about their ability to succeed when they return to study.
5 They normally have more pressing and unavoidable commitments than school leavers which compete for their attention.

How to Adapt Teaching/Learning Strategies

The differences between mature students and school leavers mean that there are many ways in which their needs should be taken into account. Some of these are:

☐ More flexible teaching and assessment — for example viewing the experience of mature students as a rich resource for learning (as described by Knowles[1]) and taking account of the different needs of mature students by methods such as independent study contracts. [2] / [3]

☐ More counselling on entry and assistance in developing or recalling study skills. [4] / [5]

☐ Understanding the perfectionism of many mature students.

☐ Recognizing the contrast between students' initial anxiety and lack of confidence and their underlying desire and capacity for taking a large responsibility for their own learning. [6]

If teaching strategies can be adapted to meet the needs of both school leavers and mature students, some of the problems faced by the latter can be overcome. To quote a previous report: 'the problem, if there is one, may well be not whether mature students are capable of university study but whether universities are capable of responding with sufficient flexibility to the challenge of mature, hard-working students who arrive with high expectations and are unwilling to accept second best'. [6]

References

1   Knowles, M S (1973) *Self-directed Learning.* Association Press, New York.
2   Jones, P J (1977) Personalising instruction through the learning contract. *Australian Journal of Advanced Education,* 6, 2, p 24.
3   Marshall, L and Bain, A (1978) *Taking an Independent Study Contract.* Murdoch University, Western Australia.
4   Gough, J E (1978) Distance education, mature age, open entry and counselling. Paper given at the conference 'Returning to study: the mature age student'. Sydney.
5   Mainsbridge, B and Carras, J (1978) Tertiary level physical science ab initio. Paper given at the conference 'Returning to study: the mature age student'. Sydney.
6   Knights, S and McDonald, R (1978) The learning needs of adult students. Paper given at the conference 'Returning to study: the mature age student'. Sydney.

Section 7:
Some Applications
of Training Technology

7.0 Introduction

ETIC '79 Tracks

As many as four of the seven papers in this Section are from Track 1, 'Self-Instructional Programmes in Practice'. These papers are Marson (7.1), Moakley on the American Military Educational Technology Complex (7.2), Symes (7.3) and Townsend (7.5) (this last appears as a report in this Section in order to integrate it with Marson). The paper by Moore and Kitchin (7.4) is from Track 3, 'Learning Environment, Practice and Presentation Techniques'.

Categories and Special Interests

Two of the papers, Marson and Townsend, have a strong Para Medical ('ParaMed') interest. Two others, Moakley and Symes, were coded 'MeDes' at Sheffield for their 'Media Design' interest, Moakley also carrying a 'Prof' code because it touches on professional aspects of educational technology.

An industrial or business interest ('Ind') is to be expected in a section on training technology applications and is found particularly in Symes and in Adamson's workshop (7.6). In both Moakley and Moore/Kitchin there is a military context, coded 'Mil' at ETIC '79. The Moore/Kitchin paper also has a strong Evaluation ('Eval') interest.

Links with Other Sections

Readers with a particular interest in Section 7 are also likely to be interested in the following contributions from other sections:

Section 4: Le Hunte (4.2), Bray (4.6).
Section 8: Roebuck (8.4), Butcher (8.5).
Section 9: Edney (9.5), Romiszowski (9.8).

7.1 Programmed Instruction — Promise, Propagation and Progress

Sheila N Marson
National Health Service Learning Resources Unit, Sheffield City Polytechnic

Abstract: This paper outlines developments in the field of self-instructional programming for nurse training. The paper begins with a brief outline of a regional research and development project originating in 1968 and centred on Sheffield University; developments are traced through to the present day national project. The following themes are developed and discussed:

(a) Subject areas and topics which have been successfully programmed and implemented, and those which have not.
(b) Presentation design and devices that have proved acceptable to the nursing profession and those which have not.
(c) Barriers to successful implementation and how they have been overcome.
(d) Present state of the art and possible future developments.

Introduction

The stimulus which produced this paper was a series of questions raised from the floor during the presentation of 'Is educational technology infectious?' at the ETIC Conference in 1977. (Heath and Townsend, 1977.) This was a paper reviewing and making predictions about the development of educational technology practices in nurse education. During a discussion on the contribution of the National Health Service Learning Resources Unit to developments, a chart was displayed which showed a steady increase in demand for self-instructional materials.

The questions raised were:

☐ *where?* — Which institutions/individuals had purchased the texts?
☐ *who?* — Who was in fact using them?
☐ *how?* — How were they being used?

As much of the effort of the NHS LRU clerical staff is directed into the production of programmed texts for nurses, these were therefore highly relevant questions to ask, with the addition of a further question:

☐ *what?* — Impact, if any, is made on the nursing curriculum by the introduction of such materials?

To borrow Townsend's model (ETIC '79), educational technology can be seen to have three dimensions:

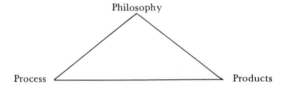

Figure 1. *The dimensions of educational technology*

The NHS LRU's main function is concerned with dissemination of the philosophy and processes of educational technology as a stimulus to the development of nurse education. To aid this function, along with other activities, two types of self-learning materials are produced:

1 Those which inform and up-date nurse teachers in the practices of educational technology.
2 Self-learning materials for some aspect of the nurse training curriculum to serve as models for good educational technology practice.

It is the second of these products I wish to discuss in this paper: the distribution and use of programmed texts in Schools of Nursing.

Early Promise

A few nurse teachers were caught up on the bandwagon of Programmed Instruction as it gathered momentum in the early and mid 1960s.

The first article written by a nurse teacher reached the nursing press in October 1963 (Whyte). Thereafter, contributions on PI continued at a steady rate, reaching a peak in 1966 (Raine, 1966; Mander, 1966; Hull and Isaacs, 1966; Buckby *et al*, 1966) and gradually tailing off in 1967 (Turner, 1967; Wilkinson, 1967). (See Figure 2.) For unaccountable reasons, no articles were published in 1965.

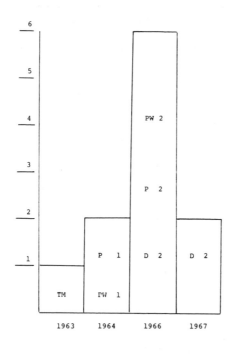

Subjects	TM	– teaching machine
	PW	– program writing
	P	– promise of P.I.
	D	– developments

Figure 2. *Published articles on programmed instruction*

The tentative questions raised in these articles hinted at a possible promised land for nurse teachers and students alike:

- ☐ 'Could the teaching of nurses be improved by use of PI? Could PI help develop student nurses in training to something nearer their full potential?'
- ☐ 'A number of difficulties permeate nurse training at the present time . . . how much technical knowledge does a nurse need to possess? . . . is the apprenticeship system adequate for present day needs? . . . what can we do about the shortage of teachers? . . . should more use be made of modern teaching techniques? . . . To some of these questions PI can provide at least a partial answer.'
- ☐ 'Could the slow learner learn as well as the fast learner but at his own rate?'

How far have these questions been answered in 1979? Has the early promise come to fruition, or 'has the bandwagon become a hearse'?

Propagation

As a result of this early interest, a three-year project was set up in 1968 to study the application of programmed instruction to nurse education. The research worker appointed was based at Sheffield University Programmed Instruction Centre for Industry.

The project was sponsored by the (then) Sheffield Area Nurse Training Committee, administratively responsible for nurse training schools covering an area stretching from Boston in the East to Derby in the West, and from Doncaster in the North to Leicester in the South.

Influential members of the Committee had attended a Conference on Programmed Instruction convened by the Kings Fund and were fired with enthusiasm for the technique. It was generally agreed, however, that before widespread spending on machines and materials was allowed more research was needed on its place in nurse education.

Findings from the Sheffield Project

The surprising thing was that, in spite of the spate of articles published in nursing journals and the number of courses and conferences on PI being held in this same period, very little use if any was being made of PI in nursing schools in the Region. Investigation outside the Region also revealed the same findings, apart from one centre of intense activity at the Luton and Dunstable Hospital School of Nursing. Two nurse teachers there were engaged in programme writing in their spare time to meet the needs of their students. A total of 30 programmes in all were produced during the period 1966-1970, a unique achievement on any count. (Hull and Isaacs, 1972)

Barriers to Progress

The first hurdle to be overcome in the Sheffield Project was that of the *knowledge gap*. Information on available programmed materials was not readily accessible to nurse teachers. At this time, 1968, programmed instruction was equated with the teaching machine; it was felt therefore that the expense involved would prevent its implementation in Schools of Nursing. There were preconceived ideas around on the kind of subjects that could be taught by the method and/or the reactions of learners to learning from programmed materials. These opinions were not based on factual evidence, for up to this time no empirical studies had been conducted. Tutors generally lacked confidence in PI as a teaching method.

Encouraging Developments

Much of the work in the project concentrated on developing the use of PI in nursing schools. This was achieved by establishing an information service and conducting a series of *evaluation studies*. Selected programmes were tested on groups of trainee nurses (approximately 1,000 students). Records were kept of their test scores before and after taking the programmes and they were encouraged to express their opinions on the technique. The programmes used in the trials were selected on the basis of an expressed training need. Topics were taken from the applied science section of the General Nursing Council's syllabus of training, ie applied anatomy and physiology. 31 programmes in all were tested.

No attempts were made to compare PI with conventional instruction; many experiments of this nature had been conducted in other fields and had not proved particularly fruitful. During the concluding 18 months of the project programmes were written to meet specific training problems, a series to teach arithmetical skills being one example.

Overcoming Common Problems

Which Topics?

Many of the commercial programmes available for nurses in the '60s were, in the author's opinion, inadequate. Attempts had been made to programme topics not suitable for such tight structuring, for example, human relations and practical nursing skills. The end result could be described as using a sledgehammer to crack a walnut. Programmed instruction was found to be suitable for teaching factual knowledge with an inherent logic. This type of knowledge is considered a necessary prerequisite to learning nursing skills, eg anatomy and physiology, mathematics and basic science.

Presentation Format

Early programmes were long and tedious to work through. The content was mainly verbal; little use was made of illustration, diagrams or allied materials like photographs, models or X-rays. The following measures were found to increase the acceptability value of programmed instruction:

1 Short sequences taking no longer than 30-35 minutes to work through.
2 Larger frames (steps of learning) than was fashionable at that time.
3 Use of skip tests before each sub-section of a programme to allow a student to save time (ie the section could be skipped if a satisfactory score was achieved).
4 Summaries at the end of each section were found useful to serve as a permanent record of material learned, or for quick revision before going on to the next section.
5 The addition of materials, eg models, X-rays, slides, tapes etc heightened the interest value.

Practical Problems

The most common practical problem encountered arose from early attempts to marry the advantage of self-pacing with the rigid time-tabled approach met in many nurse training schools. The self-pacing element was found to be disruptive of classroom routine, some students
more time than was allocated to finish. Happily, the learning climate has changed in the intervening eight years. Nursing schools are attempting to operate a more

flexible autonomous system. I would like to think that perhaps the introduction of self-instructional techniques has in some small way influenced this trend.

Attitudes

By far the biggest problem to overcome is one of attitudes. Research in the Sheffield Region clearly shows that where a teacher is convinced of the value of programmed instruction and has sufficient knowledge to select and use it appropriately, it can be a very useful learning tool. (Marson, 1971).

A national survey (Marson, 1973) demonstrated similar findings. Tutors who had attended courses on programme writing were more likely to use it in their own teaching situation. The same survey also highlighted the need for advisory and information centres to keep tutors abreast of educational developments.

With regard to learners, the Sheffield experience showed the majority have a favourable attitude. There was inconsistency in the students' attitudes: the same programme would be described as boring by one group of students and stimulating by another. Very often complaints of boredom were linked to high pre-test scores; students were in fact working through material they did not need.

Progress

A sum of money was provided by the original sponsors at the conclusion of the Sheffield project to allow the materials which had been written and/or tested, to be published for general use in the Region. This coincided with the establishment of further funding, this time from the Department of Health and Social Security, to continue the developments commenced in the Sheffield Region on a national scale. The excursion into the publication field was made very tentatively at first with little idea of its possible outcome. Sales of the publications have increased steadily from 1972.

It would seem appropriate at this stage of development to ask the questions listed in the introductory paragraph:

- ☐ *Who* has purchased them?
- ☐ *Who* is using them?
- ☐ *How* are they being used?
- ☐ *What* impact if any does the introduction of PI have on the curriculum?

To this end all nursing schools in England and Wales were sent a questionnaire to determine current use of Programmed Instruction (December, 1978).

Current Use

A 69.8 per cent return was achieved, ie 125 of the 179 nursing schools mailed responded to the survey. Of those responding, 85 were using programmes in some way or another, these centres being widely distributed in England and Wales. Fifteen schools, ie 12 per cent of the respondents, had fully integrated self-instructional programmes into the nursing curriculum. Seventy schools (56 per cent) had programmes available for student use but were much less certain of how it fitted in; in other words, to use Ian Townsend's analogy, tutors were flirting with the technique (Townsend, 1979).

The survey revealed that in the majority of schools programmed instruction is used mainly in private study times for revision and remedial purposes; only 25 per cent of the respondents used it for initial teaching purposes. This indicates there is still a credibility gap to be overcome, ie tutors need to gain confidence in programmed instruction as a teaching tool. In 28 schools (33 per cent) the programmes were shelved in the library and classified in the general book index.

Other less open methods of storage were tutors' offices and storerooms (11.76 per cent). In three schools (3.5 per cent) the books were put into classrooms during relevant study blocks. Eleven schools (13 per cent) had developed a resources centre and the programmes were integrated into self-instructional packages available in the centre.

Comments from the teachers on the effectiveness of the technique included: 'a useful tool, but the tutor must be the master'; 'introduces variety into the curriculum'; 'very good for slow learners'; 'stimulus to further study'; 'extremely useful as a teaching tool'; 'a good back up for missed classes'.

The problems encountered are still those highlighted in the Sheffield project. For some tutors and students, the use of self-instructional programmes is seen to be too time-consuming. Nursing trainees have an extensive statutory syllabus to cover in a very limited time, the bulk of their three-year training being spent working in clinical areas. Tutors are therefore reluctant to give up what they see as very precious time in study blocks to self-instructional methods.

For some tutors, the structured approach of programmed instruction is seen to be too narrow. This is a valid criticism. In this era of the 'knowledge explosion', when so much information has to be absorbed, there is a need to select very carefully topics for the programmed approach; it can be an inappropriate as well as a very effective tool.

Very confident students can find the close structuring of a programmed topic restricting; others less confident in their ability to find their way through a new subject find it very helpful. Again, by far the major problem still to be overcome is one of attitude. When a teacher becomes convinced of the value of programmed instruction then his enthusiasm transfers itself to the students.

In an earlier paragraph the question was raised: 'has the bandwagon become a hearse?' I think not. Perhaps the nearest analogy is a 'haywagon'.

Conclusion and Predictions

Nurse teachers are given a free hand to develop a curriculum within the broad framework of the General Nursing Council's syllabus of training. However, many pressures for curriculum reform are on them at the present time; external socio-cultural pressures as well as internal organizational ones. It is in this climate of rapid educational development that the full potential of educational technology in its widest sense could perhaps be realized.

References

Buckby, E, Carpenter, L and Howells, C (1966) Programmed writing. *Nursing Times,* 11th March, 62, p 326.

Heath, J and Townsend, I J (1977) Is educational technology infectious? *Aspects of Educational Technology* XI. Kogan Page, London.

Hull, E J and Isaacs, B J (1966) Two years experience of programme teaching. *Nursing Times,* 11th and 18th March, 62, pp 333, 373.

Hull, E J and Isaacs, B J (1970) Integrating programmed learning techniques into training courses in a general nurse training school. *Aspects of Educational Technology,* VI.

Mander, M (1966) Trying a teaching machine. *Nursing Times,* 30th December, 62, p 716.

Marson, S N (1971) Final report to the Steering Committee for the programmed learning in nurse training project. NHS, LRU, Sheffield Polytechnic.

Marson, S N (1973) Programmed instruction in the nurse training school. Report on a national survey. NHS, LRU, Sheffield Polytechnic.

Raine, N L (1966) An experiment in programmed learning. *Nursing Times,* 3rd June, 62, pp 763-764.

Townsend, I J (1979) Come into my parlour. (In present edition of *Aspects of Educational Technology,* XIII. Kogan Page, London.)

Turner, F (1967) More programmed teaching needed. *Nursing Times,* 13th January, **63,** p 62.
Whyte, B B (1963) Teaching machines in schools of nursing. *Nursing Times,* 11th October, **59,** p 1277.
Wilkinson, P M (1967) Programmed learning progress report. *Nursing Times,* 17th February, **63,** p 219.

7.2 The American Military Educational Technology Complex: Focus, Research and Development

F X Moakley
San Francisco State University

Abstract: With the decline in funding at American colleges and universities for research in media and educational technology, the research support has shifted to the American military. This presentation examines selected research groups and their findings, and their contribution to the development of educational technology in America. Special attention is directed to groups such as NPDRC, TAEG, AFHRL and HumRRO — agencies that produce large amounts of media research, contribute much of the current knowledge on PI, CAI and CMI, but are little known to the American educational technology establishment and are all but invisible to educational technologists abroad. This paper also looks at some of the reasons why the military media establishment exists and why it is having problems dealing with the civilian community.

NPDRC	—	Naval Personnel Development and Research Center
TAEG	—	Training Analysis and Evaluation Group, USN
AFHRL	—	Air Force Human Resources Laboratory
HumRRO	—	Human Resources Research Organization
NTEC	—	Naval Training Equipment Center.

The purpose of this paper is to focus on the activities of selected media research groups in and around the American military establishment. The results of such activities are well documented and a sampling of such reports will be available for the audience to examine.

Military support has meant much to media research in America. Early research on educational film effects was sponsored by the Navy although commonly known as the Pennsylvania State Studies. Additional military support led to early conceptual work in programmed instruction at Lowry Air Force Base, Denver, Colorado in the early 1950s. Many early media researchers, such as Tucker, Lumsdaine, Deterline, Finn and Kanter, were involved in projects funded by the Defense Department. During World War II and for the 1950s and early 1960s, the arrangement for such research was usually a contractual one between the military and a university. With the anti-military feeling generated on many campuses during the Vietnam period, this traditional arrangement was broken, most notably when the Human Resources Research Organization (HumRRO) left Georgetown University in 1969 to become a non-profit corporation after an association with the military that had lasted 19 years. For a period of time in the late 60s and early 70s, media research and development was done through groups acting independently of universities while retaining university personnel to perform the research. The services themselves created internal research organizations. Groups that already existed within the services to monitor contract research were strengthened and tasked with activities they previously evaluated.

Four of these groups will be examined in the context of media research and development. Each illustrates a somewhat different approach to the problem of media development and research.

HumRRO

The Human Resources Research Organization was established in 1951 under the George Washington University, Washington, DC, to carry out an integrated programme of research for the Army. In its early days the interest was in basic research. Studies focused on low aptitude recruits and ways in which they could be trained. The agency also conducted research on the effects of isolation. In the late 1950s and 1960s there was a move to applied training research. Pioneering work was done in the mid-1960s on systems and CAI/CMI approaches to training. In 1969 HumRRO separated from George Washington and its Army identification and conducted training research for other governmental and private agencies. In recent years, areas of emphasis have included peer training, the problems of reading as they affect training and continued work in computer managed systems. A bibliography of all their publications is available and a nominal charge is made for their reports.

TAEG

An example of an internal instructional technology group is the Training Analysis and Evaluation Group (TAEG). Supporting the Navy, this agency has been primarily involved in assessing Navy training in the areas of systems, CAI, CMI and simulation. New technologies are also reviewed for their possible application to Navy training and have included holography, video disc and satellites. The selected TAEG bibliography indicates their research interests should prove interesting to educational technologists.

Persons interested in their publications may write direct to Florida.

AFHRL

The Air Force Human Resources Laboratory has three branches that would be of interest to the educational technologist; the Advanced Systems Division at Wright-Patterson Air Force Base, Ohio; the Management Informations Systems Office at Brooks Air Force, Texas and the Technical Training Division at Lowry Air Force Base, Colorado. Wright-Patterson emphasizes theory and literature review. The AFHRL TR 74-15 is a compilation of systems research needs gathered from over 2,000 studies on instructional systems development. Technical training at Lowry emphasizes applied research that Brooks co-ordinates. The research is done both by in-house personnel and contract.

The Air Force systems effort is perhaps the best of all the military services. Air Force Publications 50-58 Volumes I-V and Air Force Manual 50-2 have served as the base for the other services to engage in systems development in training. It is interesting to note that the Inter-Service Instructional Design Manual has five volumes and is modelled after AFP 50-58.

Miscellaneous

In reviewing the materials listed in the bibliography, I discovered several other publications that would be of interest to the educational technologist.

The Air Force Manual 50-Z on *Instructional System Development* is a condensed version of Air Force Publication 50-58, a detailed *Handbook for Designers of Instructional Systems.* The 50-58 publication comes in five volumes and is the basis for the systems approach in the Air Force.

The National Laboratory for the Advancement of Education has a catalog of occupational courses designed and validated in Air Force Training. Of particular interest to this audience are the courses developed by the Laboratory in television production, audio-visual production and instructional systems development. Finally, the Directory of US Government Audio-Visual Personnel is an excellent source for one interested in the development of media in a particular area of government.

It is my hope that this brief exposure to military and government involvement in instructional technology will be of interest to you. They offer sources of low-cost information on educational technology that have application beyond the military. In many cases items will be sent *gratis* until initial printing stocks are depleted. The publications are rarely copyrighted, so they can be duplicated and used in instruction. Most publications review the current research in their respective areas and contain excellent bibliographic data, both military and civilian.

Bibliography

HumRRO
Human Resources Research Organization, 300 N Washington Street, Alexandra, VA 22314.

HumRRO (1977) *Academic Computing Directory.*
TR-78-1 *Evaluation of a Prototype Computerized Training System CTS in Support of Self-Pacing and Management of Instruction.*
TR-73-13 *The State of Knowledge Pertaining to Selection of Cost-Effective Training Methods and Media.*
TR-77-1 *Team Training and Evaluation Strategies: State of the Art.*
Miller *Designing Printed Instructional Materials: Content and Format.*
TR-75-3 *Instruction for Unit Trainers in How to Conduct Performance Training.*
TR-75-4 *Procedure for the Derivation of Mission-Relevant Unit Task Statements.*
TR-75-7 *Learner Control of Instructional Sequencing Within an Adaptive Tutorial CAI Environment.*

AFHRL
Air Force Human Resources Laboratory, Air Force Systems Command, Brooks Air Force Base, Texas 78235.
AFHRL TR-74-65 *Development of a Video System for Rapid Generation of Learning Sequences.*
AFHRL TR-74-67 *Development and Evaluation of Video Systems for Performance Testing and Student Monitoring.*
AFHRL TR-74-10 *A Theoretical Basis for Individualized Instruction.*
AFHRL TR-74-70 *Learning Strategies: A Review and Synthesis of the Current Literature.*
AFHRL TR-74-11 *A Survey of the Present State-of-the-Art in Learning Center Operations.*
AFHRL TR-75-46 *Learning Strategy Training Program.*
AFHRL TR-74-66 *An Action Oriented Review of the On-the-Job Training Literature.*
AFHRL TR-74-14 *A Comprehensive Key Word Index and Bibliography on Instructional Systems Development.*
AFHRL TR-74-15 *A Compendium of Research and Development Needs on Instructional Systems Development.*

NTEC
Commanding Officer, Naval Training Equipment Center (Code N-423), Orlando, Florida 32813.
IH-276 *Readiness Through Simulation* (1976) 9th NTEC Industry Conference, proceedings, November 9-11.
IH-294 *Resource Conservation Through Simulation* (1977) 10th NTEC Industry Conference, proceedings, November 15-17.

IH-306 *New Horizons for Simulation* (1978) 11th NTEC Industry Conference, proceedings, November 14-16.

TAEG

Training Analysis and Evaluation Group, Naval Training Equipment Center, Orlando, Florida 32813.

Report No 8 (1973) *An Evaluation of Ten Techniques for Choosing Instructional Media,* December.

Report No 12-3 (1975) *Design of Training Systems Phase IIA Report,* An Educational Technology Assessment Model (ETAM). July.

Report No 16 (1975) *A Technique for Choosing Cost-Effective Instructional Delivery Systems.* April.

Report No 23 (1976) *Learning Guidelines and Algorithms for Types of Training Objectives.* March.

Report No 39 (1976) *Training Effectiveness Assessment.* I: *Current Military Training Evaluation Programs.* December. II: *Problems, Concepts, and Evaluation Alternatives.* December.

Report No 40 (1977) *Design of Training Systems. Computerization of the Educational Technology Assessment Model (ETAM).* 1 and 2. May.

Report No 44 (1976) *Computer-Managed Instruction at Remote Sites by Satellite:* Phase I, A Feasibility Study. December.

Report No 48 (1977) *Evaluation of Microfiches as an Instructional Medium in a Technical Training Environment.* July.

Report No 60 (1978) *Use of Mnemonics in Training Materials: A Guide for Technical Writers.*

Technical Memorandum

75-1 (1975) *Trends in Industrial Training Management.* March.

77-2 (1977) *Demonstration and Evaluation of a Microfiche-Based Audio Visual System.* April.

77-3 (1978) *Interim Cost Model for Estimating Development Costs of Existing Curricula in the Naval Educational Training Command.* September.

NPDRC

Naval Personnel Research and Development Center, San Diego, CA 92152.

NPRDC TR 77-11 *Videodisc Technology Use Through 1968. A Delphi Study.*

NPRDC SRR 71-4 *Job Training Course Design and Improvement.*

NPRDC SRR 70-19 *A Survey of Training — Related Utilizations of Television.*

Support Test and Evaluation Division, Naval Training Equipment Center, Orlando, Florida 32813.

TN-53 (1976) *Evaluation of the Dukane Cassette/Filmstrip Projection System* Model 28A28A. March.

74-01 *Media Comparison for Individualized Instruction Between Super 8mm Projectors, Video Cassette/Cartridge Players and Associated Software.*

73-02 *Video Cassette Player Evaluation.*

For a Catalog of Occupational Courses — National Laboratory for the Advancement of Education, Aerospace Education Foundation, 1750 Pennsylvania Avenue NW, Washington, DC 20006.

For *Instructional System Development* — Air Force Manual 50-2, 31 July 1975 — Department of the Air Force, Headquarters, US Air Force, Washington, DC 20330.

For *Directory of US Government Audiovisual Personnel 1977* — National Audiovisual Center, General Services Administration, Order Section, Washington, DC 20409. $3.00

For *How to Prepare and Conduct Military Training* — FM 21-6 — Headquarters, Department of the Army, Washington, DC.

7.3 From Panacea Programme to Peripatetic Package

P R Symes
Standard Chartered Bank Ltd, London

Abstract: This paper is an attempt to trace the use and development of programmed learning and associated analytical techniques in the preparation of training material in the Standard Chartered Bank Group in the United Kingdom and overseas. The words programmed learning *and associated techniques* are used because it is suggested that, as part of the development from panacea programme to peripatetic package, various techniques originating from programmed learning and the theory which surrounded it and gave rise to it have been used and developed, and could now be said to be associated analytical techniques which current users may not label 'programmed learning'.

The progress from the first aspect of the title to the second aspect will, it is to be hoped, become clear. If it does not, then the presentation will have failed!

Introduction

To start at the beginning, back in 1968, a Programmed Learning Unit was formed in the Standard Bank Group Training Centre in London. You may think that 1968 was slightly behind the field in starting this sort of activity. This is so, but such techniques travel only slowly in some environments and it is possible that they would not even have arrived — much less have been adopted — if there had not been the feeling of 'panacea' about them. For it was probably because it was thought that the adoption of this new technique would, in itself, result in better training that the decision to set up a unit was made. The unit was expected to produce training material in the, then, accepted 'programmed' form using a simple teaching machine — the Bingleytutor. The sort of material which was produced for use in this machine, mainly for overseas but also for the UK, covered such topics as 'Double-Entry Book-Keeping' and 'What a Cheque Is and How It Works'. However, the machine was unsuitable for presenting training material covering routine clerical procedures.

Training Aids

It was found that routine clerical procedures were better covered by the preparation of training aids. These aids used various methods of presentation from a very simple check list to more complex booklets or folders containing specimens and algorithms. These aids were based on analytical techniques originating on the one hand from O and M techniques and on the other from programmed learning techniques. Concepts of presentation, preparation of objectives and validation were developed from programmed learning ideas.

So the manner in which this material was prepared stuck quite closely to programmed learning techniques. Those who prepared it were trained in programmed learning. The material was prepared for jobs or parts of jobs after a type of training needs survey (which is what it would be termed now, but not then) of various branches and departments. It replaced training manuals which had been laboriously produced some years previously for all jobs but never used because they were too long, too detailed and written in essay style.

But the material produced for use in London was also little used. The main reason for this was that the method had been adopted as an end in itself on the assumption that, somehow, by presenting training in this manner people would learn better — both faster and more effectively. The early proponents perhaps have something to answer for here in that many 'credulous amateurs' were taken in, in the early days. Anyway, what ultimately happened was that the unit was disbanded because the material was not sufficiently used to make preparation worthwhile; on-the-job training problems were not acute nor was there a high staff turnover. One interesting point about this exercise, however, was that the material was prepared by newly-recruited graduates who were specially trained in programmed learning analytical techniques and who were then set to work analyzing jobs and preparing training material. This training helped them to pick up a wide variety of jobs in a short space of time and made them useful to the organization very soon after joining. It also provided them with a challenge and an interesting job, in contrast to the tedious 'Cooks tours' which were the fashion for graduates on joining an organization in those days.

African Applications and Early Problems

By this time, however, it was realized that such techniques might be useful in Africa where there was an urgent training need (owing to increasing Africanization, especially at clerical level, in many countries in which the Bank operated) and where staff turnover was high and there were a large number of scattered branches, thus probably rendering a training centre uneconomical. Material was therefore first of all prepared *for* Nigeria *in* London. This did not work because of the difficulties involved in carrying out the analysis from thousands of miles away and also because there was no-one on the spot who had the time, knowledge or will to oversee the operation .

But there was perhaps at that time an even more urgent training requirement in Zambia. A project was therefore undertaken to use programmed learning to train clerks, including cashiers, in all the routine clerical procedures. The basic idea behind this was sound, using the pragmatic advantages of self-instructional material. For example:

☐ There was an urgent training need for a large number of people.
☐ These people were scattered over a large area.
☐ They were carrying out the *same* procedures in all branches.
☐ There was a high turnover of clerks.
☐ There were no qualified instructors available.
☐ Training centre facilities were already overburdened.

However, although the basic idea was sound some vestiges of the panacea syndrome remained. For example, the authorities in Zambia expected something special simply because of the technique. It was therefore decreed that *all* jobs would be presented in the programmed learning method, which was seen as something separate from other training. And not only all jobs had to be covered; every bit of all jobs had to be covered also. This meant that far too much, too detailed material, was produced.

Other problems with this project were that clerical procedures and systems changed all too often (thus causing many amendments to material), staff turnover dropped (thus rendering the preparation of each programme or aid less economical) and the material was used effectively only in certain branches. The problem of such training material being only as good as the person administering it was anticipated to some extent, in that every branch was visited by the person who prepared the material and the person who would administer it was instructed how to do so. This, however, was only effective with some people, and then only as long as they stayed in that position in that office.

In Zambia the use of Bingleytutors has been stopped but training aids continue to be kept up-to-date and used in certain branches. But whether or not the use of these techniques has been justified in this situation in Zambia is doubtful. The main points to be learned seem to be:

- [ ] To use these techniques for pragmatic reasons and not because they will in themselves make training 'better'.
- [ ] Such material is only as good as the atmosphere and motivation provided by the person who administers it; some people do not even get to the point of using it when it is available.
- [ ] Such material is only of use if sufficient people will use it (staff turnover is high) and systems do not change.
- [ ] Such techniques should be seen as part of overall training strategy, not as something separate with an end in itself.

Self-Instruction and Pragmatism in Singapore

Learning from the two experiences so far, the scene now changes to Singapore. In some ways the problems in Singapore were similar to those in Zambia. But there were other aims in using programmed learning although, by this time, that name was not used and the techniques had been expanded greatly. In Singapore there was a need to make clerical training more effective, to tighten it up and give it greater flexibility. To this end it was decided to use self-instructional material as part of the overall training strategy.

All offices in Singapore are within half-a-day's journey of the training centre. It was therefore decided to conduct all training at the training centre but to use varying degrees of self-instruction to give much greater flexibility to the training. For example, a tutor could supervise several people going through several different courses if they were studying self-instructional material; this would not be possible if he were running a course himself. Further, giving the person who prepared the material the opportunity to be responsible for administering it himself meant that he had a vested interest in its success — which the person who supervised it in Zambia did not have.

A carefully selected person was therefore brought to London and not merely trained in programmed learning but put through a specially oriented training officer's course including the analysis of training needs, job analysis and subject matter analysis, the validation and evaluation of training and various ways of presenting training (one of which was programmed learning) including algorithms, audio-visual techniques, even lectures — all based on the same rigorous, analytical approach.

This exercise has worked — much more so than the first two mentioned. I would suggest this is because:

- [ ] The right person was chosen to carry it out.
- [ ] Appropriate methods were used for pragmatic reasons; there was no 'panacea syndrome' which expected magical results from one technique or which caused 'blanket' use of one method whether appropriate or not.
- [ ] The exercise was seen as one part of an overall systematic approach to training.

The Singapore material looks less like the original programmed learning and not at all like it in some respects. It does retain certain basic principles, though, such as behavioural objectives; testing based on very practical exercises; students going at their own pace; presenting material when it is required and in easy 'chunks'.

The Singapore exercise has worked then, though it is still striving for more flexibility in training.

Peripatetic Packages in the Gulf

This leads us to another part of the world — the Gulf — which, as far as we are concerned at present, consists of Bahrain, Abu Dhabi, Doha, Sharjah and Muscat. Here there is a large central branch — Bahrain — which is 'central' to the area for our purposes, but not in political terms. There are also widely scattered units carrying out, in theory, similar clerical procedures. There is another urgent training problem also, complicated this time by a low standard of English.

Based on experience in the three areas already mentioned, a training officer was carefully chosen and trained *as a training officer*, one of his skills being the preparation of self-instructional material and its presentation in a variety of ways. Before this, a training survey was made of the whole Gulf area and priorities of training decided. It was decided that induction and clerical training should have priority and the training officer therefore recruited an assistant to help him and started the analytical work. There was assistance also from London in the early stages to give the project the necessary boost at the beginning.

It was decided that self-instructional methods would best fit the need of people in scattered branches (which have been visited by the training officer twice a year). Further, to alleviate the problem of poor English a combination of audio-cassette, text and training aid has been used. This also gives flexibility and has some 'gimmick' value.

The Gulf exercise is showing that, again, the problem of the effective use of such material is less in preparing it and more in getting it used. Material cannot be better than the person who administers it, or very rarely so. In other words, if a person who gives it out does so with an air of disdain, then the student is unlikely to be very motivated to learn. In the Gulf it is not possible to bring all trainees to the centre and the administration problem has been tackled by the bi-annual visits of the training officer and by his actual administration of training on these visits. But this cannot entirely overcome the problem.

The Gulf exercise is showing also that programmed learning has virtually disappeared. Its basics can be seen if looked for, but there are no frames to be seen, no teaching machines, no readily visible prompts or fades. However, the rigorous analysis has been done and the testing is there. Also, there is the idea of flexibility — the idea that a module or package of training can be prepared and used when needed without needing a full-time tutor available or a course running at the time. The idea also contains the element of system — that training is designed in interchangeable units which can stand on their own or link in, in a systematic manner, with other training units to make an integrated whole.

Conclusions

So we are getting near the 'package' idea. But let us look at what has lasted from the original programmed learning. In the Standard Chartered Bank Group this is:

☐ The basic 'common skills' material — Double-Entry Book-Keeping; What a Cheque Is and How It Works; but *not* in its original form — often now in booklet or audio-cassette form.
☐ Training aids, where they have been found useful *on-the-job* itself.
☐ Training aids administered in a training centre by a person with a vested interest in their success and as part of an integrated overall training scheme.
☐ The analytical techniques — now the basis of all training material on- or off-job.

So we have progressed from the 'panacea programme' to the package — but peripatetic? That may be the future. This could bring an increasing flexibility in training so that training centres can cope with any number of trainees from one to 20 at almost instant notice; this is possible if packaged material is available, plus a competent tutor. The package could be used in the centre or sent out to isolated branches, even in audio-visual form if branches have the equipment to play it back; the package is becoming peripatetic! It could also bring about the intelligent use of modern technology, but based on sound analytical principles and avoiding any panacea syndromes; for example, CCTV could be used but only after rigorous analysis of the material and its cost-effectiveness compared with other possible appropriate methods of presentation. The analytical approach will stay but its exponents will 'Beware of the Therbligs' — in other words analysis, too, will be seen in cost-effective terms. In fact, if we do not 'Beware of the Therbligs', or avoid getting carried away with the marvel of our own analysis, we will be back to where we began — with the panacea syndrome applied to analytical techniques! That is not the way forward. The way forward must be via the pragmatic use of the peripatetic package! Perhaps that could be the title of a similar discussion at the Aplet Conference in 1990?

7.4 An Evaluation of the Royal Navy Training System and Implications for Future Development

Lt Cdr J D S Moore and **Lt Cdr M J Kitchin**
Royal Naval School of Educational and Training Technology, Portsmouth

Abstract: This paper describes the design, implementation and analysis of a large scale, comprehensive evaluation of the systems approach to training, as applied in the Royal Navy. Resultant changes in the procedures used to control the design and implementation of training are discussed and particular emphasis placed on the problems of balancing cost-effectiveness and efficiency.

Introduction

The Royal Navy has been using a systems approach in the design and evaluation of its educational and training courses developed since 1971. The *de facto* application of systematic design methods evolved from the use of programmed learning packages in the early 1960s and in 1971 was formally and comprehensively introduced across the Royal Navy.

In early 1977, the Commander-in-Chief Naval Home Command, who has responsibility for most shore training, initiated an evaluation of the RN training system. The task of reviewing the experience of the previous five years was given to the RN School of Educational and Training Technology.

The terms of reference for the evaluation were as follows:

☐ *Phase 1* To review the progress made in implementing systematic design methods (commonly called 'objective' design methods in the Royal Navy).
☐ *Phase 2* To identify the latter's main strengths and weaknesses, as applied to naval training.
☐ *Phase 3* To make recommendations for the most effective and economical development of the training system (to commence after senior management consideration of Phases 1 and 2).

Summary of Methods Used in Phases 1 and 2

For Phase 1 information on the implementation of systematic training was obtained as follows. The percentage of establishment training which had become objective was taken from a previous study in which courses were described as wholly, partially or non-objective. Major career courses were re-checked individually with appropriate training establishments, using the same classification criteria.

Support courses for personnel involved in objective training were listed and their range, frequency and student throughputs compared for 1971 and 1976 in order to illustrate possible growth in the demand for knowledge and skill in the implementation and management of objective training.

For Phase 2, the following methods were applied: a sample of approximately 450 training and operational personnel were interviewed about their views on the objective training system. Interviewees were provided by 16 operational ships and submarines and 32 training establishments and authorities. Whilst the choice of interviewee was left to a liaison officer from each ship or establishment, it was emphasized that there should be a cross-section of personnel, taking into account rank/rate, branch and type of employment.

The interview questions were obtained by asking an original, smaller sample of naval personnel which aspects of objective training they considered ought to be included in a structured interview. Those interviewed were also invited to make any other comments they wished, especially those relating to strength of weaknesses of objective training and recommendations for improvement.

	March 1975		September 1976	
Wholly Objective	232	(24%)	290	(23.7%)
Partially Objective	210	(21%)	356	(29%)
Not Objectively Designed	540	(55%)	578	(47.3%)
Total	982		1224	

Rise in number of courses 24.6 per cent.

Table 1. *Overall design state of all courses*

October 1975 — September 1976

	Course Weeks		Student Weeks	
Wholly Objective	10442.1	(36.7%)	119358.2	(36.9%)
Partially Objective	7053.5	(24.8%)	96739.9	(29.9%)
Not Objectively Designed	10938.1	(38.5%)	106818.3	(33.2%)
Total	28433.7		322916.4	

Table 2. *Course throughput*

Results of Phase 1

The state of the move to objectively designed courses at September 1976 is set out in Table 1. Career courses are concerned with longer-term training and pre-joining training (PJT) courses with preparation for specialist shorter-term deployment in a ship.

Table 1, setting out the position in simple terms of numbers of courses designed and redesigned objectively, is somewhat misleading since it hides questions on the lengths of courses and their nature. When related to the figures in Table 2, it appeared that the proportion of wholly objective courses included a considerable number of lengthy courses with a high student throughput.

It was found that Training Schools' individual returns agreed very much with the actual situation, although the value of the returns was somewhat reduced by the use of the term 'Partially Objective' since this term was open to a wide variety of interpretation. Whereas 23.7 per cent of all ratings' courses were wholly objective and 29 per cent partially objective in September 1976, the equivalent career course figures were 63 per cent and 11 per cent. Non-objective courses primarily related to the technician level of training. At this level, ratings are responsible for a wide range of equipment and have to cope with a larger proportion of unpredictable situations than non-technical ratings. This combination makes the objective design of such courses more difficult and less amenable to a very rigid interpretation of objective design methods.

Actual Design Methods Applied

'Objective design' interpretations may differ from training school to training school and even from team to team. Even for low-level ratings' career courses there were variations between courses with respect to:

(a) deriving training objectives;
(b) design standards; and
(c) assessment methods.

Ranges of Courses Supporting Training

The range of support courses offered by RNSETT increased from five in 1971 to 18 in 1977. If courses are divided into three classes — Career, Training Design, and Training Execution — then the nature of the changes may be summarized as follows:

(a) The numbers of Career Courses increased from nil to five.
(b) Training Design Courses increased from three in 1971 to six in 1977, additions being Course Design and two Assessment Courses.
(c) Training Execution Courses increased from two in 1971 (the standard Instructional Technique (IT) Course, and the CCTV Production Course) to seven in 1977, the additions being three specialized CCTV Courses and two courses dealing with particular IT areas, Presentations and Instructor assessment.

The addition of career modules for Instructor Officers was a recognition of the need for all such officers to possess minimum skill and knowledge in the application of instructional technology to training.

Courses in Design and Execution together (excluding IT) showed a gain in student throughput from 119 in 1971 to 414 in 1976. Since all these courses are based entirely on demand it is considered that the substantial implementation of objective training methods in the Royal Navy between 1971 and 1976 was reflected in an increase in the need, not only for design and management skills, but also for more expertise in the selection and application of instructional media from television to audio-visual aids.

Results of Phase 2

Summary of Strengths and Weaknesses Perceived in Objective Training

STRENGTHS
The philosophy of objective training was sound and by better design work had produced effectively trained men. The training design method reduced irrelevant course content without adversely affecting trainee expertise.

The documentation allowed greater control of training by management and provided the instructor with a complete guide to the training required. It also offered a sound basis for the provision of support resources such as classrooms, workshops, equipment and audio-visual aids.

Objective training was producing a majority of motivated trainees who were achieving the standards specified. The setting down of such standards had not encouraged student mediocrity.

Task Books for On-Job Training were providing useful guidance to both trainer and trainee and were invaluable to less able trainees.

WEAKNESSES

Current job description techniques, although thorough, took too long and did not allow for the future considerations which then had to be taken into account separately by course designers. The techniques were also unsuitable for analyzing the more complex jobs at the technician level and above.

A great deal of course design and assessment was being carried out by untrained personnel, resulting in courses of a mechanical nature being produced. This situation was worsened by over-rapid job rotation of design staff and a lack of flexibility in matching the technical expertise of personnel with the needs of each design.

Design documentation and handling procedures were too cumbersome and needed considerable pruning. Slavish attention to detail resulted in course data becoming obsolescent when minor changes occurred. Because of the ponderous nature of the task, there was a reluctance to amend documentation to reflect changing requirements.

Recommendation for Phase 3

Following discussion of these points by a Ministry of Defence working party, RNSETT was asked to investigate ways of (a) reducing the time required for job analysis while making it more relevant to higher level training and future considerations, and (b) reducing the quantity of training documentation without loss of essential control information.

Concentrating, then, on ways of reducing the quantity of documentation without lessening the control function, the approach adopted covered three main areas — an analysis of existing documentation, a study of the control requirements of authorities concerned with training, and identification of the requirements of civilian award-giving bodies such as the TEC.

Existing Documentation

Naval Training documentation consisted of 11 parts. An examination of this documentation revealed the following:

1 Objectives were written in the Mager format of Performance, Conditions and Standards. These were found to be tedious and time-consuming to produce, extremely wordy and therefore leading to bulky paperwork, and appropriate only for expressing the attainment of physical skills. Additionally they were produced, and interpreted, by a wide variety of naval personnel, very few of whom were educational technologists, and this militated against both the production of satisfactory objectives and the communication of training content to managers. It was considered that single statement objectives would be easier and quicker to produce, improve communication between training establishments, authorities and operational units, and be of universal application to all areas of naval training and education.

2 The shore training specified by the Training Performance Standard and the on-job training stated by the On-Job Training Specification enable a man to do his operational job stated in the Operational Performance Standard. Clearly only two of these documents were required to give a complete picture of a

man's employment and training required.

3 The outline Operational Performance Standard was an abbreviated version of the Operational Performance Standard and it therefore duplicated much information. The outline document was intended to be produced quickly, giving authorities an early indication of training requirements and possibly saving much nugatory design work. A change in the format of the objectives forming the OPS which would enable it to be produced quickly would therefore eliminate the need for the outline OPS. A similar argument applies to the On-Job Training Specification and Task Book.

Control Requirements

The requirements of authorities concerned in the training process were identified with respect to the control information provided, and lacking, in the documentation, with the following results:

(a) The Operational Command, such as Commander-in-Chief Fleet who is responsible for all surface vessels, approves the jobs being trained for and the on-job training carried out in operational units. This was done by training establishments submitting the OOPS and OJTS at an early stage of design, followed by the detailed OPS. However, it was found that the early documents were insufficiently detailed for sound decision-making but that the OPS was unnecessarily wordy and difficult to interpret because of the style of objective employed. But if a job were expressed in the form of single-statement objectives, with the on-job training for each task indicated by a simple scale, one would have a document which could be quickly produced, would resolve all these problems and would replace three existing documents.

(b) The Operational Command also needs to be able to control the continuing cost-effectiveness of training. Feedback from operational units was generally carried out on an individual ship-establishment basis, and independent action was taken; there was no centrally controlled process of refinement of training. However, if documentation were specifically designed to enable training effectiveness to be monitored, Operational Command could identify areas in which improvements were required and state priorities for action.

(c) The Training Command needs to be able to control the use of training resources and personnel which are provided for individual establishments. Information in these areas was provided by a variety of documents and clearly needed rationalizing and presenting in such a way that the efficient use of resources could be ensured.

(d) The Ministry of Defence continues to require information on material and manpower resources and training content, so that it can continue to control large scale matters of policy, equipment and manpower provision.

New Documentation

It was clear that the main purposes of training documentation — to define and communicate training content and to facilitate control of cost-effectiveness — could be met by a rationalized and simplified documentation and approval procedure. Development work at RNSETT resulted in a six-part documentation style, which was introduced in 1978 for all new and redesigned courses, as follows:

(a) *Course Control Certificate* This document is the primary control document for a training course, recording the decisions made by authorities and the resources and manpower used in the design and conduct of the training; it enables cost-effectiveness to be controlled throughout the lifetime of a course.

(b) *Statement of Objectives* This lists, in the single statement form adopted for all objectives, the tasks comprising the operational job and indicates on a four-point scale the amount of on-job training required for each task; a single document thus enables the Operational Command to control training content.

(c) *Training and Enabling Objectives* This contains the detailed objectives of a course of shore training required for effective training management; it is also suitable, without modification, for submission to national awarding bodies for recognition purposes.

(d) *Instructional Specifications* The individual Instructional Specifications remain essentially unchanged, but are assembled in the order in which the material is taught; additional planning data is included to obviate the need for separate timetabling and scheduling, and cross-referencing is made to the Test Specification so that one has a complete specification of a course of shore training.

(e) *Test Specification* All tests in a course of shore training are combined in this document, together with details of how results are processed to give the overall pass/fail criterion for the course.

(f) *On-Job Training Specification* This contains the details of on-job training objectives, usually arranged in the form of a Task Book, in which case additional details are required for trainee guidance and administration. Although this document largely duplicates information in the Statement of Objectives, it does give more details of on-job training and its inclusion in formal documentation was insisted upon by Operational Commands to enable the operational units' on-job training load to be assessed. However, most on-job training courses are now supported by Task Books produced for the individual trainee's use, and so no additional design work is involved.

These new documents have vastly reduced the amount of paperwork and the time required to generate it, while greatly increasing its intelligibility and managerial usefulness.

Approval Procedure

The new approval procedure for a course of training is controlled by the Course Control Certificate (Figure 1 shows the first part of this Certificate) and has three main stages:

1 After being tasked to design a course, a training establishment completes Section A of the Course Control Certificate and submits it to the Training Command. The latter thus approves the resources required to design the course, and the estimated resources required to run it.

2 The Statement of Objectives is submitted to the Operational Command which therefore controls the content of training, and to the Ministry of Defence which assesses whether the course is compatible with long-term policy.

3 When the design is finished the training establishment completes Sections C and D of the Course Control Certificate and submits it to Training Command for approval of the shore training course, to the Operational Command, along with the On-Job Training Specification, for approval of the On-Job Training Course, and to the Ministry of Defence for final approval.

The approval procedure therefore gives authorities the right information at the right time so that they can act quickly and have effective control over their areas of responsibility.

PART 1	COURSE CONTROL CERTIFICATE	HMS	DATE

COURSE TITLE	REF NO	SECURITY CLASS

A. DESIGN APPRAISAL

1. Reason for proposed design/redesign †
2. New equipment/building works required
   (including TEP and D145 references)
3. Major consumable resources anticipated
   (material transport non-service accom, etc)
4. Expected annual total trainees
5. Planned number of courses per year:
6. Man-weeks anticipated for design work:
   Officer *   Civilian   Senior Rates
7. Estimated execution staff required:
   Officer *   Civilian   Senior Rates
8. Additional staff required for which no
   compensating reductions can be found
   Officer *   Civilian   Senior Rates
9. Location(s) and approximate course
   duration (training days)

10. Time-scale to complete design (weeks) 11. Estimated usage of TEP equipment 12. Estimated usage of ship/aircraft	13. Date forwarded by School:	Approval to Proceed by:	Training Command: Date:

B: OBJECTIVES 14. Statement of objectives forwarded to Operational Command. 15. Statement of OJT provided †	16. Date forwarded by School:	Parts 1 and 2 agreed by:	Operational Command: Date:
	17.	Parts 3 and 4 required for sighting Parts 1 and 2 approved by:	† YES/NO MOD(N) Directorate: Date:

C. DESIGN ACCEPTANCE

18. On-job training specification forwarded †
19. Actual man-weeks for design
    Officer *   Civilian   Senior Rates
20. Staff required for course
    Officer *   Civilian   Senior Rates
21. Course length (training days)
22. Related courses
23. Class size   Maximum   Minimum

D. TRAINEE ADMINISTRATION

24. Eligibility
25. Application procedure
26. Joining procedure
27. Seniority/advancement available
28. Associated National qualifications
29. Procedure for recording results
30. Action to be taken on failure

E. APPROVAL	31. Date forwarded by School:	Shore Course specification agreed by:	Training Command: Date:
	32.	On-Job Training specification agreed by:	Operational Command: Date:
	33.	Approval to conduct course by:	MOD(N) Directorate: Date:

† Delete as applicable   * Include rank and specialisation

Figure 1.

Control of Cost-Effectiveness

Cost-effectiveness is controlled over the lifetime of a course by Section F of the Course Control Certificate. This has annual summaries of information under two headings:

(a) *Effectiveness*. Details of the tasks unfavourably reported on from the operational environment are recorded, so that a profile of course-effectiveness is obtained. Training establishments can then be directed to improve deficiencies in training to restore adverse feedback to an acceptable level.

(b) *Manpower and Resources*. Details of trainee and staff manpower dedicated to a course, course length, trainee scores, waiting time, etc and of consumable items such as stores, transport, accommodation, are recorded annually so that the cost of a course of training can be calculated. The ideal is obviously to reduce the resources used by a course to a minimum compatible with acceptable job performance, and this document enables this to be done.

Summary

One may summarize by noting that the Naval Training System has responded to feedback about itself, which has resulted in reducing the time spent designing courses by up to 70 per cent. The quality of the designs has been improved and the quantity of paperwork has been reduced by as much as 60 per cent, while the monitoring and control of training cost-effectiveness has also been improved. At the same time, the fundamental principles of Systematic Training have been retained and have been made more effective.

7.5 'Come into my Parlour', Said the Spider . . .

Ian Townsend
National Health Service Learning Resources Unit, Sheffield City Polytechnic

Introduction

In this presentation Mr Townsend contended that the field of nurse training had been slow to take up the challenge of learning resources. Even now, two decades on, there were many to whom the term signified something contrived, something which had little or nothing to do with *their* teaching.

The speaker pointed out that his view was given away in the title. *'Come into My Parlour'*, said the Spider of educational technology . . . and in the haste to gain those glittering toys those attracted did not see the web before them and were lost.

The following is a summary of Mr Townsend's paper.

Two years ago Townsend and Heath (1977), reviewing the intake of educational technology in nursing, concluded that 'the past 10 years have seen the hesitant growth and encouragement of the process of educational technology in nurse education — who can now say what even the next year will bring?' For some time now I have suspected that little of the information available has been related to the use of learning resources in nursing. An earlier study (Townsend, 1978, 1979) took the view that interest in learning resources and the learning resource centre, reflected in some elements of resource-based learning, depended very much on the possession of an educational philosophy grounded in an educational technology approach. The study thus looked at relevant literature within and without nurse education and, through postal enquiry and visits, the adoption and practice of its components as reflected in the School of Nursing.

As regards awareness of research findings, accounts identified in general literature revealed either no significant differences, or measured improvements in learning which did not prove to be large. Most studies were descriptive, their outcomes inconclusive and more in the order of guidelines than research findings.

The literature of nurse education was sparse. Discussion in the nursing press was limited to monologues and ignored a variety of vital background factors.

Evolution

Practitioners in nurse education first met the basic ideas of educational technology through the use of programmed learning. However, programmed learning cannot claim the honour of sole genesis, although it may well have been a major contributor. A number of developments have all played a part. Nursing is slowly becoming aware of some of the potential of educational technology. As a philosophy and a process, the theory and practice of educational technology is for the most part misunderstood. Certainly there had been a very gradual change from a sporadic use of simple aids to a concern with systematizing — but this on the part of only a minority of nurse teachers. The genesis and evolution of the use of any sort of educational technology in nursing lay more in the attitudes, interests and enthusiasm of individuals than in anything else.

Present Use

Provision of resources and their use ranged from the most primitive to the most superfluous. Viewed along a scale:

'Simple AV Teacher-Support ⟶ Self-Learning, individualized Student education'

most of the use encountered — even in situations where considerable time, money and effort had been put into resource organization — was elementary. Resources *were* being used, and used enthusiastically, but their application relied more on the enthusiasm of individuals than to any planned or thought-out growth by institutions.

Achievements

Despite this somewhat pessimistic view, the educational technology approach had managed to achieve more than just a certain notoriety through its association with gadgetry. Nursing had become more aware of, and involved with, the specification of learning objectives at both an individual and a professional level. A growing number of schools were experimenting with the organization of learning resources. They were being supported in this by the existence of a cadre new to nursing: the

AV Technician, or media officer. Nurse tutors were actively involved in resource use, and one school even boasted a senior tutor post devoted to their organization. Additionally, one of the latest concepts in the profession — that of the nursing process — could arguably be considered as relying on an educational technology approach.

Structures

Few recognized structures exist which could be shown as evidence of a wide and professional acceptance. Those which do exist do not reflect any recognized national policy. Broadly, they group into three areas.

Professional

Nurse teacher training courses do contain a variable element of educational technology study. Most, if not all, schools have tutors with a responsibility for audio-visual aids. Sometimes there are audio-visual committees, whose main functions seem to be ratifying purchases or reviewing products. Both the General Nursing Council and the Joint Board acknowledge educational technology; the one through the work of its inspectors and its Education Committee, the other through its objectively specified curricula.

Paraprofessional

The emergence of media officers, sanctioned by the GNC, has been strengthened by their grouping together in a self-help organization.

Governmental

Government involvement was reflected by the seven-year existence of the DHSS-sponsored NHS Learning Resources Unit. 1975 saw the establishment of a National Training Council . . . still to make its official voice public.

Strictures

In nursing, educational technology has not made the great strides claimed for it in other areas. At a guess, many more teachers in other fields will be familiar with at least some of the main tenets by virtue of their exposure to major curriculum trends which nursing has yet to experience. However, the limited uptake of educational technology in one form or another has been owing to five factors:

(a) *Knowledge.* The most important single factor limiting its uptake is the lack of knowledge evident in the profession.
(b) *Finance.* There is no regular funding for software or staff skilled in its preparation.
(c) *Time.* Very few schools are prepared to allow tutors officially recognized periods in which to develop ideas or materials.
(d) *Structure.* There is a limited organizational and curricular structure in which resources can develop.
(d) *Support.* The inadequate, and in some cases non-existent, support offered (through knowledgeable discussion, sound administration, technical back-up and in-service programmes) is yet another limiting factor.

A tape-slide package based on his package is available from Ian Townsend at the NHS Learning Resources Unit at Sheffield City Polytechnic.

References

Townsend, I and Heath, J (1977) Is educational technology infectious? In *Aspects of Educational Technology,* XI, pp 189-95. Kogan Page, London.

Townsend, I (1978) Caring to learn: the evolution and practice of resource-based learning in nurse education. MA Thesis. York University Department of Education.

Townsend, I (1979) Talking about innovation: the resource centre revisited. (In press)

7.6 A Systematic Approach to the Future of Educational Technology

Robert M Adamson
Civil Service College

In this workshop, a tape/slide sequence was used to illustrate how one individual, the presenter, had been introduced to educational technology over the last 20 years. Various stages from 1959 — when the only visual aid he saw was a blackboard — to 1979 when the presenter suffered the problems of non-compatibility of equipment, were illustrated.

It was suggested that the lessons to be learnt from the last 20 years were that educational technologists are not getting enough publicity — people still consider educational technology a closed shop. Also, in the past resources have been wasted and developments have been haphazard. There has been competition, rather than co-operation, and duplication of effort between organizations.

The participants were asked to discuss, in two groups, the following questions:

(a) Should we plan for the future?
(b) If so, how?
(c) If so, in what areas?

Participants were also asked to consider:

☐ 'What are the needs of you and/or your organization in each area?'
☐ 'What are *you* going to do to try to satisfy those needs?'
☐ 'What are *you* going to do to try to satisfy the needs of others in those areas?'

Should We Plan for the Future?

The groups did feel that some planning should be done.

If So, How?

It was felt that this planning could not be too detailed and that a central organization should carry it out in order to draw up broad general guidelines. Their procedure might be to conduct some form of *needs analysis* amongst users, followed by the formulation of *objectives* — or at least *aims* — in various areas.

If So, In What Areas?

It was felt that there should be development of educational technology in schools and other training organizations. For example, during teacher training, more publicity about the *basics* of educational technology should be pushed for so as to avoid, for example, the 'teaching machine syndrome' being applied to mini-computers in training.

Hardware

The problems of non-compatibility of equipment were very keenly felt. Possibly this is an area that would cause great problems because of professional jealousy between manufacturers. It was thought that *some* improvement could be made if a central organization was able, for example, to inform manufacturers of users' requirements at the design stage. Another suggestion in this area was that a 'needs analysis' might highlight requirements for the development of hardware.

Software

It was thought that material for common subject areas could possibly be developed by teams from different organizations, each working on a particular aspect of the training problem. It was also thought that copyright licensing agreements between training organizations could be of mutual benefit.

Communication

It was suggested that one of the problems faced today is difficulty of communication between educational technologists, and that in the future a central recording of information, with easy access, should be made available.

Society

It was felt very strongly that there is a need to consider the human aspects of educational technology. It is feasible that social patterns will change very rapidly as, for example, min-computers become commonplace. To avoid a very efficient 'battery-hen' educational situation developing, planning is essential. It is probable that planning is needed, more to cope with the *impact* of educational technology than with educational technology itself. Over the next 10 years, as society changes, the role of the teacher/trainer will alter. Educational technologists must face up to their responsibilities.

Conclusion

Mr Adamson was encouraged to find support for his opinion that educational technologists should be planning for the future. As far as time scale is concerned it is not a matter of talking about next year or next month. With developments like mini-computers, home video, Ceefax/Oracle and Prestel, the 'future' has already arrived. As to the question of *who* should be doing the co-ordination of that planning, the answer from the participants in this workshop was: APLET.

7.7 Twenty Years On — The Development of Instructional Technology in the British Army

Maj J R J Goose and Maj P T Nolan, RAEC
Army School of Instructional Technology

In the 1950s increasing interest was being taken in the individualization of instruction for soldiers preparing for the Army Certificates of Education. Individual assignments were being written and used in Army Education Centres to cater for the wide range of intelligence, learning ability and educational background of what was a large and predominantly National Service Army.

It is not surprising, therefore, that the work of Dr Harry Kay and his associates in the field of programmed instruction, which was being carried out in Sheffield, should have interested the Research Wing of the Institute of Army Education.

The first of a long series of courses in programmed instruction was held at the Army School of Education in 1962. The protagonists of programmed instruction made great claims for its efficiency and effectiveness. The list of benefits was usually headed by 'a reduction in training costs', a subject dear to the heart of the army, and included such items as 'a reduction in training time'; 'an increase in retention levels' and 'a decrease in staffing ratios'. This latter produced some backlash amongst certain instructors who saw their jobs threatened or saw programmed learning as a threat to the thespian role of the classroom teacher which they enjoyed playing.

Despite commercial pressure to make programmed instruction hardware orientated, there were a number of attempts to introduce less costly presentation methods such as the Roneodex File with separate answer sheets. This method was also advocated because of the popular demand to eliminate, as far as possible, the cheating factor.

A few army courses in the early 1960s which had been instructor-orientated were converted wholly or in part to programmed courses. With hindsight, such courses often suffered from a lack of analysis before formulating the objectives. The wisdom of translating existing syllabuses into behavioural terms to form the objectives of programmed courses is now questioned, but job analysis as we know it today was then very much in its infancy.

In 1964 the Directors of Army Training and Army Education set up a steering committee in the Ministry of Defence to examine the possibilities of programmed instruction and to co-ordinate the work of the Programmed Learning Wing of the Army School of Education.

In 1966 the Ministry of Defence asked the Service Psychologists to examine the progress of programmed instruction in all three services. They noted in their report that developments in this field had led to the concept of a technology of training. This involved the consideration of operational task requirements; the assessment of the knowledge and ability of potential trainees, the methods and materials to be used on training courses and the assessment of training efficiency in terms of performance standard and cost-effectiveness.

It is interesting to note that in the same report the Service Psychologists saw Computer Aided Instruction (CAI) as the most promising future development emanating from programmed instruction. Apart from a continuing interes in results achieved elsewhere in this field, little progress was made at that time in CAI in the Army. No doubt the cost of such a system had much to do with this but also the developments, which were taking place as a result of the identification of the concept of a technology of training, fully occupied the small number of personnel working in this area.

By 1969 in the larger training schools in the Army there were RAEC Officers who were known as Educational Methods Advisers (EMAs) (later known as Training Development Advisers) specializing in course design based on the systems approach to training.

In the same year the Army School of Instructional Technology (ASIT) was established to develop the principles and techniques of a systematic approach.

Eleven Training Development Advisers were working in the major Army Training Schools in 1969. Ten years later, the number had risen to 18 and this does not include the eight consultants in the Training Development Wing of ASIT who provide additional back up as required and have a special responsibility for the small schools which do not have Training Development Advisers.

In the last 10 years the majority of Arms and Corps in the Army have established Training Development Teams (TDTs), made up of serving or retired officers and NCOs of that particular Arm or Corps. Where such teams exist, the TDA is also a member. The tasks carried out by such teams vary in accordance with the requirements of the particular training organization and the wishes of the Director of the particular Arm or Corps.

The latest six-monthly report from ASIT and the TDTs lists 311 projects. These include 15 Automatic Data Processing Projects, most of which concern computers in the management of learning. However, we are also interested in a number of other applications, one of which is the use of a computer to support the training of Battle Group Commanders to solve the tactical problems they may have to face in any future war. In conjunction with Loughborough University, ASIT is testing the use of holography in the training of engineers. The production of learning packages continues and many applied as levelling material before normal courses of instruction, as remedial back-up during courses, or for revision at the end. A more recent departure has been the centralized production of instructor support material, multi-media packages, to assist instructors who may not have the time, expertise or suitable equipment to produce their own.

The inclusion of enabling objectives based on the overall training objectives also assists the less experienced junior instructors as well as providing greater quality control over the instruction. Closed circuit television is being used in many ways in the educational and training fields. Present trials would indicate that its use in the training of soldiers to fire expensive missiles is not only efficient but also very cost-effective. The most mundane but nonetheless important aspects of instructional technology, such as job analysis, preparation of training objectives, course design and internal and external validation, continue to be carried out. The aim is that instructional technology should be accepted as a norm by all involved in army training and not regarded as an esoteric modern fad.

Even 20 years on, we have not yet reached that goal and still have many problems to solve. For example, the formulation of objectives in the affective domain: is it reasonable for example to attempt to formulate affective objectives in Mager's format, and is it possible to set objective standards for such items as leadership training? We have concentrated in the past on training the individual and ensuring that his performance satisfied the objectives based on an analysis of the job to be done. Is it possible to produce effective collective training objectives for groups of soldiers, eg gun crews, companies, battalions, etc, and if so, how are we to validate their training? The scope for further development is still wide but we have made great strides since our first visit to Sheffield to find out what Dr Kay had to teach us about programmed instruction.

Section 8:
Computer-Based Instruction

8.0 Introduction

ETIC '79 Tracks

This Section includes one paper, Butcher (8.5) from Track 1 'Self-Instructional Programmes in Practice', and three from Track 3 'Learning Environment, Practice and Presentation Techniques', namely, Bryce and Stewart (8.1), Cooper and Lockwood (8.2) and Shaw (8.3)

Black (8.6) which, like Butcher, appears here as a paper report rather than a full paper, was a members' informal session at ETIC '79, not formally allocated to a particular track.

Categories and Special Interests

All five papers and Roebuck's workshop (8.4) were, of course, in the 'CAI' category at Sheffield, but they also touched on a variety of other interests.

Bryce/Stewart was also in the 'MeDes' for 'Media Design' category; Cooper/Lockwood in 'Tert' for 'Tertiary Education'; Black belonged in 'TTr' for 'Teacher Training'; both Roebuck and Butcher in 'Ind' for 'Industry'; and Shaw in 'PriSec' for 'Primary and Secondary Education'.

Links with Other Sections

Readers with a particular interest in Section 8 are also likely to be interested in Landa (1.2) in Section 1.

8.1 The Application of Random-Access Back Projection in Computer-Assisted Instruction ·

Charles F A Bryce and Alistair M Stewart
Dundee College of Technology, Dundee, Scotland

Abstract: Random-access back projection, interfaced to a main frame computer, was investigated as a means of generating supportive visual material for structured, interactive computer-assisted learning packages. Detailed aspects of the associated software and hardware of the unit are discussed.

Introduction

During the last 18 months we have been very actively involved in the implementation and validation of a number of computer simulation packages and in this time we have come to the conclusion that the potential for computer-based education is considerable, although we in no way see it as a panacea.

The types of computer-based package designed so far cover a number of aspects of a biochemistry teaching course — some are used in conjunction with laboratory practicals, some with the lecture course and still others with assessment procedures (Bryce, 1977; Bryce, 1978; Bryce, 1979a and b). The programs designed are self-contained structured interactive programs which the students can work through themselves. With respect to the sometimes large difference in student ability, the use of a branched program was essential.

However, since a number of the concepts in biochemistry are largely visual and also because of the complexity of the molecules involved, some form of visual projection was necessary (see Figure 1). In addition, the CAL packages which we were designing and producing were intended to be individualized and, therefore, allowance had to be made for different students proceeding through the package by different routes. The consequence of such an approach led us to the idea of using a random-access back projection system which could be interfaced to a main frame computer.

The application of random-access projection in conjunction with computer-based branching programs is possible in other fields. Recent work in the college on the use of computer-assisted simulations in the training of senior police officers has proved to be very effective. More realistic simulations have been sought and random-access projection would provide such improvement.

Associated Hardware of the CAL Unit

Figure 2 illustrates the system which we have employed in the present study.

The visual display unit (VDU) was on-line to a DEC SYSTEM-20 main frame computer, currently capable of supporting up to 32 users simultaneously (present configuration, 256K 36-bit word memory, 2 x 200 Mbyte RP06 disc drives).

The random-access back projection equipment used was the REVOX Audio-card system composed of an audio-card monitor and an audio-card control device

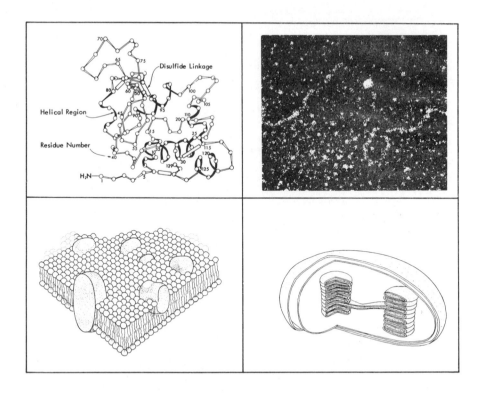

Figure 1. *Examples of the types of visual information which are*
frequently required in the teaching of biochemistry

or encoder. With this particular system, which employs a 5 x 12 grid microfiche, the selection time in going from one frame to another is a small fraction of a second, the poorest response time (ie travelling from one corner to the opposite diagonal corner) being about three-quarters of a second. This extremely rapid selection time, plus the ability to produce and display high resolution photographs and illustrations, were the features which recommended this particular projection system for the current study.

Associated Software of the CAL Unit

Features of the Computer Programming

Over the last two years we have also been actively involved in the design, production and implementation of multi-level programming using the Philips PIP system (Bryce and Stewart, 1979). Arising from this work, we demonstrated that it is often possible to compose questions, raise adjoining remarks or observations etc at different discrete levels of educational standard whilst using the same visual information. This observation was incorporated into the present package in the following way. When the student begins to study this package he or she is given relevant managing instructions for the correct operation of the unit. Following these preliminary remarks, which can be by-passed by those familiar with the system, the student is asked at which level he wishes to be assessed — fundamental,

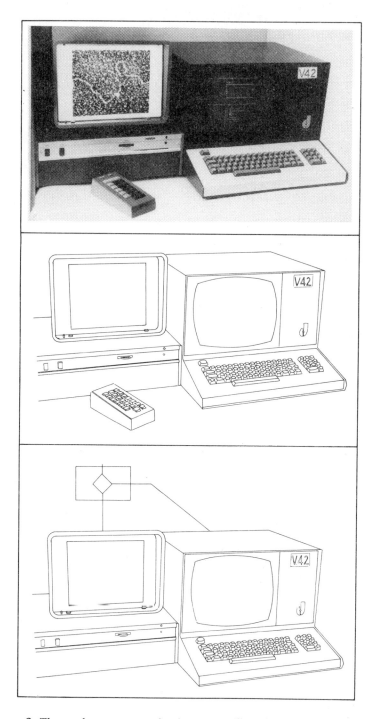

Figure 2. *The random-access projection system linked to an on-line terminal as used in the present study*

intermediate or advanced. Depending on the response to this question, the student is directed along a certain broad route through the learning package. The format of the output at this stage is shown in Figure 3.

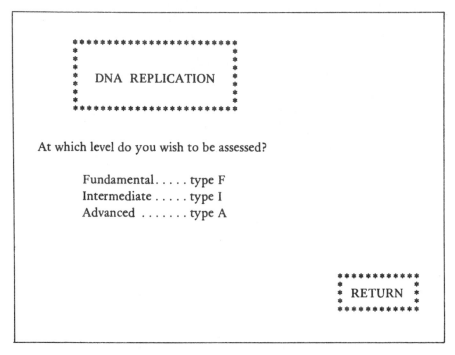

Figure 3. *Sample output from an early stage in the running of the computer-assisted learning package*

Setting the Page Size

Figure 3 also illustrates another feature which was incorporated into this package and this is apparent in the bottom right hand corner. One problem in using a VDU terminal is that frequently the output is longer than can be accommodated on the screen and so material runs off the screen before the user has a reasonable chance to read and digest the information. This can be easily overcome by using a systems command of the type:

@ TERMINAL PAGE 20⟩

which, on the DEC-20, would stop the output after 20 lines of information. Once the information is read the output can be continued by typing in certain key instructions, eg **CONTROL/Q.**

We have used this approach for some programs in the past but, in practice, this has given rise to a considerable number of problems with students as multi-users. This being the case, a sub-routine was incorporated into the present program which would carry out an identical function, ie it would not allow output to run off the screen before the user had a chance to read it. The sub-routine in use generates the grid box with the word **RETURN** in the centre. Once the student has assimilated the material he or she can continue by depressing the **RETURN** key on the VDU keyboard. This particular sub-routine has additional functions written into it and these will be discussed at a later stage.

Format of Test Questions

A typical format for the test items within the program is shown in Figure 4.

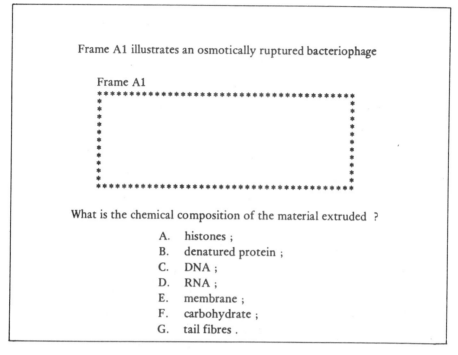

Figure 4. *The format of a typical test item*

The 'starred' frame and its associated label are generated by another sub-routine. This sub-routine only exists in the developmental program and will be replaced in the final version by a sub-routine which will, in fact, drive the REVOX random-access microfiche monitor (see later).

With regard to the actual test questions, the student responds by typing in the letter of his or her choice. This is checked by character or string matching and an appropriate message is output to the VDU. Examples of such diagnostic feedback are shown below:

'Well done . . . The X-shaped pattern is not too clear in this particular diffraction pattern. The reason for this in this case is because the fibres used were not very highly ordered.'
'Yes, well done. The distinction between deep and narrow grooves is very important when we come to consider enzyme-binding to DNA and also the binding of certain antibiotics.'
'No, wrong answer . . . Try again, this time look to see if the base pairs are at right-angles to the backbone. This should help you to distinguish between the different possible forms.'

During the program's development phase it became obvious that the system was well suited to operate in a tutorial mode in that questions plus associated visuals could be presented and, equally easily, factual accounts and their associated visuals could be presented to the students. This we used to convey either additional material or remedial material to particular groups of students.

Quantitative problems could also be managed with ease. In developing the program, it was a simple matter to incorporate a tolerable and pre-specified error in any such quantitative estimate — thus one might allow a student an error of 10 per cent or 3 per cent etc for a particular calculation. If the response is outside the range then the student is told *'Your estimate is too large (or too small), try again.'* In addition, in such a problem we felt that it was beneficial to give a step-by-step solution to the problem once the student had finished. This allowed the student to check his or her working against the correct solution, just in case he or she arrived at the correct answer by a number of compensating errors.

In earlier programs developed by us, we cycled students around a question until such time as they got the correct response. In the present package we restricted this to two attempts. If students got the correct answer first time then they progressed to another section of the program and the point to which they progressed depended on their immediate past 'track record'. If they answered incorrectly then they were looped back through that question for a second attempt. As before, the point to which they proceed within the program after their second attempt depends on whether or not they chose the correct response and also on their immediate past record.

Additional Features within the Program

It was mentioned earlier that the program was written to contain a sub-routine capable of paging the output from the VDU. This same sub-routine is also capable of certain other functions within the program.

In designing this package we felt that it would be advantageous for the student to be able to monitor his or her own performance at any point in the package. To do this, the student need only type the letter S (for score) at any point in the program where a :RETURN: is encountered. A typical outcome of this request is shown below:

total number of questions attempted	= 10
number of correct responses on first attempt	= 8
number of correct responses on second attempt	= 1
percentage score for this session	= 83.33

It is also intended to have a more detailed version of the above information which could be used at the end of the learning session. For example, by typing SE (score at end) before a :RETURN: , the student can be given the above information, the current high for a student in the same stream, plus a record of those questions which were wrongly answered. The latter could be matched up to certain terminal learning objectives held on disc for that package and an output of those achieved and those not yet achieved could be output to the student. Early exit from the program can be achieved in a similar way by typing O (for out) before :RETURN: . The student receives a message to say that the exercise is incomplete but does get a current score. It is intended to incorporate other similar request features as the program develops and is extensively validated by a number of students.

By-Passing the Encoder Keyboard

The Unit now is as described earlier (Figure 2) and is operated by two keyboards — the VDU keyboard for data input and interacting with the program and also the REVOX encoder for typing in the grid reference for the visual material (A5, E11 etc).

This we felt was a little unsatisfactory and so we considered the possibility of by-passing the REVOX encoder box. Work in this area has shown that it will be possible to construct a 'black box' which can be interfaced to the VDU terminal on line (Figure 2c). This box, which is currently being constructed, contains a logic circuit which continuously monitors the information coming from the DEC-20 computer to the terminal line. Provided that the information coming down the line is standard information, then the box allows this to proceed uninterrupted to the VDU. If, however, a reserved special character is detected, then the logic circuit takes the next 7-bit code of information and directs this to the REVOX monitor. This information never appears on the VDU screen. The 7-bits code for the microfiche grid reference (the first three for the y-co-ordinate (eg $\equiv$ C), the last four for the x-co-ordinate (eg $\equiv$ 8). This then drives the REVOX monitor to display that particular frame (C8) of the microfiche. When the visual is no longer required, a suitably coded signal brings up a blank frame. This aspect of the study is currently under active investigation and a report of the final results will appear shortly.

The application of random-access back projection is obviously useful where illustrative material is required which cannot be generated on a VDU or on a graphics terminal. However, the requirements of such visual material in an instructional program frequently demand moving as well as still pictures. A logical next step in the investigation would be to interface either film or television material with the computer.

The linking of visual material, whether still or moving, can also enhance the use of the computer in some kinds of simulation. For example, a computer-assisted simulation currently being used for the training of senior police officers is soon likely to be rendered more realistic by such an addition. The addition of random-access sound will also increase the realism, and investigation of these enhancements will begin shortly.

References

Bryce, C F A (1977) Simulations using random-generated DNA and RNA sequences. *Journal of Biological Education*, 11, p 140.

Bryce, C F A (1978) Nearest-neighbour frequency analysis — a structured, interactive program for biochemistry students. *Journal of Biological Education*, 12, p 133.

Bryce, C F A (1979a) Management of an objective test item bank for biochemistry. *Biochemical Education*, 7, p 17.

Bryce, C F A (1979b) Refined integer fit of amino acid residues from the amino acid composition of a pure protein. *Laboratory Practice*, 28, p 403.

Bryce, C F A and Stewart, A M (1979) Design and production of self-instructional learning packages in biochemistry using the Philips PIP system. *Aspects of Educational Technology*, XII, p 256.

Acknowledgements

We would like to thank Mr Duncan E Ord, Director of the Computer Centre, Dundee College of Technology, for his most helpful advice and interest in this project.

8.2 The Need, Provision and Use of a Computer-Assisted Interactive Tutorial System

Aldwyn Cooper and **Fred Lockwood**
The Open University

Abstract: Open University teaching material incorporates a variety of devices by which feedback can be provided. However, the main interactive element, over which the course team has little control, is provided by part-time staff in tutorials, by written comments on assignments and by telephone contact. The varied nature of this provision is illustrated in the paper.

Whilst the valuable contribution of part-time staff is recognized, the special needs of students studying at a distance have prompted a recent development in which the facility of interactive computer programs is exploited. A computer-assisted interactive tutorial system, designed to meet the needs of the Open University and utilizing material assembled by central course teams and intended to complement both teaching material and other feedback mechanisms, is described and illustrated. There is an evaluation of its use, and its perceived value by students, part-time staff and central academic staff is described.

A knowledge of the context within which the computer-assisted tutorial system — codenamed *Cicero* (Cooper, 1978) — is being developed is important for an appreciation of its needs, provision and use. The provision of distance teaching materials within the Open University will thus be briefly described.

For a student to gain an ordinary BA degree through the Open University, he or she has to successfully complete, by home study, six credits.[1] Entrance to the University is open to all but if a student has some previous academic qualifications he or she may obtain a number of credit exemptions but no preferential entry to the University (Open University, 1979). The precise combination of courses followed, apart from a few minor restrictions, is up to each individual student.

The Open University courses a student follows may consist of correspondence texts, set book(s), articles or extracts, additional printed material, home experiment kits, television and radio broadcasts, audio-cassettes, LPs/flexi-discs, tutorials and computer data sets or programs. This material is generated by a Course Team for each course based at Walton Hall which usually consists of central academic staff, academic consultants, an educational technologist, BBC producers, editors, graphic designers, administrative assistants, photographers, librarians, regional representatives and production planners. This team, and the authors in particular, recognize the immediate problems facing the student studying in isolation. There is no opportunity to directly question the teacher, little or no opportunity to discuss problems with fellow students and delay between the completion of an assignment and the receipt of comments about it.[2]

1 One credit is equivalent to approximately 380 hours of student study time over a period of about nine months or about 10-12 hours per week over the academic year.

2 Within the Open University summative assignments are generally divided into Computer Marked Assignments (CMAs) and Tutor Marked Assignments (TMAs). When a student submits a CMA there is usually a delay between the date of actual submission and date of processing — the cut-off date for the assignments after which all CMAs are marked. Furthermore, there may be a further two-week delay in informing the student of his performance. Even at this time a detailed account of performance may be absent and merely an overall grade provided. In TMAs a part-time tutor comments on the actual script, providing advice, guidance etc. However, there is often a long delay, two to three weeks, before this is returned to the student by which time he or she may have had to progress to new course material.

In preparing their teaching material, Open University authors thus try to provide opportunities where students can monitor their progress, check their level of understanding, measure their competence — where they can formulate their own ideas and check them against the ideas of others. Prior to the introduction of the *Cicero* System there were two main approaches by which to provide this feedback on course performance; by trying to simulate a 'tutorial in print' and by providing conventional, but limited, tutorial provision.

The simulation of a 'tutorial in print' (Rowntree, 1975) is the procedure whereby an author regards the student time spent working on his material as time spent by the student in the author's company. In such a situation it is unlikely that an author would expect students to simply read an exposition from start to finish without reacting to it in some way or producing anything themselves. They may, for example, be asked to recall items of information, define concepts, draw together arguments. justify particular statements, consult other sources, interpret data, compare different interpretations of the same data, work out examples, and so on. In short, to exercise certain study skills by which they can construct their own picture of a subject and integrate what they have just been taught with what they had learnt before. Within the Open University there are numerous terms to describe these components of the teaching material — In Text Questions (ITQs), Self-Assessment Questions (SAQs), Activities, Exercises, Study Questions, etc. These Self-Assessment Materials, which are not graded for continuous assessment purposes, are built into the teaching text. Whilst there have been several attempts to categorize these different elements (Rowntree, 1975; Zimmer, 1977; Lockwood, 1978), a simple way would be to group them into materials that

(a) look back — involving recall, restatement, recognition, identification of principles/concepts;
(b) look forward — involving the use of facts/principles/concepts to analyze, interpret, criticize, design etc;
(c) provide practice — involving either specific skills and techniques or various combinations of them. (Lockwood, 1978)

The other mechanism by which students are able to obtain information on their progress/understanding/competence is from the comments of a part-time tutor; either in a tutorial or from comments on summative assignments. Figure 1 represents the hours of tutorial provision for Social Science courses in 1977 (Durbridge, 1977). Full credit courses (those to the left of the dotted line) required tutorial provision that ranged from nine to 26 hours. (Remember that a full credit course involves about 380 hours of student study time.) Half credit courses (to the right of the dotted line) required substantially less with one course, D291, Statistical Sources requiring no tutorial provision.

This variety in the provision required is the same in other Faculties (Durbridge, 1977). Within this total time allocation the actual form of tutorial provision varies: it could be face-to-face contact, telephone contact, via audio-cassette or at day or weekend schools (Northedge and Durbridge, 1978). Furthermore, within a single course the provision may vary from Region to Region. For example, an inspection of Figure 2 reveals that the 71 students in Region 01 (London) were offered six one-and-a-half-hour face-to-face tutorials and one three-hour 'Saturday School' whilst the 27 students in Region 02 (South) were offered no face-to-face tutorials but three two-hour 'Saturday Schools' and a two-hour 'special session'. The 24 students in Region 03 (South West) were offered no 'Saturday Schools' or 'special sessions' but simply four two-hour face-to-face tutorials! This variety in the tutorial provision within a single course, illustrated in Figure 2, is not unique. Factors such as the course population within a region, the geographical distribution of students, available tutor expertise, study centre location, and policy commitments to teaching by telephone, letter, cassette or face-to-face influence the provision that can be

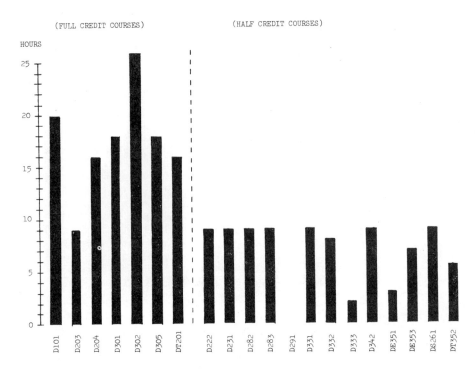

Figure 1. *Tutorial provision for Social Science courses in 1977*

offered.

Unfortunately, the two mechanisms that have been described still fall short of the special needs of students studying at a distance. The self-assessment questions and associated answers often fail to perform a diagnostic and remedial function with authors completely unaware of which questions have been answered and how. Tutorial support may not occur at the times when it is most needed, even assuming a student is able to attend the tutorial and his specific problem is being dealt with.

The area which is increasingly showing most prospect of fulfilling many of the tutorial needs of distance-learners outlined above is the computer-based tutorial system. Given adequate access, computer systems can provide the flexibility required. The Open University has always used computers as an integral, albeit limited, part of its teaching packages. Until recently, use has been restricted to the assessment field including regular Computer Marked Assignments (CMAs) and Computer Marked Exams (CMEs) on many courses.

Typically, CMAs have taken the form of a series of variants of multiple-choice questions. Each assignment is designed to test a student's knowledge of a 'Block' of a course. Student participation is mandatory. Students must answer and return a specified proportion of the CMAs to gain credit. The only feedback which the student receives on performance is a letter grade which typically arrives at least one month after completion of the exercise.

Offering, as they do, ample opportunity for collaboration between students, coupled with a generally low level of expertise in multiple-choice design by many academics, it has been increasingly argued that CMAs fulfil only a dubious

	01	02	03	04	05	06	07	08	09	10	11	12	13
	London	South	South West	West Midlands	East Midlands	East Anglia	Yorkshire	North West	North	Wales	Scotland	Northern Ireland	South East
No of students*	71	27	24	71	49	50	40	70	27	22	41	18	42
No of face-to-face sessions (x hrs)	6 (x1½)		4 (x2)	4 (x2)	4 (x1½)	3 (x1½)	5 (x1½)	5 (x1½)	6 (x1½)	7 (x1)	8 (x1)	6 (x1½)	6 (x1)
No of 'Saturday Schools' (x3 hrs)	1(x3)	3(x2)	0	0	0	1	0	0	0	3(x2)	0	0	0
No of 'special' ** sessions' (x hrs)		1(x2)	0	0	0	2(x1½)	1½	1(x2)	0	0	1(x2)	0	1(x1½)
Flexible Time							5 hrs						
No of telephone tutorials	0	0	0	0	0	3	0	0	0	1	0	0	0

* 'No of Students' includes both undergraduate and post-experience students.

** 'special sessions' includes sessions allocated from within the SCS budget and sessions allocated from the regional fund

Figure 2. *Actual tutorial provision arranged for a half credit educational studies course in 1977*

assessment function.

It is certainly true that they offer little or no educational benefit to the student. A grade gives little indication of real areas of weakness or strength in a student's performance. Further, after the elapse of one month there is little opportunity for revision of a previous Block as the course has progressed.

Despite the faults inherent in the CMA system, it does offer a model which can be developed into a useful computer-tutorial aid. In 1976, the Student Computing Service (SCS) initiated the *Cicero* project to develop a computer-based rapid feedback and tutorial service.

The base model was the extant CMA system. It was decided at the outset that questioning would still be limited to multiple-choice, that the system would be accessible to students at the 200 SCS computer terminals around Great Britain, that feedback would still be available by post but that one week must be the maximum elapsed time between the student sending off an exercise and receiving diagnostic feedback and comment.

Three courses offered themselves for the pilot run of this system. The academic staff on these courses, in collaboration with project personnel, designed series of special 'diagnostic' multiple-choice questions. Care was taken to ensure that not only were all alternatives plausible but also that individual alternatives, or combinations, were diagnostic of particular strengths or weaknesses of students. These diagnostic questions were termed the 'profile' set.

In addition to the profile set, extra diagnostic questions were designed to clarify confusions. Remedial packages of text and additional questions were written to assist the student and to fill in any lacunae of knowledge.

All students on the three courses were sent the profile questions. Participation in the exercise was entirely optional. There was no assessment function of the system. It was solely for formative purposes. Having answered the profile set, participating students had two options. They could either fill in the special form and return it to the computing service, or they could attend one of the terminal sites and use *Cicero* interactively. (This latter option was recommended.)

If the student did opt for the postal system, the type of assistance that could be given was limited. The student's answers to the profile questions were processed on the day of receipt. The system analyzed these responses, provided fully annotated answers based on the individual responses, offered the student a future study plan based on the pattern of responses and composed this whole into a feedback letter. The letter was despatched to students by return of post.

If the student used the interactive system, the procedure was as follows: having logged in to the SCS system (full instruction in the terminal use was provided) the student ran the *Cicero* program. The first act of the program was to prompt the student for the profile answers. These were then analyzed in groups determined by subject material. Annotated answers were provided, follow-up questions were asked and remedial assistance was offered. At the end of all the groups, advice contingent upon the total patterns of responses was proffered.

The main advantage of the terminal based system is in the immediacy of feedback and the possibility of follow-up and remedial assistance.

During the pilot year, some 1,100 students out of 2,000 used the system, approximately two-thirds at the terminal. This 55 per cent using a computer-based tutorial system represents a higher percentage than those regularly attending face-to-face tutorials.

It cannot be denied that, at the current state of the art in CAL/CAI, there are tutorial functions which the computer cannot come close to emulating. However, within a distance teaching environment there are a number of factors which militate strongly in favour of the adoption of more computer-based systems.

The first must be the flexibility that is offered to the student in terms of study patterns. A face-to-face tutorial scheduled many months in advance for a precise date and time is unlikely to prove convenient for a large percentage of students. It may not fit in with the pattern of their study, or their lives. Computer-based tutorials can be made available throughout the year of study allowing the student to progress at his or her preferred pace, obtaining diagnostic and tutorial support as and when required. They also allow back-tracking for revision of selected areas to be under student control.

Access through a nationwide network of terminals as provided by the Open University Student Computing Service is a step towards providing the necessary flexibility of tutorial support required for distance education. However, the demands of the disabled, the housebound and the truly 'distant', combined with limited access hours, make work on home 'delivery-systems' for computer-assisted instruction mandatory. For some time the OU has been investigating the access problem and has initiated projects to determine how developments in microprocessor and communications technology may best be applied to facilitate the introduction of computing power to students' homes.

A second favourable characteristic of computer-based systems is the objectivity and standardization that can be achieved. With a distributed teaching system it is perhaps difficult to ensure that a course is being presented in the desired manner.

It is unlikely that individual tutors will be able to free themselves of the desire to colour their tutorials with their own personal perspective on the subject matter. It should be possible with CAL material to cover a wide variety of perspectives, particularly when courses are developed by teams of academics, and to allow the student to select a view of his or her own. It has been argued that this approach without 'individuality' makes education dull, grey and unappetizing. However, the individuality of approach should be tapped and incorporated into the CAL material to give all students an opportunity to savour it.

A third bonus is the speed with which CAL material can be revised. Distance teaching systems have had to rely on the printed word and the broadcast media. The difficulty, time and cost involved in rectifying errors or updating these channels provides a daunting prospect which deters change. However, computer-based material may be changed overnight.

The final factor which may presage the acceptance of CAL tutorial systems is the impossibility of providing any other effective alternative for some courses. While course populations are large in a distance-teaching establishment such as the Open University it is reasonable to provide tutorial support on a local basis. Tutorial groups may typically be in the region of 20 students, the majority of whom would have to travel no more than 20-30 miles to attend. However, as courses become more specialized and populations tend to decline, it will be economically unreasonable to provide local support and students will have to travel too far to make national or area tutoring feasible. The answer may well be local or home-based computer tuition.

Since the pilot scheme ran within the OU, many more courses have realized these potential benefits and have initiated new applications such as diagnostic and remedial basic mathematics education. To support the increased demand a new system with a more flexible author language for academics, greater student control, increased communication facilities and enhanced record-keeping has been developed. It is now running on the university's DEC-20 computers and is available to more than 10,000 students on an interactive and postal basis.

Adult education and distance teaching are likely to increase over the next decade and with them will be the demand for effective use of computers in teaching. It is vitally important that academics realize this now and face up to the demands that will be made of them in using the new technologies. Any new system will meet resistance. However, within the OU, courses are increasingly bidding for academic support for CAL material and are investigating how it may be best incorporated as an integral course component. Assessments are being carried out on the work done thus far and information should be available shortly.

References

Cooper, A J R (1978) An introduction to the *Cicero* System. Open University Student Computing Service.

Durbridge, N (1977) A brief survey of current course team policies on tutorial provision. Open University Institute of Educational Technology.

Lockwood, F G (1978) A rationale for the use of formative assessment components. Open University Institute of Educational Technology.

Northedge, A and Durbridge, N (1978) The use of tutorials in the Open University. In *International Yearbook of Educational and Institutional Technology 1978-79*. Kogan Page, London.

Open University (1979) BA Degree Handbook. Open University.

Rowntree, D G (1975) Student exercises in correspondence texts. Open University Institute of Educational Technology.

Zimmer, R (1977) A schematic-learning model of students' interactions with old and new ideas. Open University Institute of Educational Technology.

8.3 Some Educational Uses of Computers in UK Schools

K Shaw
Sheffield City Polytechnic

Abstract: Current uses of computers in schools are to be found in administration, mathematics and computer studies courses and other subjects. This paper describes uses only in these other subjects such as biology, chemistry, economics, geography and physics. Some of the reasons why teachers are using computers and what computers are being used for are also detailed.

Introduction

One of the more recent innovations which will have a significant impact on teaching during the next few years is the introduction of interactive computing facilities into schools. Over the last 10 years or so about 1,200 schools (ie about 20-25 per cent) in the UK have acquired access to computer facilities either via teletype terminals or micro-computers. The impetus for this has come mainly from mathematics departments wishing to introduce computer studies courses into their schools. Within five years the school which does not have access to computer facilities will be the exception and it is the development of sophisticated but relatively cheap micro-computers (costing between £700 and £3,500) which will make this rapid expansion of provision possible. The educational implications of this are profound. For instance, one of the more interesting implications is the possibility of designing material in several subject areas which can be used to stimulate and develop the intellectual potential of students in ways not possible by more conventional means.

Computers, with their ability to produce a large amount of information quickly, are considered to be particularly useful as teaching aids when constraints are placed on more conventional approaches by factors such as the availability of adequate and sufficient equipment; the time required to complete long-term investigations;

the complexity of investigations involving a large number of interacting factors; the cost of obtaining and running sophisticated equipment; the demands of investigations beyond the skills of students; the problem of sufficiently eliminating the 'noise' of the real world such that relationships can be tested and explored; and safety.

Currently, one of the greatest barriers to introducing computers as an aid to teaching is the lack of high quality educational packages capable of exploiting the potential of this new resource. With this constraint in mind a few small groups of teachers have, over the last five or six years, been investigating possible ways of integrating computer-assisted learning (CAL) material into existing classroom practice. Their efforts have usually been reported in educational journals such as the *School Science Review; Teaching Geography; Economics* etc. In addition, two organized projects, the Chelsea Science Simulation Project[1] and the Schools Council Project Computers in the Curriculum[2] have between them produced 48 units of computer-assisted learning material in five subject areas: biology, chemistry, economics, geography and physics.

Perhaps the biggest single advantage of a computer is the opportunity it provides for creative interaction between the student and the computer program. Students can be placed easily in problem solving situations which require them to critically examine a problem, plan an investigation, respond to the computer prompts and questions and to interpret computer-generated results. This forces students into active participation in their learning and causes them to operate at a higher level of intellectual activity than is often achieved in more conventional learning environments.

Types of Application

In exploiting the advantages which computers have to offer, teachers have explored essentially three types of application:

(a) Simulations of laboratory experiments, industrial processes and field investigations.
(b) The construction and/or exploration, evaluation and modification of models.
(c) Academic games.

Using a simulation the student can be freed from every-day laboratory constraints allowing him to concentrate more effectively on, say, the biological aspects of the problem. In biology, unfortunately, the construction and development of simulations is difficult because the models on which the simulation is based, if they exist, tend to be very complex. Simulations are, however, finding application in the teaching of topics at school level such as enzyme kinetics, genetic mapping, evolution, competition between species, population dynamics and physiological processes. The following example from a biology unit 'Pond Ecology'[3] illustrates such a simulation. Using this unit students are able to study the interactions between trophic levels in a pond and some of the effects of man upon them. Four types of investigation are allowed:

1 Observation of populations in the pond ecosystem in a stable state.
2 The effect of varying the initial populations of the separate trophic levels.
3 The effect of catching fish and of having a closed season.
4 The effect of polluting the pond.

Figure 1 illustrates the type of interaction the student has with the computer and the sort of information the computer displays. (The student's responses have been underlined.)

The need for a unit of this kind is obvious. Although some elementary aspects of population dynamics can be studied in a laboratory, investigations of the more complex natural communities must be carried out in the field. Such investigations, besides being time-consuming, can significantly disturb habitats and although giving an important appreciation of the ecosystem, the impression is one of a static environment; there is little opportunity to control any of the variables which affect the community. Such problems can be overcome to a large extent by using a simulation.

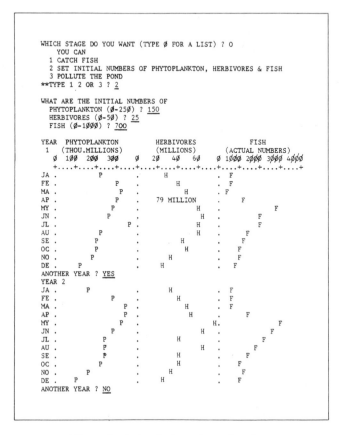

Figure 1. *A simulation of pond ecology showing the simulated aquatic system in a stable state*

Simulating Industrial Processes

A similar exercise which is valuable to chemistry teachers is the simulation of industrial processes. Current developments include simulations of the Haber process[4] for the manufacture of ammonia, the Contact process[5] for the manufacture of sulphuric acid, 'The Alkali Industry Exercise'[6] and the 'Energy Exercise'[7].

Such simulations allow students to investigate the optimum conditions for carrying out the particular process and gain an appreciation of the compromises which are necessary between chemical principles on the one hand and economic and technological constraints on the other.

This is best illustrated by reference to some sample output. Figure 2 is from the unit 'Contact'[8] which deals with the manufacture of sulphuric acid. From

investigations similar to these, students can determine apparently suitable
conditions of temperature and pressure for operating the contact process in order
to produce a high yield of sulphur trioxide. The use of a catalyst is seen to have no
effect on yield. From previous experiences, students will be aware that increasing
the temperature increases the rate of reaction. Thus, increasing the temperature,
although decreasing the yield, will result in sulphur trioxide being formed more
rapidly. The problem to solve is at what point (ie what temperature and pressure)
is this increase in reaction rate offset by the declining yield. Investigations similar
to those in Figure 3 allow this aspect to be explored in detail. A catalyst is now
seen to be of considerable importance.

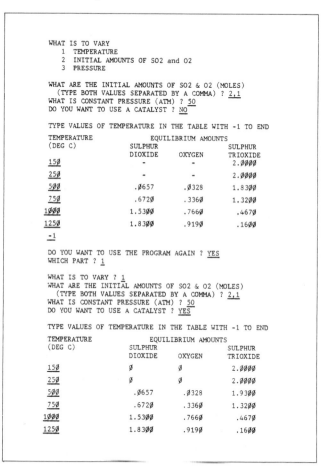

Figure 2 *A simulation of the manufacture of sulphuric acid
showing the effect of temperature and catalyst on the yield of sulphur trioxide*

The last stage of the investigation, as illustrated by Figure 4, imposes the further
constraints of producing sulphur trioxide at an economical price and operating the
process at sufficiently high yield to prevent the plant being closed down for
environmental reasons. The cost of the sulphur trioxide becomes more relevant if
this simulation is attempted by several groups working in competition.

```
WHAT IS TEMPERATURE ( DEG C) ? 500
WHAT IS THE INITIAL MOLAR RATIO SO2:02
   (TYPE TWO NUMBERS SEPARATED BY A COMMA) ? 2,1
WHAT IS PRESSURE (ATM) ? 50
DO YOU WANT TO USE THE CATALYST ? YES

MAXIMUM POSSIBLE CONVERSION OF SO2 IS 96.7%

USING ONE CONVERTER 4513 TONNES
OF SULPHURIC ACID IS PRODUCED PER DAY.


DO YOU WANT TO USE THE PROGRAM AGAIN ? YES
WHICH PART ? 2

TEMPERATURE ( DEG C) ?750
SO2:02? 2,1
PRESSURE (ATM) ? 50
CATALYST? YES

MAXIMUM POSSIBLE CONVERSION OF SO2 IS 66.4%

USING ONE CONVERTER  3098 TONNES
OF SULPHURIC ACID IS PRODUCED PER DAY.


USE AGAIN ? YES
WHICH PART ? 2
TEMPERATURE (DEG C) ? 750
SO2:02? 2,1
PRESSURE (ATM) ? 50
CATALYST? YES

MAXIMUM POSSIBLE CONVERSION OF SO2 IS  66.4%

USING ONE CONVERTER 176 TONNES
OF SULPHURIC ACID IS PRODUCED PER DAY
```

Figure 3 *A simulation of the manufacture of sulphuric acid
showing the effect of temperature on the daily production of sulphuric acid*

Simulations such as those described above enable a greater depth of understanding to be achieved than is possible through teacher exposition or reading of textbooks.

Computer-Based Models

Simple models have been used by teachers from many different disciplines. The construction, investigation and use of models, especially mathematical models, is valued for the power and economy which is associated with such forms of representing information.

In secondary schools examination of models is often limited to qualitative discussion or a simple quantitative treatment involving a few sample calculations. This is understandable because the calculations are often complex, and to perform sufficient of them to explore the model in any detail would be tedious and time-consuming. A computer program can enable the quantitative exploration of such models to be carried out rapidly and in considerable detail. Furthermore, the student is released from the chore of carrying out a large number of complicated calculations, an activity which can easily obscure the topic under investigation. With computer-based models the opportunity arises to investigate and compare alternative models and critically examine the physical or mental models on which the mathematical models are based.

```
WHAT IS TEMPERATURE (DEG C) ? 500
WHAT IS THE INITIAL MOLAR RATIO SO2:O2
   (TYPE TWO NUMBERS SEPARATED BY A COMMA)  ? 2,1
WHAT IS PRESSURE (ATM) ? 50
DO YOU WANT TO USE THE CATALYST? YES

MAXIMUM POSSIBLE CONVERSION OF SO2 IS 96.7%

USING ONE CONVERTER  4513 TONNES
OF SULPHURIC ACID IS PRODUCED PER DAY.



COSTS PER DAY (TO NEAREST POUND)

   MANPOWER       :     300
   CATALYST       :      15
   PLANT/REPAIRS  :6.2E+09
   SULPHUR DIOXIDE :  45714
   STEAM CREDIT   :  -9451
   ELECTRICITY    : 368573
   WATER          :____1354
                   ---------
   TOTAL          :6.2E+09

COST PER TONNE = 1.37E+06 POUNDS
*****POLLUTION - PLANT CLOSED BECAUSE
     MORE THAN 1% OF SO2 UNCONVERTED

DO YOU WANT TO USE THE PROGRAM AGAIN ? YES
WHICH PART ? 3

TEMPERATURE (DEG C) ? 427
SO2:O2?  1,1
PRESSURE (ATM) ? 1.5
CATALYST? YES

MAXIMUM POSSIBLE CONVERSION OF SO2 IS 99.1%

USING ONE CONVERTER  350 TONNES
OF SULPHURIC ACID IS PRODUCED PER DAY.

COSTS PER DAY (TO NEAREST POUND)

   MANPOWER       :     300
   CATALYST       :      15
   PLANT/REPAIRS  :     590
   SULPHUR DIOXIDE :   3463
   STEAM CREDIT   :    -840
   ELECTRICITY    :     292
   WATER          :_____105
                   ---------
   TOTAL          :    3925

COST PER TONNE = 11.19 POUNDS
```

Figure 4 *A simulation of the manufacture of sulphuric acid
showing the influence of several variables on daily production and cost of
manufacturing sulphuric acid*

The modelling exercise shown in Figure 5 is from a physics package, 'Radioactive Decay'.[9]

In this unit students are first introduced to some of the features of radioactive decay using laboratory experiments. A dice model of radioactive decay is then introduced. This leads to the argument that activity is directly proportional to the number of atoms of the decaying isotope. The dice model is convenient and easily appreciated and corresponds with the exponential decay observed in the laboratory. In addition, the statistical variations which are found with various size samples can be modelled by varying the number of dice used, and this model can be extended to represent a radioactive series. Unfortunately, such exercises are extremely time-

```
HOW MANY DICE ? 1ØØ
NUMBER OF FACES ON DIE ? 12
PROBABILITY OF DECAY IS 8.333331E-Ø2
THROW   DICE        DICE
        REMOVED     REMAINING       LN DICE       LOG DICE
                                    REMOVED       REMOVED
 Ø       Ø          1ØØ              -             -
 1       14          86             2.64          1.15
 2        1          85              .ØØ           .ØØ
 3       14          71             2.64          1.15
 4        Ø          71              -             -
 5       1Ø          61             2.30          1.ØØ
MORE RESULTS ? NO



HOW MANY DICE ? 1ØØØ
NUMBER OF FACES ON DIE ? 8
PROBABILITY OF DECAY IS  .125
THROW   DICE        DICE
        REMOVED     REMAINING       LN DICE       LOG DICE
                                    REMOVED       REMOVED
 Ø       Ø          1ØØØ             -             -
 1      18Ø         82Ø             5.19          2.26
 2      156         664             5.Ø5          2.19
 3      129         535             4.86          2.11
 4       87         448             4.47          1.94
·5       8Ø         368             4.38          1.9Ø
```

Figure 5. *A simulation of the dice model of radioactive decay*

consuming and tedious, involving the shaking and counting of hundreds of dice many times. A computer can be used to simulate the behaviour of a collection of dice, and thus of radioactive decay. The model can be modified to incorporate several probabilities of decay to illustrate the wide range of half lives found in radioisotopes.

The model is then developed further, as shown in Figure 6, to incorporate the growth and decay of radioactive daughter products and radioactive series.

In Economics

Science teachers are not the only ones using computers in schools to enhance the effectiveness of their teaching. In economics, for example, simulations offer a valuable opportunity to explore economic models using realistic data of considerable detail. This is an activity which is often impossible in normal teaching because of the complexity of credible models and the difficulty of performing sufficient calculations to allow adequate exploration of the economic situation being simulated.

Figure 7 illustrates a typical example taken from the unit 'Fiscal Policy' [10]. Students take the role of Chancellor of the Exchequer and control a simplified model of the economy by adjusting government spending and taxation. Some experience can be gained by analyzing an economic situation, attempting changes to affect target variables, selecting priorities for most urgent action, and analyzing the conflicts which arise between political and economic priorities.

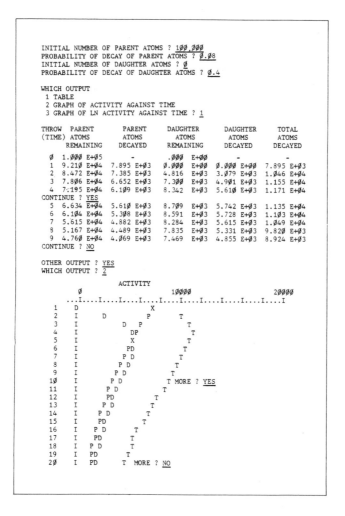

```
INITIAL NUMBER OF PARENT ATOMS ? 100,000
PROBABILITY OF DECAY OF PARENT ATOMS ? 0.08
INITIAL NUMBER OF DAUGHTER ATOMS ? 0
PROBABILITY OF DECAY OF DAUGHTER ATOMS ? 0.4

WHICH OUTPUT
 1 TABLE
 2 GRAPH OF ACTIVITY AGAINST TIME
 3 GRAPH OF LN ACTIVITY AGAINST TIME ? 1

THROW   PARENT        PARENT       DAUGHTER       DAUGHTER      TOTAL
(TIME)  ATOMS         ATOMS        ATOMS          ATOMS         ATOMS
        REMAINING     DECAYED      REMAINING      DECAYED       DECAYED

  0  1.000 E+05        -           .000  E+00        -          7.895 E+03
  1  9.210 E+04   7.895 E+03   0.000  E+00   0.000 E+00   7.895 E+03
  2  8.472 E+04   7.385 E+03   4.816  E+03   3.079 E+03   1.046 E+04
  3  7.806 E+04   6.652 E+03   7.300  E+03   4.901 E+03   1.155 E+04
  4  7.195 E+04   6.109 E+03   8.342  E+03   5.610 E+03   1.171 E+04
CONTINUE ? YES
  5  6.634 E+04   5.610 E+03   8.709  E+03   5.742 E+03   1.135 E+04
  6  6.104 E+04   5.308 E+03   8.591  E+03   5.728 E+03   1.103 E+04
  7  5.615 E+04   4.882 E+03   8.284  E+03   5.615 E+03   1.049 E+04
  8  5.167 E+04   4.489 E+03   7.835  E+03   5.331 E+03   9.820 E+03
  9  4.760 E+04   4.069 E+03   7.469  E+03   4.855 E+03   8.924 E+03
CONTINUE ? NO

OTHER OUTPUT ? YES
WHICH OUTPUT ? 2

                        ACTIVITY
         0                    10000                    20000
      ...I....I....I....I....I....I....I....I....I....I
    1   D                   X
    2   I      D         P           T
    3   I          D   P           T
    4   I            DP              T
    5   I            X               T
    6   I           PD            T
    7   I          P D           T
    8   I         P   D        T
    9   I         P D         T
   10   I        P  D         T MORE ? YES
   11   I        P D        T
   12   I        PD            T
   13   I        P D         T
   14   I       P D           T
   15   I       PD            T
   16   I      P  D         T
   17   I      PD        T
   18   I      P D        T
   19   I      PD        T
   20   I      PD     T  MORE ? NO
```

Figure 6. *A simulation of the dice model of radioactive decay illustrating the growth and decay of daughter products*

In Geography

With recent trends to include quantitative aspects into sixth form geography syllabuses many geography teachers have been looking at the potential of computer-assisted learning-type material. The Geography Association has established an organization[11] to advise on the production and use of such material and to act as a clearing house for the collection and distribution of CAL packages at all levels of the geography teaching. Typical of the material to be found in the area of geography are units on human population growth, drainage basin morphometry and industry location.

Several of the geography packages can be classified as games. Academic games, designed to assist in the teaching of material in conventional syllabuses, exist in

```
YEAR 1 : ECONOMY BOOMING

RATE OF TAX = 30
PLANNED GOVT SPENDING = 4878

POTENTIAL Y   =  24000          (I =  4592  S =  4150)
ACTUAL Y      =  23572          (C =  9987)
GROWTH        =  1.1%
UNEMPLOYMENT  = .505 M
PRICES        =  107
B-OF-P        = -550            (X =  4114  M =  4664)
RESERVES      =  50
NAT DEBT      =  8107           (G =  4878  T =  4771)
                 (+ 107)
OPINION POLL  = 56%

(TO END PROGRAM TYPE -1 FOR RATE OF TAX)  I : Gross investment in capital
*******                                                              goods
YEAR 2                                    S : Savings
                                          G : Actual Government Spending
RATE OF TAX    ? 35                       T : Total taxes levied
PLANNED GOVT SPENDING   ? 5200            C : Consumption
                                          X : Exports
POTENTIAL Y   =  24998          (I =  5301  S =  4127)
ACTUAL Y      =  23250          (C =  8709)
GROWTH        = -1.4%
UNEMPLOYMENT  =  1.104 M                   M : Imports
PRICES        =  111
B-OF-P        = -535            (X =  4042  M =  4577)
RESERVES      = -485 **CRISIS: BORROW  585  FROM FOREIGN BANKS
NAT DEBT      =  7470           (G =  5200  T =  5837)
                 (-637)
OPINION POLL  = 35%
*******
YEAR 3

RATE OF TAX   ?  35
PLANNED GOVT SPENDING   ? 4800

POTENTIAL Y   =  26118          (I =  5043  S =  4065)
ACTUAL Y      =  22360          (C =  8432)
GROWTH        = -3.9%
UNEMPLOYMENT  =  1.954 M
PRICES        =  113
B-OF-P        = -251            (X =  4086  M =  4337)
RESERVES      = -151 **CRISIS: BORROW  251  FROM FOREIGN BANKS)
NAT DEBT      =  6744           (G =  4800  T =  5526)
                 (-726)
OPINION POLL  = 21%
*******
```

Figure 7. *A simulation of the effect of tax rates and government spending on the British economy*

quite large numbers and in several disciplines, but the majority of them are board or pencil and paper-based games. Attention is now being given to developing computer-based games, which allow a complex administrative procedure to make the game more open-ended and elaborately scored. The teacher is freed from the task of refereeing and scoring so he may concentrate on giving subject advice to the students. He is also freed from the task of finding and collecting all the parts at the end of the game! These features enable computer-based games to avoid the situation in which the subject matter to be developed becomes incidental, a criticism often directed at board and card games.

Software Shortage

The success of computer-assisted learning material of the sort described above depends on several things, but of particular importance is the availability of good quality software (computer programs and any associated students' notes and teachers' guides) and ready access to computing facilities. At present in the UK there is a shortage of both of these, principally because neither the manpower resources to produce software nor the financial resources to provide computing facilities have been made available. It is to be hoped that the recently announced DES funding[12] (amounting to about £12.5 million over five years) for the development of micro-electronics applications in schools and colleges will contribute significantly to the solution of these problems.

With the advent of the micro-computer the hardware problem may well be largely resolved during the next five to 10 years but the creation of good quality software is a difficult and time-consuming process. The packages which have found widest acceptance in the teaching community to date are those which fulfil several important criteria, namely that the computer programs are portable and that associated teachers' and students' material is supplied, in order that teachers and students may make the best advantage of what may be an unfamiliar teaching resource and approach. Programs must be portable and well documented in order that they can be readily installed on a variety of computers.

As with any new development there is no shortage of poor quality or trivial CAL applications, many of which seem to be attempting to make use of the computer 'because it is there'. Such contrived use only brings CAL into disrepute. For instance, the abstract ideas of science are best taught by methods which rely on the concrete experiences of the student. It would be unfortunate if computer simulations were used as a substitute for these direct experiences. Similarly, a simulation should never be used as experimental evidence in support of the theories and assumptions on which the simulation is based. Such an argument, besides being circular, is dishonest. It is a feature of the better quality material that the originators have borne these dangers in mind and have considered what it is that the computer enables them to do which could not reasonably be done any other way.

Until micro-computers find their way into schools in considerable numbers (and until each school has several of these, as they inevitably will have if current trends in prices are maintained) the problem of organizing a class to make use of a CAL unit will remain a serious constraint.

Teletype Terminals

Currently the most common form of computer provision in schools is a teletype terminal. This is usually fixed and located in a room too small to accommodate more than a handful of students and remote from the classroom of the teacher who wishes to use it. Several methods of overcoming such constraints have been tried and the most effective modes of use appear to be the 'tutorial', 'individual', 'circus' and 'migration' modes.

With the tutorial mode the material is used as a demonstration with class discussion, the computer output being displayed on a television monitor. The individual mode is useful for students who have missed the work for some reason or who are having difficulty with a topic, or for more able students who require extension and enrichment material. Using the terminal on their own they can work through appropriate units at their own pace, the high level of motivation associated with CAL type activities making this a particularly valuable alternative. In the circus mode, however, the CAL material forms just one of several activities available. The migration mode involves groups of students travelling to an establishment such as a local polytechnic where several terminals can be made available for individual use as far as possible.

Micro-Computer Potential

The greater organizational flexibility associated with easily transported micro-computers will alleviate many of the organizational constraints associated with CAL. Shortly (in two to three years) there will be multi-user, multi-program micro-computers with high resolution colour graphics available. Such devices are going to offer considerable opportunities but also difficult challenges to the ingenuity of teachers to attempt topics and methods of teaching which might be thought desirable but which are currently not possible. When these machines are harnessed to videodisc systems (these are already available in the USA and Canada) they will have a tremendous impact on the secondary school classroom. Already it appears that currently available micro-computers are having a profound effect on not just what is taught in the classroom but how teachers interact with their pupils. The teacher's role will be considerably modified.[13] What is certain is that over the next few years we shall see a new resource emerging in homes and schools which is of far wider application than the training of potential employees of the computer industry. It is a resource which enables teachers and parents to extend and challenge the intellectual talents of their students and children in ways never before possible. It is to be hoped that this resource will be rapidly exploited and wisely used.

References

1   The Chelsea Science Simulation Project. Director: R Lewis, Educational Computing Unit, Chelsea College, University of London. Funded from 1971 - 1973 by Chelsea College.

2   The Schools Council Project Computers in the Curriculum. Director: R Lewis, Educational Computing Unit, Chelsea College, University of London. Funded from 1973 - 1977 and 1978-1981 by the Schools Council.

3   Tranter, A J and Leveridge, M E (1978) Pond ecology. In Leveridge, M E (ed) *Computers in the Biology Curriculum,* Chapter 4. Edward Arnold, London.

4   Edens, R and Shaw, K (1978) *Haber, A Unit on the Synthesis of Ammonia.* Edward Arnold, London.

5   Edens, R and Want, D (1978) The manufacture of sulphuric acid. In Shaw, K and Want, D (eds) *Computers in the Chemistry Curriculum,* Chapter 3. Edward Arnold, London.

6   Easton, M J, Johnstone, A H and Reid, N (1978) Computer managed chemistry teaching for secondary and tertiary students. *British Journal of Educational Technology,* 9, 1, pp 37-41.

7   Easton, M J, Johnston, A H and Reid, N *Ibid.*

8   Edens, R and Want, D *Ibid.*

9   Samways, B and Masterton, R D (1978) Radioactive Decay. In Chaundy, D C F and Masterton, R D (eds) *Computers in the Physics Curriculum,* Chapter 7. Edward Arnold, London.

10 Endall, J C, Fox, D W, Killbery, I and Green, W (1978) Fiscal policy. In Kilberry, I and Randall, K V (eds) *Computers in the Economics Curriculum,* Chapter 7. Edward Arnold.

11 GAPE, The Geography Association Package Exchange. Director: D Walker, Department of Geography, University of Loughborough.

12 DES Discussion Document: *Microelectronics in Education: A Development Programme for Schools and Colleges.*

13 Frazer, R E *Interactive Teaching with Microcomputers as an Aid.* Newsletter No 1. Obtainable from Department of Mathematics, College of St Mark and St John, Plymouth.

8.4 Computer-Based Training for Office Tasks

A Roebuck
Provident Management Services Ltd

In this workshop, held in conjunction with a display at the Conference Exhibition, Mr Roebuck showed how the Provident Group had used the Mentor type of computer-assisted learning to help solve the problem of training in small, dispersed units.

The Group

The principal companies of the Provident Group are: Provident Personal Credit Ltd, Practical Credit Services Ltd, PMSL Computer Services, Whitegates Estate Agency Ltd, and People's Bank Ltd. Provident's main interest is in consumer credit and it provides credit to over 1.5 million customers through its 430 branches. Each Branch has a Manager who is responsible for the growth of his Branch, security of collections, administration and co-ordination of a force of Agents.

The Need for Self-Instructional Learning

The increasing day-to-day pressures of a rapidly growing business leave Branch Managers with insufficient time to train staff properly, particularly new employees. A vicious circle develops:

Figure 1.

Mentor

To break this circle and improve the effectiveness of training, *Mentor* was used from early in 1977. *Mentor* makes it possible for a lesson writer to develop lesson material on the computer, in accordance with recognized programmed learning techniques. This material is then presented to students on an individualized basis through a visual display unit, enabling them to follow a course at their own pace and without an instructor present.

Successful CAL applications to date in the Group include:

Visual Display Unit Operator Training

This is aimed at clerks with little or no computer knowledge who are moving on to on-line systems from clerical systems and provides an introduction to the hardware used. Using the *Mentor* Edit Facility it is relatively easy to alter any small items in a lesson and several versions of this lesson have been created to personalize it as much as possible.

Teleprocessing Computer System

Six Provident branch offices are on-line to a central computer through a Real Time Teleprocessing (TP) system and this number is increasing. A suite of lessons encompasses: the need for the new system; the hardware involved; the individual transactions (eg registering a new customer or issuing credit); interpretation of the management information; and statistics which the system produces. These lessons are used in conjunction with a User Manual.

Demonstrations

After an initial period of familiarization with the *Mentor* language it is possible for an author to sit down at a VDU and write the lesson directly on to the computer. This can then be checked and de-bugged very quickly using the Edit Facility. This was found to be ideal for short technically simple lessons suitable for demonstrations, open days, appreciation courses, etc.

Induction Training

It is proposed to develop an existing introduction to Provident into a full induction lesson. Any new employee at any of Provident's subsidiaries which are on-line will be able to sign into the lesson.

Simulations

It is possible to use *Mentor* to simulate other systems. This has proved particularly useful when students have no knowledge of the system they will be using or if, for any reason, the 'live' system is unavailable or not cost-effective for training purposes. Using *Mentor*, simulations of various Real Time systems have been created. One of these comprises an instructional lesson on Premis, the Whitegates Estate Agency system, and then a simulation of the actual system.

Conclusion

It has taken very little time for people with no computer knowledge to become competent authors writing simple lessons. The original projected figure of 100 hours of lesson writing for every hour of on-screen material has been improved upon significantly with experience.

Finally, initial feedback from students suggests a generally favourable attitude to computer-assisted learning. This has proved particularly true with regard to VDU operator training.

8.5 Computer-Assisted Instruction (CAI) and Programmed Learning in British Airways

H S Butcher
British Airways Sales Training

Introduction

Mr Butcher described how Programmed Instruction techniques have been applied in British Airways to construct a computer-assisted instruction (CAI) course in Airline Passenger Reservations.

British Airways had eight separate CAI courses comprising about 230 hours of training. Passenger Reservations was the largest and most used course. From this programme trainees learned to record passenger reservations and to book seats needed through flight inventory records.

The following is a summary of Mr Butcher's paper.

The Problem

British Airways employs over 50,000 staff at 350 locations on all five continents. Business such as passenger bookings, departure control of flights etc is processed through computer terminals linked by a communication network to the main computer at London Airport.

There are 3,500 terminals, used by about 10,000 staff. These figures are expected to increase when other functions become computerized (such as freight and passenger accounting etc). Much training is needed, and is given on the computer terminals. Some terminals (about 150) are used only for training, but most (3,350) are also used in the normal day-to-day work on location. Any terminal can be used at any time for studying the CAI programmes.

The Universal Training Simulator

Any of the British Airways computer terminals can operate in 'Training Agent Mode' using a special sign in code. This means the system will respond to all inputs completely realistically. But all records and inventories in the system will remain untouched and unaffected by the inputs. The main disadvantage of this is that the students receive no instruction or remedial responses from the computer, but the advantage is that it enables students to practise without fear of changing any records and inventories. It responds automatically, rather than analytically, to any input.

The second system is called UTS (Universal Training Simulator). UTS is a CAI language and is programmed on-line into the system by the course author. The system can be used for linear and branching programmes, and has a testing and marking facility which tells each student how he or she is progressing.

UTS is used in a variety of ways, but most teaching is done by using proven programmed learning principles. The programming approach is eclectic, but mathetic principles, such as Demonstrate/Prompt/Release cycle and covert responding, are widely used.

Developing the Passenger Reservations Programme

The target population and their needs for this course were carefully analyzed, the prime factors being:

1 To cater for nationals of countries in all five continents.
2 There are widely differing training needs at many of the 350 locations.
3 Both experienced and inexperienced staff need training.

When the course was written, it was found it took a student an average time of 90 hours to complete. The basic design of the course was modular (or block) as shown in Figure 1. Each of these blocks is a self-contained unit of instruction that

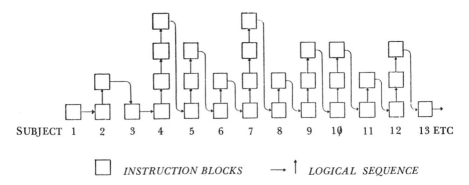

| SUBJECT | 1 | 2 | 3 | 4 | 5 | 6 | 7 | 8 | 9 | 10 | 11 | 12 | 13 ETC |

☐ *INSTRUCTION BLOCKS* → | *LOGICAL SEQUENCE*

Figure 1. *Block system*

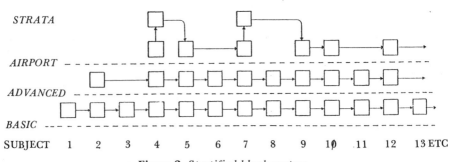

STRATA

AIRPORT

ADVANCED

BASIC

| SUBJECT | 1 | 2 | 3 | 4 | 5 | 6 | 7 | 8 | 9 | 10 | 11 | 12 | 13 ETC |

Figure 2. *Stratified block system*

takes a student an average of 20 minutes to complete. They are arranged in a logical sequence. In its original version the course design required all students to complete all blocks. In a number of locations this meant that some trainees learned transactions they would not need to use in practice. To overcome this problem, the blocks were split into strata as shown in Figure 2. The *Basic* stratum contains 2,000 frames and requires 30-35 hours study time. It aims to train staff to meet the needs of 90 per cent of all passengers requiring reservations. For many locations this is sufficient. It should be noted that the terms *Basic* and *Advanced* do not refer to difficulty or complexity, but to frequency and probability of usage.

The *stratified block system* has the following features:

1 Three strata, *Basic*, *Advanced* and *Airport*.
2 270 (approximately) separate blocks of instruction.

This effectively means that student(s) can have:

3 30 to 90 hours' training according to need.
4 Differing paths which can be followed through the instruction.

The programme is also adaptive. The complete course consists of 5,000 frames although a student, subject to ability, may complete as many as 6,000 or as few as 4,000.

When students are taking the complete course (90 hours) they can comfortably work up to six hours of instruction per day — 30 hours per week. However, this can be varied according to requirements. Students can be reasonably productive after 30 hours of instruction.

The results of regular self-tests are displayed to the students, so they are fully aware of their progress as they proceed through the course. The average number of students who use the reservations course is 400 per year. The number for all courses averages 1,000 per year.

Evaluation

As British Airways have a large number of staff requiring training in London, courses for London staff are often used by the course authors for testing the programmed learning material. Amendments are made as necessary during this time. It took two man-years to prepare and write the reservations course at a cost of £20,000 (including material).

At large locations, such as London, it is easier to use this course in a classroom. As the programme is adaptive each student receives training to suit his or her individual needs and the appropriate remedial response if an error is made. So an instructor becomes in effect a supervisor and can comfortably handle up to 20 students per class, as against a maximum number of 10 studying the same subjects in conventional chalk and talk classrooms. So productivity is doubled.

The programmed system costs approximately £30,000 less to run for a year during which time development costs are more than paid for. Over a period of five years the savings are enormous.

The reservations course, in particular, has been successfully adapted and marketed to a number of other airlines. It often forms a part of a total package in which the purchasers receive a complete working reservations system, including a share of a computer and its associated communications network, and all the training necessary to operate the system. British Airways has two computer networks. One is used just for British Airways. The other parallel network is used by other airlines and is rented to them. It is anticipated that this will gain much additional revenue for British Airways.

8.6 Computer-Managed Learning in a Postgraduate Service Course

T R Black
The New University of Ulster

The author described an application of the Keller Plan approach to a service course in which the computer substituted the provision. In particular, the computer provided feedback based on post-test performance. In the *Falcon* system developed here by the author the program classified student performance into three categories: (a) Mastery, (b) Doubt and (c) Non-mastery (Black, 1978). This allowed an alternative to proceeding or remedial assistance, such as oral discussion with the tutor, submission of corrections for items missed, or a unique progression through subsequent modules.

In *Falcon*, a performance feedback statement was generated on the basis of sub-scores on the homogeneous parts of the test. The recommendation as to what is done next is based upon how many of the sub-scores were in the Mastery, Doubt or Non-mastery ranges. (See Figure 1.)

Comments and statements were kept on cards for three reasons: (i) each test deck is used only half-a-dozen times a year — therefore not justifying permanent disk storage; (ii) the tutor has direct access to comments and can make alterations by simply changing selected cards; (iii) statements can be of unlimited length. Since the program is content free, any subject tutor could employ it as a feedback mechanism.

The author described an example of this approach, an in-service course for experienced teachers leading to the Diploma in Advanced Studies in Education at The New University of Ulster. Two units common to all students were 'Research Design and Structure' and a dissertation. The first included an introduction to general principles of research design and applications of elementary descriptive and inferential statistics.

The students (experienced teachers) rarely have any mathematical background and constitute a very heterogeneous group with respect to subject interest, scientific and mathematical ability.

	Master (M)		PERFORMANCE
Sub-scores	Doubt (D)	generate	FEEDBACK
	Non-mastery (N)		STATEMENT

AND

Number of M, D,		RECOMMENDATION
N sub-scores	generates	STATEMENT

Figure 1. *Instructional decision-making using post-test results in the* Falcon *system: diagnosing learning problems plus recommending subsequent action*

In order to deal with the fear of science and mathematics, frequent feedback on problems and encouragement for success were essential. Two pre-instructional diagnostic tests on basic maths skills and nine modules of one week were designed to facilitate student learning. Each module consisted of a detailed study guide outlining the objectives of the unit, recommended readings and practice problems in the text (which has answers in the back), and suggested additional resources, plus the post-test. This test is criterion-referenced, with the three possible categories of performance described earlier: mastery, doubt and non-mastery. The tests are primarily multiple-choice, but there are some open-ended items. Comments on the quality of response are in the feedback deck and the tutor marks the appropriate choice on the answer card.

In a weekly students' meeting, an hour was used to discuss questions arising from the previous week's post-test. After a break, there was a brief lecture introducing the next topic and any remaining time was used to sort out individual problems on previous new material. The students have until roughly the following Tuesday to read, do practice problems, and complete the post test. If answer cards and any long answers are posted to the instructor by early Wednesday, they are computer processed and individual feedback is ready for the Thursday evening class (see Figure 2). Under no other system could sizeable numbers of students

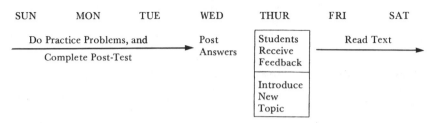

Figure 2. *Work pattern for statistics portion of 'Research Design and Structure' unit*

submit work one day and get detailed results by the following evening. It should be noted that while a new topic is introduced weekly, there is no obligation (though it is desirable) to return answer cards by the following week. This allows a limited amount of self-pacing within the limits of the university semester.

In the Spring semester of 1977, 14 students took the unit; in 1978 there were 23 and this year there have been 22. The performance of these groups on examinations has been encouraging, indicating a reasonable level of mastery of skills and knowledge. Each year, at the end of the course, a 50 item questionnaire is distributed to gather more information to help improve the unit. While the items on the questionnaire were designed to provide the tutor feedback on specific aspects of the unit and how it was taught, several sub-sets provided information for a more general analysis. Five variables were used from the questionnaire, plus three others from available data, listed as follows:

(a) *P-learn.* Perceived learning, how much the student felt he had learned.
(b) *Demand.* How demanding (time-consuming, difficult, etc) this part of the unit was felt to be.
(c) *CML.* Computer managed learning feedback: student attitude towards this.
(d) *Attitude.* General attitude towards the statistics portion of the unit.
(e) *Materials.* Attitude towards learning materials (text, study-guides, etc).
(f) *C-Tests.* Class tests, the grade received on the two class tests.
(g) *Time.* Time spent per module (in hours).
(h) *Maths.* The score on the initial pre-instructional diagnostic test on basic mathematics skills needed to understand the text.

The author reported that analysis of the 1978 questionnaire showed perceived learning tending to be rated above the middle mark, but somewhat surprisingly this variable did not correlate with class-test scores or time spent at all, though, as expected, it did so positively with general attitude and attitude towards the learning materials. Students obviously felt the course to be quite demanding, and yet several wrote comments saying they did not see how one could learn statistics other than by getting involved in 'doing' them. While the students tended to feel the computer managed learning (*Falcon*) feedback was valuable, this feeling did not correlate with any other variable. This does not mean it had no effect on learning, but simply that there is no association between student attitude towards it and any of the other variables.

There was an interesting negative correlation between attitude towards learning materials and how demanding the work was seen to be, though the attitude towards materials tended to be quite high. It seems to indicate a tendency of high attitude towards materials, low perceived demand (and *vice-versa*). There was also a not surprising correlation between general attitude and attitude towards the learning materials.

The class-tests mean was in the middle of the II(ii) range, and grades were distributed over the entire spectrum and yet there was no association between grades and any of the other traits. It is possible that grades (as long as one passes) are not as strong an influence on attitudes as one might expect, at least for these students. Also of interest was the time spent, an average of 6.2 hours per week per module. Though there was a considerable dispersion of times among students, it is not difficult to understand why, as working teachers, they might consider this a demanding course of study. Finally, it is noted that there was a high mean score on the diagnostic test, indicating that their mathematics background was not as bad as they felt it was.

One interesting result had been found when investigating an isolated item. Ten per cent of the marks for the unit were based upon the number of the nine modules in which the students demonstrated mastery. This could be achieved either by adequate initial scores on post-tests *or* by submitting corrections on sections for which mastery was not demonstrated. The relevant question asked whether or not students would have followed the recommendations of the computer feedback if they had not been given points for demonstrating mastery. Ten said probably, but 11 marked occasionally, rarely, or never. Comments indicated that pressure for time was probably the reason, and this 'carrot' seemed to make a difference. This is interesting because it is often felt that post-tests should be for feedback alone and results should not affect assessment.

In summary, it appeared that in most cases the fear of the statistics portion of the unit was overcome and learning did occur. The drawback was obviously the large demand upon their time as working teachers. This will be an essential focus for improvement in the future.

More extensive use of the potential of the *Falcon* system will be attempted, for example, establishing multiple routes through the learning materials, providing a choice of optional modules in such areas as non-statistical approaches to research, measurement technology and advanced topics in statistics.

The *Falcon* CML system would become available for use through remote terminals and micro-computers. This should increase the accessibility of computer managed learning to more teachers and lecturers as a tool for facilitating learning in the classroom.

The author argued that since such a system is not dependent on interactive terminals nor on any specific learning style, it could be of great value in providing feedback in distant learning situations.

Reference

Black, T R (1978) An introduction to the *Falcon* system: Facilitating learning by computer managed learning. The New University of Ulster. (mimeo)

Section 9:
The Management of
Education and Training

9.0 Introduction

ETIC '79 Tracks

Papers in this Section are drawn from all three tracks. At Sheffield, Adderley *et al* (9.1) appeared in Track 1, 'Self-Instructional Programmes in Practice'. Moors (9.2), Scobbie and McAleese (9.3) and Wyant (9.4) were in Track 2, 'Learning Design'. Ely (9.5) and Hammond and Wilson (9.6) were presented in Track 3, 'Learning Environment, Practice and Presentation Techniques'.

Categories and Special Interests

Adderley *et al*, Scobbie/McAleese, Wyant, and the Romiszowski workshop (9.8) were coded in the 'EdMan' for 'Educational Management' category. So was the workshop linked with the Scobbie/McAleese paper.

Moore, Ely (paper and workshop), Hammond/Wilson, and the Edney workshop (9.7) were coded 'SupS' for 'Support Systems'. Moors was also coded 'Evaluation' ('Eval'); Hammond/Wilson, 'Mil' for 'Military'; and Edney, 'Ind' for 'Industry'. There was also an 'Ind' code for Romiszowski, and a 'Tert' for 'Tertiary Education' code for Scobbie/McAleese.

9.1 Time Off for Innovation

Ken Adderley, John Pearce, Joanna Tait and David Williams
Brighton Polytechnic

Abstract: Teachers and lecturers often begin educational development work, but find that their good intentions are frustrated by lack of time, insufficient support from senior colleagues and central resource units and the low esteem with which this work is regarded.

The Educational Development Unit (EDU) of Learning Resources at Brighton Polytechnic has established an EDU Release Scheme in an attempt to alleviate these difficulties. The scheme provides a reduction in lecturers' class contact hours so that they may undertake clearly identified projects, which are approved by the appropriate Course and Faculty Boards. Lecturers are then given every possible support by EDU and other Learning Resources staff, and the usefulness of their work is increasingly being acknowledged by both colleagues and students.

The EDU Release Scheme has operated for five years and continues to grow. It currently involves 34 lecturers from five out of the six Polytechnic Faculties, and projects have ranged from investigation and evaluation of available teaching and learning materials to design and production of specialized learning packages and video-tapes.

The paper concentrates on the problems involved in establishing the Release Scheme, the types of practical support that lecturers have needed, and the nature of the educational development work achieved.

Background

One of the reasons frequently given for the general lack of innovation in teaching and learning in further and higher education is that lecturers do not have the time to do the work, and that colleges rarely allocate specific time for such activities.

The Educational Development Unit (EDU) at Brighton Polytechnic was designed so that it would provide, among other facilities, *time*. Lecturers could be seconded part-time to the EDU with a corresponding release from part of their teaching commitment in order to work on possible solutions to teaching and learning problems which they had encountered. As a result, the EDU has gradually built up the EDU Release Scheme by which lecturers are freed from a proportion of their contact hours to carry out carefully specified projects. To date, 56 Release Projects have been undertaken, involving 43 members of the teaching staff. These have involved lecturers in the sciences, art and design, engineering and social science, and included projects such as the introduction of individualized and independent learning, case studies, games and simulation; the production of workbooks, learning packages and video-tapes; and the establishment of specialist resource centres. More details are given later in this paper.

The extensive spread of Release Projects throughout the Polytechnic and the diversity of projects undertaken indicate the need for:

(a) close contact between educational development and teaching staffs and a good understanding of their academic priorities and problems; and

(b) a wide range of services to support the projects, at each of the planning, production and implementation stages.

This has been possible at Brighton Polytechnic because the EDU is a small but integral part of Learning Resources.

Learning Resources is a central service department that provides an appropriate complex of *library*, *media* and *educational development* services at each of the four main sites of the Polytechnic. Within it there are also a limited number of central support services that include technical facilities, library media services, EDU production services and library technical services. The 'site' and 'central' services are organized in such a way as to offer the most appropriate service to users, and a high degree of integration and collaboration occurs throughout Learning Resources.

At each site are based Learning Resources' key contact people, whose job is to be in close touch with the needs, problems, priorities and proposed developments of the staff and students. These are the Course Resources Officers (CROs) each of whom has responsibility for the Learning Resources services required by a course or group of courses. They are qualified librarians, and take direct responsibility for the provision of print and media resources which are made available to the staff and students of their courses through the libraries of the Polytechnic. Additionally they help to identify other needs of lecturers and direct them to the appropriate Learning Resources staff — for example, for assistance with course design, improvements to classroom facilities, specialist audio-visual requirements, and the opportunity to join in the EDU Release Scheme.

Assisting with course design and operating the EDU Release Scheme are two of the specific tasks of the Educational Development Assistants (EDAs). EDA appointments (which are Learning Resources posts) are made on a faculty basis to experienced teachers having a declared interest in improving the teaching and learning processes. The present number of EDAs is extremely small at 2.7 full-time equivalent (FTE) (in addition to the EDU Co-ordinator) and comprises two part-time EDAs who are responsible for the faculties in which they also teach, and two full-time non-teaching EDAs. However, it is intended that eventually there should be one EDA with an appropriate academic background for each of the six Polytechnic faculties.

The roles of the CRO and EDA can be seen to be complementary, and together they form mutually supportive teams in the various faculties. Sometimes both the EDA and the CRO will co-operate with a lecturer on his or her project and sometimes they will contribute separately. At other times their main concern will be to ensure that other sections of Learning Resources are providing the required support. This means that each Release Project has, through the EDA-CRO network, ready access to production, library and audio-visual services, as well as to the EDU's general consultancy service covering teaching and learning activities.

Setting up an EDU Release Project

The initiation of an EDU Release can be considered to have two essential parts — the official provision and costing of the Release time, and the generation of the project idea itself. These are developed into a written specification and submitted for approval to the relevant Faculty Boards and the Learning Resources Committee of the Academic Board.

The EDU has at present in its staffing establishment, 2.2 FTE posts specifically to support EDU Releases. This support takes the form of a transfer of part-time lecturing funds, or, exceptionally, the salary for a full-time post, from the EDU to the appropriate department, so that adequate cover can be arranged for the reduced class contact hours of the Released lecturer. In this way no extra teaching burden should fall on the other members of the department's teaching staff — an important consideration in creating an acceptance of the usefulness of educational development work. For certain departments where there is a comparatively low student: staff ratio, EDU Releases are not supported as just described but the department benefits from an improvement in its student:staff ratio equivalent to the Release time involved, and also from the projects undertaken. Such unsupported Releases currently amount to a further 3.2 FTE, and in all 34 lecturers are involved in EDU Releases for the academic year, compared with six in 1975/76. Most of these are for periods of between one and three terms, for one or two days a week — this being the usual span, but some are renewals or extensions of a previous year's Release Project.

The preparation for an EDU Release usually occurs in the Spring or Summer term of the preceding academic year, frequently involving a quick round of consultations between the EDU Co-ordinator and Heads of Departments, and that is the time when the second part of the initiation — the generation of specific project ideas — takes place. There have been several different sources of ideas, for example, Departmental Boards of Study, Heads of Departments liaising with the EDU Co-ordinator, Educational Development Assistants, Course Resources Officers, students and CNAA Course Proposals, but most commonly it is the lecturer himself or herself who originates the project idea. It is discussed fully with the appropriate EDA and CRO, and depending on the nature of the project, with EDU Production Services, as well as other teaching colleagues. The Head of the Department is consulted, and with his or her agreement, outline approval for the Release project is then sought from the Boards of Study, Faculty Boards and the Learning Resources Committee at their summer term meetings.

At this stage a detailed specification of the Release is drawn up with the aims of estimating the amount of Release time required, assessing the feasibility of the project, identifying its objectives, outlining a scheme of work and suggesting a form of evaluation. However, the specification is not intended to tie the lecturer to a prescribed schedule, but rather to allow him to think out on paper a possible framework for the project. It is our experience that lecturers re-think, develop and improve their original plans during the Release time, and indeed they are given every encouragement to do so. The drafting of the Release Specification is usually undertaken by the EDA in close collaboration with the lecturer and the appropriate CRO, and the Release proposal is passed for final approval to the Board of Study, Faculty Board and the Learning Resources Committee. An example of a Release Specification is given in Figure 1.

During the development of the EDU Release Scheme the Release Specification has acquired an increasing importance and it is interesting to consider both the explicit and implicit purposes of this document. Three of the more obvious purposes are to produce a framework for the project, to inform the appropriate staff in Learning Resources and academic departments, and to obtain official approval for the Release project. More subtle than these, but still fairly explicit, is to ensure that the responsibility for the innovative educational department work lies clearly with the academic Departments and Faculties, for it is in them that the power and influence of an academic institution such as Brighton Polytechnic reside. Similarly, the approval of the Release Specification by the Boards of Study provides official recognition of educational development and makes it 'public' knowledge within the Departments and Faculties — both purposes being important in helping to achieve academic respectability for this type of work. One of the distinctive features and emphases of polytechnics was to be their role as teaching institutions — but in general teaching and learning are still not recognized as having comparable value to research and thus two of the hidden purposes of the Release Specification are for educational development to begin to achieve greater equality with research, and for it to become an accepted part of the institution's work.

Some Examples of Release Projects

As mentioned earlier, the variety of Release Projects is considerable. However, to gain a more informed appreciation of their scope a little more detail is required, and the following summary of current projects in Table 1 provides a brief description of the proposed content of each.

```
┌─────────────────────────────────────────────────────────────────────┐
```

EDU RELEASE PROPOSALS 1978/79   LEARNING RESOURCES EDUCATIONAL DEVELOPMENT UNIT

FACULTY OF ART AND DESIGN   Educational Development Assistant: Joanna Tait

                                   Course Resources Officer: John Priestley

---

Proposal from Department of: VISUAL COMMUNICATION
On Behalf of: DON WARNER
For Release time equivalent to: 0.13 FTE – 1 day/week, Autumn and Spring terms

---

1. Subject Area: Typographic Design

2. Target Population: BA Graphic Design
                            1st and 2nd year students
                            Numbers: 90

3. Project Synopsis: To produce a teaching/learning package that will give
                            students a basic understanding of typography which they
                            will be able to use and develop throughout the test of the
                            course in projects which demand the effective use of words
                            in design.

4. Composition of   The package will include a handout/booklet with reference
   Materials: or extracts from other books, a collection of slides
                            with related notes, and possibly a videotape composed of
                            extracts from related film and video material already
                            available.

5. Educational   To make the package available to all lecturers and students
   Development Aims: working in this area and of use to them as and when
                            required.

                            To form the first collection of prepared teaching and
                            learning materials in this field in the department.

6. Application of   See 5 above
   Materials:

7. Deadlines: The materials will be produced in the Autumn/Spring terms
                            1978/9 and first used in the Autumn term 1979.

8. Evaluation: Evaluation will consist of individual feedback from
                            students and staff, a short questionnaire, and a
                            subjective evaluation by staff in the quality of
                            typographical design in student projects done after the
                            package has been used, and in third year assessments.

9. Involvement of Other   It is intended to involve other staff teaching typography
   Teaching Staff: so that the package can also be used by them as required.

10. Educational   Quiet working area.
    Development Unit: Assistance from Course Resources Officer and AV Media
                            Unit Leader in searching for and acquiring existing
                            relevant materials.

                            Assistance from AV Media Unit Leader and EDU Production
                            Services in production.

Figure 1. *An example of an EDU release specification*

FACULTY	DEPARTMENT	SUMMARY OF RELEASE PROJECT
Art and Design	Combined Arts Fine Art Visual Communication 3-D Design	Setting up Textile library – CNAA requirement. Instructional videotapes on printmaking techniques Structural learning materials on typography Tape-slide interviews with practising ceramicists

Engineering and Environmental Studies	Building
	
	Electrical Engineering
		Handouts and AV materials to improve students'
		  drawing skills
		Improved laboratory worksheets
		Sets of slides on history of man-made environment
		Media materials on the range of building processes
		Computer-assisted games to simulate planning
		  and estimating
		Learning packages in electrical circuit theory
		Setting up a collection of learning materials
		  for Complementary Studies in the revised
		  CNAA degree
		Learning packages for first-year students
		Production of structured learning notes on
		  analogue and digital electronics

Management and Informatics	Business Studies
	
	Finance and Accountancy
	
	Mathematics
		Case study materials to integrate disciplines
		  within Business Studies
		Structured learning materials with objective
		  tests
		Private study guides for engineering students

Natural and Life Sciences	Applied Chemistry
	
	Applied Physics
	
	Pharmacy
		Developing teaching and assessment methods and
		  materials for Project Based Studies in the
		  revised Combined Sciences CNAA degree.
		As above, and including "Semester I – Case
		  Studies in Physics" Unit
		Production of teaching and learning materials,
		  mainly for laboratory techniques otherwise
		  requiring repeated demonstration.

Social and Cultural Studies	Community Studies
	
	Communication and European Studies
		Collection and production of media materials
		  for social sciences skills training
		Preparation of structured learning materials for
		  Media Resources Option in CNAA Librarianship
		  degree
		Completion of videotapes on Swedish libraries
		Preparation of learning packages in French.

Table 1. *Current Release Projects*

A look at the nature of these Projects reveals an evolutionary rather than a revolutionary development of Release Projects — very much in keeping with general educational trends. The use of media is increasingly being accepted as a legitimate and valuable method of communication and presentation, and as a means to an end instead of an end in itself. There has also been an increasing emphasis in many Projects on learning rather than direct teaching, with lecturers designing individualized learning materials in a variety of formats. More recently there is evidence of some movement towards independence in students' learning with plans related to project-based case studies and the establishment of 'learning laboratories' where students can select from a wide range of learning materials. Two further trends worth noting are the greater involvement of the student in the learning process, for example by the use of games and simulations and, more generally, an increasing recognition of the importance of evaluation in the teaching and learning processes.

From the foregoing it seems apparent that, almost without exception, the

Release Projects are based on at least one of the following general educational objectives:

☐ to improve the quality of students' learning;
☐ to solve problems in the teaching process; and
☐ to make more effective use of lecturers' time.

To illustrate this and to demonstrate the initiation of the Projects four Release Schemes will be described in greater detail. The first three are current projects, and the fourth was carried out in 1975-77.

(1) Lecturers in Fine Art (Printmaking) provide a short introductory programme in printmaking techniques for all students in the Faculty of Art and Design. However, some students miss part or all of this introduction, and others do not require the techniques until later in their course when they find they need to revise and reconsider them. Consequently, lecturers have spent a lot of time repeating the same basic information to a variety of small groups and individual students. The purpose of the Release Project was two-fold, to avoid undue repetition of the introductory programme with its necessary preparation, and to reduce the time spent with individual students on basic instruction and revision. To achieve this a book of printmaking sources and resources, a tape-slide sequence of examples of general techniques and a video-tape of specific techniques have been prepared, and all three of these are to be placed in the library for use by both students and lecturers.

(2) A lecturer in Electrical Engineering was concerned about the lack of impact on students' learning produced by teaching groups of 60-80 using a fairly formal lecture technique. The large number of students attending and the teaching method employed gave the students little opportunity to apply the knowledge they were acquiring, and made it difficult for the lecturer to discover if individual students were experiencing difficulties. He therefore embarked on a Release Project to develop a number of programmed texts for students to use individually. This involved him in formulating learning objectives, designing tests, structuring the material, incorporating questions and problems into the text, and selecting background reading and references. The programmed materials were then given to the students, and the lecture time used in a different and more flexible way. Students could work through the material in the classroom, referring to the lecturer as they encountered difficulties, or they could come to the classroom for the answers to specific problems which they had identified in their own time. They could also, of course, approach the lecturer at other times. The role of the lecturer had changed significantly and he now spent most of his time helping students, individually or in twos and threes. He was able to guide them through their problems and help them to apply the knowledge and techniques learned from the programmed materials.

(3) A new Media Studies option for an established BA degree in Librarianship has recently been validated by the CNAA and is being offered from September 1979. An EDU Release has been established to prepare case-study materials illustrating the use of media in a variety of libraries.

(4) When the CNAA BSc degree course in Combined Studies (Applied Science) was introduced, it was designed to use the first half-term to offset students' deficiencies in either Physics or Chemistry and so attempt to achieve a common standard in these two main subjects. This part of the course was called 'Balancing Studies', and the Physics lecturers chose to teach their component through individualized learning packages backed up by strong tutorial support. This would allow the student to spend proportionately more time on those areas of the basic Physics with which he or she was least

familiar. Consequently, a group of EDU Releases was negotiated to prepare and test the learning packages, and to develop the existing Learning Laboratory in the Physics Department where the package could be kept, together with any necessary 'hardware' such as a slide projector, video-cassette and audio-cassette players, and a calculator, and where students could work at any convenient time.

Release Projects in Practice

Given the scope and variety of Projects within the EDU Release Scheme, a range of support services has been needed. These have included: typing and secretarial help; printing; graphic design; production of media in general, but particularly video-tapes — shot in the studio and on location, slides, photographs and overhead projector transparencies; library searches for print and non-print materials; the introduction of new library services; guidance in structuring learning materials and acquiring student feedback; and the provision of funds for visiting other colleges.

Because of the nature and integrated functions of Learning Resources, many of the services required can be provided through its own network. It is the EDA, for instance, who assists in the structuring of learning materials, helps obtain student reactions, makes contact with other appropriate lecturers and institutions, and generally tries to ensure that the Project develops as planned. CROs provide the necessary links with the libraries, as well as working with the EDA on the general progress of the Project. EDU Production Services provide a media and print production service along with graphic design expertise, while other Learning Resources services can be drawn on as required. The lecturer, EDA and CRO meet at intervals — depending on the needs of the individual and his or her Project — to review progress, plan ahead and consider any problems that may have arisen.

Of course, there are problems! Personality clashes can sometimes occur, jeopardizing the success of the project. Consequently the highest priority is placed on establishing good personal relationships between the lecturer and the Learning Resources staff with whom he or she is involved. Informal discussions are often held to attempt to identify potential problems before they are overtaken by events. Each lecturer has his or her own way of working and relating to others. Some wish to work alone with the minimum of consultation and support and some respond to frequent discussions with a number of colleagues. So a flexible arrangement exists for each working group to allow the organization of, for example, discussion sessions and meetings, to suit the lecturer's wishes.

Many lecturers find it difficult to work in their departmental staffrooms, which are usually shared with several other colleagues. Students constantly drop in, *ad hoc* meetings are arranged, and departmental problems are never far away. Learning Resources has, therefore, set aside one quiet room for those Released lecturers who wish to use it. This room provides a refuge from departmental pressure and is also close to most of the support services they are likely to need.

Time presents another problem. In spite of reduced class contact hours it is often difficult to reserve the appropriate block on the time-table. To try to overcome this, proposed Releases are discussed at the earliest opportunity with the departmental time-tabler so that he or she can plan the necessary half-day or whole day free from teaching commitments. It has become clear that time in units of less than half-a-day tends to disappear without trace, and it is such a vital resource that it must be guarded carefully. Linked with this is the problem of pacing a Release Project so that the seemingly generous 'one day a week for a year' does not insidiously become 'four weeks to the deadline'. The EDA and the CRO have a very important role to play in avoiding such last minute panic.

Where EDU Production Services is involved, there can sometimes be a conflict between the professional standards of highly skilled production and design staff and the basic expectations of the academic lecturer. This was raised critically at one Departmental Board of Study as the aspiration to Rolls-Royce standards of quality when what were required were Mini standards! Although this was clearly an over-statement of the point, the achievement of an appropriate standard of production can only occur if all the relevant parties discuss this at an early stage of the Release Project.

Lecturers who have participated in the EDU Release Scheme have usually accomplished what they set out to do, become more enthusiastic about their work and have been able to influence the attitudes of their departmental colleagues. Because their work is based on *actual* teaching and learning problems the danger of these lecturers becoming alienated from their colleagues is minimized — in contrast to the situation which can arise when members of staff are seconded full-time on to courses outside their own institution.

The Wider Context

The main aim of this paper has been to describe how time has been found for lecturers to carry out innovations in teaching and learning. Release Projects are now well spread throughout the Polytechnic and will have extended to all faculties and departments by 1979/80. But how do these projects relate to the priorities of the Polytechnic as a whole? And what is their importance to Learning Resources?

There is a growing correlation between the purposes and content of Release Projects and two important current Polytechnic concerns:

1 *The Academic Development Plan*
   This gives a forecast of new courses proposed by departments and faculties and courses which will be required to undergo re-approval, for the next five years. Putting this plan into action requires academic departments to make preparations and solve problems, and Release Projects are increasingly being related to these situations. For example, a CNAA course proposal may identify the need to prepare certain materials and resources, and may indicate that the EDU Release Scheme has been, is being, or will be used to assist.

   Increasingly EDAs and CROs are involved in course teams preparing course proposals and re-submissions. EDU Release time is not normally given to lecturers to help them prepare the actual course proposal since this has increasingly been accepted as a necessary aspect of all lecturers' professional work. However, Release Projects are often a direct result of implications identified during this process of course development.

2 *Student: Staff Ratios*
   There is constant pressure on all departments to achieve a 10:1 student:staff ratio[1] and some recent Release Projects have attempted to improve the efficiency of teaching methods without reducing the effectiveness of students' learning. A lecturer may, for example, avoid repeating a demonstration of a particular experiment to students by producing a video-cassette of the demonstration, which can be used on many subsequent occasions.

The importance of the EDU Release Scheme to Learning Resources was the second question posed. In general, central services, such as Learning Resources, are very vulnerable to irrelevance and stagnation and have a history of becoming white elephants which are unloved and not valued by the teaching staff for whom they were ostensibly created.

---

[1] Memorandum from the 'Pooling Committee — monitoring of student/staff ratio', (1972). The Delany Report, DES.

The Learning Resources department at Brighton Polytechnic has developed a comprehensive and integrated range of services rather than the more common pattern of separate library and educational technology units. The failure of earlier comprehensive systems elsewhere may well have been due to their lack of emphasis on educational issues in both their development and operation. Brighton Polytechnic's model for Learning Resources depends for its success on the internal integration of its contributing activities and the external integration of its services with the needs, attitudes and wishes of academic departments.

This latter integration depends on how successfully Learning Resources staff can link with and move into departments so that they make an effective contribution to their work. It is the EDAs and CROs who hold this strategic position, not only through the services they provide directly and their membership of Boards of Study, course planning teams and working parties, but also through their role as gatekeepers — opening appropriate 'gates' into Learning Resources for teaching staff with particular needs. This entry into Learning Resources from the academic departments is greatly strengthened by the EDU Release Scheme, which has established the means by which teaching staff become an integral part of Learning Resources while they are on Release. Their close working with Learning Resources staff and use of its facilities results in an increased commitment to educational development work by all concerned, and often means that the lecturer, on returning to his department, shares the usefulness of many of his experiences with his colleagues.

Conclusion

The EDU Release Scheme is an institutionalized yet flexible arrangement representing an unusual and attractive middle-path between the extremes of *laissez-faire* individual initiative and direction by the Polytechnic's top management. A central agency, below this high level, has obtained the resources and the brief to encourage, co-ordinate and facilitate individuals' initiatives and relate the whole activity to the institution's academic development and policy. The scheme provides an importantt form of internal staff development, involving a growing number of teaching staff, and has the potential for improving the educational health of the whole institution. It may also be an essential element for the vitality and continuation of a comprehensive Learning Resources complex.

Acknowledgements

We wish to thank all our Polytechnic colleagues in Learning Resources and academic departments who have taken part in EDU Releases over the past few years, thereby making this paper possible. We would also like to acknowledge the major contribution of Clive Hewitt, Head of Learning Resources, who originally conceived the idea of the EDU Release Scheme.

9.2 A Model for Evaluating Educational Programmes

D C Moors
Department of Education, Nova Scotia, Canada

Abstract: The model which will be described is designed to assist in the evaluation of educational programmes including those of an occupational training nature. It is intended to provide those persons who are involved in the planning and delivery of such programmes with a means whereby they will be able to arrive at a number of conclusions relative to programme effectiveness.

Numerous articles deal with theoretical treatments of programme evaluation. While accepting the common factors of the Brooks (1965) and the Suchman (1969) definitions of evaluation, this presentation will concentrate on providing a workable option for those who wish to evaluate an educational sequence or activity. In the final analysis this option recognizes the emphasis of Hyman and Wright (1967) on evaluation research as ' . . . fact finding methods that yield evidence that is objective, systematic and comprehensive.'

The Timing of Programme Evaluation

Programme evaluation usually occurs in one of two ways:

1 Either an evaluation plan is established and agreed upon during the overall planning and development of the programme, or
2 A decision to evaluate is taken well into (or following) the programme operation (ie when the planning and development phases of the programme are finished).

This model will assist either approach. For those situations which relate to 1 above, this model suggests a series of steps or systems should be followed during the programme planning process continuing through the development and delivery stages of the education programme. As the education programme evolves through these stages, the information which is necessary for the suggested evaluation sequence should become available and utilized within the model sequence.

In those instances when the programme planning, development and/or operation have been complete prior to the decision to evaluate, relating to 2 above, the activities suggested within the model sequence provide the opporunity to document and clarify many of the variables related to and involved within the programme. Because some past information may be forgotten or otherwise be unavailable, the output of this second approach will not be as precise as that of the 'Planned Evaluation'. Even in such circumstances, the information generated can be useful. Once organized, it will provide the basis for an on-going evaluation should the programme be continued or reactivated.

Technical Information on the Model

The modelling technique employed is known as *logos* and has been described by Silvern (1972). This model contains 12 major sub-systems beginning with 1.0,

Initiative Evaluation Process, and terminating with 12.0, Distribute Report.

The first level of detail describes in general terms the various steps of the process with very little, if any, guidance as to the nature of activities which might occur within any of the sub-systems.

The sequence of activities through the model is indicated by arrowhead lines (➡) and *not by the numerical indicators*. In most instances the correspondence of the numerical indicators to the system sequence occurs because of a visual or organizational effect which assists the reviewer.

In some cases information which becomes available to the model through activities in one sub-system is utilized in a subsequent sub-system. This information becomes available to the subsequent sub-system through a feed-forward signal ⒡⒡

At times information which becomes available through activities of one sub-system leads to a re-analysis of the activities of previous sub-systems. Such instances are indicated by a feedback ⒡ signal.

A number of terms are used throughout the narrative. Some of these are as follows:

(1) *Programme* This refers to the operation being evaluated. A programme can refer to an academic class, a provincial welding training programme at a number of locations, or an overall educational/training department.

(2) *Programme Sponsors* Groups (either formally or informally structured) who have an interest in some aspect of the programme which is being evaluated. This interest is frequently legislated or specified within a contractual arrangement between the agencies who are involved in the planning and operation of an education programme. Sponsors can be government departments, training and/or certification agencies etc.

(3) *Programme Components* The various parts of a programme which actually are, or are intended to be, delivered to the clients represent programme components. There are two broad categories: (a) courses of instruction, and (b) support services etc. Eg, an academic upgrading programme might provide classes in science, language and mathematics. These three subjects would represent programme components. Programme components may also be described in more global terms, such as a vocation component, an academic component and a technical component. Thus, the term programme component can be general or specific.

(4) *Programme Processes* The programme processes represent the various activities which permit the total programme sequence to occur. These may be further defined in terms of a number of specific processes. Some examples would be: Programme Planning Processes, Programme Development Processes, Programme Operation Processes, Programme Evaluation Processes, and Programme Management Processes.

There will be occasions in which the programme processes will not be mutually exclusive sequences. For example, the management process will most likely be a part of other processes in that all processes usually require some type of supervision.

Entering the Evaluation Model

While the model was designed to flow in a sequential manner from system 1.0 to system 12.0, it is also possible (with slight revisions) to use the model to evaluate something less than a complete educational programme. For example, programme personnel might only be interested in answering a particular programme-related question, such as, 'Do the graduates of our training programme achieve employment?' If this hypothesis, or those of a similarly limited nature, represents the total evaluative interest the model may be employed during the questioning process. In such instances the evaluation sequences would be accomplished by entering the model at sub-system 1.0 and moving directly to sub-system 7.0, by-passing sub-systems 2.0 to 6.0 inclusive.

While this would be an effective means of answering limited programme related questions, it also includes an evaluation cost factor. Any reduction in the effort required to answer programme related questions conversely limits the information which is generated as a result of the evaluative activities. This, in turn, limits the degree to which the information will assist in answering overall programme related questions.

In summary, attempts to answer rather broad programme related questions such as, 'What aspects of the programme are effective in assisting graduates to achieve employment?' should involve an activation of the complete model sequence. Questions of a less global nature, such as, 'Do our graduates qualify for (or secure) college entrance?' may lead to a by-pass of various sub-systems within the model.

Levels of Detail

The model at the first level of detail (the larger boxes only in Figure 1) is quite general, providing limited guidance and direction for accomplishing the activities required within the various sub-systems. Concurrently, the user of the first level of detail can exercise greater flexibility in deciding upon, or selecting, the necessary sub-system activities. Higher levels of detail provide more specific direction to users, thereby reducing choice of flexibility with the model sequence.

The present narrative describes the rationale for each of the sub-systems at the first level of detail and suggests a number of sub-systems which might be included at the second level.

SUB-SYSTEM 1.0 – INITIATE EVALUATIVE PROCESS
This represents the point of initial entry into the evaluative process. Usually this activity can occur as the result of a variety of requests by an agency. For example, a school board might wish to evaluate a primary grade programme and the decision to conduct an evaluation, therefore, initiates the evaluative process. Another example would be a request made, or decision taken, to evaluate or assess some component of an educational programme. The specifics of this second example would include such instances as an attempt to examine the appropriateness of the assessment materials associated with a curriculum package. A third example would be a situation in which the evaluation process was being planned in conjunction with an overall plan to establish a programme or to initiate a course. All of these examples lead to a decision to plan and conduct some type of evaluation process.

Some suggested activities which may form a part of this sub-system include naming the programme to be evaluated and meeting with an agency representative who is able to generally describe the objective(s) of the programme. If it is appropriate at this point, general problem areas upon which the subsequent evaluation process may concentrate would also be outlined and, to any degree possible, the evaluation plan should be laid out.

It is important to provide a general statement of purpose for the evaluative process at this point. This statement need not be specific or limiting. It should simply serve to provide direction for subsequent activities. One effective means of stating the purpose is in terms of the prospective use of the evaluation results by those who requested the evaluative process.

These activities within sub-system 1.0 could then be described in a second level of detail expansion as indicated in Figure 1.

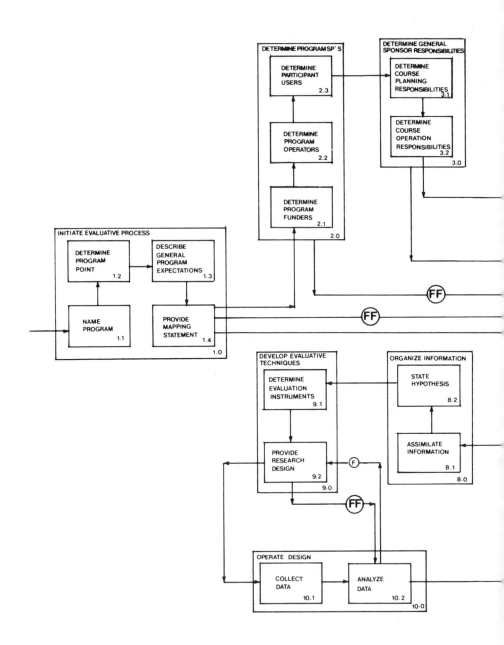

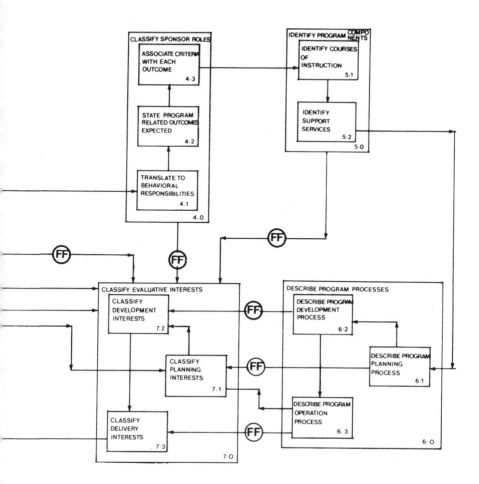

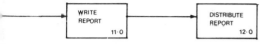

Figure 1. *Programme Evaluation Model*

The Sub-systems of 1.0 therefore include:

1.1 Name Programme
1.2 Determine Programme Point
1.3 Describe General Programme Expectations
1.4 Provide Mapping Statement

SUB-SYSTEM 1.0 ⓕ 7.0 – CLASSIFY EVALUATIVE INTERESTS
It is possible that some activities associated with sub-system 1.0 will lead to the identification of areas of subsequent evaluative interest. For example, it might be immediately evident that programme staff are interested in assessing the occupational relevancy of their curriculum. Such interests should be noted and held for processing in sub-system 7.0 activities. Thus, some information from sub-system 1.0 may be fed-forward ⓕ for use in 7.0 activities. This process of noting evaluative interests and storing them for 7.0 activities occurs throughout sub-systems 1.0 to 6.0 inclusive.

SUB-SYSTEM 1.0 → 7.0 – CLASSIFY EVALUATIVE INTERESTS
In some situations the activities of 1.0 lead to the conclusion that an extensive process by which the various programme related factors become documented during activities of 2.0 to 6.0 (inclusive) would not be of interest to those persons for whom the evaluation is being prepared. In such cases, the evaluation sequence should ignore sub-systems 2.0 to 6.0 (inclusive) and proceed directly from 1.0 to 7.0.

This 1.0 → 7.0 signal would be logical in those situations in which the evaluative interests as defined in 1.0, were sufficiently limited so that their role within the programme could be isolated. For example, if the purpose of the evaluation was simply to determine if the assessment tests actually reflected the content of the curriculum *and* if the programme personnel were not interested in any additional programme related questions that might surface, the 1.0 → 7.0 signal would be an appropriate sequence. In cases when this by-pass option is to be exercised, those persons for whom the evaluation report is being prepared should be thoroughly briefed on the implications of this limited questioning approach. The primary implication which must be understood in such situations relates to the limited applicability of the answers to limited questions.

SUB-SYSTEM 1.0 → 2.0 – DETERMINE PROGRAMME SPONSORS
Activities associated with this sub-system will result in the naming of programme sponsors. Programme sponsors represent groups and/or agencies who maintain programme related responsibilities.

Programme sponsors can usually be identified because they provide some assistance or service to a programme. Such assistance can take the form of contributing to programme funding, carrying out programme operations and/or being instrumental in the subsequent employment or further education of programme participants. These three classifications can serve as a convenient basis upon which to identify programme sponsors.

Expanding the first level of detail for sub-system 2.0 therefore provides a suggestion for the second level of detail found in Figure 1.

2.1 Determine Programme Funders
2.2 Determine Programme Operators
2.3 Determine Participant Users

SUB-SYSTEM 2.0 ⓕ 7.0 – CLASSIFY EVALUATIVE INTERESTS
Any evaluative interests that become apparent during sub-system 2.0 activities

should be noted and held for 7.0 activities.

SUB-SYSTEM 2.0 ⇥ 3.0 – DETERMINE GENERAL SPONSOR RESPONSIBILITIES
Activities within sub-system 3.0 are designed to permit the sponsors to begin to
define their programme objectives. While this definition will be finalized during
sub-system 4.0 activities, the requirement of 3.0 includes an indication of the programme areas over which the named sponsors hold or exercise jurisdiction.

If the evaluation is being planned during the programme planning sequence, 3.0
activities may be accomplished as a part of the responsibilities of the planning
committee. One approach to the activities of this sub-system would be to define
broad areas of programme activity and then to name the appropriate sponsor(s)
(from sub-system 2.0) for each of the defined programme activities. This would
result in statements which, for example, named the agency responsible for the
instructional process, the department responsible for programme funding or the
commission which assumed responsibility for student/client assessment, selection
and post-course certification.

Should no planning committee be available, the evaluators might gather the
required information from a representative of the agency operating the programme.
It would assist the process if this representative also had an historical appreciation
of the programme. In other cases it might be possible to directly contact the
agencies/groups defined in 2.0 activities. Again the broad areas of programme
activity such as planning, development of materials and operation could serve as an
initial basis upon which to determine general sponsor responsibilities.

Figure 1 indicates the sub-systems which would be included in the second level
of detail of sub-system 3.0. These sub-systems include:

3.1 Determine Course Planning Responsibilities
3.2 Determine Course Operation Responsibilities

SUB-SYSTEM 3.0 ⓕ 7.0 – CLASSIFY EVALUATIVE INTERESTS
Again, evaluative interests, as they become apparent during 3.0 activities, are noted
and held for 7.0 activities.

SUB-SYSTEM 3.0 ⇥ 4.0 – CLARIFY SPONSOR ROLES
This sub-system permits the sponsors to expand upon the information of the
previous sub-system. The requirement is that each of the programme sponsors
defines their relationship to the programme in terms of behavioural objectives.

Consistent with the principles of behavioural objectives, the sponsor(s) should
be assisted in defining their programme relationship in terms of the behaviours by
which their particular responsibilities are maintained or effected. The behavioural
objectives should also include the intended result of the sponsor carrying out a
stated responsibilitity. This outcome should also be stated in behavioural terms.
Finally, for each objective which a sponsor defines, assistance should be given
in establishing a measure by which success in meeting the objective may be assessed.

The second level of detail for sub-system 4.0 is indicated in Figure 1. The sub-
systems include:

4.1 Translate to Behavioural Responsibilities
4.2 State Programme Related Outcomes Expected
4.3 Associate Criteria With Each Outcome

SUB-SYSTEM 4.0 ⓕ 7.0 – CLASSIFY EVALUATIVE INTERESTS
Evaluative interests as indicated in 4.0 are fed forward for 7.0 activities.

SUB-SYSTEM 4.0 → 5.0 – IDENTIFY PROGRAMME COMPONENTS
The activities represented in 5.0 will require the assistance of the organization primarily responsible for programme operation and delivery. As such the evaluator can expect to involve in this sub-system sequence the sponsor group or groups acting as delivery agents. The term 'Programme Components' as used in the present model refers to those aspects of the programme which are intended to be or are actually delivered to the programme clients. Programme components not only refer to the subjects to be taught but also the support services which are delivered to the programme clients. Support services in most instances would refer to counselling and guidance activities, employment support activities, etc. In short, programme components refer to those aspects of the programme intended to be consumed by the clients.

The process of identifying the programme components should begin with an attempt to list the names of the courses which are involved in the programme which is being evaluated. Whether or not it is necessary to provide a detailed listing or outline of the topics included in each of the named courses is determined by the nature of the evaluative questions which are subsequently identified in 7.0 activities. As a rule of thumb, the evaluator should ask for the available course names and outlines. This information can be retained for future reference should it become necessary.

The strategy for detailing support services should be similar. The listing of the sub-system 5.0 should include only the support services which are necessary and sufficient for the operation of the programme or are likely to be of subsequent interest within the evaluative process.

Figure 1 presents the sub-systems which would be involved in the second level of detail of sub-system 5.0. These include:

5.1 Identify Courses of Instruction
5.2 Identify Support Service

SUB–SYSTEM 5.0 ⓕ 7.0 – CLASSIFY EVALUATIVE INTERESTS
Evaluative interests as they become defined in 5.0 are again noted and stored for 7.0 activities.

SUB-SYSTEM 5.0 → 6.0 – DESCRIBE PROGRAMME PROCESSES
Some categories of programme processes were defined in the introductory section of this paper. It was noted that any combination of the suggested programme process categories could exist within a programme. For example, the planning, development and operation processes usually can be found. However, the management process or the evaluation process is frequently a part of each of the planning, development and delivery processes. In other cases the development process is part of the delivery or planning processes and does not exist at an autonomous level. Therefore, the activities of 6.0 should not only identify the various processes which exist, but describe the manner in which these processes function and/or interact with each other. A number of questions may assist the identification of these processes. Such questions would be:

☐ What contingencies are available by which programme plans are established?
☐ Is there a planning committee that meets? If the planning committee has been identified in an earlier sub-system (for example during 3.0 activities) the evaluator should meet with them and document the process by which programme planning occurs or has occurred.
☐ Which processes permit curriculum development?
☐ How, where and by whom does programme delivery occur?
☐ Is there a plan for monitoring the operation of the programme?

☐ Is there a regular programme assesment or evaluation process which occurs? If so, describe it.

Suggested sub-systems which permit this type of questioning are outlined in Figure 1. The sub-systems involved in the second level of detail include:

6.1. Describe Programme Planning Process
6.2 Describe Programme Development Process
6.3 Describe Programme Operation Process

SUB-SYSTEM 6.0 → 7.0 — CLASSIFY EVALUATIVE INTERESTS
The evaluative interests or questions which have been identified and fed forward during previous sub-system activities should be reviewed. The activity of this sub-system should permit a classifying or ordering of these interests on the basis of broad categories which have been evident. The most obvious categories for classification are those which relate to the programme processes as clarified through 6.0 activities. Consequently, the evaluators should review the 6.0 information and classify evaluative interests in terms of the various processes which have become evident.

The sub-systems of 7.0 are presented in Figure 1. The figure also presents sub-systems 6.1, 6.2 and 6.3 in order to indicate the manner in which the information on the various programme processes feeds forward to the 7.1, 7.2 and 7.3 sub-systems. Therefore, the sub-systems are described as:

7.1 Classify Planning Interests
7.2 Classify Development Interests
7.3 Classify Delivery Interests

SUB-SYSTEM 7.0 → 8.0 — ORGANIZE INFORMATION
Activities within this sub-system permit the consolidation or organization of the information which has been documented in sub-systems 1.0 to 7.0. The organization process reflects an incorporation of the Stake (1967) model and represents a critical integration of the documentation activities.

Through such an integration it should be possible to associate each sponsor, as identified in 2.0, with their programme related objective(s) as generally stated in 3.0 and refined in 4.0. These objectives are reflected in the delivery of a programme component which has been identified in 5.0. The programme processes which have been identified in 6.0 are related to the appropriate sponsors, objectives and programme components. Finally, each of the evaluative interests as classified in 7.0 are organized within the information system. This level of organization will permit an understanding of the relevancy of the defined evaluative interests to the overall programme factors. The specific questions which will be addressed during the subsequent research should be clearly defined and appropriately stated in terms of testable hypotheses.

The second level of detail for sub-system 8.0 is shown in Figure 1. The sub-systems include:

8.1 Assimilate Information
8.2 State Hypothesis

SUB-SYSTEM 8.0 → 9.0 — DEVELOP EVALUATIVE TECHNIQUES
Activities in this sub-system are directed toward identifying the research instruments and activities which will be employed during the subsequent sub-systems. This would involve securing the appropriate instruments to be used in answering the evaluative questions as defined in 8.0. Examples of such instruments are

questionnaires, performance-rating tasks, work sample tasks and on-site observations. These instruments may be available from a number of sources or may be developed as a part of the evaluation process. In addition to identifying types of instrumentation, the research plan should be precisely described. This is usually represented by a well organized research design.

Thus in Figure 1, the higher order sub-systems suggested are:

9.1 Determine Evaluation Instruments
9.2 Provide Research Design, with the Ⓕⓕ signal to 10.2

SUB-SYSTEM 9.0 → 10.0 — OPERATE DESIGN
The research design as outlined in 9.0 is now activated. As this usually involves visits to training sites in order to collect data, the operators of the programme should be properly briefed prior to the arrival of the data collection group. Beyond collecting the data, activities in this sub-system would include the statistical analysis of the data that has been collected.

Figure 1 displays two second level of detail sub-systems for 10.0 They include:

10.1 Collect Data
10.2 Analyze Data

Notice the feedback signal 10.2 Ⓕ 9.2. This signal recognizes the possibility that the data analysis might provide inconclusive answers to the hypotheses which are being tested through the research design. In such circumstances those responsible for the evaluation would be required to determine whether or not further research activities are warranted.

SUB-SYSTEM 10.0 → 11.0 — WRITE REPORT
A report, outlining the evaluation process, defining the evaluation interests and summarizing the results of the data collection and analysis should be prepared. It is frequently of benefit to circulate a draft copy of the report to those who originally commissioned the evaluation activity. Frequently, this type of activity permits a refinement of the information in the final report thereby providing a more meaningful final product.

SUB–SYSTEM 11.0 → 12.0 — DISTRIBUTE REPORT
The report should be presented to and discussed with the group or sponsors who initiated the evaluative request.

9.3 Course Planning Teams: The Roles of Participants

John Scobbie and Raymond McAleese
Universities of Aberdeen and Melbourne

Abstract: The *planning* of instruction is seen by many to be the main focus for the educational technologist. This paper examines a course team and how it plans instruction in higher education. It is therefore an attempt at defining the essential elements in course team planning. The paper examines the roles played by four individuals (or groups of individuals): the media specialist; the educational specialist; the subject specialist; the student-assessor. It is suggested that a number of tensions exist in the teams. Such tensions can be understood in terms of poor role definition and competing roles. The roles of the media and educational specialists exhibit role-shift (peripheral to central). It is argued that such teams may well not succeed unless there is careful consideration given to social interaction skills and management principles.

Background

One of the central tenets in educational technology is the rational planning of instruction. Often it is assumed that teachers are completely responsible for the planning of new instruction; calling on outside help only when required. The subject specialist is therefore seen as being the pinnacle of a loose team of individuals such as media personnel (eg television producers, researchers, writers, graphic artists, designers, photographers and printers), with additional involvement by students.

Recent thinking and Open University experience have prompted many to consider that instruction can only be planned by a definite team of colleagues working as equals. (For a description of the Open University system see Lewis, 1971 a, b and c and Stanton, 1978 *inter alia*.) The work in this paper, however, arose out of an experiment conducted by the University of Aberdeen to plan and produce a series of learning packages in the Faculty of Law and in the Botany Department. In his application to the Nuffield Foundation, under their Small Grants Scheme for Undergraduate Teaching (who partly funded the work referred to in this paper), McAleese states the aims and objectives thus:

> 'The project aims are to produce and evaluate two parallel series of learning packages consisting of video-cassettes, textual material and self-assessment tests. The packages will be produced as a co-ordinated, four-cornered project team exercise (subject specialist, educational specialist, media specialist and student representative). The effectiveness of the project team will also be evaluated in a participative, observation study.'

The application spelled out the intentions behind the course team and an aim was set for the team.

> ' . . . as well as producing and evaluating the learning packages, we intend to evaluate the role of the project team in producing such material. The team will be co-ordinated by a graduate production assistant from the television service who will be seconded to the project for six months. Each team will consist of four members who will be jointly responsible for seeing the project through. In each case, a student will be invited to join the team as a full working member.'

This paper is a first attempt at evaluating the project team. (Details of the project as a whole can be found in Scobbie and McAleese, 1979.)

Course Teams

Ideas on the development of Course Teams have emanated from the work of curriculum development teams, where a project is originated and executed not through the work of one individual, but by the team effort (eg Humble and Simons, 1978). Team teaching in its planning phase (see for example, Shaplin and Olds, 1976), follows a similar tactic. However, some authors writing a course design seem to take little account of the *process* of course planning (eg Dallas *et al*, 1976).

Division of Labour

Inherent in any team is a division of labour and the resulting reliance on specialists. Division of labour means that teams can be composed of media, educational and subject specialists. Sometimes, student members are co-opted or asked to join such teams. The orgins of such team work can be found in the changing role of the teacher in education:

> 'One of the most exciting and important things that has happened to the concept of teaching in many years . . . has been the current departure from the image of the teacher as an isolated adult working in lonely professional solitude . . . ' (Denemark, 1969).

This breaking down of the isolation of the teacher has led to the introduction of specialist helpers at different levels. Engel (1974), writing about medical education, advocated the use of educational assistants to augment the traditional medical illustrator and the medical subject specialist. Such specialists were seen by Engel as providing the 'head' to the planning body. Recently, polytechnics, colleges of further education and central institutions in Scotland, are using course teams to plan new courses. (This has been caused largely by the need to prepare courses in great detail for bodies such as the Council for National Academic Awards.)

The Open University

In the Open University, course teams are set up to plan, write and edit units. These Open University teams are composed of subject specialists, representatives from the broadcasters, a member of the Open University's Institute for Educational Technology and from time-to-time, legal experts, designers, printers and others. These teams are often cumbersome and it is sometimes alleged that some of the members take little or no part in the work.

Francis Castles has observed that, with the sophisticated means of communication used by the Open University, tensions arise as a result of the division of labour and that it is important to have a clear delineation of spheres of responsibility. Our own research pointed to difficulties in defining roles exactly, and indeed as was found in the Open University the operation of an educational partnership may evolve as a result of a trial and error approach over a period of time. Francis Castles goes on to say:-

> '. . . at the Open University, the Course Team is encouraged to provide constructive criticism. Since the line between constructive and destructive comment is at best a tenuous one, bitter disputes are sometimes engendered in the context of course team discussion.'

The problems do not only exist in well known examples, as this paper will indicate, but also in less ambitious situations. Indeed some have argued that a small team is better than a large one. The intimacy of the small team (such as set up at University of Aberdeen) may be beneficial; curriculum development by committee, while attractive from a research development and diffusion (RD and D) standpoint, is not well suited to university course planning. There are a number of reasons for this. First, despite the exciting and important changes that have taken place in teaching, much of the planning work for teaching is still undertaken independently by the lecturer 'working in lonely professional solitude' (Denemark, 1969). Not only does the lecturer perform in private, he plans his course in privacy as well. Second, curriculum development by committee is difficult due to problems of getting a committee together when people have full timetables. As there is no norm that people work in committees, the planning of individual work programmes tends not to take into account joint planning. Third, it may be that highly success-ful 'elitist-researcher' or 'elitist-teacher' lecturers (Halsey and Trow, 1972) are not good at co-operative activities. Certainly, comments made by individuals who have had to work in highly structured teams indicate a wide range of inter-personal conflicts at a professional as well as a social level. (See Forman and Richardson, 1977).

University of Aberdeen Experiment

The course teams adopted in this project varied considerably. Although at the outset, the concept of learning packages; a combination of textual, audio-visual (in the form of video-cassettes) and self-assessment tests was broadly defined, the subsequent production of such learning packages involved fundamental differences in the formation and interaction of the 'teams' working on the two very different disciplines of *Law* and *Botany*. Details of the different course teams can be found in Scobbie and McAleese (1979), and the data for this analysis is based on both subjective and objective observations of the project teams and their progress, made by Scobbie, the Media Specialist and by McAleese, the Educational Specialist. Such data by its nature must be open to interpretation although it is alleged to be an accurate account of the day to day interaction of team members. It is with this caveat that we make our observations.

The Model

The initial model for participants and their roles was set up. Four basic participants or groups of participants were identified as follows:

(1) The subject specialist.
(2) The media specialist.
(3) The educational specialist.
(4) The student assessor (ie the consumer).

From Figure 1, it is possible to perceive the probable interactions between each participant. In practice, however, the roles of participants and their degree of participation varied enormously and continually evolved as the project progressed. However, the expected role definition was as follows:

Subject Specialist

Traditionally, he is the lecturer responsible directly to his students for the assembly and presentation of learning material. At the University of Aberdeen when a need for audio-visual aids to learning is identified, the subject specialist who may be a professor, reader, lecturer or head of department has traditionally contacted the media specialist, ie. a producer/director, termed a 'production assistant', within the university television service. The roles in this situation are more easily defined, the subject specialist provides the content, and the media specialist analyzes the

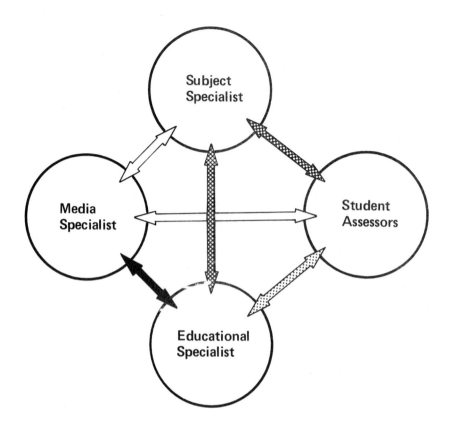

Figure 1. *Course team planning — probable interaction between participants*

content and recommends methods of presenting the material. On agreement of content and style of presentation, the production assistant may then produce a television programme. However, this traditional role had to be altered in the team content as can be seen in Figure 1.

Media Specialist

Traditionally, his role has been to translate subject content into an audio-visual programme. In the current situation, the person involved is a former teacher and an experienced audio-visual, television and film producer. Although the medium employed is television, he is able at his discretion to work with the range of media available (eg film, location and studio video-recording, stills photography, animation, graphics design etc). Often the media specialist will work closely with the subject specialist researching and writing the script to achieve the aims and objectives of the subject specialist and on the budget available to execute the project, the role of the media specialist can shift from a service role to a project leader role. In this case, the role was that of team co-ordinator.

Educational Specialist

Usually, he is someone trained in psychology and/or education, and in this project he was a lecturer in education. Of the main participants, the role of the educational specialist is least well-defined. Indeed, part of this project had been to assess what role such an individual can effectively play. Specifically, the educational specialist was the originator of this project and so his initial role was more central than one would normally expect.

Student Assessor

At the end of the day, the student is the consumer and his role must be to determine the effectiveness of the material presented to him. This is a particularly difficult role to fulfil. In practice, several students played this role, and as a result, there is no clear role definition. The initial expectation was to have one individual working as an integral team member.

An Analysis

As was suggested, the whole concept of team planning is brought under critical scrutiny in this paper. The tensions we discovered in our project have also been found in the production of Open University Courses but their significance is not fully appreciated. For example:

'Certain conflicts and crises occur in most course development projects; they are part of the 'creative tension' of any collaborative art.'
(Forman and Richardson, 1977.)

The multi-media programmes have been made in *Botany* and *Law*. They are and will be used in teaching and learning. All of us involved in the project have survived the experience and we have learned a number of valuable lessons.

There are general principles that apply to both the Law and Botany Projects, although the subjects were vastly different in content, style and approach. In each case, a gap in knowledge was identified and it was thought that a learning package would go a long way towards plugging the gap.

Teams of specialists were formed in both disciplines, Scobbie and McAleese being the only two specialists common to both projects. At the outset of the Botany project, there appeared to be a very sound team structure with clear definition of roles, and the aims and objectives to be achieved by the individuals. Professor Charles Gimingham was regarded as the subject specialist and delegated the work of researching and writing the draft scripts to a group of post-graduate students who acted as demonstrators during tutorials where the learning packages were primarily intended to be used. The formation of this sub-group while spreading the work load successfully, created new roles and problems in communication. As the numbers increased, the role of co-ordinating the personnel and the material became more difficult.

In the Law project however, all the written material was provided by one man (the subject specialist), Robert Hunter, Senior Lecturer in Jurisprudence. This certainly simplified communication and meant that there was a continuity in style and development of content.

There is however, little doubt that any planning by a Course Team causes tensions. They have been analyzed in terms of 'role strain' (eg Goode, 1960). That is, due to differences between the role that someone plays, or is seen to play, and the role they are expected to play or want to play, both social and management tensions exist.

McAleese observes that role strain in this project was due to three contributing factors:

1 Poor role definition for participants.
2 Role competition between participants.
3 Role shift of participants.

1 POOR ROLE DEFINITION

As a result of the novelty of the venture, different individuals perceived themselves in different ways. While Scobbie was the link man he was perceived differently by the subject specialist, by the educational specialist and by the student assessor.

No clear definition of exact roles was made explicit at the outset. This can be done, but does not necessarily rule out role competition between participants, nor role shift in participants.

2 ROLE COMPETITION

Role competition can arise because of poor role definition. Here different individuals expect to, or are perceived as wanting to do different things. In particular there was a very strong role competition between the media specialist and the educational specialist with regard to the overall direction of the project.

3 ROLE SHIFT

Role shift is a result of role competition. Individuals who experience role strain will shift their role definitions. This can happen in two ways. First, individuals can shift from marginal to central role or secondly, from central role to marginal. A marginal role for an individual defines him as having little control of the direction of the project. Role shift was found in all four groups.

Conclusions

The role analysis suggests that the prime problem in such work is with role definition. Conflicts do arise concerning the roles of individuals who are working on equal terms with similar aims and objectives — in this project to achieve an effective series of learning packages.

McAleese states that roles must be defined and guidelines agreed explicitly at the beginning. There has to be an individual with benign control. There has to be a plan that details objectives, team organization and participant roles. And this document should be agreed to and negotiated at the beginning.

Scobbie, while accepting that an individual with benign control is essential to direct the project, is more sceptical regarding the laying down of rigid role definitions at the outset. Inevitably, as the project evolves, individuals will contribute more or less as they are directed or think fit, and there must follow role competition and role shift. It is agreed however, that social awareness is an essential ingredient for successful planning. Individual members of teams must be sensitive to the aspirations, needs and feelings of others.

At the end of the day it is the subject specialist and the student who have most to lose or gain. There must be an acceptance of the corporate nature of planning and teaching. Any project must have a coherent viewpoint originating from the subject specialist. The educational specialist must know when to intervene and when to withdraw (what McAleese terms the 'adaptive interventionist'.) The media specialist is a catalyst within the team. He must be able to facilitate, cajole, and counsel his colleagues. Only when agreement is reached on the composition of a Course Planning Team and the members' commitment to their respective disciplines accepted, will there be a more effective method of teaching and learning.

References

Dallas, D et al (1976) *Studies in Course Design,* 1. UTMU, London.

Denemark, G N (1969) Co-ordinating the team. In Lucio, W H (ed) *The Supervisor: New Demands, New Dimensions* ASCD, Washington, DC.

Engel, C F (1974) Educational assistants, *The Lancet,* 9 September, pp 573-75.

Forman, D C and Richardson, P (1977) Course development by team: some advice on how many cooks does it take to spoil the broth. *Educational Technology,* 12, pp 30-35.

Goode, W J (1960) A role theory of strain. *American Sociological Review,* 25, 4, 483-96.

Halsey, A H and Trow, M (1972) The British university teacher. In Butcher, H J and Rudd, E (eds) *Contemporary Problems in Higher Education. An Account of Research.* McGraw Hill, London.

Humble, S and Simons, H (1978) *From Council to Classroom: an evaluation of the diffusion of the HCP.* Schools Council Research Studies/Macmillan, London.

Lewis, B N (1971, a, b and c) Course production at the Open University. *British Journal of Educational Technology,* 2, 1; 2, 2; 2, 3.

McAleese, R (1978) Staff development in the University of Aberdeen: a study of roles. PhD thesis, University of Aberdeen.

Scobbie, J and McAleese, R (1979) Course team planning: a report to the Nuffield Foundation. University of Aberdeen.

Shaplin, J T and Olds, H F (1964) (eds) *Team Teachings.* Harper & Row, New York.

Stanton, H E (1978) The Open University: Comments of an interested observer. *Vestes,* 3, 4, pp 18-21.

Workshop Report

Following the above paper, there was further discussion at a workshop conducted by Mr Scobbie.

9.4 Getting it All Together: or a Systems Approach to Technical Education Curricula

Tom Wyant
Thai-German Technical Teacher College, Bangkok

Abstract: At past ETIC meetings I have presented papers that detailed how management techniques could be used to answer technical education questions. (Wyant, 1971, 1972, 1973.) This paper joins together a number of separate theories to detail how they have been used to design a systematic form of curriculum development for technical education in a developing country, Thailand.

Base Facts

At the Thai-German Technical Teacher College, which is a part of the King Mongkut's Institute of Technology, North Bangkok Campus, Thailand, one of the degrees that we offer is that of Master of Technical Education.

To get the degree, an agreed number of educational units (modules) have to be completed. One of the units is Curriculum Development. The work, and necessary knowledge and experience, for this unit is that the Master will produce a curriculum development design that details a time-table for a two-week unit of training, a systems framework of Thai industry pointing out where the probable trainee is positioned, teaching operations, tests, handouts and teaching apparatus that may be used.

Unit Organization and Training

In the time given for the unit, Masters learn and use many management techniques. The teaching is supported by examples, learning experiences, handouts and taking part in current College curriculum development activities.

For their curriculum development work, Masters are requested to use a systems design that has been designed in the College. The steps in the systems design are:

1.0 Systems Framework (Systems Diagram)
   Design the outline of a system or organizational structure that points out where the work position (job) is fixed. Detail the actions and interactions that take place.
2.0 Job Detail (Job Description)
   List the operation and other details.
   Number off the operations.
3.0 Job Structure (Job Specification)
   Detail the knowledge, experience, abilities and behaviours necessary for each operation.

4.0 Knowledge and Abilities List (Duty List)
Make a list of the knowledge and abilities that a trainee will need to learn, to get to get to a quality worker level.

5.0 Levels List (Duty Grading)
Using the list from 4, compare the levels of importance and quality or other details that may be related; for example, teacher's time, teaching apparatus, tests, etc.

6.0 Teaching Unit Network (Topic Network)
Make a network of the knowledge and abilities, detailing the connections between them.

7.0 Time-table
Design a time-table, within the given limits, for teaching the curriculum.

8.0 Teaching Support Material (Software)
Develop teaching/learning units, tests, apparatus, etc as needed.

I will point out how this works by using an example that we developed for a short two-day training event to teach two part-time workers how to help in our Resources Centre. The first step, designing the systems framework, details the position of the trainee in the organizational structure.

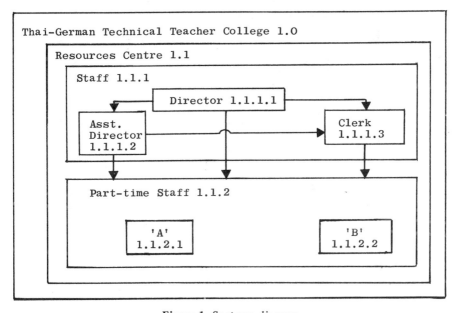

Figure 1. *Systems diagram*

Having detailed the trainee's position in the organization, the second step is to write up the job detail form (job description) of the trainee's work. The job detail form is based on the examples and opinions given in the BACIE booklet *A Guide to Job Analysis* (Boydell, T 1970).

JOB DESCRIPTION

Job title : Resources Centre Assistant

Department: Resources Centre

Location : Room 104, Faculty of Education and Science, KMIT.

Function : To assist in the administration and smooth running
            of the Resources Centre.

Hours of
work   : Monday - Friday, 09.00 - 17.00 hrs.
            (Lunch   12.00 - 13.00 hrs.)

Responsible to   : Director, Asst. Director, clerk.

Responsible for : nil

Authority over   : nil

Duties and Responsibilities :

1. To check that all the books in the Resources Centre are :

   (a) Referenced (b) Carded (c) Pocketed (d) Covered.

2. To produce index cards for all books.

3. To assist in the control and checking of all the other
   resources held in the Centre.

4. To carry out such duties as may be requested by the permanent
   staff of the Centre.

Salary : To be agreed.

Signed :   March 1978

T.G.Wyant
Director, Resources Centre.

Figure 2. *Job description*

The job detail form leads into step 3: job structure (job specification). This details the knowledge and experience of the quality worker.

Job Specification		
Duties and Responsibilities	Knowledge	Skill
1. Book checking		
(a) Referenced	i That a reference number consists of 3 digits and a decimal value (Dewey), also author code and accession numbers.	Recognise number quickly.
	ii Accession books (English, German & Thai)	Identify
	iii Establishing details of books; number of pages, illustrations, date, place, publisher, etc.	Locating data and entering neatly into books.
	iv System of filing books on shelves.	Establish location of book by number and code.
(b) Carded	i Details that should appear on the book card.	Recognise missing or incorrect data or detail.
	ii How to make out cards	Neat typing
	iii Filing and purpose of cards	Filing under various headings
(c) Pocketed	i Where to locate pocket	Check position and replace if required
(d) Covered	i Why cover is necessary	How to make and affix covers.

Signed: _T.G. Wyant_   March 1978
T.G. Wyant
Director, Resources Centre

Figure 3. *Job specification*

Steps 4 and 5 detail all the operations in the job, parallel with all the knowledge and abilities needed. A five-point scale highlights the degrees of importance and learning which seems hard.

Duty Grading					
Topic	Knowledge	Skill	(a) Import.	(b) Learn. Diff.	(a+b) Grade
1(a)i	Dewey system		5	4	9
		Recognise	5	3	8
ii	Access.books		4	4	8
		Identify	3	2	5
iii	Book data		3	2	5
		Locate-enter	2	2	4
iv	Filing books		4	2	6
		File	3	2	5
(b)i	Book card		3	2	5
		Check data	3	1	4
ii	Author/Subject cards		4	2	6
		Type neatly	5	3	8
iii	Filing		4	2	6
		File	4	2	6
(c)i	Location		3	1	4
		Check-replace	2	1	3
(d)i	Covering		1	1	2
		Make-affix	1	2	3

Signed: _[signature]_

T.G.Wyant
Director, Resources Centre

March 1978

Grading system: 5 - Must know
4 -
3 - Should know
2 -
1 - Could know

Figure 4. *Duty grading*

The scale points may be used in step 6 when the network of the learning and training activities is completed. The network outlines the dependencies existing between activities and points out the different measures that may be taken in step 7.

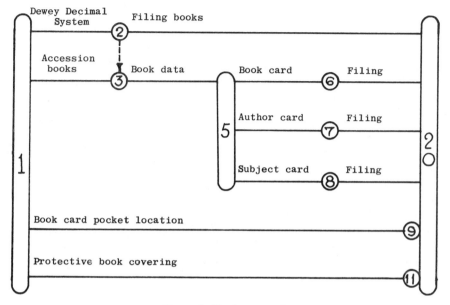

Figure 5. *Topic network*

In step 7, the time-table, the network and the levels list are used to produce a time-table that will be well constructed, and details the way to be taken by the trainee to learn the knowledge and abilities that are needed.

In the last step the Masters have to produce tests, learning units, teaching apparatus, etc based on the network.

Support advertising material is designed and produced as well.

Opinions and Observations

The work produced so far by Masters, using this step-by-step process, has been of a high quality and of great value to the Institute. Some of the ideas have been used to forward the Institute's work on curriculum development.

Other management techniques used in the unit range from Information Mapping developed by Robert Horn which the Programmed Instruction Centre for Industry at Sheffield was instrumental in presenting in this country in 1974 (this technique is used in the production of handouts), to the Buzan technique of 'patterning' (Buzan, T, 1973). Not all learners take kindly to the 'patterning' technique, although personally I use it all the time for note-taking, meetings, testing ideas, etc. It is very useful for expanding thoughts, and has possibilities for discovery learning.

It is interesting to see in a developing country how new ideas are valued and quickly tested and adapted in direct comparison with the UK where new ideas come to be viewed with distrust, or disgust. A friend once said to me, 'British Education is like a rice pudding, you can take a good kick at it and make a sizable dent but, in a very short space of time it will resume its normal soggy shape.'

When new ideas do not come easily, it may be useful to look again at past ideas and suggestions that have been put forward. Most of them, not having been approved by persons in authority, are painlessly put to sleep — or left to die a natural death. A number of the ideas, once put forward, were good and very valuable but were in the wrong place, at the wrong time, for the wrong persons. An example is Basic English, a list of 850 words that still gives a chance to cover all forms of writing, reading and discussion. It was suggested before the war, used in the war and then not used again. When I see my Asian friends painfully reading theoretical English text books I picture how much easier it would be written in Basic English.

In a small way I have used Basic English and Information Mapping together when producing handouts in Thailand. The pleasure, approval, interest and reactions of the readers are payment enough for the hard work and time that was necessary to produce them.

note: Apart from the illustrations, 95 per cent of the foregoing paper has been written and presented in Basic English.

References

Boydell, T (1970) *A Guide to Job Analysis*. BACIE, London.
Buzan, T (1973) 'Use Your Head'. BBC Television.
Wyant, T G (1971) In (eds) Packham, Derek, Cleary, Alan and Mayes, Terry *Aspects of Educational Technology*, V. p 393. Pitman, London.
Wyant, T G (1972) In (eds) Austwick, K and Harris, N D *Aspects of Educational Technology*, VI. p 103. Pitman, London.
Wyant, T G (1973) In *Aspects of Educational Technology*, VII. p 300. Pitman, London

9.5 The Dynamics of an Information System for Educational Technology

Donald P Ely
Director, ERIC Clearinghouse on Information Resources, Syracuse University, USA

Abstract: The Educational Resources Information Center (ERIC) data base is one of the largest repositories of educational information in the world. The ERIC Clearinghouse on Information Resources, located at Syracuse University, is responsible for acquiring, processing and disseminating documents and indexing the periodical literature in the field of educational technology. This paper outlines the procedures and problems of acquiring information on a worldwide basis; reports on a study of ERIC users; explores the potential for computer-based searching of the ERIC system. A proposal is made for extending the ERIC data base to include educational technology information on an international scale.

Introduction

Samuel Johnson is reported to have described two types of knowledge: knowing a subject ourselves or knowing where to find information about a subject. Traditionally, education has emphasized the former — helping students to acquire knowledge. The current information explosion seems to require the other type of knowledge — providing the learner with the means to locate information.

The information industry, as it is often called, is made up of people who handle information. Oettinger (1975) outlines the dimensions of the industry by describing those who work in it and their functions:

☐ The creators — research and development, advertising, computer programmers, authors, composers, poets.
☐ The processors – data processing services, legal services, bank and credit card services, insurance agents, security brokers.
☐ The collectors — libraries, data retrieval services, the intelligence community.
☐ The communicators — education, telephone, telegraph, radio, television, postal services, mobile radio, newspapers, book and periodical publishers, motion pictures, theaters, agricultural extension agents.
☐ The information equipment producers — computer and related equipment, radio and television sets, paper, photo equipment and supplies.

The focus of this paper is on the collectors and communicators, those people who gather data and information which others have produced and make it available through live and mediated channels to those who need it.

Information Needs

By moving closer to education and educational technology, we can consider data and information in terms of a specific set of users. Let us examine an array of information needs which a typical practising educational technologist might require in any given day:

☐ Title, description and source of programmed learning materials for a basic course in developmental psychology.
☐ The location, cost and scope of post experience courses in educational technology.
☐ Two or three evaluation instruments which would assess teaching effectiveness.
☐ A critical review of a new film.
☐ Cost data on the use of computer-assisted instruction.

Reasons for Seeking Information

These contrived information needs are representative of a host of daily information seeking behaviours displayed by educational technologists. While we do not know specifically what purposes educational technologists have in needing information, a recent study in the United States (Hood and Blackwell, 1976) revealed that reasons for seeking information varied with the position held in the educational community. However, there are some similarities exhibited among the populations studied: teachers, school administrators, higher education personnel and governance groups. The five most frequent reasons for requiring information, in order of priority, are as follows:

1 Keeping aware of developments and activities in education.
2 Finding answers to specific questions.
3 Identifying new sources of assistance for improving work.
4 Developing alternative approaches to solving problems.
5 Identifying new educational programmes, methods, materials, or products (ERIC/TE, 1977).

This list seems sufficiently generic to assume that educational technologists would seek information for the same purposes, perhaps with some realignment of priorities. This is a hypothesis for further research.

Sources of Information

There is much more research on where educators go to seek information. The study which looked at purposes also surveyed sources used by the various sub-groups within education. (Hood and Blackwell, 1976)

Item	Average	Rank
Face-to-face discussion or conferences with people in my own organization	1.35	1
Notes and files in my own office	1.46	2
Educational newsletters, bulletins, announcements	1.72	3
Telephone calls to people in my own organization	1.76	4
Educational journals	1.80	5
Personal library	1.85	6
Memos and correspondence	1.87	7
Face-to-face discussion or conference with people in other organizations	1.88	8
Telephone calls to people in other organizations	1.92	9
Library or resource center in my own organization	1.95	10

Table 1. *Frequency of use of 10 information sources based on unweighted averages of 14 sub-audiences (1 = Often, 2 = Sometimes, 3 = Rarely)*

The principle which applies here is that professional educators seek information from sources which are most accessible and credible. The search for information is not necessarily undertaken with the idea of maximum return, but according to the principle of least effort. However, this principle can be observed in almost any facet of life and is not limited to information seeking. It is a principle which must be considered when designing an information system.

When participants in the Hood and Blackwell study were asked to indicate reasons for preference of information sources, the most frequent responses, in rank order, were: (i) 'is likely to have the information I want;' (ii) 'is near at hand or easily accessible;' (iii) 'is responsive to my particular problem or question;' (iv) 'is easy to use;' and (v) 'is usually available when I need it.' Again, access is a key factor in seeking out information as is the reliability of the source.

Preferred Products and Formats

The need for specific, practical information is confirmed by Mick and Paisley (1972) in a study of 9,737 educational personnel in 13 states in the US. When asked to indicate the form in which information is the most useful the rank order of preference was: (i) how-to guidance 73.06%; (ii) research reviews 70.80%; (iii) current awareness 52.00%; (iv) case studies 47.53%; (v) original research 11.13%. There were only minor differences between each of the 15 personnel types surveyed.

The Educational Technologist as an Information Seeker

Educational technologists probably prefer information which is desired by both practitioners and chief administrators. This prediction, as well as the previous estimates, is based on the various linkage roles which the educational technologist plays. Unlike any professional educator, other than the librarian or curriculum development specialist, the educational technologist is concerned with information in performing day to day tasks. Whether it is the source of a specific product or the report on a successful practice, the educational technologist as a member of a course team is expected to locate, retrieve, interpret, recommend, and adapt information for use by others, primarily teachers and learners.

Where, then, does the educational technologist turn for information? Like other educators, he or she would consult sources close at hand: personal files, personal library, and journals; then people close at hand in face-to-face or telephonic communication. Such searches are usually for the relatively simple information needs. For example: What is the address of the National Film Board of Canada? Where can I locate information about cost-effectiveness of computers? Who is successfully using simulation to teach values? A substantial number of daily information requirements can be met by nearby and accessible sources. The satisfaction is directly related to the amount and quality of the resources and the searching skills of the individual. (Some information searchers are successful because of a good network of professional friendships and a large telephone budget.)

Journals

Journals serve a current awareness function. Information in journals tends to be more current and specific. Special features such as book reviews, lists of new publications and materials and advertisements help to fill the need for information on trends, issues and current events. While periodicals fill a very important need, the decision as to which journals to read regularly is an individual matter. The *Current Index to Journals in Education,* which is part of the Educational Resources Information Center (ERIC) system, indexes 27 journals in the field of educational technology. The *British Education Index* includes most of the same educational technology journals as CIJE.

The remaining information sources include non-copyrighted, unpublished material such as project reports, speech texts, research findings, locally produced curriculum materials, conference proceedings and other ephemeral materials. The ERIC system in the US has attempted to seek out, acquire and process these materials since 1966.

The ERIC System

One organization, the ERIC Clearinghouse on Information Resources at Syracuse University, is charged to gather, process and disseminate information in the field of educational technology. To fulfil this charge, representatives of the Clearinghouse routinely contact potential sources of information and encourage individuals and organizations around the world to submit manuscripts, reports and non-copyrighted publications for consideration. All documents are reviewed by professionals from the content area and are either accepted or rejected. The current acceptance rate is about 60 per cent. The general criteria applied in reviewing each document are: currency, timelines, relevance authority, thoroughness, and quality of presentation.

When a document is accepted, an abstract is prepared and the document is announced in a monthly index, *Resources in Education.* This index provides a readable abstract for each entry as well as a full bibliographic citation, availability information, and the ED (ERIC Document) number that serves as an address for locating the document in the system. Cumulative issues of the subject, author, and institution indexes are published every six months.

The full text of the document is available in the ERIC microfiche collection for about 85 per cent of the items announced in RIE, with full availability information for the remainder. Microfiche are located in libraries and other institutions which subscribe to the service and individual copies of microfiche (and, in most cases, hard copies) are available through the ERIC Document Reproduction Service.

Another facet of the ERIC system is the indexing of journal articles. The *Current Index to Journals in Education* (CIJE) announces significant articles from more than 700 major professional publications with brief descriptions of the content and complete bibliographic citation, but copies cannot be supplied by ERIC. If a journal is not available through local sources, it may be possible to order a copy from University Microfilms International.

International Dimensions of ERIC

The ERIC system has grown to over 350,000 citations. A recent check showed 4,689 items from or about the United Kingdom, 4,891 from Canada, and 1,337 from Australia. The magnitude of items now in the system has led to an increasing use of the computer to search the data base. Tapes of all document and journal input are available. Three commercial services in the US[1] make ERIC available on-line to subscribers. Satellite connections with two of these data bases make them available in some areas of Europe, Asia and Australia. The time saved by interactive searches has to be compared with the cost of computer time. Off-line searches are less expensive but require some waiting time. A computer search of the data base yields the same information as the printed indexes but it is still necessary to go to the microfiche collection or the journals to find the text of the materials cited.

The ERIC system has proved to be sound in its basic design as an information system. The ERIC format has been adopted by the Council of Europe for its European Documentation and Information System for Education (EUDISED) and the Government of Canada is exploring its use for a national educational data retrieval system.

The Potential for an International Information System

These efforts in the English speaking world seem to point to the ERIC system as having the necessary components and formats to establish an international data base in education. Co-ordination of ERIC in the US, EUDISED in Europe and the new Canadian system would form the basis for an extensive data base. In addition, AUSINET in Australia would add a significant body of educational literature from that part of the world.

The combined data base would encompass literature from all areas of education, which seems to be an appropriate scope. The literature of educational technology would be an integral part of the data base, which is consistent with the position that the field permeates some aspect of nearly every area of knowledge. The extent to which educational technology is well represented in the data base is directly related to the extent and quality of the input.

The ERIC Clearinghouse on Information Resources in the US will continue to search far and wide for documents and process those which have merit. A new initiative is being made by ERIC to solicit international documents with emphasis on materials in English. Educational technologists in Europe, Canada and Australia should be sure that their interests are represented by the education data bases in their respective nations. If educational technology is covered in all current data bases, it would appear that the non-copyrighted literature of the field is under control.

The next step would be the amalgamation of all existing data bases in education to form an international information system. The politics and economics of such an effort might be major problems for a long time. Meanwhile, access to all systems by an institution or agency in any country ensures a fairly comprehensive coverage of the education literature. Rather than depend upon co-ordination by an inter-

1 Bibliographic Retrieval Services (BRS), Lockheed Data Systems (Dialog) and Systems Development Corporation (Orbit).

national organization or a governmental agency in a single nation, the individual organization can provide its own co-ordination. Use of the multiple data bases is facilitated by adoption of the ERIC format and procedures.

The Danger of False Security

There is a sense of security when information is available. This sense of security is enhanced when the information is readily accessible. The danger here is believing that a comprehensive bibliographic search adds validity to any proposition As data are stored on shelves, or microfiche or on computer tapes, they become useful only when 'right' questions are asked. Only then does data become information and contribute to decision-making. (Ely, 1973)

The quantity of information available in the field of educational technology is exceeding the capacity of the individual professional to evaluate its usefulness. There is a need for *better* rather than more information. Therefore, those who review documents for inclusion in existing information systems should exercise better quality control by tightening evaluation criteria. Users are too often disappointed with the quality of information received from existing sources.

Focus on the User

Information systems can be improved by considering the special needs of users. Too many information systems exist because they are technically possible. All too seldom do the designers of such systems consider the individual who will use them.

An analysis of such studies as Hood and Blackwell (1976) and Mick and Paisley (1972) would help an information specialist to determine the criteria for information input. Knowing the purposes for seeking information, the preferred formats and the types of information sought are key elements for designing any system. More research needs to be done to explore the unique information needs and information seeking behaviours of educational technologists.

Conclusion

We live in an information-rich society. We are overloaded with information from multifarious sources. Educational technologists have special information needs which are filled from a variety of sources, probably on an idiosyncratic basis. Several studies have been completed which explore the purpose, source and satisfaction of information seeking among educators. Educational technologists have not been studied as a special group.

There are several data bases in education currently available in various parts of the English speaking world and there is some attempt to use compatible procedures and formats. If educators in general and educational technologists specifically are to use all data bases, co-ordination has to be accomplished within an institution or agency which subscribes to all existing data base services.

Improvements in the current information environment for educational technologists should be preceded by a study of the information needs of the population. Input criteria and output potentials should be altered accordingly. Existing schemes should be modified rather than to create new systems. Eventually, consideration should be given to the establishment of an international information system in education which includes all aspects of educational technology.

The ability to control and use information is at the heart of almost any enterprise. For educational technologists it may be the key to survival.

References

Ely, Donald, P (1973) The myths of information needs. *Educational Researcher*. April, pp. 15-17.

ERIC/TE (1977) *The Market for Education Information*. ERIC Clearinghouse on Teacher Education, June. Washington, DC. (ED 138 593).

EUDISED R & D Bulletin. (1978) Strasburg: Documentation Centre for Education in Europe.

Hood, Paul and Blackwell, Laial (1976) *The Education Information Market Study*. System Development Corporation, October. San Francisco (ED 135 411).

Mick, Colin and Paisley, William (1972) *Developing a Sensing Network for Information Needs in Education*. Institute for Communication Research, September. Stanford, California (ED 006 622).

Oettinger, Anthony and Shapiro, Peter (1975) Information industries in the United States. *1975 Britannica Book of the Year*, p 18.

Workshop Report

Using the ERIC System

Donald P Ely
Syracuse University

The purpose of this session was:

1 to extend the knowledge of each participant regarding ERIC's purpose and use;
2 to review the ERIC access tools; and
3 to introduce procedures for computer searching.

Background Information About ERIC

The ERIC system has been gathering 'fugitive' materials, such as speeches, reports, conference papers, resource guides, and curriculum materials in the field of education since 1966. At the end of 1978 there were approximately 147,000 titles. About 1,200 new titles are being added each month. In addition to the material found in RIE, the ERIC system has been indexing and annotating journal articles since 1969, with a total of 186,000 completed as of the end of 1978.

Approximately 77 per cent of the documents announced in RIE are available in microfiche and hard (xerox) copy from EDRS. About 7 per cent are available in microfiche only, either because of the print quality of the original document, or because the author wished to make the hard copy available elsewhere. About 13 per cent are available only from other sources.

ERIC Clearinghouses acquire documents from individuals and through acquisitions arrangements made by the ERIC Facility. Documents are processed at the Clearinghouses and sent to the ERIC Facility with a resume form containing bibliographic information, index terms, and an abstract. There the résumé forms are further edited, and the information transcribed onto computer tapes. The computer tapes may be purchased outright, but most users ot the tapes gain access to them through the three major database vendors, Lockheed, Systems Development Corporation, and Bibliographical Retrieval Services. The documents themselves are sent to EDRS, where the microfiche is made, and xerox and microfiche copies are distributed to users.

Clearinghouses also subscribe to journals in their scope areas, from which articles are indexed and annotated; the résumés are sent to the CIJE contractor, and printed to form the monthly *Current Index to Journals in Education*. This information is also transcribed onto computer tapes.

Resources in Education

An entry for every document submitted by a Clearinghouse, called a résumé, appears in RIE. There are three indexes from which you may gain access to documents: subject, author, and institution.

Information provided includes author, title, source, publication date, number of pages, descriptive notes, availability and EDRS prices. A document that is not available in microfiche or hard copy from EDRS (and therefore not found in an ERIC microfiche collection) will contain the line, 'Document not available from EDRS.' In that case, an alternative availability source is provided.

Each document résumé also contains the indexing terms assigned by the Clearinghouse subject specialists to describe the concepts contained in the document's content. The starred, or major descriptors, are those chosen to reflect the most important concepts in that particular document and they appear in the Subject Index of RIE with this title listed under them. In addition to the descriptors, which are part of ERIC's controlled vocabulary and found in the *Thesaurus of ERIC Descriptors*, Clearinghouses may assign identifiers which are specific terms that provide access to documents through proper names of people, tests, geographical locations, projects, etc. Starred identifiers appear in the RIE subject indexes.

Subject experts in Clearinghouses write a 200 word abstract for each document, intended to provide enough information for users to determine whether or not the material is relevant to their needs.

The Thesaurus of ERIC Descriptors

The *Thesaurus of ERIC Descriptors* is the key to locating the terms which are used to index materials in *Resources in Education* and the *Current Index to Journals in Education*. The *Thesaurus* contains the terms (called descriptors) used by the Clearinghouses to index documents and journal articles. The terms are arranged alphabetically in the first part of the *Thesaurus*. A hierarchical and rotated listing of terms follows.

In the alphabetical list, each term in use is found in bold face type, sometimes followed by a scope note (or definition) (SN); synonym (UF) for which the term is used, if any; and narrower terms (NT); broader terms (BT); and related terms (RT). The searcher may find additional useful terms by studying the lists of narrower, broader, and related terms. The 7th edition of the *Thesaurus* also provides postings for each term, which tell how many times the term has been used to index documents in RIE, or journal articles in CIJE.

Current Index to Journals in Education (CIJE)

The monthly *Current Index to Journals in Education* (CIJE), published by Oryx Press, includes citations, index terms, and annotations for articles from over 700 educational journals. Access to journal articles is provided through subject, author, and journal contents indexes.

Each main entry in the *Current Index to Journals in Education* includes the title of the article and the journal citations, so that the user is able to locate it in a library collection or through the University Microfilms reprint service. The indexing terms, or descriptors, and identifiers and an annotation also appear in the entry.

Computer Searching of ERIC Data Base

The ERIC indexes are available not only in printed form but on computer tape. Computer searching provides an effective alternative to manual searching particularly in the case of a complex search. Not only does computer searching take less time but it also retrieves more citations because of the information contained on the tapes and the way in which the computer accesses the information. Computer searchers express their queries in specific ways.

The more specific the search, the fewer citations will be retrieved. In complex searches the computer saves hours of searching manually through indexes under several headings. It also eliminates the effort involved in judging whether particular articles cover the combination of subjects desired.

9.6 Use of an Optical Mark Reader in Army Selection

D R F Hammond and P L Wilson
Royal Army Education Corps

Abstract: The Army is currently examining the value of an Optical Mark Reader (OMR) — the Dataterm 3 — in its selection procedures for adult, and some junior, male recruits. This report first describes the nature of Army selection and the problems initially met with OMR. A summary of the corrective advice received from leading OMR users and interested parties is next presented, along with a provisional solution for the Army's OMR problems. Finally, conclusions and recommendations based on our OMR work are reported.

Army Selection and Need for OMR

All adult, and some junior, male recruits from England, Wales, Ulster, and Eire must initially attend the Recruit Selection Centre (RSC) at Sutton Coldfield. There they take a standard set of five pencil-and-paper cognitive tests used to assist selection and allocation decisions for all forms of non-commissioned entry to the Army. In addition, they are given a comprehensive briefing on all Army jobs available. When this centralized selection system was begun in 1971, it was envisaged that recruits would also answer an Occupational Interests Guide. The resulting Guide data would, it was hoped, permit selective job briefing. Thus, instead of each recruit having to study all Army jobs, information would only be presented on those in which he was interested (as assessed by the Guide) and for which he had the suitable abilities (as measured by the five tests). The version of the tests used in 1971 had predominantly open-ended items requiring a constructed response. Though these could not be marked as quickly as multiple-choice questions, RSC testing staff working at their maximum capacity could score them fast enough for job allocation decisions to be made on schedule. However, adding the Guide to the selection procedures increased the marking time and accompanying strain on the testing staff to unacceptable levels. Consideration was thus given to the introduction of a rapid automatic marking system for the five tests and the Guide. This would necessitate changing the tests to a multiple-choice format so that respondents' data could be converted by an OMR to a form suitable for computer scoring. As the tests were in need of updating, the decision was made to revise them accordingly in case OMR marking was later used. Following a survey of available OMR systems, it was resolved in 1972 to purchase the Dataterm 3 OMR manufactured by Data Recognition. The initial intention was for this OMR to convert recruits' test and Guide data to punched tape which would be fed into an RSC terminal linked to the IBM Call System for computer scoring. Eventually, it was hoped to replace the IBM connection by a link to one of the Army's own computers. An OMR answer sheet was therefore designed for the Guide and a general-purpose one was developed later for the new multiple-choice tests under construction by psychologists at the Army Personnel Research Establishment (APRE). On both forms an answer was indicated by joining two guide marks with a vertical line. For example, selecting option B in a question would be shown on the answer sheet as in Figure 1.

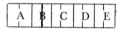

Figure 1. *Method of answering original Army OMR answer sheets*

The Army's Two Problems with OMR

It had been expected that these two OMR answer sheets would be correctly completed by recruits. However, two serious problems arose. First, many recruits did not join guide marks by the required vertical lines, but instead drew varying shapes of mark covering part, or none, of the area read by the OMR. This caused it to reject around 25 per cent of answer sheets for both the Guide and the only multiple-choice test (Arithmetic) in use at the time. Such a reject rate was unacceptably high as valuable time had to be used in amending incorrectly completed forms for re-running on the OMR. This delayed job allocation decisions. The second difficulty was caused by a few recruits drawing a vertical line down that part of the answer sheet containing response guides for questions near the end of the test. This blind guessing was apparently carried out when the test time-limit was running out and pressures to attempt all the questions were greatest. As the OMR could not detect such guess lines, these recruits gained a higher test score than others unaware of this ruse. (On average, one fifth of such blind guesses would be correct.) As the Guide was untimed, there was no similar pressure to guess blindly, and guess lines were not drawn on its answer sheet. It was realized that these two problems could only be solved by redesigning both OMR answer sheets. Accordingly, the decision was made to seek corrective advice from leading OMR users and interested parties in the British Isles. This would, it was hoped, not only overcome the present difficulties, but would avoid introducing unforeseen ones.

Advice Received on OMR

It is not possible to reveal the eight firms or organizations that we identified as OMR users because their OMR information was given in confidence. For reference purposes, they have thus been labelled A to G in Table 1. They raised several useful points concerning hardware and software aspects of OMR, and these have guided the revision of the Army's answer sheets and usage of its OMR equipment. Their advice and other relevant information will now be discussed under the headings, 'hardware' and 'software'. (As the hardware subject labelled 'OMR accuracy research' is regarded as particularly important, hardware issues will be considered first.)

Hardware

Table 1 summarizes the relevant issues and the information obtained from our contacts. The contents of this table will now be described in detail.

OMR Accuracy Research

From Table 1, it can be seen that only C is systematically checking the accuracy with which OMR converts data from answer sheets to a form acceptable for input to computers. This began after the discovery that a small percentage of answer sheets had been incorrectly processed by their Dataterm 3. Fluctuations in current OMR's read-head were thought to have caused this problem. Now every sixth form run through the OMR is also hand marked to ascertain the OMR's accuracy. If such research confirms the existence of a low but persistent OMR error rate, C will cease to use OMR. This is because the possibly damaging consequences of wrongly marked work for the candidates involved are considered unacceptable.

D uses an Opscan 17 OMR as part of their automatic system for scoring answer sheets completed by school children. It is normally assumed that the OMR processes these sheets accurately and so no systematic checks are made. However, if a school teacher complains that a candidate has been given an unusual score (either too high or too low for his estimated ability), D will examine the relevant answer sheet for possible OMR errors. The few justifiable complaints received are viewed as evidence of the OMR's accuracy. This may be an over-optimistic conclusion since it relies, perhaps unwisely, on the integrity and conscientiousness of the relevant teachers. Multiple responses (which are discussed in paragraph 25) were blamed for such infrequent OMR errors.

Like D, E does not systematically check how accurately answer sheets are processed by their own OMR, an Opscan 17. But it was claimed that some of the University Departments served by E do examine the accuracy of OMR processing for all sheets read, while others perform random checks. Although no OMR errors were reported to have been found, clear details of these checking procedures were not produced by E.

While these comments may cause concern about the use of OMR for processing answer sheets, it must be remembered that hand marking can also introduce scoring errors. The crucial question is whether the extent of the inaccuracy caused by OMR unacceptably exceeds that associated with hand marking. Only research can answer this.

Prior to their discussions with us, G, probably like many OMR users, had never questioned the accuracy of OMR processing. However, on learning about our worry over possible OMR inaccuracy, G also decided to investigate the relative effectiveness of OMR and hand marking for scoring answer sheets. Currently, they contract a commercial firm to use its OMR (of unknown make) for processing answer sheets completed by local school children. G now propose to hand mark a batch already scored by OMR and compare the error rates.

OMR Reject Rate

This refers to the percentage of answer sheets rejected and hence unread by the OMR. As Table 1 shows, OMR reject rates generally appear low and acceptable according to the users contacted. But, to achieve them, the redesigning of answer sheets was found necessary by A and B.

The high reject rate for Type 1 forms at C was blamed on their unsupervized completion in students' homes and the need to fold them for posting. (C and D form design is discussed under 'Software'.) This was to reduce the errors made by candidates when answering poorly designed forms. In addition, B, C and D employ

OMR Hardware Issue	ESTABLISHMENT						
	A_1	B_1	C_1	D_2	E_2	F_3	G_4
OMR Accuracy Research	None	None	Yes	No Systematic Research	No Systematic Research	None	None
Annual Processing Load — number of sheets	150,000	300,000	300,000	120,000	2,000	Not applicable	120,000
OMR Reject Rate	2%	<2%	Type 1 forms 20% Type 2 forms 4%	2%	1%	Not applicable	Unknown[5]
OMR Sensitivity	High	High	Low	Middle	Unstated[6]	Unstated[6]	Unknown[5]
OMR Warm-up Time	None	None	15 minutes	None	None	Unstated[6]	Unknown[5]
OMR Maintenance and Servicing	Initial Problems	Initial Problems	Initial Problems	Initial Problems	Initial and continuing problems	Not applicable	Not applicable

1   Use DATATERM 3 OMR.
2   Use OPSCAN 17 OMR.
3   Consultants on production of OMR answer sheets but do not use an OMR directly.
4   Use a commercial firm for OMR processing and do not know make of OMR employed.
5   'Unknown' = organization unable to supply information.
6   'Unstated' = not necessarily 'unknown', but not mentioned by organization.

Table 1. *Information from contacts on OMR hardware issues*

personnel to inspect and amend (where necessary) candidates' responses on the answer sheets in order to avoid their rejection through incorrect completion (eg faint marks). This practice is also followed by E. Using manpower for this purpose is expensive, however, and raises questions about the cost-effectiveness of automatic marking systems based on OMR. Apart from poor form design and candidates' errors, the main causes of OMR rejection seem to be power surges and the use of answer sheets stored in unsuitably humid conditions. F reported that rejection rates of up to 11 per cent have occurred due to humidity problems.

OMR Sensitivity

It is usually possible to vary an OMR's sensitivity to marks on answer sheets by appropriately turning the OMR read-head. When this is adjusted upwards to give high sensitivity, candidates' faint responses can be detected. Unfortunately, smudges, creases and folds may then be interpreted as responses by the OMR. Keeping the OMR tuned at a high level of sensitivity may also strain it, leading to an unacceptable number of breakdowns. By de-tuning the read-head, these problems can be overcome, but candidates' faint responses may then be missed by the OMR. As Table 1 reveals, our contacts were in disagreement about the most suitable level of OMR sensitivity. This was partially because they differed on the perceived importance of these OMR errors.

OMR Warm-Up Time

This is the time (if any) which must pass following the connection of power to the OMR before effective processing of answer sheets can begin. To some extent, the amount needed seems to depend upon the type of OMR used. As shown in Table 1, both users (D and E) of the Opscan 17 reported that none was required. In contrast, research by one user (C) of the Dataterm 3 indicated that the warm-up should not be less than 15 minutes, or unreliable processing would result. However, only two minutes was considered necessary by its manufacturer (Data Recognition). Neither A nor B used any warm-up time for their Dataterm 3.

OMR Maintenance and Servicing

From Table 1, it can be seen that all OMR users had experienced initial difficulties with the maintenance and servicing of their equipment. Such problems have largely been solved for users of Dataterm 3 by increased direct contact with Data Recognition. This allowed them to explain their grumbles clearly to the manufacturer who then took appropriate remedial action! D now regarded maintenance and servicing of their Opscan 17 as adequate. However, E's problems with their Opscan 17 were continuing to such an extent that they were considering the purchase of a Dataterm 3. This would, they hoped, be easier to maintain and service. E's difficulties arose following the withdrawal of maintenance cover by Scandata in December 1977. This firm had provided the service after the business failure of Britain's Opscan distributor. No one else is currently offering to maintain Opscan.

Software

The pertinent issues and the information acquired from our contacts will now be fully discussed.

Response Lines

Most contacts with a clear policy on the matter preferred form designs requiring candidates to show their answers by drawing horizontal lines between, or inside (if appropriate), the relevant response guides. They felt that such lines were easier to draw than vertical ones, though little, if any, research seems to have been done on this subject. Only H advocated the use of diagonal lines, but no evidence was cited in their support.

Response Guides

The majority of our contacts used lozenge-shaped (ie long and narrow) response guides of various types. The sole establishment (C) employing guide-marks is now giving consideration to dropping them in favour of a lozenge-shaped guide. It should, however, be noted that no research has been carried out to determine the most suitable response guide.

Grid Lines

These usually refer to the lines printed on forms to separate the boxes containing response guides. Their purpose is to guide candidates on where their responses can be placed. Contacts with a policy on such lines disagreed about their value. So research could usefully be conducted to clarify this matter.

Answer Box Groupings

This refers to the use of gaps between successive groups of answer boxes in order to divide the answer sheet into visually manageable portions. Without such gaps, a candidate may unintentionally lose his place on the form, missing out one or more boxes. Such an error is called 'slippage' and is undetectable by the OMR. Thus, unless spotted by human inspection, this can result in the candidate being given an undeservedly low score as some or all of his answers would be in the wrong boxes. Most contacts designed their forms to include gaps between groups of answer boxes. However, F do not follow this procedure and so their forms may encourage slippage errors. Some forms used by D and E have answer box groupings, while others do not. Colour shading is also employed by D on certain forms for the same apparent reason that gaps are inserted between answer box groupings.

Location Marks

These are only used on forms designed for the Dataterm 3. Each consists of a pair of horizontal lines which define the start and finish of a reading line. There is always a location mark in the first column of a form. The gaps between such marks can be varied at the form design stage. Using wider location marks increases the permissible thickness of response lines drawn by candidates. This, in turn, means that their lines do not need to be as straight as when the narrower location marks are employed. By thus demanding less skill from candidates, it is likely that fewer of their answer sheets will be rejected by the OMR because of incorrect completion. The use of wide location marks is especially advantageous when forms are to be answered under examination conditions.

Because of the accompanying stress, most candidates cannot then draw straight lines. A, B, and C used forms with five location marks to the inch. This density may have been selected as it is conventional in the printing trade. However, wider location marks (eg four to the inch) may be more appropriate. Research could usefully be conducted to determine the most suitable density of location marks.

Drop-Out Colours

The term 'drop-out colour' signifies that the relevant colour is not detected by OMRs. When selecting such colours for OMR forms, the most important criterion to use is their legibility to candidates. Magenta is favoured by several contacts, but there was disagreement over the suitability of other colours. Thus, while B argued against the use of blue and brown, these were approved by D and E. Research is clearly needed to identify the most suitable colours for OMR forms. OMRs should be tuned for the particular drop-out colour on the forms being processed at any given time.

Colour Shading

As mentioned earlier, colour shading is employed by D to form answer box groupings, thus preventing slippage errors. It is also used by A and F to help candidates distinguish between dense groupings of lozenge-shaped response guides.

Back to Back Printing

It is essential that the printing on OMR answer sheets is accurately positioned, and that the forms are guillotined correctly. This is to ensure that candidates' responses on the forms appear under the precise paths followed by the OMR read-heads and are thus interpreted by them. Faulty printing and/or guillotining would lead to responses being misinterpreted or forms rejected. Using an OMR form printed back-to-back (ie on both sides) can cause these problems as the position of the printing may vary slightly from side to side. Despite this danger, answer sheets with back-to-back printing are employed by A, D, E and G. D add to the risk by including such forms in answer sheet booklets which, they admit, are associated with more OMR errors than single page answer sheets. These may, in part, be due to variations in the accuracy of the guillotining from page to page.

Answer Changing

Candidates should, if they wish, be able to change their answers on OMR forms. All our contacts (except, possibly, H, whose policy is unknown) allowed this option, though the particular methods of changing an answer depended upon the type of OMR employed. With the Opscan 17 a rubber is used to remove unwanted responses in pencil, and answers can be changed as often as desired. This simple procedure can also be followed for forms processed by the Dataterm 3. However, it is likely to detect poorly rubbed-out marks along with the intended response, misinterpreting the lot as a multiple-response error.

For this reason, none of the Dataterm users permitted answers to be changed by this method. Instead, they followed the procedure recommended by Data Recognition. This involves cancelling the unwanted response by shading a small defined area beneath it, and then marking in the new answer. Unfortunately, candidates are not able to re-mark the original response if they later wish to do so. Such a disadvantage should be borne in mind when considering the use of the Dataterm 3. One possible, though laborious, way of solving this problem is to write the reselected response at the side of the answer box and then to mark all the answers to that question. The OMR would interpret this as a multiple-response error, and can be made to alert the OMR operator accordingly. He would then ensure that the relevant form is hand marked, giving credit, where appropriate, to the reselected response.

Multiple-response Error

A genuine multiple-response error is committed when the candidate wrongly marks more than one answer to a question. If it is uncorrected before processing, the Dataterm 3 will interpret all such responses as valid. However, this problem can be overcome by appropriately programming the computer linked to the OMR for scoring purposes. This would trigger an alerting system in the OMR, and, as already discussed, the relevant answer sheet can be hand marked. By contrast, the Opscan 17 reads only the darkest mark in a multiple-response and so programming cannot be used to detect such errors. Thus users of this OMR should always correct these mistakes before their answer sheets are processed to avoid scoring inaccuracies. However, D do not correct them, simply accepting the darkest mark read by their Opscan 17 as the candidates' true response. This is a dubious practice, especially as their few (admitted) OMR errors were blamed on multiple-responses. Users of a Dataterm 3 without suitable programming could, of course, be similarly criticized if they failed to correct this type of error before processing forms. B and C are immune from this censure and their answer sheets are appropriately amended where necessary.

Marking Implements

Most contacts recommended HB pencils for answering OMR forms. This is because they do not make a glossy mark or smudge easily. (These are common causes of OMR errors.) Though A also advocated black felt-tip pens, F criticized such pens as their heads became flattened after only a little use. This produces unacceptably thick marks which, in turn, may cause OMR reading errors. Like F, Data Recognition favoured black Pentel fibre-tip pens for form completion, but these are expensive. Moreover, their marks are indelible, so answers cannot be changed on OMR answer sheets processed by Opscan 17.

Completion Instructions

Most contacts insisted that candidates and their supervisors should be given clear instructions on how to complete OMR answer sheets. This is particularly important for candidates of low intelligence, with no experience of such forms.

Possible Solution for Army's OMR Problems

Using the information received from our OMR contacts, a new answer sheet was designed for the new multiple-choice Arithmetic test. This form has the following features:

- (a) horizontal response lines;
- (b) uninterrupted, rectangular, lozenge-shaped, response guides;
- (c) grid lines;
- (d) gaps between response guides and between grid lines;
- (e) answer box groupings;
- (f) four location marks to the inch;
- (g) magenta drop-out colour;
- (h) no colour shading;
- (i) no back-to-back printing;
- (j) a facility for answer changing.

In addition, suitable programming has been written for the computer linked to the RES dataterm 3 so that multiple-response errors can be detected and subsequently rectified by hand marking. HB pencils were chosen as the marking implements to be used by candidates. The final software innovation has been the preparation of thorough OMR completion instructions for verbal administration to candidates by experienced supervisors. These instructions are supplemented by a simple summary on the answer sheet.

On the hardware side, the RSC Dataterm 3 has been tuned to a high level of sensitivity and the warm-up time increased from five to 15 minutes. RSC trials are currently being conducted using the new Arithmetic form in order to check the OMR's accuracy and reject rate. While only initial results are available, these are encouraging. Only two out of 250 answer sheets were inaccurately read by the Dataterm 3, and in each case the error was only one mark out of 80. As these two forms were processed consecutively, it is suspected that the problem was caused by a power surge which led to peaking. When the errors were detected by hand marking, all the answer sheets were reprocessed, this time correctly, by the OMR. No pre-checks or amendments had been performed when these forms were first read by the Dataterm 3, and yet the reject rate was only 2 per cent. When the relevant answer sheets were rectified, this was reduced to zero on each of 10 subsequent re-runs. Moreover, no blind guessing was found.

Conclusions and Recommendations

On the usage of OMR, generally, it is concluded that there is a need for research on both the hardware and software aspects in order to give adequate guidance to users. Currently they seem to select OMR procedures on a solely subjective basis. Specifically, studies could usefully investigate the comparative accuracy of OMR processing and hand marking, and the most appropriate response lines, response guides, grid lines, location mark density and drop-out colours. As far as the use of OMR in Army selection is concerned, it is concluded that the encouraging results from preliminary RSC trials indicate the suitability of the newly designed answer sheet. But it is recommended that further RSC trials should be carried out as soon as possible to check (i) the comparative error rates between the Dataterm 3 and hand marking; (ii) the OMR's reject rate; and (iii) that the problem of blind guessing has been overcome.

Workshop Report
9.7 A Technology for Job Mobility Through Training and Education

P J Edney
Food Drink and Tobacco Industry Training Board

In the workshop, Mr Edney described a scheme developed in the training board to train workers in new skills required by the need to change jobs and keep pace with new technologies.

Mr Edney gave a brief history of the scheme and traced its origin from about 1976. Research has shown that a majority of workers still do not change their place of work during their working life. However, many people have to adapt themselves to changes in working methods and procedures or use their existing skills in different ways as a result of constantly changing technology.

The method adopted consists of setting up a skills profile for the person involved, to identify the skills he already has, and see how best these can be used in order to satisfy the demands required in the new task or job. All unnecessary learning is reduced to a minimum and avoided as much as possible.

Job descriptions are designed in terms of responsibilities rather than what is is to be done. Hence it is desired that statements should indicate exactly what is actually done, and this should be expressed in language which is easily understandable.

The world of work is one of the areas in which the organization is involved. The organization often views the world of work from a very different perspective to that viewed by the various existing agencies such as careers guidance and employment agencies. Many of the problems are due to a misunderstanding of the situation. For example it is assumed that a manager of a bottling factory could manage a shoe factory. This, of course, is not necessarily true. There is a need for concern with people and characteristics which are matched with job requirements and this calls for a totally new approach.

Mr Edney then illustrated the point by looking at a number of examples in which he conducted a skills analysis. He proceeded to conduct a systems analysis of the job under consideration so that the various basic functions could be clearly identified and could be expressed in specific objective terms.

He proceeded to demonstrate the difficulty involved in determining the level of complexity that was demanded in identifying an element which was, in turn, related to behaviour or skill and knowledge. Thus although functions appeared similar there were differences in levels of performance.

Frequently, the manner in which an occupation is identified involves the process of task analysis which identifies the behavioural elements required in a wide range of jobs. From such a matrix a variety of elements can be taught which can subsequently be collated in order to increase the versatility of a person's job prospect, as he would have a range of skills and knowledge which could be suited to satisfy demands over a wide spectrum.

A more sophisticated approach now involves the use of computers which can compare the skills he has in one particular field with that which he is most likely to be suited to in the event of a change. Thus, if his present job makes him redundant computers may determine the next best job he can be easily trained to take up with the minimum amount of skills redundancy and as little retraining as possible. This is referred to as 'maximizing on transfer'. This job matching process needs to take into account the details of behaviour elements which need to be trained, sharpened, transferred etc.

Because of this method of job evaluation it is now possible to design a curriculum for schools and for further education. It also helps employers and employees (and those concerned with finding and matching the needs of the industrial market).

9.8 The Management of Large-Scale Instructional Technology Projects

A J Romiszowski
Brazil

Objectives of the Workshop

Many large-scale applications of educational technology seem to run into problems, either when (a) an originally successful small-scale ('micro') project grows in size or is 'multiplied' (applied in many institutions); or (b) a project is planned as a large-scale ('macro') project right from the start, but the techniques that it uses have been developed and tried out mainly in 'micro' situations. Problems may occur at three stages:

1 training system and materials development (the 'manufacturing' stage);
2 implementation and dissemination of the system (the 'distribution' stage);
3 long-term operation of the system (the 'utilization' stage).

Very few guidelines exist on how to predict and avoid problems in 'macro' projects, although many retrospective analyses of such problems exist. This workshop brought together nearly 30 educational technologists, concerned with the design or operation of large scale training projects, in an attempt to pool their experiences and opinions on how to predict and avoid problems. The chief objective was to construct a list of likely problem areas in small, medium and large scale training projects, using the concept of 'scale effect' to identify the types of problems which become of prime concern to the project manager as the scale of the project grows.

Key Problems When the Factor was:	FACTORS WHICH CREATED PROBLEMS			
	1. Number of Students	2. Frequency of Use of Centre	3. Quantity and Variety of Materials	4. Number of Staff in Centre
Small	Justify existence and costs of centre	Part-time staffing Limited budget	Integrating self-instruction with traditional courses	Need for jacks of all trades
Medium	Loss of personal contact	Organizing; utilization Queuing problems	Storage and retrieval problems.	Need for specialists and teamwork 'team-building'
Large	Predicting demand Losses and damage	Loss of flexible study hours	Need to decentralize. 'Satellite departments'	Personnel: — training — motivation — control

Table 1. *Matrix of problems encountered in a resource centre, owing to the 'scale effect' (Adapted from Cowan, 1975)*

Conceptual Framework

John Cowan (1975) described the concept of 'scale effect' in relation to the problems appearing during the growth of a resources centre. The present author (Romiszowski, 1978) has summarized John Cowan's findings as a matrix relating specific growth factors to the problems that they created (see Table 1).

During the workshop the participants attempted to construct a similar matrix (conceptual framework) to classify the problems encountered in the development, implementation and utilization of instructional systems.

Methodology

Three groups were formed, to consider separately the problems of:

(a) instructional system design and development
(b) implementation of instructional systems
(c) long-term management of instructional systems.

Size-bands were defined for each group as follows:

	Group (a) criterion	Group (b) criterion	Group (c) criterion
	Number of instructional designers on the project	Number of 'client' institutions in the project.	Number of students ('consumers') per year using the instructional system
Small project	1 to 5	1 to 5	about 100
Medium project	10 to 20	10 to 20	about 1,000
Large project	about 50	about 50	about 5,000

Table 2.

Through the use of brainstorming techniques each group attempted to list the key problems for the project manager in each of the size-bands. The ideas were then brought together and complemented or criticized in large-group discussion.

Results

Each group suggested some types of problems that exist in projects of any scale but tend to grow as the size of the project grows and other types of problems that are particularly critical in projects of a certain scale. The main types of problems mentioned are summarized in Table 3.

Comments and Suggestions

The amount of time available severely limited the possible achievements of the workshop. Final discussion barely touched on the possible solutions to the problems identified. Also, the list of problems is as yet tentative and incomplete. Many participants considered that further sessions of the workshop would be useful (perhaps at future conferences).

Some doubts were expressed as to how far one could go in developing a generic model for the prediction of project management problems. To what extent are the problems of any specific project unique to that project and not capable of being systematically predicted? However, consensus was reached that as projects grew, so did the need for project management skills (they become more critical and more complex). Whereas the small-scale project might rely chiefly on the manager's personal leadership skills coupled to relatively *ad-hoc* and informal planning/

	STAGES IN WHICH PROBLEMS ARE ENCOUNTERED		
Key problems when the project is:	(a) Instructional Design/production Stages	(b) Implementation/ dissemination Stages	(c) Long-term Management and Control
Small	Promoting a creative approach Adapting project to existing skills	Availability of resources Personnel changes and personalities	Integration within the institution Performing long-term evaluation
Medium	Standardizing the language and documents Scheduling time and budgeting	Creating 'receptive' environment Controlling 'drift' in the system	Maintaining individualization Staff development, control, delegation
Large	Co-ordination of several teams Task-scheduling and teamwork Planning regular validation/learning opportunities (for the designers)	Support of the 'supra-system' Ensuring long-term resources Controlling waste of resources/time Ensuring the system is 'self-correcting'	Management information systems that work Support-staff requirements Student opinions, objectives, welfare Systematic procedures of project management
Factors which create problems in projects of any size but which increase in critically increase as the project grows	Changes in the team or in the team management Duration of the design stages and continuity in time Sheer quantity of materials to be produced	Training of the teachers/monitors Extent of centralized control Maintenance of interest/momentum Ensuring adequate installation budget	Overcoming tendencies towards 'inertia' Establishing effective command-chains Predicting and defining future changes in system Ensuring adequate running resources
		the 'Dog-food Syndrome', ie the distinction between the *consumer* and the *client* and their respective needs and attitudes.	

Table 3. *Matrix of problems encountered in instructional system development/use*
(Drawn up by the participants in the workshop)

control procedures, the medium-scale project demands more sophisticated skills and planning/control instruments. The large-scale project depends for its success on the systematic utilization of a range of scientific management techniques (such as PERT, MBO, PPBS, etc) in just the same way as any other complex industrial manufacturing/distribution/after-sales-service system.

How to adapt such scientific management techniques to educational and training projects was considered an area worthy of further study.

References

Cowan, John (1975) Scale effect and its relevance to resource-based learning. *Aspects of Educational Technology*, X. Kogan Page.

Romiszowski, A J (1978) Alguns cuidados na aplicação de technologia educacional em grandes projetos de treinamento. (Some points to watch when applying educational technology in large-scale training projects.) Brazilian Association of Training and Development. Proceedings of 1978 Conference.

Section 10:
The Role of Educational Technology

10.0 Introduction

ETIC '79 Tracks
The two papers in this final section, Lawless (10.1) and Leedham (10.2) were both presented in Track 1, 'Self-Instructional Programmes in Practice'.

Categories and Special Interests
Lawless was in the 'MeDes' for 'Media Design' category. Leedham was coded 'Prof' for 'Professional Aspects', as were the workshops by Boydell and Pedler (10.3), Green and Morris (10.4), and Rowntree (10.5).

Boydell/Pedler was also coded 'Eval' for 'Evaluation'. Walsh (10.6) was in this latter cateogry and also in 'Tert' for 'Tertiary Education'. Green/Morris, as an annual look at 'Strategies and Presentation of Learning', was also coded 'Strats'.

Links with Other Sections
Readers with a particular interest in Section 10 are also likely to be interested in Moakley (7.2) in Section 7.

10.1 Information Processing : a Model for Educational Technology

C J Lawless
The Open University

Abstract: The basic model of educational technology as it emerged 20 years ago was based on behaviourist or stimulus-response (S-R) views of learning then dominant in psychology. This model, behavioural objectives, active responding, self-pacing and knowledge of results, remains influential in spite of much criticism, notably of the insistence on behavioural objectives (MacDonald-Ross, 1973) and the fact that effective instructional practices have been developed which do not fit easily into the model, and for which eighteenth-century craft technology provides a better analogy (Atkin, 1967-8). A theoretical or knowledge base is important to prevent practices becoming 'rote-by-numbers' procedures (Glaser, 1976) and since educational technology is concerned with learning it must retain links with theoretical and experimental work. In this field there has been a 'shift from behaviourism to cognitive psychology' (Wittrock and Lumsdaine, 1977, p 218) which can probably be dated from the publication of *Cognitive Psychology* (Neisser, 1967), so that it can be claimed, 'Modern cognitive psychology is today's dominant theoretical force in behavioral science' (Glaser, Pellegrino and Lesgold, 1978, p 495). Hence the importance of investigating it as a basis for the design of instruction.

The Information Processing Model

Cognitive psychology is concerned with 'complex perception, the organization of memory, language thinking, and in general the complicated processes which underlie the intellectual side of human life'. (Broadbent, 1975, p 163.) The basic model of these processes provided by cognitive psychology is an information processing system which views the learner as an *active* processor of information rather than as a *passive* receiver of stimuli and emitter of responses. Among the factors which have shaped the information processing approach have been computer programming and work on artificial intelligence. Computer models are only analogies, they are 'incredibly simple' (Ausubel, 1968, p 122) when compared to 'the complexities of human mental processes' (Neisser, 1967, p 9).

The basic model illustrated below is based on Newell and Simon (1972, p 20), Atkinson and Shiffrin (1971, p 82) and Gagné (1977, p 53) and covers a number of controversial issues such as the relationship of structure to process (Reynolds and Flagg, 1977) and the existence of two or even three memories in the processor area (Bower, 1975). Such issues are comprehensively discussed by Lindsay and Norman (1972).

A vast amount of information constantly comes through the senses into the sensory register where a small proportion is selected by conscious attention (control process) and perceptual skills (stored in the long term memory) and enters the processor, probably in the form of visual and aural images. Only a limited amount of information can be held in the processor and for a short time (though this can be extended by conscious rehearsal). The processor carries out the main work of the system of encoding or transforming the incoming images into concepts for entry into the long term memory (LTM) or store. The form in which the information is encoded is crucial and is determined by the nature of the images, basic encoding skills and the cognitive structure in the LTM. Constant interaction

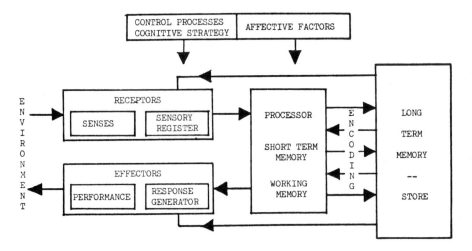

Figure 1. *The information processing system*

occurs between the processor and the LTM so that the form in which information
is encoded and the structure into which it is incorporated are greatly influenced
by each other. The form in which information is stored determines how easily it
can be retrieved. The way in which items, concepts, ideas are grouped (structured
or formed into schemata), the number and richness of their inter-connections
rather than the amount of information or number of items, determines their
availability.

Retrieval is a more complex procedure (Atkinson and Shiffrin, 1971), involving
successive 'searches' of the information stored in the cognitive structure of the
LTM until relevant information is located and transferred to the processor for
use in problem solving. The richness of the cognitive structure or schemata in
terms of valid inter-connections will determine the ease of the search and the extent to which the learner can transfer this information to the solution of unfamiliar
problems. When a solution has been arrived at in the processor, information is
passed to the response generator where it is cast into the appropriate form, speech,
writing or other physical action. This leads to performance providing the individual
has the appropriate physical capability. Such transfer of learning requires a high
level of processing or problem solving skills and is an important element in the
type of objectives implied by this approach (Voss, 1978).

Outside the system, but acting on every part of it, are affective factors and
control processes. Affective factors include motivation and attitudes, including
attitudes to the subject matter itself (possibly influenced by a previous teacher),
to the manner in which it is presented and to the person who presents it. Control
processes or cognitive strategy are the conscious decisions that an individual makes
to determine the way information is processed into the LTM and retrieved to solve
problems. Essentially they are focused on the processor where they can involve
rehearsing, imaging, decision rules, structural or organizing devices, or problem-
solving procedures. These processes are conscious and can be developed and
improved and provide the key to effective learning. Hence the importance of
developing the individual's control processes is one of the primary implications

of the information processing approach for the design of instruction.

Two further issues need to be considered: individual differences and the role of language. First, this approach highlights a wide range of individual differences in cognitive structure, in processing skills and in cognitive strategy or control processes, all of which have implications for the design of instruction. Secondly the role of language is crucial for the whole process, particularly in the encoding and storing of information. Highly developed language skills are an essential prerequisite for processing the information associated with academic learning while deficiencies must inevitably lead to a low level of processing and poorly organized cognitive structure.

Applying the Model

(1) Analyzing the Information

In applying this model the first task is to analyze the information to be processed by the student, the course content in other words, and to establish its real nature, the meaning of the concepts and the underlying relationships between them. Making and using relationships between concepts is what understanding and learning are all about. Relationships make up a structure which is an important aid to the student in storing information and building up his own cognitive structure. Superficially, the information processing model appears most relevant to content-oriented courses, mainly in higher education, since it is concerned with processing knowledge. It is also applicable to task-oriented courses since it is concerned with the internal processes behind performance of the task. This provides a multi-dimensional approach which is wider than 'traditional' educational technology's requirement that all purposes expressed in activity or behavioural terms.

Techniques for analyzing the content of instruction are both general and specific to particular subject areas. The procedures described here are general with wide applicability but it must be recognized that different academic disciplines not only use different types of concepts, different sets of relationships but provide different ways of looking at the world (Schwab, 1964, Hirst, 1974). While recognizing different kinds of analysis for varieties of purpose and types of subject matter, one issue is paramount. The purpose of such analyses is to establish and to clarify the relatedness of the elements or concepts of subject matter.

Wilson (1963)	Lewis (1974))	Klausmeier and Goodwin (1975)
Isolate concepts	Define concepts in turn	Define concept
Model cases	Examine antonyms/	List relevant attributes
Contrary cases	synonyms	List irrelevant attributes
Related cases	Valid/invalid examples	Examples
Borderline cases	Borderline cases	Non-examples
Social context	'Confuser' concepts	Taxonomic relationships
Practical results	'Pervasive' concepts	Principles
Results in language	Analyze for vagueness,	Sample problems
	ambiguity and opacity	Vocabulary
	Apply Kelly grid proce-	
	dure to establish differ-	
	ences and similarities	

Table 1. *Three techniques of concept analysis*

The techniques compared in Table 1 show a high degree of similarity, they represent a general, common-sense approach to the analysis of subject matter. Wilson (1963) provides a particularly good treatment of the basic issue of identifying concepts in contrast to many works which provide no guidance at all on the first vital step of answering the question 'What is a concept?'. Lewis (1974) gives procedures for establishing the relationships between concepts. Essentially the result is a network of concepts such as that illustrated in Figure 2. Although all the 'concept boxes' are linked with each other, this does not lessen the usefulness of such a network. What is needed is an analysis of the nature of these relationships. One way of categorizing relationships is to divide them into *causal* (X happens because), *teleological* (X happens in order that) or *structural* (X is made up of). Alternatively, operations that a student is expected to make can be specified, *change* (recall, transform . . .), *describe* (attitudes, limitations . . .) or *relate* (order, exclude, analogy . . .). (Merrill, 1973).

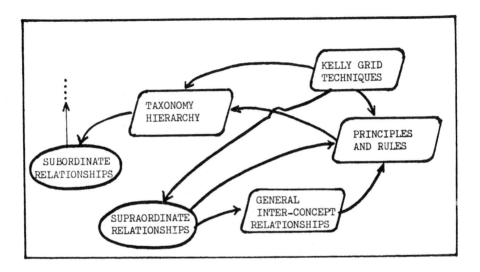

Figure 2. *Concept analysis of concept analysis*

'Specialist' analysis techniques include those to identify prerequisites or components, 'entailment structures' (Pask and Scott, 1972) or 'learning-prerequisite relationships' (Reigeluth, Merrill and Banderson, 1978). Other types of analysis procedure include taxonomies, flow charts and decision trees ('algorithms') and hierarchies (Gagné, 1977, White and Gagné, 1974) which relate to both subject matter and to associated activities. These techniques are not new, but at all levels of education information is given and knowledge is taught in isolated packets lacking any indication to the student of how it is linked to other sections even of the same course. This reflects the position that course designers, teachers and lecturers are themselves often unaware of the underlying structure of their subject matter.

This stress on the information to be processed does not mean that the performance expected of the student should be ignored. ' . . . a cognitive theory of instruction must indicate how knowledge is related to performance both in its acquisition and subsequent performance'. (Olson, 1976, p 119-120.)

Analyzing the information which lies behind performance requires a more rigorous approach than specifying behavioural objectives, recognizing that not all objectives are behavioural. Where there is a task to be performed behavioural objectives can be specified along the lines of Mager (1962) but analyzing the knowledge behind performance is still important. The purpose of content-oriented courses is to build up the student's cognitive structure to provide long term capacity of interpreting and 'increasing control over the environment' (Holloway, 1978, p 2). Attempts to specify behavioural objectives for such courses are often artificial and misleading, resulting in lists of subject matter dressed up with fancy verbs! Real changes in behaviour occur over long periods not from short pieces of instruction. With content-oriented courses activities may have a *sampling* function rather than being objective as such, though this does not remove the need to develop students' skills in these activities.

Where courses are part of an established discipline or recognized area of knowledge, the way a master-performer operates is a starting point (Lewis, 1974). From the analysis of master performance the areas of competence to be developed or practised in a particular course are selected, though the tasks derived from such an analysis may have a complementary sampling function. Realism is important in relating student performance to that of the expert operating on the frontiers of a discipline. Student performance will be essentially second-hand and should be recognized as such (Resnick, 1976). In cases where specific master performance is lacking, students' knowledge can be sampled by activities appropriate to the level of education, writing essays, preparing project reports, producing a dissertation etc. The competencies involved in these activities, however, still have to be acquired by students, yet all too often little attention is given to them in much conventional instruction. Two points need to be made about competence analysis. The order and components of master or expert performance revealed by analysis will not necessarily indicate how a student starting from a low level can acquire the expertise. A second aspect of analysis (error analysis) is to identify the type of things experts do *not* do and why they do not do them (Lewis, 1974). The development of a more rigorous approach to student performance is implicit in the information processing model from its focus on quality in processing as well as on the quality of the product. 'But rather than just specifying the behaviors needed to succeed on such tests, cognitive objectives are developed by analyzing the psychological processes and structures that are sufficient to produce the needed behaviors'. (Greeno, 1976, p 123.)

(2) Developing the Process

In the past educational technologists have concentrated on manipulating the stimulus by changing the teaching materials in order to produce the correct student response. However, the information processing model emphasizes changing the learner so that he can handle the stimuli he receives, ie information presented by different media. In practice this means enabling the student to develop learning ability which, in terms of the basic information processing model, focuses attention on the 'control processes' (Atkinson and Shiffrin, 1971) or 'cognitive strategy' (Gagné, 1977). Although the flow of information in the model is a closely integrated, almost unitary, process it is convenient for practical purposes to see it in three basic stages: encoding, storing/organizing and retrieving.

At all levels of education little attention is given to developing processing abilities on the assumption that students have already acquired them or will do so by exposure to subject matter. Four examples will demonstrate how ineffectively students process the information they receive, even at the higher education level. Richards (1929) found that Cambridge students exhibited a wide degree of misunderstanding, in some cases verging on the ludicrous, of poems given to them for comment. He attributed this misunderstanding to lack of training in reading and poor background knowledge. Lack of reading competence among Harvard students was found by Perry (1959) over 20 years of running reading development clinics. These students exhibited a high level of ability to recall factual details of passages read but lacked understanding of the purpose of their reading and were unable to describe the basic meaning of what they had read. Turning from reading to the interpretation of information presented visually, Abercrombie (1960) found that medical students provided widely differing interpretations of (X-ray) radiographs and she shows how this resulted from ' . . . the way his schemata of recently received, specialized information about techniques of radiography are related to older, more generalized, schemata of the kind that "things which are alike in some respects are alike in others" ' (p 79). Although frequently cited as a milestone in the use of groups in teaching (which indeed it is) Abercrombie's (1960) work is also of great importance for its stress on the importance of processing. The fourth example is provided by Marton (1975) who investigated how Swedish students studied. He distinguished between 'surface' processors, who concentrated on the form of what they were learning, and 'deep' processors who actively sought connections with previous reading, aimed at basic concepts and developing an overall structure. Two major points emerge from these studies. First, if highly selected university students process information so badly, the problem is likely to be worse at lower levels. Indeed information processing needs to be seen as a major factor in the achievement of academic attainment and, therefore, a major objective of instruction. The second point is the integrated relationship between process and structure in all four studies. Processing skills cannot be seen as separate from subject matter.

Many courses use a variety of media, lectures, seminars, practicals, print and sundry audio-visual methods to present information to students. It is important to recognize the effects of particular media (their 'bias' (McCluhan, 1964)) since students do not interact directly with structured knowledge but as it is presented through particular media. Students need to develop abilities to process information from different media and this must involve seeing through their limitations (Salomon, 1972). Considerable attention is given to improving reading skills, but it is likely that students process information poorly from other media as well. Are such processing skills general, or are they specific to particular subject matter? If seen as general, then special courses on improving reading and developing problem solving skills, for example, would be required. The answer, obviously, is that there are both general and specific processing skills varying with the type of course and all courses require a modicum of general skills to start with. Any work on study skills, such as reading improvement, must have some content on which to be developed. The problem of general courses in study skills is that students find it difficult to relate them to their experience of studying particular subject matter (Gibbs and Northedge, 1977). Applying or transferring general skills at anything above the basic level requires a high level of versatile cognitive strategy. A model sequence might involve firstly general basic skills, then, secondly, the development of specific subject area skills and general skills in the context of specific subject matter. A third stage, the transfer of high level learning skills to different subject areas, is the mark of a sophisticated, versatile learner.

Building up concept relationships in the cognitive structure lies at the heart of the information processing model. This involves a rich pattern of valid but flexible relationships; valid in the sense of being related to structures of knowledge in the world outside the individual and flexible in the sense of wide applicability which is the essence of understanding and critical thinking. A course of instruction should both enable the student to build up specific relationships with the subject area of the course and to develop general structuring skills. How relationships should be developed is not easy to prescribe. The nature of subject matter and the experience of the learner are clearly crucial, but the key practical question is whether learners should be *told* relationships between concepts or whether they should *discover* them for themselves. No global prescription is possible, clearly relying on telling is likely to lead to a superficial level of learning while it is impracticable for students to 'discover' everything. A 'discovery' element needs to be built up in the cognitive structure, a dimension associated with cause and effect, so that the student can incorporate new information received from telling; what Ausubel (1968) refers to as 'meaningful reception learning'. Awareness of the importance of making connections between new and existing knowledge is the important quality, devices such as 'advance organizers' (Ausubel, 1968) which acquaint the learners with the overall structure of the subject matter, and developing an overview by a 'spiral curriculum' (Bruner, 1966), have been shown to be effective, but the long term aim must be for the student to develop techniques of working out structure for himself.

No student starts a course with a *tabula rasa*. There is an existing cognitive structure that will assist or interfere with the acquisition of new knowledge. Nor should it be assumed that adding new information to existing cognitive structure will be easy. Norman (1978) identifies three ways in which the cognitive structure is developed: accretion, re-structuring and tuning. Accretion is the easiest (relatively, at least!), involving adding new information of a similar type to existing structure. In contrast re-structuring is the most difficult since it can involve abandoning existing structures to which the student has strong emotional attachment. This can be compared to the idea of a paradigmatical shift or scientific revolution (Kuhn, 1962) where a model or paradigm is subject to increasing strain by new discoveries until it is replaced by a new one. Northedge (1976) illustrates this problem, recounting his difficulty in accepting that light was reflected from objects to the eye, rather than 'something' going from the eye to the object, 'At first the new notion was so different that it was virtually incomprehensible . . .' (p 69). The third way in which cognitive structure is altered is tuning, in which aspects of structure are applied to a problem and become successively refined by practice to allow more efficient problem solving. Recognition of these processes and their relation to the purposes of instruction cannot be left to chance.

Retrieving in the information processing model can be seen as problem solving, though the input aspect can be similarly viewed, involving problems like 'What is the meaning of this passage? How do these ideas relate?'. There is a considerable literature on the theoretical aspects of problem solving, much of it in the cognitive psychology, information processing field, notably *Human Problem Solving* (Newell and Simon, 1972). Indeed from a cognitive psychology point of view learning can be seen as problem solving (Eisenstadt, 1978). As with the input aspect the general/ specific dichotomy is crucial and this is illustrated by the work of Larkin and Reif (1976). They investigated how students could develop a general learning ability, namely the ability to learn from text a working understanding of new relations, definitions or laws in an introductory physics course. After analysis of the skill, it was explained to students who were given extensive examples to work on. Not only did students' skills improve in the specific subject area but there was also evidence of transfer to other fields. This work illustrates three basic principles for developing problem solving skills. Firstly it involves the whole information processing model and, secondly, it is integrated into the students' current learning experience. It also recognizes that learning skills are not acquired merely through exposure to subject matter, but require conscious attention by teacher and student. Specific problem solving skills need to be identified and their relationship to general skills established as requisites for successful learning. Although certain skills can be formalized into routines (Reif, Larkin and Bracket, 1976) or algorithms (Broadbent, 1975), it has to be recognized that '. . . more complex skills including many socially valued skills, cannot be taught explicitly and they may have to be 'taught' through demonstrations or *modeling* and/or through making allowances for learning through trial and error or *meddling*!' (Olson, 1976, p 119.)

Work on developing students' learning skills has largely been aimed at helping students with severe learning difficulties rather than with the design of instruction itself. While some research in this area has been based on short, artificial tasks, there is a growing body of work on student learning of complex, extensive subject matter (Pask, 1976a, 1976b) under normal instructional conditions (Laurillard, 1978). The information processing approach provides a framework within which this work on 'learning to learn' can be directly related to the design of instruction. Creating awareness in the student of his learning processes and their potential for improvement is the first priority, '. . . when people become aware of their own learning in different respects, they will be better equipped to deal with various sorts of learning difficulties' (Säljö, 1978, p 7). Secondly, developing learning skills must start from where the student is, from his existing patterns of work and perceptions of study tasks. This contrasts with approaches which provide a 'cook book' approach unrelated to the students' actual situation (Gibbs, 1977). As Perry (1959), showed, techniques are of little value unless associated with purpose; to use techniques students have to be aware of their appropriateness and this is the third point. Fourthly, of those who have tackled the problem, Abercrombie (1960), Beasley (1973) and Gibbs (1978), have used free discussion group techniques, but the challenge to instructional designers, particularly of self-instructional materials is to develop individual approaches to this problem. Finally, the aim of 'learning to learn', which could be taken as the aim of an information processing based educational technology, is to develop a learner who can design his own learning, 'a self-organizing learner' (Thomas and Harri-Augstein, 1976) or a 'versatile learner' (Entwistle, 1978), who is able to adjust his learning strategy to the demands of particular learning tasks.

Since each individual's cognitive structure, processing ability and cognitive strategy are different, if not unique, instruction needs to take account of a wider range of individual differences than speed of working. Glaser (1976a) identifies three different levels in terms of initial competence (prerequisites), different learning styles and alternative terminal attainments. The second of these three conditions, different learning styles, relates to the work of Pask (1976a, 1976b, Entwistle, 1978) who has identified 'holist' and 'serialist' learners and has shown the serious effects when learners adopt a mismatched strategy. Pask identifies 'holist' learners with 'comprehension' learning and 'serialists' with 'operation' learning, but he also indicates 'versatile' students who can adapt their style to the demands of the task. Much of this work is still tentative. Are learning styles fixed or can they be adapted? Are 'holists' 'better' learners than 'serialists' or is it simply a question of matching style to the appropriate strategy? Similarly, are 'holists' what Marton (1975) calls 'deep processors' and, if so, should this be an ideal for learning improvement? Such issues must play an important part in a cognitive approach to the design of instruction. Individual differences in outcome can differ either in level or in nature. Different types of learning outcome are particularly relevant in the humanities, allowing for creativity and differing purposes; areas where attempts to apply the one-dimensional approach of traditional educational technology have been controversial.

That children also differ in their stage of intellectual development has been shown by Piaget. With adults Perry (1970) has proposed a hierarchy of stages of development, from conventionalism through relativism to commitment. Intellectual development in this sense is a part of the individual's cognitive structure and failure to learn can result where there is a mismatch between level of intellectual development and the demands of a learning situation. Students entering university, used to clear authoritative teaching, often find it difficult to come to terms with a relative, propositional approach. Although Baron (1975) has advocated a component rather than a hierarchical view the importance of intellectual development remains.

Although too complex a subject for detailed treatment in this paper, language is a key factor in the whole information processing system (Carroll, 1976), since it is the means by which information is processed, stored and organized. Without a high level of language skills information will only be processed superficially. In designing instruction account must be taken of subject areas which have their own language or 'jargon', and areas like philosophy which give special meanings to words in everyday use. The effects of learning in a second language, or in a first language whose basic structure differs from that of the course originator, are also important issues. What is important is that the student develops a satisfactory cognitive structure to accommodate such variations in language use.

Although the information processing model has its origins in cognitive psychology, this in no way excludes affective information from attitudes or emotions. Indeed these must be seen as influential components of mental structure which cannot be ignored by those concerned with teaching and learning. The use of the terms 'instruction' and 'design of instruction' should not be taken in the sense of 'teacher direction or building' (McKeachie, 1974, p 162) but in a more general sense which includes self-instruction and even self-designed instruction. Indeed the stress on the learner as an active processor of information and the importance of his processing ability in determining the outcome of instruction is essentially non-directive and student-based. The information processing model offers educational technology a multi-dimensional approach that could well prove adequate for the next 20 years.

References

Abercrombie, M L J (1960) *The Anatomy of Judgement.* Hutchinson, London.

Atkin, J M (1967-8) 'Research styles in science education' *Journal of Research in Science Teaching,* 5, pp 338-45.

Atkinson, R C and Shiffrin, R M (1971) The control of short-term memory, *Scientific American,* 225, pp 82-90.

Ausubel, D P (1968) *Educational Psychology: A Cognitive View.* Holt, New York.

Baron, J (1975) Some theories of college instruction. *Higher Education,* 4, pp 149-72.

Beasley, V J (1973) Autonomous group discussions and academic success, *Vestes,* 16, 2, pp 11-19.

Bower, G H (1975) Cognitive psychology: an introduction. In Estes, W K (ed) *Handbook of Learning and Cognitive Processes,* 1. Lawrence Erlbaum, Hillsdale, N J.

Broadbent, D E (1975) Cognitive psychology and education. *British Journal of Educational Psychology,* 45, pp 162-76.

Bruner, J S (1966) *Toward a Theory of Instruction.* Belknap, Harbard, Cambridge, Massachusetts.

Carroll, J B (1976) Promoting language skills: the role of instruction. In Klahr, D (ed) *Cognition and Instruction,* pp 3-22. Lawrence Erlbaum, Hillsdale, N J.

Eisenstadt, M (1978) Problem solving. *Course D303 Cognitive Psychology Unit 24.* Open University Press, Milton Keynes.

Entwistle, N J (1978) Knowledge structures and styles of learning: a summary of Pask's recent research. *British Journal of Educational Psychology,* 48, pp 255-65.

Gagné, R M (1977) *The Conditions of Learning* (3rd edn), Holt, Rinehart & Winston, New York.

Gibbs, G (1977) Can students be taught how to study? *Higher Education Bulletin,* 5, 2, pp 102-18. (Summer.)

Gibbs, G (1978) Intervening in student learning — a practical strategy. Paper presented to the 4th International Conference on Higher Education. University of Lancaster.

Gibbs, G and Northedge, A (1977). Learning to study — a student centred approach. *Teaching at a Distance,* 8, pp 3-9.

Glaser, R (1976a) The processes of intelligence and education. In Resnick, L B and Glaser, R (eds) *The Nature of Intelligence,* Lawrence Erlbaum, Hillsdale, N J.

Glaser, R (1976b) Cognitive psychology and instructional design. In Klahr, D (ed) *Cognition and Instruction,* pp 303-23. Lawrence Erlbaum, Hillsdale, N J.

Glaser, R, Pellegrino, J W and Lesgold, A M (1978) Some directions for a cognitive psychology of instruction. In Lesgold, A M, Pellegrino, J W, Fokkema, S D and Glaser, R (eds) *Cognitive Psychology and Instruction,* pp 495-517. Plenum, New York.

Greeno, J G (1976) Cognitive objectives of instruction; Theory of knowledge for solving problems and answering questions. In Klahr, D (ed) *Cognition and Instruction,* pp 123-59. Lawrence Erlbaum, Hillsdale, N J.

Hirst, P H (1974) *Knowledge and the Curriculum.* Routledge & Kegan Paul, London.

Holloway, C (1978) Learning and instruction. *Course D303 Cognitive Psychology Units 22-23,* Open University Press, Milton Keynes.

Klausmeier, H J and Goodwin, W (1975) Learning and human abilities. *Educational Psychology.* Harper and Row, New York.

Kuhn, T S (1962) *The Structure of Scientific Revolutions.* University of Chicago Press, Chicago.

Laurillard, D (1978) The processes of student learning. Paper presented to the 4th International Conference on Higher Education, University of Lancaster. (August 29-September 1.)

Larkin, J H and Reif, F (1976) Analysis and teaching of a general skill for study of scientific text. *Journal of Educational Psychology,* **68,** pp 431-40.

Lewis, B N (1974) *New Methods of Assessment and Stronger Methods of Curriculum Design.* (The first annual report on a research project sponsored by the Ford Foundation.) Institute of Educational Technology, The Open University, Milton Keynes.

Lindsay, P H and Norman, D A (1972) *Human Information Processing: An Introduction to Psychology.* Academic Press, New York.

MacDonald-Ross, M (1973) Behavioural objectives — a critical review. *Instructional Science,* 2, pp 1-52.

McKeachie, W J (1974) Instructional psychology. *Annual Review of Psychology,* 25, pp 161-93.

McLuhan, H M (1964) *Understanding Media: The Extensions of Man.* McGraw-Hill, New York.

Mager, R F (1962) *Preparing Instructional Objectives.* Fearon, Palo Alto.

Marton, F (1975) What does it take to learn? In Entwistle, N and Hounsell, D (eds) *How Students Learn* (Readings in Higher Education, 1) Institute for Research and Development in Post-Compulsory Education, University of Lancaster, Lancaster.

Merrill, M D (1973) Content and Instructional Analysis for Cognitive Transfer Tasks. *A V Communication Review,* **21,** 1, pp 109-25.

Neisser, U (1967) *Cognitive Psychology.* Appleton-Century-Crofts, New York.

Newell, A and Simon, H A (1972) *Human Problem Solving.* Prentice-Hall, Englewood Cliffs, N J.

Norman, D A (1978) Notes towards a theory of complex learning. In Lesgold, A M *et al. Cognitive Psychology and Instruction,* Plenum, New York.

Northedge, A (1976) Examining our implicit analogies for learning processes. *Programmed Learning and Educational Technology,* 13, 4, pp 67-78.

Olson, D R (1976) Notes on a cognitive theory of instruction. In Klahr, D (ed) *Cognition and Instruction,* pp 117-20. Lawrence Erlbaum, Hillsdale, N J.

Pask, G (1976a) Conversational techniques in the study and practice of education. *British Journal of Educational Psychology,* **46,** pp 12-25.

Pask, G (1976b) Styles and strategies of learning, *British Journal of Educational Psychology,* **46,** pp 128-48.

Pask, G and Scott, B C E (1972) Learning strategies and individual competence. *International Journal of Man Machine Studies,* 4, pp 217-53.

Perry, W (1959) Students' Use and Misuse of Reading Skills. *Harvard Educational Review,* 29.

Perry, W G (1970) *Forms of Intellectual and Ethical Development in the College Years: A Scheme,* Holt, Rinehart and Winston, New York.

Reif, F, Larkin, J H and Brackett, G C (1976) Teaching general learning and problem solving skills. *American Journal of Physics,* 44, pp 212-17.

Reigeluth, C M, Merrill, M D and Banderson, C V (1978) The structure of subject matter. *Instructional Science,* 7, pp 107-26.

Resnick, L B (1976) Task analysis in instructional design: some cases from mathematics. In Klahr, D (ed) *Cognition and Instruction,* pp 51-80. Lawrence Erlbaum, Hillsdale, N J.

Reynolds, A G and Flagg, P W (1977) *Cognitive Psychology.* Winthrop, Cambridge, Massachusetts.

Richards, I A (1929) *Practical Criticism.* Routledge & Kegan Paul, London.

Säljö, R (1978) Learning about learning. Paper presented to the 4th International Conference on Higher Education, University of Lancaster. (August 29-September 1.)

Salomon, G (1972) Can we affect cognitive skills through visual media? An hypothesis and initial findings. *A V Communications Review*, **20**, 4, pp 401-22.

Schwab, J J (1964) Structure of the disciplines: meanings and significance. In Ford, G W and Pugno, L (eds) *The Structure of Knowledge and the Curriculum*, pp 6-30. Rand McNally, Chicago.

Thomas, L F and Harri-Augstein, E S (1976) Learning to learn: the personal construction and exchange of meaning. In Howe, M (ed) *Adult Learning*. Wiley, London.

Voss, J.F (1978) Cognition and instruction: toward a cognitive theory of learning. In Lesgold, A M, Pellegrino, J.W, Fokkema, S D and Glaser, R (eds) *Cognitive Psychology and Instruction*, pp 13-26. Plenum, New York.

White, R T and Gagné, R M (1974) Past and future research on learning hierarchies. *Educational Psychologist*, **11**, pp 19-28.

Wilson, J (1963) *Thinking with Concepts*. Cambridge University Press, London.

Wittrock, M C and Lumsdaine, A (1977) Instructional Psychology. *Annual Review of Psychology*, **28**, pp 417-59.

10.2 Staffing and Consultancy : UNESCO Enquiry into Modern Educational Techniques

J Leedham
Rothley, Leicestershire

Abstract: For three years APLET discussed and researched the idea of founding a professional institute for educators and trainers who employ modern educational methods. The idea was put on one side because it was felt that such an institute would be too large for APLET to absorb. It was no surprise to find that in 1978 UNESCO commissioned an enquiry in over 20 countries to establish common criteria for such professionals. This paper and the symposium represent an overview of the present state of the enquiry. It is highly relevant to our membership and bears directly on the question of consultancy with which the Association is properly concerned.

Introduction

Both developing and industrialized countries are expanding their hopes and requirements. Universally, education is looked upon as the means of meeting these demands. At the same time communication techniques and systems organizations are developing rapidly and will soon be developing faster. The needs and techniques are fusing so as to change the traditional role of the teacher. Some institutions such as Tele-Niger, PETV of the Ivory Coast, The Open University in the UK, The Federal German Institute for audio-visual and others now have years of experience in the *staffing* of systems which employ such modern educational techniques. In seeking to create an awareness of the critical need for the adaptation of traditional teaching roles to modern requirements UNESCO is commissioning a world-wide study of institutions whose experience and problems could benefit both formal and non-formal systems now in process of modernizing their own methods and techniques.

Identification of Tasks

There are now several categories of staff who use modern educational techniques which are published by the industrialized countries. These categories have developed into 'taxonomies of competencies' more simply 'lists of abilities', which may be formidable in their sub-divisions. Such a category is that recently issued by the Association for Educational Communications and Technology of the USA. Entitled 'Guidelines for the Certification of Media Specialists' it lists the competencies required by staffs in most of the States of the USA who are concerned in media production or management in formal educational institutions. A division is made between the fields of competency for media specialists and those of technicians in media management although some common functions and responsibilities are recognized. It maintains the professional standpoint that the education and training specialists and some technicians must be qualified as teachers. The further categorization of functions and competencies are allied to the status of the staffing role. A similar recent publication, 'A Study of Professional Roles and Competencies in the Field of Development and Training', was issued by the American Society for Training and Development which broadly represents the non-formal training agencies in the USA such as Government and Federal Training Institutions, The Armed Forces, Banking, Commerce and Industry. Their categorization of competencies is dealt with differently in that although staffs are deemed to be educationally as qualified as in the formal sector they need *not* be qualified teachers. Moreover certification as to media competency is not expected but the ability to handle modern educational communication involving television, radio, computers and media packages is essential. Compared with such situations the position in developing countries so far as staffing is concerned could be represented by considering any of the massive training schemes in South America or elsewhere. Here the use of radio, television and programmed communication techniques are fully exploited in attempts to improve the basic quality of education and social behaviour. Field workers in such situations are often volunteers of a primary education standard and are related to their communities sociologically. Such an organization is operated in the North East of Argentina by INCUPO, (Instituto de Cultura Popular), whereby a basic staff of 50 prepare and disseminate programmes to many thousands of radio listeners. These 'listener-learners' are assisted by a range of voluntary 'teachers' — Delegado Zonal — and 'monitors' who work with regional and provincial directors. Their categorizations lie within the terms of their basic education — primary, secondary or tertiary. It could only be the 50 permanent staff who would form the basis of a comparative study; similar is the case of Tele-Niger, which has recruited staff for 15 years to operate at specialist level in programme preparation — simply on the basis of psycho-techniques and local 'on-the-job' training. The identification of tasks from such diverse backgrounds so that there is helpful comparability is difficult. The efforts of reporters to achieve such identification inevitably leads to long diagnostic lists which explain a local situation adequately but confuse an overall assessment. UNESCO circulated a suggested identification matrix which in a modified form is stated below. .

Although institutions found some difficulty in matching their situations to such a matrix its modified form could provide a useful tool as to job identities. In this respect, Planners include conceptualizers, Producers employ media presentations of all types, Distributors employ evaluation techniques, Technical Support includes production and maintenance. At the moment, such a simplified matrix would seem to satisfactorily identify tasks at a preliminary enquiry stage. The role of the professional teacher as paramount in task identification is stressed several times by contributors; markedly from countries having strong professional teacher unions. Other submissions are less precise but there is a general level of agreement that the role of the 'educator' must be seen as paramount. Equally it is appreciated that

Function					
Activity	A Planners	B Producers	C Distributors	D Users	E Technical Support
Control Administration					
Educational Control and Design					
Technical/ Artistic Control					
Supporting Roles Technical					

Table 1.

diversified tasks emerge from new systems of managing education and that administration rarely acknowledges the fact of these new identities. New roles go unrecognized and unrewarded.

Functions

The submission on behalf of the Ivory Coast, for example, lists among the considerable diversification of role in educational broadcasting the sub-division and breakdown of roles of the 'pedagogue' or educationalist. In the preliminary stages of production he works to a document or schedule which calls for:

1 Defining the objective of the topic.
2 Listing entry behaviour.
3 Inter-relationship with major sequences of study.
4 Organizing initial stages of learning.
5 Stipulating the required materials.
6 Defining the role of the learners.
7 Elaborating the multi-media or support situations.
8 Defining the teacher role.
9 Defining evaluation procedures.
10 Listing training schedules or time-tables.

This view of a 'teacher's function' aptly illustrates what competencies are required in addition to those of a classroom teacher. The Federal Republic of Germany in its submission which accounts for procedures in the Institute for Audio-visual Aids in Science and Education covering most of the Federal States' requirements for educational audio-visual material, categorizes the functions of its 34 'subject experts' in the following manner:

'Execution of production (listed in a flow chart of 10 processes). This includes the *selection* of authors, technical advisers and producers, the *supervision* of drawing up exposés, treatments, scripts, photo lists and other manuscripts from specific didactical, creative and economic viewpoints and the *presentation* of the production in approval (evaluation) circumstances'.

The list of competencies here requires specifically the pedagogical supervision of all the process. Moreover the role of a subject expert in these circumstances is limited categorically to a maximum period of eight years with five years as the quoted optimum period before the teacher returns to the class or lecture room. It is worth noting that all contributors stress the need for educational control of production. Not all are able to indicate its achievement so precisely.

Within organizations employing such staffs there is also a hierarchy of administration and support staff which is part of the process. For example in the situation quoted from Germany the Institute numbers the following staff:

1 Director	1 Head of Management
1 Head of Law Department	2 Heads of Production
1 Head of Technical Department	1 Head of Administration
34 Subject Experts	4 Editors of Printed Material
2 Public Relations	3 Office Staff
6 Librarian/Data Experts	3 Research Staff
5 Production Assistants	2 Developing Technicians
4 Testing Technicians	3 Maintenance Engineers

If a function category is constructed as follows it appears to cover all these roles and those of other submitting institutions.

Policy Creators
Administrators
Subject Specialists
Advisers or Educational Specialists
Production Staff
Technical Support Staff

The considerable sub-divisions then necessary must be the aim of a synthesis of studies yet to be completed, but useful contributions will come from a ratification of its broad categorization likely to be globally accepted so that job titles can be secured. This possibility appears to hinge around the consideration of such a matrix as follows.

FUNCTIONAL FIELD

	Media Production	Media Management	Advanced Development
Creators/Directors			
Subject experts/ Conceptualizers			
Advisers/Distributors			
Producers/Designers			
Technical Support Staff			

Table 2. *Institution using modern techniques*

The necessity for simplification to this level appears essential. There is already a mushroom of job designation which will distil endeavour unless broad categories are now agreed. Further diversification can occur at national level, but these broad categories could direct attention to the needs for new roles and new training schemes.

Profiles

The submission from the Institut National de L'audio-visuel (France) provides some guide to profiles in advanced institutions whether in industrialized or developing countries:

Director	Should be able to direct the group and administer the technical and artisitic activity. He should possess a pedagogical background including the theory of education at all levels and a thorough knowledge of the techniques of audio-visual communication. Hold a Master Degree with Specialised Diploma. Have at least two years similar experience elsewhere at director level.
Librarians)	Intellectual, artistic and manual abilities.
Data Personnel)	Aptitude for working educationally with all age groups.
Media Management)	Ability to analyze and synthesize media materials.
Specialists)	Chartered librarian or equivalent.
	Three years experience including radio, television and documentation before assuming departmental responsibility.
Production Staff)	Intellectual, artistic and manual abilities
Technical and)	Able to translate situations into visual-graphic terms for
Artistic)	learners at child and adult ages.
	Possess considerable affinity for users of the material.
	Diploma in Art/Communication Studies at university level.
	Wide experience in media production units.
Educational)	Considerable intellectual ability.
Specialist/)	Thorough knowledge of pedagogical theory especially.
Adviser)	as concerned with audio-visual learning.
	Grasp of broad sociological principles.
	Ability to liaise with administration and production.
	Teacher with Master of Education level specialism.
	Qualifications in specialist field of audio-visual such as video.
Technical Staff)	Experience of techniques and apparatus concerned with
Maintenance and)	presentations including video.
Production)	Ability to co-operate well with other staff.
	Brevet de technician superior (City and Guilds Final).
	Two years experience in a production-diffusion centre.

Other national submissions carry contributions which could be identified with such a preliminary diagnosis. The resulting profiles would be nationally indigenous but could adequately describe the jobs resulting from the function matrix previously outlined.

Training

Training systems for staff using modern educational techniques appear to exist at the following levels:

External	:	Either inside national provision or outside it. Often one or two years.
Internal	:	Within the Institution's own provision. Usually one year or less.
Continuous		
In-Service	:	Usually internal or localized short course provision.
No Training	:	On-the-job experience, year by year.

There is insufficient space in this paper to deal with the highly detailed training schemes and curricula submitted from various countries. It is hoped that the symposium to be associated with this paper will examine the topic in some detail. It appears that most industrialized countries with sophisticated educational systems can list a training schedule which encompasses aspects of current educational technology. Often the statements are ahead of the actual training situation and it is very doubtful if any conventional curriculum is capable of adapting to the fast evolving communication scene. In many cases (the UK is a good example) classroom practice is ahead of many initial training systems so far as modern techniques are concerned. In less industrialized countries with unsophisticated educational systems there are now many established television and radio training schemes which by-pass the conventional classroom. Staffs for such systems are usually the product of 'on-the-job training'. There is considerable evidence that such systems of training are preferred to expatriate experience which frequently leads to a measure of disillusionment.

It would appear that a rational categorization of training for qualified teachers capable of using modern techniques in sophisticated education institutions could now be made on a global basis. Still to be rationalized are the tremendously important training categories for developing and rural economies.

Status of Staff

Accepting status to mean 'standard or regard paid to such staff, the working conditions, remuneration and other material benefits accorded to them relative to other professional groups' (ILO/UNESCO definition) it is fair to say that there is evidence that staff who use modern techniques have a special status when they work for a massive institution such as a national television/radio service, open or distance learning university or within the higher education framework. Consideration of the two matrices already quoted suggests that such staffs can be globally categorized if the effort is now made to do this. Such media specialists are generally required to have higher education. The very fact of being a 'specialist' constitutes a supervisory role. This appears to be true even in the most rural systems. Certainly, the evidence so far presented by the submissions points to a status equal to or superior to the supervisory grade of the general service teacher, together with leave and salary benefits on the same relative scale. One distinctive difference is drawn by the *non-formal* agencies in the USA whose members appear to enjoy a salary scale considerably in excess of their equally qualified counterparts in the *formal* sector.

A simple illustration of the difference in role between the subject or general teacher and the media specialist is to compare the situation in larger secondary schools. The establishment of a library resource area with supporting aids has created posts of improved status for the specialist. The major concern is then one of mobility. He is at the top of his particular 'tree'. Within television and radio networks he may well be in competition with professionals who are not teachers and his way upward may well only be via administration. This point was clearly seen in the submission from Federal Germany and their insistence that teachers move out after five years' specialization appears to have been successful in that such teachers have gained status posts in universities and major establishments on leaving the media specialized service. Whilst the question of status does depend upon the recognition of professional skills and qualifications, it must never be over-looked that the onward sweep of technology and the increasing call for education, gathers up staff who occupy quite traditional roles and transforms them into educational technologists on-the-job. In part it is the recognition and refinement of this phenomenon that will finally endorse status.

Conclusion

It is useful here to raise again the idea presented by Dr E M Buter in 1977 to that year's APLET Conference. We should consider staffing of major educational enterprises using modern techniques as follows:

(a) *The macro level* which represents top administration and planning staffs often found at governmental level, but also including regional and area administrators with financial authority.

(b) *The micro level* which represents the staffing at teacher-pupil level wherever that may be.

(c) *The meso* or intermediate level where staffs change plans into programmes so that children and adults may learn.

It is at the latter level that attention should be focused. There are some difficulties at macro level especially those concerned with mobility, but, by and large, professionally qualified staffs will find their level; it remains to create the classification and career prospects for them. At micro level the situation turns on initial training schemes for teachers and technicians. There are reasonably adequate outlines for technicians, but for teacher-producer-programmer the solution lies in the creation of a meso level transfer. It is at the meso level where the lack of staff and professionalism occurs.

It is hoped that response to this paper, either in the immediate discussion or during a later symposium, will examine the following themes:

(a) Is there a need to categorize jobs in modern educational establishments so that the educational technologist has a distinctive career or ought teachers to adapt to evolving requirements more quickly?

(b) What qualifications do we expect a consultant in educational technology to possess?

(c) Is not educational technology already out-dated in that modern communication media carry their own systems procedures which can be fitted into national or regional circumstances?

Workshop Report
10.3 Educational Technology and Significant Learning?

Tom Boydell and Mike Pedler
Sheffield City Polytechnic

The title of this session was deliberately posed as a question, as our aim was to look at the nature of significant learning and hence to discuss what contribution, if any, educational technology might make to such learning.

Significant Learning

We felt, for reasons that might become apparent later, that we should involve the participants as much as possible during the workshop. We therefore asked them to think of five or six occasions when, they felt, they had learned something really significant. These occasions could be any at all during their lifetime; some might have been short, sharp events, others might in fact have lasted some time — days, weeks, months, or even years. But no matter how long or short, each had to be identified by the person concerned.

Having recalled five or six such occasions, we then asked participants to complete a form (as in Table 1) giving the main outcomes and the main characteristics (described briefly, using adjectives or short phrases), of each event.

Significant Learning Experiences	Outcomes	Characteristics
1 2 3		

Table 1

Having done this, everybody was then asked to walk about in the middle of the room and to meet and talk to someone with whom they would like to share their experiences. This personal pairing sharing-discussion lasted for approximately 30 minutes.

Some Outcomes of Significant Learning Experiences

Some of the outcomes were collected orally and posted on a flipchart. These are shown in Table 2, together with some other contributions from our research in this area (elaborated in more detail in Pedler and Boydell, in press).

From this Workshop	From other occasions
A wish to know more	Maturity
Development of a skill	Confidence (often mentioned)
eg — reading/writing	
— riding a bicycle	Desire for more experiences
— driving a car	
Realization of limitations/potentials	More flexible and relaxed
in a given area	approach to personal relationships
Possibility of other life styles	Less tied to things
without conflict with others	Concern for my wife
Reduction/comparison of freedom	More self-questioning
Reassurance/disappointment	Realization of how much I can do
Affirmation of self by others	for myself as a person
Wish to repeat a performance	
Ability to compete	Feeling of completeness
Awareness of own feelings	Independence
A nice sense of achievement	New sense of personal capabilities
'There is no such thing as snow'	
Change in perception/philosophy of life	

Table 2

Model of Development

The data in Table 2 indicates, we believe, that significant learning is on the one hand highly individualized, as the outcomes are very specific to individuals whilst at the same time it shows that certain clusters of related features begin to emerge, such as:

☐ making one's own mind up, thinking for oneself;
☐ confidence, maturity, independence;
☐ interpersonal relationships;
☐ motivation, direction, purpose in life;
☐ self-awareness;
☐ modes of consciousness, feelings about life and death, spiritual development.

This ties in with various models of development, one of the best known of which is Maslow's hierarchy of motivational needs (Maslow, 1968). We have considered a number of such models elsewhere (Pedler and Boydell, in press) from which Table 3 is reproduced.

It is our contention that two types of learning can take place, namely a quantitative incremental, gradual type (within the stages of Table 2) and a qualitative, step-jump, 'question-change' type, between stages, from one stage to another. In these terms, the great majority of the significant learning outcomes of Table 2 fall into the second category.

What sort of process is involved, then, in this qualitative change? A number of specialists have focused attention on this issue (eg Piaget 1968, Kohlberg 1969, and Langer 1969) and proposed a model of dis-equilibration. Thus, qualitative development takes place as a result of perturbation, surprise, dis-confirmation, as in Charlesworth's (1969) model of the 'role of surprise in development', from which Figure 1 is derived.

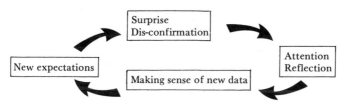

Figure 1. *Role of surprise in development*

This corresponds well with the characteristics of significant learning events as reported at the Workshop. Table 4 lists some of the feelings and perturbations the workshop participants experienced during these events.

Level (Alderfer[1])	Ethical/Moral Development (Loevinger[2] and Kohlberg[3])	Ways of Knowing (Various)	Interpersonal Style (Loevinger[2], Argyris and Schon[9])	Needs, Motivation (Maslow[10]) Preoccupation (Loevinger[2])	'Potentials' (Wilber[11,12])	'Dys-ease' after (Wilber[11])
Growth	Integrated – reconciling inner conflict[2] Moral principle[3]	Inspiration, intuition[4] Coalescence of knowing and being[5] Prehension – non-duality (ie polarity)[6] Growing confidence, acceptance that apparent opposites are not in conflict[7]	Move from tolerating to cherishing individual differences[2]	Self-actualization[10] Identity[2]	Transcending of space-time (Maslow) Mythological awareness (Jung)*	Transpersonal anxiety
	Autonomous –coping with inner conflict[2] Social Contract legalistic[3]	Imagination[4] Emergence of prehension[6] Beginning to make no-right-answer decision[7]	Recognition of mutual interdependence and others' needs for autonomy[2]	Esteem (own)[10] Development,[2] Self-fulfilment[2]	Existential freedom Authenticity (Perls)* Centredness Being mode (Fromm[8])	Existential anxiety – fear of death, of the void
Relatedness	Conscientious – internalisation, commitment to rules and norms of particular group[2] Authority, rule and social order[3]	Imagination[4] Duality[6] may appear Realization that perhaps there cannot be a right answer Luxury version of having knowledge – depends on social prestige[8]	Reciprocal but often mutual trust; often extended only to those in narrow in-group[2] Model II – minimally defensive interpersonal relations[9]	Esteem (from others)[10] Achievements[2]	Civilization Culture Social membership Language Law Logic	Double-binds Social alienation Conflict War 'Normal neuroses' Games People Play (Berne)* Acquisitive Society
	Conformist – adherence to external rules and norms[2] Good boy approval[3]			Belongingness[10] Things, appearance, reputation[2]		
Existence	Opportunistic – rules recognized, obeys out of fear of being caught[2] Instrumental egoism[3]	Material knowledge[4] Distinction between knower and known[5] duality[6]	Exploitive, manipulative, varying degree of dependency[2] Model I – defensive, competitive, controlling, fearful, withholding feelings, relative unconcern for others[9]	Safety[10] Advantage, control[2]	Deliberate self-control Civility Verbal Communication	Chronic low-grade emergency (Perls)* Depression as out-of-touch with one's body (Lowen)* Having mode (Fromm)[8]
	Impulse ridden – no recognition of rules; fear of retaliation[2] Obedience and punishment oriented[3]	There must be an answer seen in terms of right/ wrong, good/bad, us/ them[7] Having knowledge – minimum to do one's job[8]		Physiological[10] survival Bodily feelings, especially sexual and aggressive[2]	Pride, drive to success Righteous indignation Romantic love	Panic anxiety Guilt Hatred Depression as retro-flected Rage[20] Fear

Table 3. *A synthesis of some development theories*

* Cited in Wilber[11] (see References)

Excitement	"I want to go to bed"
Awe	"I want to get on with it tomorrow"
Relief	
Competent	Relief
Shattering	Pleasurable
Stimulating	Disappointment
Embarrassing	Sense of achievement
Fear	

Table 4

Of course, we do not always learn from such perturbations; sometimes we may take non-developmental tracks, as in Figure 2 (from Pedler and Boydell, in press).

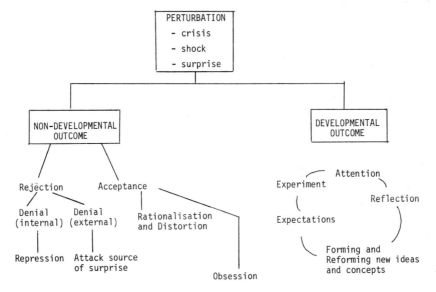

Figure 2. *Non-developmental tracks*

Educational Technology and Significant Learning?

What, then, is the role of educational technology in such qualitative, step-change learning?

To some extent, the answer to this depends on one's concept of educational technology. However, some possible approaches, raised for further thought, might include:

☐ Structured packages for achieving outcomes such as those in Table 1. (See eg Pedler *et al*, 1978.)

☐ Design strategies that involve surprise, confusion, perturbation. (This might also be said to be the direct opposite of most current 'good educational technology practice'!)

☐ Packages, resources etc for helping people make sense of and hence learn from, surprises, confusions and perturbations that occur as a part of normal everyday working and living.

References

Aldefer, C (1972) *Existence, Relatedness and Growth.* Collier Macmillan, New York.

Argyris C and Schon D (1975) *Theory in Practice.* Jossey and Bass, San Francisco.

Charlesworth, W R (1969) The role of surprise in cognitive development. In Elkind and Flavell (eds) *Studies in Cognitive Development*, pp 257-314. Oxford University Press, New York.

Deutsch, E (1969) *Advanta Vendanta, A Philosophical Reconstruction.* East-West Center Press, Honolulu.

Fromm, E (1978) *To Have or to Be?* Jonathan Cape, London. (Also Sphere Books, 1979.)

Kohlberg, L (1969) Stage and sequence: The cognitive developmental approach to socialization. In Goslin, D A (ed) *Handbook of Socialization Theory and Research*, pp 347-480. Rand McNally, Chicago.

Langer, J (1969) *Theories of Development.* Holt, Rinehart and Winston, New York.

Loevinger, J (1966) The meaning and measurement of ego development. *American Psychologist*, 21, 3, pp 195-206. (March)

Maslow, A (1968) *Toward a Psychology of Being.* Von Nastrand, New York.

Pedler, M J and Boydell, T H (in press) Is all management development self- development? In Beck and Cox (eds) *Advances in Management Development* (in press) Wiley, Chicester.

Pedler, M J, Burgoyne, J G and Boydell T H (1978) *A Manager's Guide to Self-Development.* McGraw-Hill, Maidenhead.

Perry, W G (1970) *Forms of Intellectual and Ethical Development in the College Years.* Holt, Rinehart and Winston, New York.

Piaget, J (1968) *Six Psychological Studies.* University of London Press, London.

Wilber, K (1977) *The Spectrum of Consciousness.* Theosophical Publishing House, Wheaton, Illinois.

Wilber, K (1975) Psychologic perennis: the spectrum of consciousness. *Journal of Transpersonal Psychology,* 7, 2, pp 105-32.

Workshop Report
10.4 Mapping the Field of Educational Technology

Jon Green
Middlesex Polytechnic
Anita Morris
South Thames Polytechnic

Introduction

Educational technology was first defined some 12 years ago in the Brynmor-Jones

Report as: 'the development, application, and evaluation of systems, techniques and aids, to improve the process of human learning'. Although this definition has stood the test of time it was soon realized, especially by those who had had some experience working in the field, that the newcomer may find this all-embracing concept difficult to pin down.

Background to the project

Thus, during the period 1974-76, a group of practitioners within the membership of the Network of Programmed Learning Centres held two weekend working sessions. They produced the first draft of a 'hierarchy of topics' and under the operational headings of analysis, design, implementation and evaluation, a 'hierarchy of objectives' that was considered to be pertinent to the field of educational technology. These crude hierarchies were then referred to as 'maps of the field of educational technology'.

In order to obtain a consensus of their correctness these 'maps' were presented by Jon Green and Andrew Trott at a workshop session at the 1977 APLET conference.

During the following year the original notion of 'maps of the field' was expanded to include a conceptual model of the roles (as suggested by the University of Concordia, Canada) that an educational technologist would be expected to perform.

And so another workshop at ETIC '78 considered these roles and their associated competencies.

Aims of the present workshop (ETIC '79)

This workshop was intended to carry on from the one held at ETIC '78. The recommendations made by the members of that workshop had been implemented during the year and it was anticipated that members of this workshop, by adopting a 'systems thinking approach' would reach a consensus on the processes within the system and then check the model of the role and the related list of competencies that had been prepared for the validation process. Then, if time permitted, to use the presented model as a guide to describe other previously defined processes.

Workshop organization

Participants would discuss with a 'partner' the presented 'model' ie:

   (a) an in-put out-put diagram of the validation process, and
   (b) the related list of general and specific competencies. (See Appendix.)

and after a period of 15 minutes, report back on their amendments and additions.

Outcome of the workshop

The intended outcomes were not achieved. This was due to lack of time. However, within the time limit of 45 minutes two themes emerged:

   (a) The difficulty of modelling reality to show competencies (defined as 'a high degree of ability in performance') would probably be best overcome by constructing a three-dimensional model, rather than a two-dimensional in-put-out-put model.

(b) The investigations recently completed by audio-visual instruction and the Council of Europe should be noted and maybe incorporated into the present scheme.

Consideration for future development of the project

The original notion of defining the field of educational technology for the new-comer has now been extended to include a three-point development plan which will provide 'source information' for: the content of a training programme and the specification of an experience profile for an educational technologist.

The plan can be outlined thus:

1   The *big* picture or map of the educational technology system to show purpose, processes and content.
2   Three-dimensional models of the processes and content to show roles, functions and competencies.
3   List or map of general or 'core' competencies.

This plan was to be forwarded to the Network of Programmed Learning Centre by its members at their next meeting. Their decision will in turn be forwarded to the participant members of the ETIC '78 and ETIC '79 workshops.

Appendix: *Map of the Process*

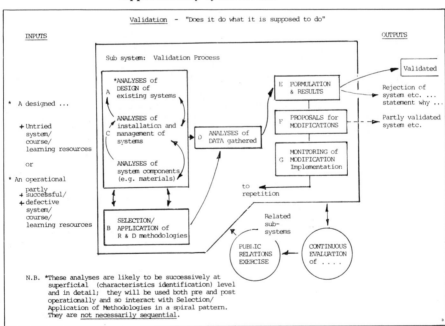

<u>Roles and necessary competencies of a Validator</u>

The general statements below indicate the range of skills a validator
needs and, simultaneously, together spell out the roles he may need
to undertake. The most important ones are broken down overleaf as
a series of task sets. It should be noted that at this level the
individual tasks within sets are not necessarily sequential.

<u>General Role</u>

> The selection and application of R & D methodologies to the
> study of teaching/learning systems in order to 'prove' -
> or where necessary improve - their performance to a
> predetermined level of effectiveness.

<u>General competencies/requirements:</u>

The validator must be able to carry out:

- Analyses of :

  - the design of existing education/training schemes
    or systems

  - the installation and management of existing
    educational or training systems

  - data gathered from validation investigations

- Formulation of the results of validation investigation and
  of proposals for modification to the systems or materials
  under review.

- Moderation of the implementation of proposed modifications.

N.B. these apply to systems and learning resources at all levels.

The validator should also be able to undertake:

- The maintenance of a public relations exercise with clients.

- The maintenance of an on-going evaluation of all current
  validation procedures.

10.5 Educational Technology to Educational Development — A Bid for Survival ?

Derek Rowntree
The Open University

Derek Rowntree introduced his workshop by explaining that he would present the outline of his paper and then open up a discussion.

The main points made were as follows:

There were three main recognizable types of educational technology:

(a) Tools ed tech
(b) Systems ed tech
(c) Reflections ed tech

The first two were explained in their historical context and several controversial statements and questions were put forward.

The third item, 'Reflections ed tech', was described in more detail, covering such major items as participation, sense of values, intuition, open attitude, improvement and critical reflection, as related to the function of the educational technologist.

Making the point that educational technology should be seen in the new light of educational development, the presenter outlined several aspects of knowledge which included:

(a) change and development;
(b) self-knowledge;
(c) knowledge of values;
(d) pedagogical knowledge; and surprisingly
(e) subject matter knowledge.

The ensuing discussion was lively and wide ranging, several points being made regarding the function of an educational technologist (a) as a team member and (b) as an individual linked to staff development and in-service training.

10.6 Evaluation : Dialogue between Education and Technology

Denise Walsh
Ballarat College of Advanced Education, Mt Helen, Victoria, Australia

Evaluation of students, teachers and materials is a difficult task and one which seems to be given less thought than the more interesting one of planning courses and materials; it means so many different things and is used for so many purposes that general discussion seems fruitless. In this workshop, conducted by Ms Walsh, an attempt was made to provide a common experience on which to ground some discussion of evaluation processes. In his *Handbook of Simulation Gaming in*

Social Education, (1974) R Stadsklev sums up evaluation of games in the following manner and Ms Walsh sought to extend his remarks to a wider field. He maintains that to evaluate games is a troublesome problem. There is a tendency on the part of a large number of people to evaluate a game simply on the basis of how valid it is. Validity, in this instance, is usually described as a true and accurate representation of reality. However, in the September 1973 issue of *Simulation/Gaming News*, Garry Shirts suggests that:

> This is a sterile, unproductive and outdated notion of validity. Such an approach is appropriate for the research designing a simulation to be used in the testing of hypotheses, but not for the person concerned with education simulations . . . Educational simulation should be considered valid if it teaches what it purports to teach, regardless of its form and content. Reality is certainly one of the concerns of the designer but in many situations he may want to exaggerate, abstract, distort, and simplify reality, just as the author, artist, and film maker do, in order to teach the ideas and concepts he wants to teach.

Allen Feldt summed it up at the 1973 fall meeting of the National Gaming Council:

> You can't evaluate games as a generic type. You can only evaluate a game in a context, under certain circumstances. You can't talk about its use in all circumstances, any more than you can evaluate the utility of the telephone. It's what goes into it and comes out of it that's important, not the device itself. It's just the instrument through which information is transmitted.
> (Stadsklev, R 1974, p 44).

The discussion ranged over many aspects of the question of evaluation which included reference to the gap between theory as evidenced in educational writings and practice in the field, to the differences across cultures as evidenced in experiences related from different countries and from different aspects, eg, industrial training, social science and hard science education. One issue raised was that of the professionalism of teachers who seemed to be considered less 'professional' than doctors in that their judgments needed to be backed up by other evidence. As seems appropriate in such an open-ended discussion, no conclusions or recommendations were reached except, perhaps, that no generalizations can be reached on such a topic.

All the participants made a contribution in some form or other about the difficulties of evaluation of changes in attitude. General agreement was reached that there are many occasions when evaluation is at the discretion of the teacher, that it may take a very subjective approach and should not be influenced by outside factors such as cost-effectiveness.

Closing Address

Norman Willis
Council for Educational Technology

Mr Willis considered it important that the theme of ETIC '79 had been retro-spective, even if many contributors had not kept to that theme. 'There are lessons to be learned, very valuable lessons, from the years which have gone past,' he said, 'and we ignore them at our peril.'

To illustrate this point, Mr Willis dipped into the pages of *Visual Education* of 1959-60, when he himself had been the journal's editor. For example, in August 1959 the journal had reported 'an experiment with closed circuit television which is said to have potential in certain areas of technical college and university work.' An editorial had observed that 'the medium has potential which is worth exploring'. However, a decidedly vituperative editorial of the same year had declared, 'Teaching by television can only result in replacing the teacher . . . it would mean the same lesson at the same time by the same teacher for all schools.' Mr Willis reminded ETIC '79 delegates that some of the ideas lying behind that particular reaction had not died.

At other times the pages of *Visual Education* had, however, shown more opti-mism. In November 1960, an American writing on CCTV had concluded his article with the words, 'Unless in the decade ahead we broaden our image of television to be something more than just an electronic extension of what already is, then truly we can be ashamed. It will mean we have not been brave enough or creative enough to ask the difficult questions.'

Flicking further forward through the pages of *Visual Education*, to 1961, Mr Willis quoted from an article by Dr R L Reid of Aberdeen on teaching machines. 'Teaching machines,' Dr Reid had written, 'deal with individual pupils and it is the special relationship that they permit between structural material and pupil that is their essential feature . . . There is no doubt that adequate research in this field could establish a new technology of instruction.' Thus, Dr Reid had perceived the beginnings of such a technology some four years before the concept of educational technology had emerged in the Brynmor Jones Report of 1965.

Derek Rowntree's popular workshop (10.5) of ETIC '79 had argued the way from educational technology to educational development, thus 'recoiling from that word technology'. 'Indeed', said Mr Willis, 'I have a feeling coming from this con-ference of retreat from specialism, of retreat from technology.' Mr Willis neither applauded nor argued with this attitude but urged delegates to apply educational technology thinking to their own approach to educational technnology, or what-ever name delegates might choose to give it.

Mr Willis urged delegates to be determined in applying educational technology. At ETIC '79 he had found a number of sources of inspiration for his belief that if you are determined to win, win you will. One source had been Francis Moakley's paper (3.1) relating the story of the Television Phoenix at San Francisco State University.

Mr Willis urged educational technologists to work co-operatively with teachers.

There was an enormous complexity of individual learners, as Clive Lawless had
pointed out in his paper (10.1), but it was necessary to try to cope with those
variations. Improving teaching methods had to be a team effort. 'What the educational technologist brings to the team,' said Mr Willis, 'is his own specialist
contribution, his knowledge of presentation, editing, questioning, ordering and
analyzing which can be added on to the subject specialist's knowledge of the
subject and turned into something which in the end is better for the student . . .
If educational technology is not a practical subject which is to do with improving
the way in which students learn, it isn't worth the time — and it *is* . . . We must
be prepared to get mud on our boots.'

Dipping into his *Visual Education* files again, Mr Willis then produced another
salutary gem: 'When a new teaching aid makes its appearance, two schools of
opinion immediately, and often without much examination, become vocal — the
extreme opponents and the extreme supporters. To the diehards it is yet another
gadget, probably very entertaining but with no significant contribution to make
to classroom work. At the other extreme, the cranks, dazzled by its novelty, greet
it with open arms and make extravagant claims for it.' 'And,' added Mr Willis, "the
novelty" that all that was about may just have been the taperecorder'.

Then Mr Willis turned to a pressing present-day problem, micro-electronics,
whose impact on our society was going to be greater, faster and more radical than
had been the case with television. 'How many of us,' asked Mr Willis, 'are going to
remember the dead teaching machines starved of programmes? . . Remember how
unused teaching machines created a well of opposition.' Mr Willis reminded delegates how Keith Shaw's paper (8.3) had drawn attention to the terrible problem of
finding people who could prepare programmes for computer-assisted learning. It
could be the teaching machine software problem all over again. Writing programmes
took time and training — to be successful 'they need careful, creative testing and,
above all else, they need system change, otherwise it doesn't work!'

'Teaching itself is going to change very considerably. You straddle the divide
between technology and process . . . You are the people whose expertise, founded
on those 20 years of experience which too many of you at this conference have
not wanted to consider, are the ones whose experience put you at the forefront
of this change. If you believe, you are the ones who are going to win. If you don't
we shall do it wrong and this country will end up as a banana republic . . . If we get
it wrong this time, there will not be a second time because we shall have gone so
far down the league there won't be a way back . . . That's why I welcome the idea
that this conference this year should be retrospective, bringing back to your minds
the opportunities the past has given, the problems that have been met and overcome.

'In order that from that foundation of experience you can build new structures,
you must think forward and I look forward to ETIC '80 when you will be able to
talk and discuss among yourselves the ways in which you will push forward into
the twenty-first century, building upon the experience which you have gained as
educational technologists over the last 20 years.'

Keyword Index

adaption 31
affective learning 174
algorithms 35, 47, 189
analysis: job/task 53
Analysis of Covariance 194
Analysis of Variance 192
analysis: problem 46
analysis: topic 53, 165, 166
analysis: skills 53, 123
anasynthesis 46
assessment 79, 198, 213
attention 36
audio-card 246
audio-cassettes 85
audio-visual aids 53, 78, 79, 121, 183, 198, 203, 211, 239

backward chaining 133
Bloom's taxonomy 16, 22, 75, 134, 154
booths — see carrels
branching programming 32
Business Education Council 87

carrels 90, 186
case studies 20, 30, 36
cognitive learning 22, 94, 128, 153, 174
cognitive structure, 340
competency-based 203
computer aided instruction (CAI) 242, 246, 259, 269, 271
computer-based models 262, 287
computer managed learning 17, 37, 90, 223
computer marked assignments 252
concept analysis 335
correspondence study 74
cost-effectiveness 109, 237
counselling 214
course planning 297
cues 188
curriculum development 9, 16, 47, 68, 177, 184, 298, 304
cybernetics 16, 37, 73

degaussing 116
distance learning 72, 77, 132, 252
design of instruction 42, 117, 126, 134, 153, 164

educational development 278, 358
educational technology staff 99, 148
EFL 109
evaluation 58, 67, 79, 207, 273, 287, 358
evaluation models 68

fading 188
feedback 59, 83, 122, 203, 252, 274
flexistudy 94
fog index 106

games 20, 128, 169
group instruction 56, 78, 155

handouts 146, 195
heuristics 35, 48

independent study 213
individual differences 40
individualized instruction 33, 45, 57, 88, 91, 149, 161, 190, 242
information processing 333
information systems 310, 333
instructional media 187
instructional objectives 46, 116, 120, 128, 132, 160, 165
instructional technology management 328
interactive computing facilities 258
interpersonal skills 128, 138

job aids 123
job descriptions 233, 327
job evaluation 327

Keller Plan 68, 158, 274
Kent Mathematics Project 151

laboratory training 58

learning packages 133, 143, 148, 172, 211, 229
learning resources 237, 278
lecture handouts 62, 88
lectures 56
lesson plan 121, 170
library resource centre 89, 92
linear programme 32

mass-audience courses 203
mastery testing 157
mathetics 46
mature students 213
media design 184, 297
media research 222-225
mediated programming 185
micro-computers 164, 258, 268
microfiche 148
micro-teaching 184
motivation 17, 36, 63, 117, 159
movies 206

National Extension College 92, 94, 95
network analysis 121
note-taking 62

objectives 195, 230, 233, 238, 240, 243
objective tests 88
Open University 85, 92, 131, 227, 333-43, 358
optical mark readers (OMRs) 318

pacing 90
peer instruction 143
post-test 192, 274
pre-test 191
proctors — see Keller Plan
programmed instruction 11, 31, 45, 48, 123, 135, 144, 148, 186, 189, 195, 216, 226, 242, 269, 271
programme writing 131
psycho-motor skills 53, 86, 94

questionnaires 80, 120, 126, 138, 145

recall 57
reinforcement 38, 146
resource-based learning 77, 87, 96, 155
resource centres 98, 110, 208, 328
resource workshops 89
retraining 326
role-playing 26, 126
Royal Navy training model 116

SAKI 12
self-assessment 122, 253
self-directed learning 193
self-pacing 160
seminars 79
semi-programmed course units 195
simulation 138
simulators 271
software 267
sound/slide presentation see tape/slide
status of staff 348
stimulus 183
student attitudes 59
study skills 85, 213
systemic approach 180
systems approach 189, 230, 330

tape/slide 38, 108, 111, 187, 239, 240
taxonomies 344
teacher assistants 205
teacher training 180-185, 189-195, 274
team teaching 50, 59
Technician Education Council 91
team teaching 50, 59
tele-type 258, 267
television: cable 100, 109
television: educational 37, 98
testing 205, 249
textual design 102, 107
tours 58
Trainer Guide 126-129
training systems 347
Training Services Agency 87
training within industry (TWI) 123
training workshops 138, 143

validation 122, 355
video-cassettes 109
visual aids see audio-visual aids
visual display unit (VDU) 245, 269

workbooks 148
worksheets 88, 145

Author Index

(alphabetical list of authors, including co-authors not present as delegates)

Adamson, R M 240
Adderley, K 278
Addinall, E 20, 29
Anderson, E W 116
Atherton, B 45

Banks, B 151, 157
Belsey, V R 108
Black, T R 274
Boydell, T 349
Bray, L M 148
Bryce, C F A 245
Butcher, H S 271

Clarke, J 111
Cooper, A 252
Cooper, N 111
Corfield, G 111

Daly, D W 158

Edney, P J 326
Ellington, H I 20, 29
Ely, D P 310, 316
Evans, L F 136

Goose, J R J 242
Green, B 94
Green, E E 203
Green, J 359

Hammond, D R F 318
Harris, N D C 172, 178
Hartley, J 62, 102, 107
Hawkins, C A 67
Hills, J 87
Hills, P J 208
Holmberg, B 72
Hudson, E 111

Kay, H 11
Kitchin, M J 230

Landa, L 31
Larcombe, A J 151, 157
Lawless, C J 333
Leedham, J 343
Le Hunte, R J 123
Lockwood, F 252

McAleese, R 297
McDonald, R J 213
Marson, S N 216
Megarry, J 77
Mills, J T 111
Mitchell, P D 36
Moakley, F X 98, 222
Moore, J D S 230
Moors, D C 287
Morris, A 359
Moyes, R B 208

Noble, P 87
Nolan, P T 242
Nunan, E 180

Pearce, J 278
Pedler, M 349
Percival, F 20, 29
Pettman, L 109

Race, W P 195
Roebuck, A 269
Romiszowski, A J 45, 328
Rowntree, D 131, 364

Sakamoto, T 164
Scholl, P 185
Scobbie, J 297
Shaw, K 258
Soremekun, E A 53
Stewart, A M 245
Symes, P R 226

Tait, J 278
Tourret, A 151, 157
Townsend, I 237
Trueman, M 62, 102, 107

Walsh, D 358
Watts, P J 172, 178
Webb, F J 111
Wellington, J 108
Wilkinson, G M 143
Williams, D 278
Willis, N 367
Wilson, P L 318
Wood, A 189
Wyant, T 304